Acknowledgments

A number of people lovingly tried to dissuade us from editing a book pre-tenure. They were correct that this endeavor took significant time and energy, but we are nevertheless glad we embarked on this journey together.

At the University of Tulsa, we thank our fellow media studies faculty—Benjamin Peters, Mark Brewin, Justin Owen Rawlins, and Jennifer Lynn Jones—for their intellectual excitement for this project and for their support throughout, as well as Gina Rubio-White for all her help. We thank Hana Saad for working with us on this book as part of her Tulsa Undergraduate Research Challenge project. We are grateful for our students, with whom we enjoyed discussing how and why we use Instagram, especially when it comes to food. We also thank TU's Office of Research and Sponsored Programs, the Kendall College of Arts and Sciences, and the Department of Media Studies for funding that supported research for this book, printing the book's images in color, and indexing.

At the University of Illinois Press, we thank our editor, Danny Nasset, as well as Mariah Schaefer, Tad Ringo, and Dustin Hubbart. We greatly appreciate the work of Deborah Oliver for copyediting and Cynthia Savage for indexing. We also thank our anonymous readers for their helpful feedback on the book manuscript.

Many thanks to one of our multi-talented contributors, KC Hysmith, for the incredible cover photo of our book.

I, Emily, thank my husband, Chris, and my rescue pup–writing buddy, Raven, for their love and support, which make everything worth it. I also thank my Food Media students for fearlessly diving into the world of food Instagram with me, often becoming fantastic (but still critical!) food photographers. I also thank Zenia for editing this book with me, and for writing the introduction together, which was a special and truly collaborative experience.

I, Zenia, thank Emily for taking the leap on this book project together. It has been a pleasure and a rich learning experience to collaboratively research, write, and think through what food and Instagram mean to each other. Thank you to Justin and Maksym, my whole heart. To a lifetime of beautiful meals together.

Finally, we both thank this book's contributors for working with us on this project. When we first circulated this book's call for abstracts, it drew many fascinating submissions, from which we selected these stellar seventeen. We are proud of, and delighted by, the final result. We hope all of you are too.

From Seed to Feed

How Food Instagram Changed
What and Why We Eat

ZENIA KISH AND EMILY J. H. CONTOIS

In 2017, the Tea Terrace café on London's Oxford Street launched a new menu item called the Selfieccino, designed to entice millennial crowds. It continues to be wildly popular today. For about $7, customers e-mail a selfie to the café's Wi-Fi-enabled cappuccino maker, which prints their face onto the surface of a cappuccino or hot chocolate using flavorless, sepia-toned food coloring (fig. 0-1). "For us, today's dining experience is no longer just about having great food and drink," explained the shop's director, Ehab Shouly. "It's all about creating unique experiences that our customers can document on Instagram and social media."[1] The Selfieccino fulfills desires for camera-ready food experiences, selling a drink that begs to be photographed, and a photograph made to be drunk. Combining two of the most popular photo genres on Instagram—food and selfies—this caffeinated self-portrait satisfies social media's constant hunger for personalized, and often promotional, content. It also underscores how food images offer unique insights into the changing visual culture of our digital age.

Two years after the advent of the Selfieccino, many writers reflected on what had most changed food and eating during the previous decade.[2] Unsurprisingly, Instagram topped many of these lists. Launched in October 2010, the app boasted one billion users worldwide by mid-2018, and encouraged many chefs to cook for looks. "Instagrammability"—that is, an appealing, photogenic quality worthy of being widely shared via the platform—has become a culinary incentive to fill reservations and grow a line out the door. For some chefs, customers' obsession with taking food photos so disrupted the dining experience that they banned flash photography.[3] Beyond "grammable" foods gorgeously plated on attractive dishes, restaurants seeking to go viral invested in eye-catching wallpaper, photography-enhancing lighting, decorative floor tiles, exterior feature walls, and a revival of colorful, neon signage.[4] By 2019, it was estimated that 78 percent of U.S. restaurants engaged with the platform.[5]

Food and dining have always fed eaters' sense of status, but Instagram further transforms Jean Anthelme Brillat-Savarin's timeworn aphorism linking food and identity into "you are what you post."[6] Although more than half of the platform's global user base is aged thirty-four and under, a wide range of people from professional chefs to recipe bloggers, farmers to tourists, are rearranging their spaces and altering their photo-taking practices to produce food images "for the gram."[7] Instagram provides an ostensibly free platform to both everyday users and a growing crop of influencers and content creators who challenge conventional categories of producer and consumer by blurring lines between branding, food criticism, and visual diary-keeping.[8] These categories have been collapsing under the weight of digital media convergence and the entrepreneurial gig economy for some time.[9] But the specific relationship between food imagery and Instagram has an outsized effect as these various actors seek access, audiences, and authority.

Building on her foundational research on food blogs, Isabelle de Solier expands Marshall McLuhan's famous declaration to consider food and new media, asserting that "the medium *shapes* the message."[10] We agree that platforms communicate different messages in accordance with their respective structures, which also shape society in various ways. And yet, Twitter and Facebook have drawn sustained scholarly attention, while Instagram has not.[11] When we searched Google Scholar in February 2021, it returned 7.34 million results for academic publications on Twitter and 6.38 million for Facebook, but only 1.43 million for Instagram. A number of scholarly volumes have also been published in recent years on the topic of digital food. In addition to de Solier's study of food blogging, Signe Rousseau's *Food and Social Media: You Are What You Tweet* marked an early foray into the field.[12] A number of thoughtful edited collections and special issues explored and extended digital food's terrain.[13] Tania Lewis's *Digital Food: From Paddock to Platform* further defined a critical research agenda, while Jonatan Leer and Stinne Gunder Strøm Krogager (also contributors to this book, chapter 13) honed a set of research methodologies in their edited collection.[14] And yet, in each case, Instagram remains a relatively marginal focus.

In the beginning, critics pegged Instagram as the site for Polaroid-shaped pictures of millennial brunches, pets, and babies—subjects often coded as displays of white affluence and leisure. Its presumed feminization and superficial consumerism slowed its cultural legitimacy and its scholarly assessment. As a result, the first book dedicated solely to Instagram was not published until 2020.[15] In this book, we expand on such analysis to examine Instagram's cultures and affordances (that is, the capacities it offers users) through one of its most popular and codified subjects: food. Although situated within the broader context of

FIGURE 0-1. Selfieccino images, the Tea Terrace, London.

Instagram, our focus is more specifically turned to food Instagram, a quasi-genre on the platform distinguished by recognizable aesthetic conventions, the presence of both everyday users and industry professionals, and a shared focus on representations of food, eating, and food-related phenomena. We consider how users engage food Instagram to construct identity, to seek influence, and to negotiate aesthetic norms, institutional access, and cultural power, as well as social and economic control.

As such, food Instagram provides ripe opportunities for interdisciplinary conversations, particularly between the academic fields of media studies and food studies, as well as with new media studies, cultural studies, gender and sexuality studies, and other approaches to analyzing digital food cultures. In this book, we consider what theories and methodologies in each field might be fruitfully brought to bear in the study of Instagram, and food Instagram specifically. We have made every effort for this book to be accessible to not only fellow academics but also to students and general readers. The authors are drawn from media studies, food studies, communication, American studies, history, science and technology studies, sociology, anthropology, and political science. Many are teachers. Two are practicing artists. One is a journalist. One is an influencer in real life. We have learned much from them and know readers will too.

In this introduction, we preview and synthesize the work of our twenty-three contributors, whose seventeen chapters engage this book's key themes: identity, influence, and negotiation. We also situate the study of food Instagram within the history of visual representation and photography, the concept of food porn, and the platform's specific affordances, architecture, and style. Then, in an effort to demonstrate the interdisciplinary possibilities at the juncture of media studies and food studies, we dive into Instagram's visual ecosystem, systematically analyzing it from soil and seed to our digital feed, and beyond.

Food Instagram: A Prehistory

For all that Instagram might have changed, photographing and sharing food images are not novel. The platform is only the latest inheritor of a rich history of artistic traditions fascinated with the visual pleasures of food and eating. From the earliest identified cave paintings by Homo sapiens depicting hunting scenes through Song Dynasty paintings of royal banquets and luscious Renaissance still lifes of edible delicacies, visual depictions of food have served many cultural functions. Encompassing everything from ritual invocations for a successful hunt to the display of wealth, sensual indulgence, and symbolic plenitude, food is an enduring visual fixation, embedded in broader cultural and material contexts that complicate its meaning.

The invention of photography in the early nineteenth century introduced new relationships between human subjects and visual reproduction, which have relevance for the study of food Instagram today. Louis Daguerre revealed his technique for producing daguerreotypes on coated pewter plates in 1839, signaling the arrival of photography amid the rapid expansion of industrial capitalism.[16] As technology improved the medium's speed of development and ease of reproduction, commercial portrait studios became so widespread beginning in the 1840s that over 90 percent of daguerreotypes created were estimated to be portraits of people, anticipating the later popularity of selfies.[17] For visual theorist John Tagg, the portrait signified "both the description of an individual and the inscription of social identity," while also acting as a commodity whose ownership conferred social status.[18] Beginning with William Henry Fox Talbot's 1845 photograph, "A Fruit Piece," food was another popular subject of early photography because, unlike people, it didn't move and was easily arranged for painterly still lifes.[19]

Walter Benjamin noted that the commodification of photography coincided with the industrialization of food and agricultural production in Europe. The tension between photography as art and as commodity was increasingly tipping toward commodification, he explained, as it became more fashionable as a medium. This aesthetic shift "unmasked a photography which is able to relate a tin of canned food to the universe, yet cannot grasp a single one of the human connections in which that tin exists."[20] It is revealing that Benjamin selects the fetishization of a mass-produced food item as a reference point for his argument about the commercial artifice of photography: as both food and photography became more culturally visible as commodities, their modes of production were increasingly hidden from view.

George Eastman's 1888 introduction of the Kodak handheld camera signaled the transformation of photography into the first participatory mass medium, presaging its later centrality for Instagram. "Eastman originated not only a camera but also a radical reconception of the boundaries of photographic practice," Tagg writes. "People without training or skills now took pictures of themselves and kept the intimate, informal or ill-composed results in family albums."[21] The unrehearsed aesthetic introduced with the personal camera shifted portraits and food photographs away from the more painterly nineteenth-century style toward a new visual sensibility focused on how the camera uniquely captures form, color, and shadow. This sensibility not only underwrote a revolution in amateur photography but also birthed a new industry of visually oriented food advertising.[22] In cookbooks, photography both displaced and intermingled with other illustrations to communicate recipe instructions, as such images also cultivated a sense of identity and possibility for home cooks.[23] Today, Buzzfeed's Tasty videos take such compressed representations of cooking time and labor to a new level, especially on Instagram where the account boasts more than forty million followers.

Long before the Selfieccino, then, photography was an active agent in the commodification of both portraiture and food, at the same time that it democratized access to diverse sensual pleasures and amateur media production. The addition of high-quality digital cameras to smartphones in the late 2000s reflects a similar transformation in accessibility and now-instantaneous photographic production and distribution. It set the stage for visually oriented social media to exponentially expand their consumer base.

The birth of Instagram is embedded in this history, condensing visual pleasure and commodification into a digital app identified with selfies, food porn, and branded content. Initially launched as a photo-sharing app for Apple's iPhone, its aesthetic style was distinguished by square posts, filters emulating vintage photographs, and a minimalist visual interface. These modernist and retro impulses are folded into the name itself, which combines "instant" with "telegram." The techie portmanteau suggests that Instagram was envisioned to revolutionize mobile social media on the same scale as the telegraph, which linked continents for the first time through instantaneous communication.[24] In January 2011, Instagram introduced the hashtag feature, transforming the platform from one of linear chronology to a networked database of tagged and machine-sortable content.[25] Although users continued to perceive Instagram as an independent entity for years afterward, Facebook purchased Instagram in April 2012 for $1 billion—double Twitter's offer for the company—before the platform had ever turned a profit, indicating recognition of food pics' significant value.[26]

The architecture and business model of the company have continued to evolve rapidly. Instagram began exploring limited advertising on the platform in late 2013, rolling out extensive marketing tools in September 2015; shortly thereafter the platform overtook Twitter in user numbers.[27] In the intervening years, a complex economy of influencers sprouted, transforming large groups of followers into a new type of currency. Instagram has provided an additional tool for users and communities to speak for themselves in notably visual ways. In chapter 5, for instance, Robin Caldwell explores how tags like #blackgirlcooking foster digital culinary communities by and for Black women cooks. But access to platforms like Instagram has not curtailed oppressive experiences, such as culinary cultural appropriation. Indeed, many influencers gain their status on Instagram through existing social privilege. Despite its democratic potential, Instagram still often reinforces existing dynamics of power, especially when considering how race, ethnicity, gender, sexuality, and social class are stitched into the platform's rampant harassment culture.[28]

Other notable Instagram developments include the switch to an algorithmic (rather than chronological) feed in June 2016. This change altered user relationships with the platform as content became more personalized in anticipation of what our algorithmically sculpted profiles would "like." The new Stories feature followed in August 2016 (incorporating Snapchat's popular ephemeral content messaging), and IGTV launched in June 2018 to compete with YouTube's popular video content. Mid-2020, the platform added Reels to compete with TikTok and began allowing creators to monetize their content through direct audience sponsorship, opening up new revenue streams and business models for influencers.[29] With such developments, Instagram adopted various social media platforms' most compelling features, turning them to their advantage, especially for food.

I Know It When I See It: Food Porn

Some critics characterize food Instagram's images of delectable dishes as food porn. Film and media scholar Linda Williams describes pornography as "a genre that tends to suspend narrative in order to scrutinize the sights and sounds of interpenetrating bodies."[30] Food porn similarly fixates on decontextualized visuals as it incites other sensory experiences. These images express a passion that bursts from the frame, in part because of the sensuality of food itself. Food porn elicits an ambivalent gaze that at once objectifies, covets, and adores. Even when represented as static visuals, food porn often intimately represents movement, such as closeups of oozing egg yolks, or triggers it, such as the viewer's own salivation. The equivocal food gaze is complicated throughout this book. In chapter 1, Michael Z. Newman analyzes the Instagram account Hot Dudes and Hummus, which applies a pornographic style to seductive photos of food *and* to the muscled, often partially clad men, depicted holding bowls of chickpea dip. In chapter 3, Gaby David and Laurence Allard further theorize what they call food porn's "meal gaze," a synthesis of the male gaze and commodity fetishism of digital food images. In chapter 17, Sarah E. Tracy documents how Instagram privileges sight, a sensory hierarchy she tries to subvert with her students through multisensory engagement with food and food media in the classroom.

Viewing food porn from a different angle, writer Molly O'Neil defines it through its aspirational elements as "prose and recipes so removed from real life that they cannot be used except as vicarious experience." Food studies scholar Anne McBride remarks on how it makes food "seem increasingly out of reach to the average cook or consumer." These ideas take their cue from Roland Barthes's 1950s *Mythologies*, in which he dubbed a similar phenomenon "ornamental cuisine." He analyzed the elaborate and intricately embellished dishes within the pages of *Elle* magazine, writing that "the prevailing substantial category is surface sheen: visible effort has been made to produce glazed, carefully smoothed finishes." Devoted to visuality and appearances, it consisted of both "a dream cuisine" and "an advertising cuisine," one "at once close up and inaccessible," particularly for *Elle*'s primarily working-class readers.[31]

Barthes's analysis seems to have anticipated Instagram's characteristic aesthetic focus on surfaces and hyper-ideal objects, often captured in an overhead shot, as well as the sentiments of class-based desire and aspiration. Food porn creates fetishistic distance between producers and consumers, even as Instagram creates new possibilities for prosumption—that is, the consumer is also an active producer of content for the platform—which Katherine Kirkwood explores in chapter 11. This distance unfolds through dynamics of inclusion and exclusion for both producers and consumers along lines of class, status, expertise, and access.

In this line of thinking, food porn marks foods, ingredients, cooking practices, and representational modes that are perceived as available to only an elite few.

Food porn's evolution over the last several decades also informs the study of food Instagram. The terms "food porn" and "gastro-porn" first emerged in the late 1970s.[32] As Ariane Cruz writes, "we might understand gastro-porn as a visual and literary rendering of porno chic in the realm of the culinary arts," given the related historical developments of pornography's "socio-cultural, political, and technological developments" in the 1970s alongside the rise and proliferation of food porn.[33] Indeed, such images originated in legacy media in full-color magazine spreads, on food television shows, and in food films, a genre where "food fills the screen."[34] In the 2000s, food porn jumped to the Internet with the rise of food blogging.[35] At each moment "food porn" labeled different practices and conjured different audiences, but it continued to express a visual aesthetic of glossy surfaces and exaggerated ornamentation with a touch of explicit seduction. Food porn also enacts the power imbalances and objectification inherent to much of porn itself, often across gendered bodies and labor.

Throughout much of the 2010s, the food Instagram genre built upon these aesthetic precedents. A codified, visual style of well-lit, carefully positioned, and artfully filtered shots took on a nearly hegemonic status, particularly for branded content. A global convergence of Instagram-friendly aesthetics has been noted everywhere, from book covers to makeup and graffiti styles, but trendy restaurants and home kitchens have become perhaps the most iconic stages for Instagrammability. The app grew and sustained a digital space uniquely ravenous for food porn, at the same time that it purportedly democratized the tools and expertise to create and share such food images.

By the late 2010s, however, some users began to resist Instagram's aesthetic norms. While nonetheless curated, users produced unfiltered, less edited, and even "ugly" images, performing authenticity as an act of rebellion. Such stylistic shifts incited some writers to decree that the Instagram aesthetic was over.[36] Culture, technology, and marketing critics mostly attributed this shift to the tastes and practices of younger Gen Z users, especially their use of Finstas—that is, "fake" private Instagram accounts intended for a small, trusted audience.[37] Two chapters in this book explore different deployments of such aesthetics. Within the infinitely Instagrammable New Nordic cuisine of Copenhagen's food scene, Stinne Krogager and Jonatan Leer examine how chef Umut Sakarya transgresses such aesthetic norms with gastronomic and political consequences (chapter 13). And Sara Garcia Santamaria explores in chapter 14 how far-right political leaders in Italy and Brazil use anti-food-porn images on Instagram in an effort to represent and cultivate populist sentiment.

Instagram's food porn and anti–food porn open up new lines of inquiry, even as food porn has become so ubiquitous that it seems to have lost any coherent meaning. For example, David and Allard discuss how Instagram users attach #foodporn to essentially any image of food (chapter 3). Yet, even as it grows diffuse, food porn serves as a richly complex analytic that provides multiple avenues for theorizing and interpreting food media. It is more than just a gag or hashtag. Food porn's intellectual pathways address separately—or more ambitiously, *together*—the aesthetics of food, the politics of food labor and production, the historical and economic context of food consumption, and the dynamics of power and identity, inclusion and exclusion throughout the food system.

Rather than pin down a precise meaning of food porn in the 2010s or predict what it will mean in the 2020s, the chapters in this book reflect on how food porn acts as a floating signifier. We, as editors and authors, ask: how have food porn's use and meaning changed across historical and cultural contexts, and how might it be deployed in the future by Instagram users and academic researchers alike? How and why do people, including many Instagram users, invest so deeply in the concept, even as they want it to accomplish different things at different moments? Is it good to think with, and is it good for us? With such questions in mind, food porn emerges hand in hand with Instagrammability throughout this book as a key concept.

Instagram Affordances, Architecture, and Style: Reshaping the Aesthetics of Food

The platform architecture of Instagram transforms not only the way we produce and consume food, but also how we look at it. The app's signature aesthetic style combines with its ease of use to produce what Lachlan MacDowell identifies as "a new cultural logic of the visual."[38] Incorporating the food porn aesthetic, this visual logic spills out across food Instagram through additional features explored in this book, especially its temporal and spatial organization, distinctive celebrity aesthetics, and interplay between image and text.

These features are all implicated in the *affordances* of Instagram—that is, the capacities a media technology or application offer users, or what it allows its users to do.[39] Media studies analysis of affordances foregrounds the relationships between subjects and technologies, stressing how both users and the technologies are shaped by their interactions. It therefore resists technological determinism, or the assumption that a media technology's features prescribe how people will use them. With their concept of imagined affordance, Peter Nagy and Gina Neff stress that affordances arise through the intersecting motivations and assumptions of technology designers, the beliefs and expectations of users, and the material and operational qualities of technologies.[40] Conceptually, affordances help social media researchers explore how technologies (like platforms) are designed to suggest behaviors and uses, even as users repurpose them in unexpected ways.[41] Robin Caldwell, for instance, examines the unique affordances of Instagram for nurturing and sustaining social bonds among Black women cooking their way through social distancing during the COVID-19 pandemic (chapter 5). As we explore throughout the rest of this section—and as many of our contributors chart across the book—food Instagram takes up the platform's affordances in myriad ways when users negotiate and adapt its design to their needs and desires.

Instagram registers temporality through the flow of rapid image scrolling, with square photos framed by white space, redolent of a film strip or the staccato view of a landscape streaming through the windows of a train. Such remediation of older media forms into the Instagram scroll is ideally suited to the attention economy's demand for constantly updated content. Populated by users and advertisers, the feed is algorithmically curated to refresh what is newest or most engaging at any given moment: "insta" is in the name itself, suggesting seamless representation of the present.[42] The immediacy of food photographs is a particularly good match for Instagram's perpetual appeal to liveness. Because food photographs must be captured quickly, before the ice cream melts or the steaming dish cools, they seem to ask the viewer: *don't you wish you were here, now, in the instant when you could taste this delicious dish before it's gone?*

Instagram's insistent present tense is further shaped by the narrative logic of seriality. Users are provided endless opportunities to update their profile or publish a story, "invited by the structure of the user interface as well as by the feedback of the community to post again and again, to like, to comment on pictures, and to comment on comments."[43] The serial impulse populates Instagram galleries stored as archives of presents past, documenting accumulated experiences like episodes. The daily rhythm of eating—as well as the conventions of food presentation, including the common shapes of dishes and silverware—provide connective tissue across individual posts. These visual templates of seriality punctuate photo diaries with shots of travel and exotic meals, while also cultivating brand identities across curated posts from food bloggers and merchants. In this sense, Instagram speeds up the rate of food imagery production. Alex Ketchum illustrates how, compared to the much slower publishing rates of cookbooks and restaurant pamphlets by feminist eateries in past decades, Instagram's near-constant need for attention means restaurant owners "must release at least one new story ever twenty-four hours" (chapter 16).

Instagram's spatial layout structures its temporality, using blank space to frame each image as the most important thing to look at *now*. The grid view of individual accounts flattens the passing of time by incentivizing users to curate their images by harmonizing color palettes and aesthetic styles (as Tsugumi [Mimi] Okabe explores with dreamy pastel hues in chapter 2), rather than emphasizing change over time. This aesthetic convergence extends through the platform across global spaces, as revealed in the Selfiecity project led by Lev Manovich. His team's analysis exposed surprising stylistic repetition across a sample of fifty thousand Instagram photos gleaned from thirteen cities around the world, including in color patterns, filter selection, and subject matter.[44] Considering food, specifically, Fabio Parasecoli and Mateusz Halawa document a "Global Brooklyn" aesthetic that similarly appears in hip food spots around the world, purposefully designed to be Instagrammed.[45] The space of Instagram therefore reaches beyond the screen to encompass the places where we eat and cook that are redesigned to create the right balance of trendiness and distinction, mirroring the tendency of selfies to attempt to individuate through "extremely repetitive patterns."[46]

One of these spatial patterns common to food Instagram is the flat lay, which photographs artfully arranged recipe ingredients or beautifully curated dishes from directly above. Descended from the photographic practice of knolling—a bird's-eye image of a set of things, such as a toolkit, laid out on a flat surface—the flat lay was long popular in fashion magazines and has been widely taken up by digital food photographers.[47] This photographic style transparently reveals the consumption of the gaze by borrowing a familiar commercial aesthetic, but it also draws attention to the work of the curator or chef in selecting desirable ingredients and kitchen tools. In chapter 6, Dawn Woolley and Zara Worth deploy their Instagram artworks to critique how these commercial cultures have infiltrated the foodscape, especially through ideas like "clean eating" propagated by Instagram's imagery and hashtags.

Instagram is also defined by its architecture of shareability: it is an engine for connecting people, brands, and content. Users access Instagram content through many portals—one's feed, account grids, the explore function, search hashtags, and external links that lure users onto the platform or steer them out— which promote Instagram's prominence among digitally networked publics.[48] The platform is central to what José van Dijck calls the "culture of connectivity," which she defines as "a post-broadcast, networked culture where social interactions and cultural products are inseparably enmeshed in technological (and legal-economic) systems."[49] Alongside its photographic content, the social connections, followings, followers, and likes logged on Instagram are its most important product. Joceline Andersen examines these connective affordances for food systems in chapter 15 by documenting how farmers across North America strategically interact with each other in private groups to share the farming fails, gripes, and technical questions that do not advance their brand but build solidarity among peers.

The chapters in this book address not only the diverse food aesthetics of Instagram's visuality, but how its visual cues work in concert with language and text through geolocation tagging, captions, comments, and hashtags. Textual content is an indispensable and often overlooked element in Instagram meaning making. For example, feminist food business owners include captions far lengthier than other users, emphasizing their political messages as much as grammable images (chapter 16). In Tara J. Schuwerk and Sarah E. Cramer's study of food Instagram influencers, men used aggressive capitalization in captions and text positioned over images far more often than women influencers, acting out dominant gender conventions through textual style (chapter 9). These textual elements are all the more important as they adopt and extend the platform's dominant visual logics. Instagram engineers noticed in 2015, for instance, that nearly half of all comments on the platform contained emoji, illustrating how even comment fields are being colonized by pictographs.[50] In this book, authors offer different entry points for examining the interplay of image and text. Some analyze images screen-captured from Instagram's mobile app and website, which maintain the platform's visual and textual formatting (see chapters 2 and 14, for example). Others include just the photographs themselves, extracted from the surrounding interface (see chapters 8 and 13, for example).

Hashtags are another set of textual practices shaped by Instagram's visual logic. They are the only way to actively search images on Instagram, serving an indexing function by linking images to seemingly stable textual meanings.[51] Food influencers, for instance, use hashtags to label content that is paid brand promotion, marking the discretionary boundary between "authentic" and sponsored content (see chapters 8, 9, and 12). Kris Fallon argues that hashtags on Instagram (inherited from Twitter) often serve less of an indexing function and instead operate according to the logic of memes: they emerge as collective practices, typically lack an identifiable author, and follow the rapid growth and disappearance of viral trends.[52] Under this logic, hashtags are most often used to accrue attention rather than as search terms. Illustrating this point, a digital marketing strategist in 2020 advised food bloggers to label their images with the top trending food tags, identified as #Food, #FoodPorn, #Yummy, #Foodie, and #Delicious, to grow their engagement.[53] While these tags may be employed to build visibility for one's content, the strategist warns not to rely on them too heavily because they are in competition with so many other posts sharing the same hashtag. Hashtags thus mimic memes more broadly: participating in such an "ephemeral collective" can promote an individual's visibility as easily as it can smother it.[54]

Geotags are another type of frequently used textual identifier, logging the place where a photo was taken either in the location field, or by adding a geo-modified tag such as #NYeats or #HKfoodie. As a form of what Henri Lefebvre calls "spatial practice," geotags combine with images of everyday activities to narrate and visualize space in transformative ways.[55] For instance, picturing a global city through food-focused geotags, such as #Bangkokfood, both reflects and reinterprets how we understand it in space and time. Emily Buddle delineates the limits of this practice, documenting how geotags can also raise safety concerns for food workers, such as certain livestock farmers in Australia targeted by protesters who located farms via Instagram (chapter 10).

Exploring how food-related identities, communities, and business models take shape across the digital architecture of Instagram highlights their diverse visual and textual logics. Instagram is not a monolith; it is more useful to approach it as a collection of corporate entities and communities of practice organized in alternately predictable and subversive ways.[56] Against this backdrop, studying how everyday users, influencers, and workers in food and agricultural industries engage with food Instagram provides a unique lens for studying social media and modern life.

Exploring Food Instagram's Feed Supply Chain

A significant area of food studies scholarship focuses on food systems, evolving from discussions of commodity food chains to more complex analyses of food systems as networks with multiple stages, nodes, and processes of connection and exchange.[57] What happens when we view Instagram through this model, considering the flows from seed to our visual feed on the app and beyond? Although we do not provide a full accounting of how food systems or Instagram function as visual economies, this framing offers openings for scholars in both food studies and media studies to play with the points of contact between these distinct but overlapping ecosystems.

Central to both is the production of value through visually appealing products that are consumed first through the eyes. Instagram does not just *represent* our food system, or elements of it, through photographs. It helps to *produce* food systems through its visual economy, linking farms to food bloggers to restaurants to eaters in novel and potentially profitable ways, connections explored by all authors in this book. Further, just as Instagram sells seemingly immediate access to friends, brands, and celebrities, so too food Instagram reproduces the illusion of frictionless access to beautiful food. As various chapters in this anthology demonstrate, the platform helps to foster the fantasy of shortened food (and image) supply chains through its aesthetics of liveness, intimacy, and authenticity. Exploring Instagram's *feed* supply chain thus offers a method for teasing out how digital visual economies are reshaping what and how we eat.

Raw Inputs

The food system starts with raw materials, such as soil, fertilizers, air, water, seeds, and livestock. As a platform, Instagram requires a vast array of inputs, from electricity and computer code to capital and labor. As a visual medium, additional raw inputs include photogenic food, such as the colorfully indulgent unicorn lattes and FreakShakes analyzed in chapters 7 and 11. At the time of this writing, #eatingfortheinsta had surpassed five million posts. Indeed, food Instagram's appetite for visual content privileges the combination of attractively curated spaces, people, and objects, such as well-manicured yet disembodied hands cradling props and walls painted or papered to provide whimsical backdrops.

Similar to most food systems, food Instagram's inputs are rarely truly raw. They must be purposefully selected, prepared in various ways, and made camera-ready. As detailed in the food porn discussion, the production of beautiful food often requires enormous amounts of labor. Instagram users celebrate some of this labor through behind-the-scenes photos of the process of creating food, or images of it. In chapters 10 and 15, Buddle and Andersen explore how farmers and livestock producers depict their daily work through posts, while Ketchum describes how a feminist chocolatier Instagrams herself drafting a cookbook and selecting truffle ingredients (chapter 16). Indeed, Instagram cofounders Kevin Systrom and Mike Krieger promoted the platform's preferred "behind-the-scenes content" from its inception.[58] For food, showing *just enough* of the transformation from raw ingredient to finished product conveys a sense of authenticity and intimacy that draws people to Instagram.

These curated depictions of labor, however, hide at least as much as they reveal. The majority of workers involved in growing, harvesting, processing, transporting, and preparing foods are largely invisible to the end consumer, except when part of the food chain breaks, as happened in 2020 when the COVID-19 pandemic shut down U.S. meatpacking plants and interrupted supply chains worldwide. The visual economy of food Instagram relies on—and indeed profits from—a similar occlusion of the many types of labor that support the production of food images, from farm workers to overseas content moderators scrubbing our feeds of offensive posts.[59] As David and Allard observe in chapter 3, the "Uberization" of the restaurant industry in France is leading to the further erasure of its labor force through "ghost kitchens" and exploitative food delivery services such as Ubereats, which use Instagram to sell the image of more direct access to desirable food regardless of the impact on workers.

Celebrity also fuels the Instagram feed chain. While many flock to the platform to build fame and influence (Instagram outputs that are discussed below), the input of existing celebrity power established Instagram's distinctive brand in its early days. Rapper Snoop Dogg was the first recognizable star to join Instagram in early 2011, when he posted a filtered shot of himself wearing a suit and holding a can of Blast by Colt 45, a new caffeinated alcoholic drink (fig. 0-2).[60] It was unclear whether the post was an overt advertisement or not ("nobody knew, and nobody asked"), but it is notable that the first high-profile

FIGURE 0-2. Snoop Dogg's first Instagram post, in 2011.

celebrity on Instagram used a novel food product as a prop, ushering in a type of media influence that fused fame with ambiguous brand marketing.[61] The platform's—and advertisers'—expectation of frequently updated content also encourages celebrities, including chefs, food television hosts, and health gurus, to share public glimpses into their everyday lives. Celebrity pics of their daily meals legitimize and commodify the proliferation of what Yasmin Ibrahim calls banal imaging, which aestheticizes mundane nonevents through visual rituals that feel within reach of ordinary people.[62] In this way, food images rendered by and through the lens of celebrity help to encode the stylized yet accessible everyday aesthetic of Instagram more broadly.

This visual ecosystem wouldn't exist, however, without another primary input: attention. In the attention economy, attention is understood to be both *scarce* because of natural, technological, and social limits, and *measurable*, allowing it to function as a type of capital.[63] Whether rooted in leisure, hope, or wages, the labor of everyday users on Instagram to create and organize content, like, and comment is easily quantified. This digital accounting facilitates the commodification of our "relationships, preferences and habits" for advertisers and other data brokers.[64] Instagram devours an ever-changing menu of raw and processed inputs, demonstrating some of what fuels the platform's ravenous drive for fresh content.

Production

Within the global food system, production most often refers to the growing, cultivation, and processing of foodstuffs before they reach consumers. It is also a stage that speaks directly to the experiences, motivations, and challenges of food producers themselves, which some elect to share on social media platforms like Instagram.[65] The platform's culture and technological affordances facilitate multiple ways for food producers to represent and discuss their work.[66] Indeed, posting about food on Instagram produces many things: visual and textual content for the platform; quantifiable user engagement; and various forms of data for the company to mine, analyze, and potentially sell. As a social network, it also produces subjects, audiences, rituals, and new forms of influence, which we focus on here.

Just as early photographed portraits provided a way to communicate individual and collective identity, Instagram offers a space to perform our senses of both self and sociality. The performance of self is often enacted through what Lee Humphreys calls media accounting, which constructs authenticity through ritualized "practices of documenting, chronicling, and cataloging" our presence on social media.[67] If we are, to some extent, what we eat, then keeping a photographic meal diary as a form of media accounting can serve different functions. Creating "digital gastronomic memoirs" that document daily consumption, for instance, can establish intimacy with one's followers.[68] Meanwhile, diet brands (see chapter 2) and wellness influencers (see chapter 9) use Instagram to provide normative instruction on how to cook, eat, and look.

Instagram's visual practices can also capture and represent the photographer's subjectivity in ways that become conventional or even codified.[69] On food Instagram, disembodied hands caress latte mugs or hold ice cream cones, while feet or toes stick out below handheld food items shot from above. The combination of food and selfies has become integrated into Instagram's "platform vernacular," which Gibbs et al. define as a social media platform's "unique combination of styles, grammars and logics."[70] Partially disembodied food selfies are a vernacular expression that Alise Tifentale and Lev Manovich call the anti-selfie, depicting "a person's body but not her/his face." They serve not as a portrait in the classical sense, but as a record of participation in an activity embedded in a particular place.[71] In food photographs, partial incorporation of the self acts as a metonym for the full subject in action, demonstrating how cooking, eating, and other food-related activities are important to the production of self, including expressions of identity such as gender, sexuality, race, and social class.

Beyond established celebrities, Instagram also produces influencers, who mobilize the platform to create new forms of fame that now constitute a multibillion-dollar advertising industry.[72] Influencers manifest what Graeme Turner calls the demotic turn, which has seemingly democratized access to celebrity while accelerating the production of the personal brand as a new micro-celebrity industry.[73] Self-branding monetizes—or renders economically valuable—the production of an "ordinary" yet exceptional self that is packaged as media content.[74] This form of subjectivity increases influence by cultivating an aesthetic of authenticity and trustworthiness, while expanding influencers' visibility through complex algorithmic interactions.[75] Food is a particularly evocative medium for bolstering personal influence because it combines relatability with—in the case of food porn—aspirational desire, publicizing everyday consumption in a way that thrives in Instagram's visual economy.

The entanglement of food and celebrity threads through this book, from explicit engagement with food influencers to food's proximity to other forms of celebrity branding. Yue-Chiu Bonni Leung and Yi-Chieh Jessica Lin highlight how Hong Kong food influencers navigate digital leisure and labor within the city's complex blend of international and local food cultures (chapter 8), while Schuwerk and Cramer analyze health and diet discourses among Instagram wellness influencers (chapter 9). Kirkwood observes how food celebrity flows between traditional, legacy media (such as television and print journalism), and digital media, including Instagram and IGTV (chapter 11). KC Hysmith weaves together reflections on food aesthetics from her life as both an Instagram influencer and a scholar who critically researches the platform (chapter 12). Finally, the national cuisines of Denmark, Italy, and Brazil intersect with the politicization of celebrity in contributions from Krogager and Leer (chapter 13) and Garcia Santamaria (chapter 14). These diverse case studies and methodological approaches to food, fame, and social media form a rich seam connecting food studies and media studies, suggesting the importance of nurturing this emergent scholarly conversation.

The production of individual subjects on Instagram, whether through media accounting or celebrity culture, takes place within hyper-connected social contexts. From farmers to food entrepreneurs, producers cultivate networks of current and potential consumers through their visual feeds as a way to build their markets and maintain trust. For instance, the livestock producers examined by Buddle (chapter 10) and organic farmers by Andersen (chapter 15) share field-level images on Instagram in order to reach across urban-rural divides and address the alienation and lack of transparency that can characterize our food system.

Regional identities also find visual expression on Instagram by constructing a sense of place through food. As Newman analyzes the Instagram account Hot Dudes and Hummus, he demonstrates how these images serve as soft power nation branding that erases political questions about Israeli occupation and militarism in the region through a utopian gallery of "Israel's Yummiest" (chapter 1). Turning to the southern United States, Deborah Harris and Rachel Phillips explore how the culinary identity of the New South becomes condensed into the humble biscuit, which is experiencing a second life as a destination delicacy (chapter 4). The meaning of the South in this context, however, is ambivalent: the Instagrammable interiors of New South biscuit restaurants project a modern multicultural cosmopolitanism to tourists and diners, even as restaurants' visual feeds belie racial inequalities across their workforce and clientele more familiar from the Old South. In such ways, Instagram's modes of production always take place within asymmetrical relations of power and access within and beyond the digital realm.

Distribution and Consumption

Distribution and consumption are typically separate stages in the food system supply chain. Distribution encompasses everything from food processing to transportation via truck, air, or sea to markets both local and global. The system also depends on the circulation of food images via marketing and advertising, package labels, cooking shows, and other forms of representation. Consumption describes buying and preparing food, as well as eating it. It also casts consumers as food system stakeholders, although access and power are unevenly distributed. The politics of food and consumption are made poignantly visible on Instagram, as branded content and monetization of attention often rely on social constructions of class, race, and gender that perpetuate inequalities. In this book, these politics are evident in Schuwerk and Cramer's investigation of predominantly white health and wellness influencers hawking expensive nutritional supplements with little consideration of their own identities and privileges (chapter 9). Indeed, the systemic sexism and racism of restaurant and food industries bleed into food Instagram in unsavory ways. For example, *Man vs. Food* host Adam Richman lost his television program for posting fat-phobic comments on Instagram, and *Bon Appétit* magazine editor Adam Rapoport resigned after photos of him in brown face surfaced on the platform.[76]

Despite this visibility, the processes of distribution, circulation, and consumption are difficult to tease apart on Instagram because of the technological affordances of digital media. For example, consumption is often simultaneous with the act of distribution, as each individual feed is algorithmically produced and delivered at the moment that one opens the app to consume it. Further, unlike food, digital media consumption is not a singular act; each image can be consumed and recirculated indefinitely. We therefore adapt the food chain model here to reflect these complex processes and to specifically discuss dynamics of prosumption, dissemination, and consumers themselves.

Social media apps like Instagram are factories of prosumption. While the construct of the prosumer is not new, having been first named by futurist Alvin Toffler in 1980, it has acquired new currency in the world of Web 2.0, especially for food and digital media. George Ritzer identifies the rise of U.S. fast-food chains as an early modern prosumption lab that trained customers to take on a growing share of producing their own meal by carrying food to their table, building their own salad at the salad bar, and busing their dishes.[77] This corporate model of putting consumers to work was adapted to online life, which is increasingly defined by user-created content. Debate among media scholars continues regarding how exactly value is created for social media companies through user prosumption.[78] Yet it is clear that retaining and increasing user attention is what allows Instagram, Facebook, Twitter, and other media to expand ad sales, data collection, surveillance, and overall revenue. In 2019, Instagram generated $20 billion in ad revenue, which exceeded YouTube's total revenue of $15 billion and comprised over a quarter of parent company Facebook's overall revenues for the year.[79] Instagram markets social connection to users and capitalizes on those dense networks to offer users up for targeted advertising, including collecting and deploying "big food data."[80]

On a platform like Instagram, the prosumer frame is necessary but insufficient to describe user practices: they not only produce and consume content, they also distribute it through likes, comments, shares, regrams (the Instagram equivalent of retweets), memetics (the creation and spread of memes), and expanding social networks. Through these interactive practices, the circulatory economy of Instagram distributes food media content along vectors of social connectivity, virality, aesthetics, lifestyle, and celebrity.[81] A number of chapters in this book explore how food Instagrammers use such strategies to mold their online personas and procure socially valuable "culinary capital," that is, "how and why certain foods and food-related practices"—such as taking, posting, and consuming food Instagram photos—"connote, and by extension, confer status and power on those who know about and enjoy them."[82] At the same time, food Instagrammers boost circulation of real products, from cakes and unicorn lattes to hummus and biscuits. The identity of posters and their imagined audiences on food Instagram also shape which foods get pictured and which do not. As one Hong Kong food influencer laments in chapter 8, traditional brown foods like red braised pork are "not eye-catching in the world of Instagram" and are regrettably becoming less popular among eaters.

Regulatory structures can also shape Instagram circulation, and call for more sustained scholarly attention. The U.S. Federal Trade Commission's (FTC's) endorsement guides direct social media influencers to disclose if they are being compensated by the brands they promote online, including clearly marking posts with tags such as #ad or #sponsored. These guidelines are nonbinding, however, and enforcement has been weak, leading to the FTC's efforts to formalize these rules and increase penalties.[83] For food influencers, stricter regulation could affect their relationships with both the brands they represent and their audiences, undercutting their performances of authenticity, transparency, and ordinariness, as Leung and Lin (chapter 8) and Hysmith (chapter 12) highlight. Emily Truman explores another curious case of curtailed Insta-circulation in chapter 7, in which an independent New York café, the End Brooklyn, successfully settled a trademark infringement case with Starbucks in a battle of unicorns. The New York café owners created an original drink called the Unicorn Latte, but when Instagram users widely applied #unicornlatte to Starbucks' Unicorn Frappuccino novelty drink, the café owners successfully argued that it damaged their trademark.

Instagram obsessions can also motivate people to circulate through and consume real places beyond the digital feed in new ways, popularizing Instagram-tailored locations such as New York City's iconic Museum of Ice Cream.[84] Sometimes these trends carry a significant and detrimental environmental footprint. For example, the social cachet of Instagramming beautiful landscapes has increased visits to national parks, monuments, and natural wonders, but some visitors are quick to skirt the rules in order to get that perfect shot, which can risk ecological damage and even devastation.[85] Instagram has not just changed what and how we eat. It has changed our relationship to our communities, the land, and the people who care for them. All too often, the Instagrammer's mentality can be one of capture and extraction, as much as cultivation and care, revealing further insights into digital consumer habits within our food system.

Waste

Our food system creates significant waste, whether from the mismanagement of food production, distribution processes, retail overstock, or individual consumption practices.[86] Instagram creates its own rubbish. Some is literal food waste. For example, Kirkwood discusses how Instagrammers purchase Canberra café Pâtissez's famous FreakShakes for the sole purpose of photographing them (chapter 11). Other food grammers acknowledge how they sometimes purchase multiple items just to capture the one Insta-worthy shot. Such food waste is not unique to the Instagram economy, but rather illustrates how wasteful norms in our larger food system extend into and prop up the digital economy. More benignly, many of us may waste time and energy on Instagram, seduced and comforted by its infinite scroll.

Instagram also indexes growing concerns about the digital economy's ballooning waste streams. Facilitated by the shift from film to digital cameras, we can all now take copious photos without concern for cost or physical storage space, often oblivious to the carbon footprint of these technologies. Instagram supports the illusion of transcendent digital immateriality—what Sabine LeBel calls the technological sublime—but its surface beauty erases the environmental toll of regularly upgrading (and disposing of) our digital devices, which are often exported to toxic dumps in the Global South.[87] Similarly, Instagram obfuscates the ecological costs of storing vast photo and video archives on power-hungry data servers. Accounting for 10 percent of global electricity demand, the Internet has been described as "the largest coal-fired machine" on the planet; these energy demands are bloated by the extensive "exhaust" or waste data produced by our digital photography and social media practices.[88]

Instagram also produces waste in the sense of "garbage" content. Like Twitter, Instagram is full of bot accounts, fake followers and posts, trolls, and other fraudulent or toxic behavior. This has led to the creation of a subindustry of content moderators hired to clean up our online trash, mostly consisting of low-wage laborers in sites like the Philippines, India, Bangladesh, and Sri Lanka.[89] Instagram thus participates in a broader digital colonialism that exports both physical e-waste and digital detritus to be managed and disposed of by an exploited labor force kept largely out of sight of users in wealthier countries. As our mapping of food Instagram's visual ecosystem reveals, our desire for friction-free access to food images warrants reform as much as our global food system's problems and inequities.

Reading Map

This book's subtitle echoes its three sections. "Part I: Identity" unpacks the notion "you are what you post" as it examines how representations of food and eating on Instagram shape and reflect gender, race, class, regionality, and nationhood, as well as health, the body, and the self. Building on this foundation, "Part II: Influence" examines not just influencers but also how Instagram functions as a persuasive platform in a number of areas, including food marketing, health messaging, consumer perceptions of meat production, and the relationship between Instagram and legacy media. Although Instagram's affordances shape its particular power, users have devised ways to negotiate and reimagine Instagram's visual logics and what uses they can serve. "Part III: Negotiation" thus examines how restauranteurs, politicians, farmers, and professors have used Instagram to resist aesthetic norms, enact feminist politics, express political critique, reimagine consumer relations, and devise new pedagogical goals.

These three sections lend thematic structure to the book's chapters, but they also open up dialogue between them. Nearly every chapter explores the themes of identity, influence, and negotiation, placing different weight on each. To extend the book's reach beyond academia, each section also incorporates one or two shorter, reflective essays that complement the traditional scholarly chapters. These essays apply the Instagram themes of identity, influence, and negotiation as they merge theoretical perspectives with art, professional practice, community building, and pedagogy in innovative ways.

Of course, there is even more to explore in the realm of food Instagram. In the afterword, we sketch potential trajectories for further research. Taken as a whole, this book confirms Instagram's primacy as a visual social platform par excellence, one that has profoundly shaped what and how we eat, how we define and express ourselves, and how our food system functions and flows.

Notes

The authors would like to extend warm gratitude to Justin Rawlins and Diana Garvin for their insightful feedback on and suggestions for this introduction.

1. Sarah Lee, "Picture Perfect? How Instagram Changed the Food We Eat," *BBC News*, December 29, 2017, www.bbc.com/news/uk-england-london-42012732.

2. See, for example, Pete Wells, "8 Ways Restaurants Have Changed in the Past Decade," *New York Times*, December 17, 2019, www.nytimes.com/2019/12/17/dining/restaurant-trends-pete-wells.html; Tim Hayward, "From Avocados to Instagram: The Decade in Food," *Guardian*, December 9, 2019, www.theguardian.com/food/2019/dec/09/tim-hayward-decade-of-food-supper-clubs-avocados-instagram; Lee Breslouer, "The Food Trends That Defined Us in the 2010s," HuffPost, December 27, 2019, www.huffpost.com/entry/food-trends-2010-decade_1_5df930aee4b0d6c84b7488d7.

3. Helene Stapinski, "Restaurants Turn Camera Shy," *New York Times*, January 22, 2013, www.nytimes.com/2013/01/23/dining/restaurants-turn-camera-shy.html.

4. Meredith Wood, "How Instagram Changed the Restaurant Industry," *Fundera* (blog), December 17, 2019, www.fundera.com/blog/instagram-restaurants; Aaron Goldfarb, "Hold the Cone!" Taste, September 4, 2019, www.tastecooking.com/hold-the-cone-ice-cream-instagram-wall/.

5. Alicia Kelso, "Restaurants Rethink Marketing, but Facebook Remains King," Restaurant Dive, August 15, 2019, www.restaurantdive.com/news/restaurants-rethink-marketing-but-facebook-remains-king/560950/.

6. Jean Anthelme Brillat-Savarin, *The Physiology of Taste: Or Meditations on Transcendental Gastronomy*, trans. M. F. K. Fisher (New York: Vintage, 2009), reprint; Pierre Bourdieu, *Distinction: A Social Critique of the Judgement of Taste*, trans. Richard Nice (Cambridge, MA: Harvard University Press, 1984); Peter Naccarato and Kathleen LeBesco, *Culinary Capital* (New York: Bloomsbury Academic, 2012).

7. J. Clement, "Distribution of Instagram Users Worldwide as of April 2020, by Age and Gender," Statista, April 24, 2020, www.statista.com/statistics/248769/age-distribution-of-worldwide-instagram-users/.

8. Alice E. Marwick, *Status Update: Celebrity, Publicity, and Branding in the Social Media Age* (New Haven, CT: Yale University Press, 2013); Keia Mastrianni, "The

Case for Food Criticism in Charlotte," *Charlotte Magazine*, January 20, 2020, www
.charlottemagazine.com/the-case-for-food-criticism-in-charlotte/. See also note 67.

9. Alexandrea J. Ravenelle, *Gig and Hustle: Struggling and Surviving in the Sharing Economy* (Oakland: University of California Press, 2019); Brooke Erin Duffy, *(Not) Getting Paid to Do What You Love: Gender, Social Media, and Aspirational Work* (New Haven, CT: Yale University Press, 2017).

10. Isabelle de Solier, "Tasting the Digital: New Food Media," in *The Bloomsbury Handbook of Food and Popular Culture*, ed. Kathleen Lebesco and Peter Naccarato, 54–65 (New York: Bloomsbury Academic, 2018). While we agree that much can be gained by examining multiple platforms produced by the same user, our aim in this book is to recuperate the minimal attention scholars have thus far given Instagram specifically.

11. Elizabeth Kaufer, "Instagram: The Next Big (Academic) Thing?," *Rough Consensus* (blog), February 12, 2015, https://blogs.oii.ox.ac.uk/roughconsensus/2015/02/instagram-the-next-big-academic-thing/.

12. Isabelle de Solier, *Food and the Self: Consumption, Production and Material Culture* (London: Bloomsbury Academic, 2013); Signe Rousseau, *Food and Social Media: You Are What You Tweet* (Lanham, MD: Alta Mira Press, 2012).

13. Peri Bradley, ed., *Food, Media and Contemporary Culture: The Edible Image* (London: Palgrave Macmillan, 2016); Kathleen LeBesco and Peter Naccarato, eds., *The Handbook of Food and Popular Culture* (New York: Bloomsbury, 2017); Tanja Schneider, Karin Eli, Catherine Dolan, and Stanley Ulijaszek, *Digital Food Activism* (New York: Routledge, 2017); Tania Lewis and Michelle Phillipov, eds., "Food/Media: Eating, Cooking, and Provisioning in a Digital World," special issue, *Communication Research and Practice* 4, no. 3 (2018); Karen Klitgaard Povlsen and Jonatan Leer, eds., *Food and Media: Practices, Distinctions and Heterotopias* (New York: Routledge, 2018); Deborah Lupton and Zeena Feldman, eds., *Digital Food Cultures* (New York: Routledge, 2020).

14. Tania Lewis, *Digital Food: From Paddock to Platform* (New York and London: Bloomsbury Academic, 2020); Jonatan Leer and Stinne Gunder Strøm Krogager, eds., *Research Methods in Digital Food Studies* (New York: Routledge, 2021).

15. Tama Leaver, Tim Highfield, and Crystal Abidin, *Instagram: Visual Social Media Cultures* (Cambridge, UK: Polity, 2020).

16. Elaine M. Power, "De-Centering the Text: Exploring the Potential for Visual Methods in the Sociology of Food," *Journal for the Study of Food and Society* 6, no. 2 (Winter 2003): 9–20.

17. John Tagg, *The Burden of Representation* (Amherst: University of Massachusetts Press, 1988), 43.

18. Ibid., 37.

19. Susan Bright, *Feast for the Eyes: The Story of Food in Photography* (New York: Aperture, 2017).

20. Walter Benjamin, "A Short History of Photography," *Screen* 13, no. 1 (Spring 1972 [1931]): 5—26; 24.

21. Tagg, *Burden of Representation*, 54.

22. See, for example, Susanne Friedberg, *Fresh: A Perishable History* (Cambridge, MA: Harvard University Press, 2009).

23. Elizabeth J. Fleitz, "Third Course: Rhetoric(s) of Visual Design in Basic Cookbooks," chapter 4 in "The Multimodal Kitchen: Cookbooks as Women's Rhetorical Practice" (PhD diss., Bowling Green University, 2009), 96–131; C. Anne Wilson, ed., *The Appetite and the Eye: Visual Aspects of Food and Its Presentation within Their Historic Context* (Edinburgh: Edinburgh University Press, 1991).

24. Lachlan MacDowell, *Instafame: Graffiti and Street Art in the Instagram Era* (Chicago: Intellect, 2019), 53.

25. The tagging of images makes them much easier for search engines to recognize and sort. Bernd Leiendecker, "Of Duck Faces and Cat Beards: Why Do Selfies Need Genres?," in *Exploring the Selfie: Historical, Theoretical, and Analytical Approaches to Digital Self-Photography*, ed. Julia Eckel, Jens Ruchatz, and Sabine Wirth, 197–98, (London: Palgrave Macmillan, 2018); Alise Tifentale and Lev Manovich, "Selfiecity: Exploring Photography and Self-Fashioning in Social Media," Selfiecity.net, 2014, accessed at http://manovich.net/content/04-projects/086-selfiecity-exploring/selfiecity _chapter.pdf.

26. Salvador Rodriguez, "As Calls Grow to Split Up Facebook, Employees Who Were There for the Instagram Acquisition Explain Why the Deal Happened," CNBC. com, September 24, 2019, www.cnbc.com/2019/09/24/facebook-bought-instagram -because-it-was-scared-of-twitter-and-google.html.

27. Leaver, Highfield, and Abidin, *Instagram*.

28. Taylor Lorenz, "Instagram Has a Massive Harassment Problem," *Atlantic*, October 15, 2018, www.theatlantic.com/technology/archive/2018/10/instagram-has -massive-harassment-problem/572890/.

29. Arielle Pardes, "Instagram Will (Finally) Pay Influencers," *Wired*, May 27, 2020, www.wired.com/story/instagram-finally-pay-influencers-badges-igtv-ads/.

30. Linda Williams, "Skin Flicks on the Racial Border: Pornography, Exploitation, and Interracial Lust," in *Media Studies: A Reader*, 3d ed., ed. Sue Thornham, Caroline Bassett, and Paul Marris (New York: New York University Press, 2009), 279.

31. Molly O'Neill, "Food Porn," *Columbia Journalism Review*, October 23, 2003, www.ora.tv/homepage/2016/8/29/1; Anne E. McBride, "Food Porn," *Gastronomica: The Journal of Critical Food Studies* 10, no. 1 (February 1, 2010): 38–46; Roland Barthes, *Mythologies* (New York: Hill and Wing, 2012), 142, 143–44.

32. Tisha Dejmanee, "'Food Porn' as Postfeminist Play: Digital Femininity and the Female Body on Food Blogs," *Television and New Media* 17, no. 5 (July 1, 2016): 429–48; Ariane Cruz, "Gettin' Down Home with the Neelys: Gastro-Porn and Televisual Performances of Gender, Race, and Sexuality," *Women and Performance: A Journal of Feminist Theory* 23, no. 3 (November 2013): 323–49; Signe Rousseau, "Food 'Porn' in Media," in *Encyclopedia of Food and Agricultural Ethics*, ed. Paul B. Thompson and David M. Kaplan, 1–8 (Dordrecht: Springer Netherlands, 2013); Erin Metz McDonnell, "Food Porn: The Conspicuous Consumption of Food in

the Age of Digital Reproduction," in *Food, Media, and Contemporary Culture: The Edible Image*, ed. Peri Bradley, 239–65 (London: Palgrave Macmillan, 2016); Nathan Taylor and Megan Keating, "Contemporary Food Imagery: Food Porn and Other Visual Trends," *Communication Research and Practice* 4, no. 3 (2018): 307–23.

33. Cruz, "Gettin' Down Home," 331.

34. Francine Matalon-degni, "Trends in Food Photography: A Prop Stylist's View," *Gastronomica* 10, no. 3 (Summer 2010): 70–83; Anne L. Bower, ed., *Reel Food: Essays on Food and Film* (New York: Routledge, 2004), 6.

35. Dejmanee, "Food Porn."

36. Taylor Lorenz, "The Instagram Aesthetic Is Over," *Atlantic*, April 23, 2019, www.theatlantic.com/technology/archive/2019/04/influencers-are-abandoning -instagram-look/587803; Carrie Battan, "The Rise of the 'Getting Real' Post on Instagram," *New Yorker*, October 1, 2019, www.newyorker.com/culture/culture-desk/ the-rise-of-the-getting-real-post-on-instagram.

37. Scott Ross, "Being Real on Fake Instagram: Likes, Images, and Media Ideologies of Value," *Journal of Linguistic Anthropology* 29, no. 3 (2019): 359–74; Jin Kang and Lewen Wei, "Let Me Be at my Funniest: Instagram Users' Motivations for Using Finsta (a.k.a., Fake Instagram)," *Social Science Journal* 57, no. 1 (2020): 58–71.

38. MacDowell, *Instafame*, 3.

39. Scholars in media studies have adopted the concept of affordances from James J. Gibson, who first developed it in ecological psychology to theorize how environments make different actions possible for animals, and later Donald Norman, whose work married cognitive science and design. See Taina Bucher and Anne Helmond, "The Affordances of Social Media Platforms," in *The Sage Handbook of Social Media*, ed. Jean Burgess, Alice Marwick, and Thomas Poell (New York: Sage, 2017); James J. Gibson, *The Ecological Approach to Visual Perception* (Hillsdale, NJ: Lawrence Erlbaum Associates, 1986); Donald Norman, *The Design of Everyday Things* (New York: Doubleday Business, 1990).

40. Peter Nagy and Gina Neff, "Imagined Affordance: Reconstructing a Keyword for Communication Theory," *Social Media and Society* 1, no. 2 (2015): 5.

41. See, for example, the application of affordances in the work of Nagy and Neff, "Imagined Affordance"; Joshua McVeigh-Schultz and Nancy K. Baym, "Thinking of You: Vernacular Affordance in the Context of the Microsocial Relationship App, Couple," *Social Media and Society* 1, no. 2 (2015): 1–13; Esther Weltevrede and Erik Borra, "Platform Affordances and Data Practices: The Value of Dispute on Wikipedia," *Big Data and Society* 3, no. 1 (2015): 1–16.

42. Indeed, the temporality of the ever-present was built into the platform's pre-2016 versions, in which posts were dated by the minutes, days, or weeks elapsed to the present moment, rather than by their fixed date in the past. For a complication of Instagram's temporality, see Nadav Hochman and Lev Manovich, "Zooming into an Instagram City: Reading the Local through Social Media," *First Monday* 18, no. 7 (2013), https://doi.org/10.5210/fm.v18i7.4711

43. Sabine Wirth, "Interfacing the Self," in Eckel, Ruchatz, and Wirth, *Exploring the Selfie*, 228–229.

44. Hochman and Manovich, "Zooming into an Instagram City."

45. Fabio Parasecoli and Mateusz Halawa, *Global Brooklyn: Designing Food Experiences in World Cities* (London: Bloomsbury, 2021).

46. Wirth, "Interfacing the Self," 213.

47. Megan Willett, "Everyone's Obsessed with 'Knolling' Their Stuff and Putting the Photos on Instagram," Business Insider, May 14, 2015, www.businessinsider.com/instagram-flat-lay-trend-knolling-2015-5.

48. Sarah Florini documents how networked publics move between platforms to take advantage of their different affordances and work around their limitations with a focus on Black transplatform publics. *Beyond Hashtags: Racial Politics and Black Digital Networks* (New York: New York University Press, 2019).

49. José van Dijck, "Flickr and the Culture of Connectivity: Sharing Views, Experiences, Memories," *Memory Studies* 4, no. 4 (October 2011): 401–15, 404.

50. Instagram Engineering, "Emojineering Part 1: Machine Learning for Emoji Trends," *Instagram Engineering Blog*, May 1, 2015, https://instagram-engineering.com/emojineering-part-1-machine-learning-for-emoji-trendsmachine-learning-for-emoji-trends-7f5f9cb979ad.

51. Elizabeth Losh, *Hashtag* (New York: Bloomsbury, 2019).

52. Kris Fallon, "Streams of the Self: The Instagram Feed as Narrative Autobiography," in *Proceedings of the Interactive Narratives, New Media and Social Engagement International Conference*, ed. Hudson Moura, Ricardo Sternberg, Regina Cunha, Cecília Queiroz, and Martin Zeilinger (2014): 58.

53. "The Best Food Hashtags for Instagram in 2020," SocialBuddy, https://socialbuddy.com/best-food-hashtags/.

54. Fallon, "Streams of the Self," 58.

55. Henri Lefebvre, *The Production of Space*, trans. Donald Nicholson-Smith (Oxford, UK: Blackwell, 1991).

56. MacDowell, *Instafame*, chapter 4.

57. See, for example, Raj Patel, *Stuffed and Starved: The Hidden Battle for the World Food System* (New York: Melville House, 2007); Warren Belasco and Roger Horowitz, *Food Chains: From Farmyard to Shopping Cart* (Philadelphia: University of Pennsylvania Press, 2008); Philip Howard, *Concentration and Power in the Food System: Who Controls What We Eat?* (New York: Bloomsbury Academic, 2016); Alejandro Colás, Jason Edwards, Jane Levi, and Sami Zubaida, *Food, Politics, and Society: Social Theory and the Modern Food System* (Oakland: University of California Press, 2018); Fabio Parasecoli, *Food* (Cambridge, MA: MIT Press, 2019).

58. Sarah Frier, *No Filter: The Inside Story of Instagram* (New York: Simon and Schuster, 2020).

59. In 2019, Facebook released content moderation data for Instagram for the first time. In the third quarter of 2019, Instagram removed over two million posts classed as either sexual exploitation of children, terrorist propaganda, promotion of self-harm, and drugs or firearm trafficking. Daniel Carnahan, "Facebook Has Released Instagram Content Moderation Data for the First Time," Business Insider,

November 15, 2019, www.businessinsider.com/facebook-shares-instagram-content
-moderation-data-for-first-time-2019-11.

60. MG Siegler, "Snoopin' on Instagram: The Early-Adopting Celeb Joins the
Photo-Sharing Service," TechCrunch, January 19, 2011, https://techcrunch.com/2011/
01/19/snoop-dogg-instagram/.

61. Frier, *No Filter*, 36.

62. Yasmin Ibrahim, "Instagramming Life: Banal Imaging and the Poetics of the
Everyday," *Journal of Media Practice* 16, no. 1 (2015): 42–54.

63. Tiziana Terranova, "Attention, Economy and the Brain," *Culture Machine* 13
(2012): 1–19.

64. MacDowell, *Instafame*, 55.

65. Tobias Linné, "Cows on Facebook and Instagram: Interspecies Intimacy in
the Social Media Spaces of the Swedish Dairy Industry," *Television and New Media*
17, no. 8 (December 2016): 719–33; Helena C. Lyson, "Social Structural Location and
Vocabularies of Participation: Fostering a Collective Identity in Urban Agriculture
Activism: Social Structural Location and Vocabularies of Participation," *Rural Sociology* 79, no. 3 (September 2014): 310–35; T. M. Stevens, N. Aarts, C.J.A.M. Termeer,
and A. Dewulf, "Social Media Hypes about Agro-Food Issues: Activism, Scandals
and Conflicts," *Food Policy* 79 (August 2018): 23–34; Nadra Nittle, "Can YouTube
Give Farmers a Financial Boost?," Civil Eats, February 25, 2020, https://civileats.
com/2020/02/25/can-youtube-give-farmers-a-financial-boost/; Jean Burgess, Anne
Galloway and Theresa Sauter, "Hashtag as Hybrid Forum: The Case of #agchatoz,"
in *Hashtag Publics: The Power and Politics of Discursive Networks*, ed. Nathan Rambukkana, 61–76 (New York: Peter Lang, 2015).

66. This is an example of how Instagram can facilitate Foucault's concept of
"heterotopia"—that is, different, simultaneous realities that serve as counterpoints
to the status quo—a concept that Leer and Klitgaard Povlsen explore in *Food Media*
and that Schneider, Eli, Dolan, and Ulijaszek also briefly consider in *Digital Food
Activism*.

67. Lee Humphreys, *The Qualified Self: Social Media and the Accounting of Everyday Life* (Cambridge, MA: MIT Press, 2018), 12.

68. de Solier, "Tasting the Digital." For an example, see Glenn Villeneuve's photo-
documentation of his meals (www.instagram.com/glennvilleneuve/).

69. Michele Zappavigna, "Social Media Photography: Construing Subjectivity
in Instagram Images," *Visual Communication*, 15, no. 3 (2016): 271–92.

70. Martin Gibbs, James Meese, Michael Arnold, Bjorn Nansen, and Marcus
Carter, "#Funeral and Instagram: Death, Social Media, and Platform Vernacular,"
Information, Communication and Society 18, no. 3 (2015): 255–68, 257.

71. Alise Tifentale and Lev Manovich, "Competitive Photography and the Presentation of the Self," in Eckel, Ruchatz, and Wirth, *Exploring the Selfie*, 180–81.
See also Larissa Hjorth and Natalie Hendry's discussion of emplaced visuality in
"A Snapshot of Social Media: Camera Phone Practices," *Social Media and Society* 1,
no. 1 (2015): 1–3.

72. Susie Khamis, Lawrence Ang, and Raymond Welling, "Self-Branding, 'Micro-Celebrity,' and the Rise of Social Media Influencers," *Celebrity Studies* 8, no. 2 (2017): 191–208.

73. Graeme Turner, *Ordinary People and the Media: The Demotic Turn* (Los Angeles: Sage, 2010). See also Joshua Gamson, "The Unwatched Life Is Not Worth Living: The Elevation of the Ordinary in Celebrity Culture," *PMLA* 126, no. 4 (2011): 1061–62.

74. Turner, *Ordinary People and the Media*.

75. Alison Hearn and Stephanie Schoenhoff, "From Celebrity to Influencer: Tracing the Diffusion of Celebrity Value across the Data Stream," in *A Companion to Celebrity*, ed. P. David Marshall and Sean Redmond, 194–211 (Malden, MA: John Wiley, 2016); Kelley Cotter, "Playing the Visibility Game: How Digital Influencers and Algorithms Negotiate Influence on Instagram," *New Media and Society* 21, no. 4 (2018): 895–913.

76. Ben Beaumont-Thomas, "Man vs Food Star Has Show Taken Off Air After 'Thinspiration' Rant," *Guardian*, July 2, 2014, www.theguardian.com/tv-and-radio/2014/jul/02/man-vs-food-adam-richman-thinspiration-rant-man-finds-food; Dade Hayes, "Bon Appétit Editor Adam Rapoport Resigns After Race-Based Controversies Grip Condé Nast Title," Deadline, June 8, 2020, https://deadline.com/2020/06/bon-appetit-editor-adam-rapoport-faces-social-media-storm-race-based-pay-inequity-conde-nast-brownface-1202953974/.

77. George Ritzer, *The McDonaldization of Society: An Investigation into the Changing Character of Contemporary Social Life* (Newbury Park, CA: Pine Forge Press, 1993); George Ritzer and Nathan Jurgenson, "Production, Consumption, Prosumption: The Nature of Capitalism in the Age of the Digital 'Prosumer,'" *Journal of Consumer Culture* 10, no. 1 (2010): 13–36.

78. Christian Fuchs, "Labor in Informational Capitalism and on the Internet," *Information Society* 26, no. 3 (2010): 179–96; Adam Arvidsson and Elanor Colleoni, "Value in Informational Capitalism and on the Internet," *Information Society* 28, no. 3 (2012): 135–50; Jakob Rigi and Robert Prey, "Value, Rent, and the Political Economy of Social Media," *Information Society* 31, no. 5 (2015): 392–406; Siva Vaidyanathan, "The Incomplete Political Economy of Social Media," in Burgess et al., *Sage Handbook*, 213–30.

79. Rob Price, "Instagram Reportedly Generated $20 billion in Ad Revenue in 2019—Even More Than YouTube," Business Insider, February 4, 2020, www.businessinsider.com/instagram-20-billion-ad-revenue-2019-report-2020-2.

80. Deborah Lupton, "Cooking, Eating, Uploading: Digital Food Cultures," in Lebesco and Naccarato, *Bloomsbury Handbook*, 66–79.

81. See, for instance, Tania Lewis, "Digital Food: From Paddock to Platform," *Communication Research and Practice* 4, no. 3 (2018): 212–28.

82. Lebesco and Naccarato, *Culinary Capital*, 3.

83. John Constine, "FTC Votes to Review Influencer Marketing Rules and Penalties," TechCrunch, February 12, 2020, https://techcrunch.com/2020/02/12/ftc-influencer-marketing-law/.

84. Alyssa Bereznak, "Can Real Life Compete with an Instagram Playground?" *Ringer*, August 9, 2017, www.theringer.com/tech/2017/8/9/16110424/instagram-playground -social-media; Sophie Haigney, "The Museums of Instagram," *New Yorker*, September 16, 2018, www.newyorker.com/culture/culture-desk/the-museums-of-instagram; Sapna Maheshwari, "A Penthouse Made for Instagram," *New York Times*, September 30, 2018, www.nytimes.com/2018/09/30/business/media/instagram-influencers -penthouse.html.

85. Rebecca Jennings, "Everyone Wants to Instagram the World's Most Beautiful Canyon. Should They?" Vox, July 11, 2019, www.vox.com/the-goods/ 2019/7/11/20686194/antelope-canyon-instagram-page-arizona-navajo.

86. See, for example, Christian Reynolds, Tammara Soma, Charlotte Spring, and Jordon Lazell, eds., *Routledge Handbook of Food Waste* (New York: Routledge, 2019).

87. Ingrid Burrington, "The Environmental Toll of a Netflix Binge," *Atlantic*, December 16, 2015, www.theatlantic.com/technology/archive/2015/12/there-are -no-clean-clouds/420744/; Amanda Starling Gould, "Restor(y)ing the Ground: Digital Environmental Media Studies," *Networking Knowledge* 9, no. 5 (2016); Marcus Hurst, "How Polluting Is the Internet?," CCCB Lab, January 21, 2014, http:// lab.cccb.org/en/how-polluting-is-the-internet/; Mél Hogan, "Big Data Ecologies," *Ephemera: Theory and Politics in Organization* 18, no. 3 (2018): 631–57; Sabine LeBel, "Wasting the Future: The Technological Sublime, Communications Technologies, and E-waste," *Communication +1* 1, no. 1 (2012), https://scholarworks .umass.edu/cpo/vol1/iss1/7; Mark Wilson, "Smartphones Are Killing the Planet Faster than Anyone Expected," *Fast Company*, March 27, 2018, www.fastcompany .com/90165365/smartphones-are-wrecking-the-planet-faster-than-anyone-expected.

88. Kevin Lozano, "Can the Internet Survive Climate Change?," *New Republic*, December 18, 2019, https://newrepublic.com/article/155993/can-internet-survive -climate-change; Sarah T. Roberts, "Digital Refuse: Canadian Garbage, Commercial Content Moderation and the Global Circulation of Social Media's Waste," *Wi: Journal of Mobile Media* 10, no. 1 (2016): 1–18.

89. Emma Grey Ellis, "Fighting Instagram's $1.3 Billion Problem—Fake Followers," *Wired*, September 10, 2019, www.wired.com/story/instagram-fake-followers/; Lorenz, "Instagram Has a Massive Harassment Problem"; Sarah T. Roberts, "Digital Refuse: Canadian Garbage, Commercial Content Moderation and the Global Circulation of Social Media's Waste," *Wi: Journal of Mobile Media* 10, no. 1 (2016): 1–18.

PART I

Identity

@hotdudesandhummus and the Cultural Politics of Food

MICHAEL Z. NEWMAN

Hummus, a puree of chickpeas mixed with lemon juice, oil, garlic, and tahini, served as a dip with bread, chips, or vegetables or as a sandwich filling, has been experiencing an extended moment as an object of desire in many parts of the world. Its status as a magnet for attention in memes and popular food culture may seem out of proportion to its humble appeal as a vegan mush that can be a snack, an appetizer, a side, or even a whole meal. Its migration from the Middle East to other parts of the world has set hummus up to serve as an emblem of our globalized, industrialized foodscape. It is the kind of dish that typifies how regional cuisines transform as they are exported from one place to another, especially from non-Western cultures to the United States, the United Kingdom, and other wealthy countries where elites consume Otherness as authentic or exotic "foodie" experiences.

"Hummus" is Arabic for chickpea, and there is no controversy over the dish's origins: the Levant, the land that is now Israel, Palestine, Lebanon, Jordan, and Syria. As a food claimed by more than one people as a national dish, hummus is a contested and highly charged symbol as well as a form of sustenance. Food, as Arjun Appadurai writes, is "a peculiarly powerful semiotic device," but its meanings vary by place and time, and by the differences among communities making and eating it.[1] As foods travel, their symbolic functions shift to match the agendas of the global food industry and local consumers. Hummus has different meanings in North America or Europe than it has in the Middle East, where it is more likely to bear the burden of weighty political and cultural disputes.

In North America and Europe, hummus is often marketed as a healthy snack food and the companies selling it to consumers surely do not want to politicize the product by identifying it explicitly with one or another side in a long-standing conflict between Israel, Palestine, and neighboring states. While some brands for sale in the United States do have names or visual identities that are products of a particular national source, such as Sabra (Hebrew slang for "Israeli") and Cedar's (national symbol of Lebanon), hummus is not typically marketed as a national dish in the United States outside of diasporic communities, and consumers may not recognize national signifiers. (By contrast, some foods are strongly identified with nations of origin, e.g., Chinese, Mexican, or Italian food.) In the Middle East, then, hummus is prized as a national dish by multiple rivals, while in Europe and North America it has an identity not so much at odds with its Middle Eastern identity as distanced from it by the changing contexts of consumption.

Into this mix of symbolic struggles and contested meanings comes @hotdudes andhummus (hereafter Hot Dudes and Hummus), an Instagram account that debuted in 2016 and quickly collected a moderately large number of followers after some celebrity and media attention drew the notice of social media users. Hot Dudes and Hummus belongs to a genre of Instagram accounts in which attractive young men, sometimes shirtless, pose with a particular object. These photos might be submitted by other users, or all produced or curated by the account holder. Hot Dudes and Hummus (41,800 followers in 2020) followed Hot Dudes Reading (1.1 million followers in 2020), Men and Coffee (377,000 followers in 2020), and HotDudesWithKittens (159,000 followers in 2020). The appeal of these accounts seems primarily to be objectification of the male body for the users whose objects of sexual desire are male, but by adding an object of desire that is not sexualized, the photos in these feeds narrativize what might otherwise be pure beefcake. Hot Dudes and Hummus adds one additional layer of meaning: its bio reads "Israel's yummiest," and its photos are—if not exclusively (it can be hard to tell from the visual evidence) then overwhelmingly—of Israeli men, especially men in Tel Aviv. "Yummiest" is of course a double entendre: the hummus is yummy, and so are the dudes. In combining imagery of desirable bodies and foods, this Instagram account bundles two of the platform's yummiest subjects whose appeal have made it so successful with its young and female-skewing user base.[2]

In combining images and captions, the Instagrammers who post at Hot Dudes and Hummus offer a reliable combination of masculine sex appeal, typically with subjects smiling and staring into the camera to acknowledge the viewer's desire, and the appeal of consuming food, itself a form of pleasure. Many of these images are rather generic and a bit suggestive. A shirtless man with well-defined abdominals smiling and looking at the camera, holding a plate of hummus as if to offer it up, carries the caption "Six pack Sunday making a comeback! 😎 Tag a friend who'd eat that 👋." Nothing particularly marks this image or caption, posted on September 30, 2018, as Jewish or Israeli. But many posts do use both imagery and captioning to locate Hot Dudes and Hummus in Israel, whether by framing shots against identifiable landmarks or locations, or by mentioning Jewish holidays or the Jewish sabbath in captions, as in an April 28, 2018, post of a bare-chested, smiling hummus eater captioned "happy weekend and good shabbes [sabbath] hummus lovers." Some posts also directly engage with LGBTQ+ themes, as in several identified photos of the Tel Aviv Pride Parade.

Unlike other hot dudes Instagram feeds, then, Hot Dudes and Hummus has a layer of geopolitical meaning, and it functions as a form of strategic communication. As with much of social media, this Instagram feed aims to influence, but not in the service of celebrity branding or promoting makeup or apparel. The account was started as a class project by Israeli students to brand Israel in a positive and depoliticized light. This activity is an example of "citizen diplomacy," the creation of a nation brand independent of state agents to cultivate a positive image of a country with a problematic brand.[3] In particular, the effort in this diplomacy campaign works by identifying Israel as a liberal country on the Mediterranean coast inhabited by beautiful people and welcoming of LGBTQ+ persons by representing images of attractive men in Tel Aviv for the visual pleasure of both male and female users. This campaign showcases Tel Aviv as a cosmopolitan, secular city in order to decouple Israel from its image as an occupier of Palestinian territory.

Hot Dudes and Hummus matches these images with a symbol of Israeli identity, a national culinary dish with widespread positive associations that is recognizable to Instagram users outside of Israel, if not as a quintessentially Israeli icon, then as a familiar popular food. This is a soft sell, but its agenda is the same as any propaganda: influencing mass opinion. Hot Dudes and Hummus is directed to Israeli hearts and minds, but more importantly to those outside of Israel whose view of the state is less than fully positive. This makes the feed one instance of a broader public diplomacy effort, known as Brand Israel, to soften the state's reputation by associating Israel with images of a progressive society in place of images of armed conflict and occupation.[4] Unlike some other representations of hummus as the common culture that unites Israeli and Arab societies, this account claims hummus as an Israeli point of pride to match the attractive bodies of Israeli men. While the targets of this appeal are gay men and straight women, the creators succeeded in particular at reaching non-Israeli female Instagram users.[5]

In discussing Hot Dudes and Hummus in a book about food and Instagram, I am most invested in the hummus, but the sexualized men are also crucial to the semiotics of this social media account and the representations it offers. The men are the bait to hook the attention of the global audience. As in some versions of television food porn, the sexualized body presented to arouse the viewer's erotic pleasure is matched by the display of food in a "fetishized emphasis on the desirable object" for the purpose of "maximizing the audience's desire."[6]

These hot men on Instagram are also a suggestion that the appeal of hummus could be as generic as that of sexualized bodies, hardly unique to one culture or state. At the same time, there is a rhetoric of Israel as a source of attractive people to match the appeal of its "yummy" culture. Israeli global sex symbols like Gal Gadot and Bar Refaeli are also crucial to this appeal of Brand Israel. So is the prevalence of LGBTQ+ visibility and pride in representations of Israel as modern and progressive, a branding approach that includes sexualized male bodies in an effort to promote Israel as an oasis of tolerance within the region, and a Mediterranean beach destination for tourism.[7]

But just what does this popular feed of photos say about hummus, and about its varied and contested meanings? The polysemic status of hummus makes this an appealing Instagram account, but it also prompts us to question the political and cultural values conveyed by this particular appeal. It speaks, as well, to a more fundamental level on which foods and bodies are produced and consumed in contexts of local, national, and global politics and aesthetics. Images of these foods and bodies, communicated from one location to another, express some meanings that travel well across global platforms, but they also gain new or different meanings produced in local instances of reception. In this chapter, then, I probe the contradictory, incompatible, or merely disparate possible con- notations of the food (as well as the men) in Hot Dudes and Hummus, whose surface-level simplicity and straightforwardness belies its potential to contain many meanings.

Hummus in Israel-Palestine

Hot Dudes and Hummus aims to showcase the culture of Israel in an apoliti- cal and positive light for an international audience of Instagram users who may not attach huge significance to hummus. But in the Middle East, hummus is a highly charged and potently symbolic food. The choice of hummus positions the dish as a token of Israeli identity. Israel is a relatively young state, having won its independence in 1948, and its Jewish population is made up largely of immigrant settlers from distinct regions of the diaspora: European Ashkenazi Jews who came from Russia, Ukraine, Poland, Germany, and nearby places; and Middle Eastern or North African Mizrahi Jews who came from the Arab world, includ- ing Morocco, Yemen, and Iraq. While each group of immigrants to Palestine or Israel brought its own foodways, the new state also claimed many of the local Arab dishes as Israeli, including falafel and hummus. Mizrahi Jews would not have commonly eaten hummus, as it was part of the cuisine in the Levant and in particular in Palestine and Lebanon. It would have been completely foreign to Europeans who settled in Palestine in the first half of the twentieth century. Hummus became increasingly popular in Israel when it began to be produced industrially in the 1950s and '60s and marketed as an affordable and filling dish associated with its Mizrahi population.[8] The store-bought plastic tubs of hummus would come to be seen as less authentic than the hummus made from scratch at a restaurant that specializes in it, a *hummusiya*.

One of the cultural contradictions of hummus within Israel is that it is prized as a national dish and at the same time strongly associated with Arab culture, especially among elite Israeli foodies who value authenticity.[9] Because of their connection to the land and their long history in the region, Arabs are often seen by Israelis as the best purveyors of hummus, and *hummusiyot* in Arab locations such as Acre and Abu Ghosh are highly regarded. Meanwhile, a "hummus war" has been waged between Israel and Lebanon over the Guinness World Record for the largest serving of hummus, a point of national pride but also a contest of legitimacy. To many Arabs and to supporters of Palestinian rights, the Israeli claim on hummus as a national dish is part of a broader Zionist appropriation of land and culture.

A further wrinkle in this complex identity for hummus in the Middle East is that it is a markedly gendered food, which is a key element in the choice of hummus as a match for sexually objectified male bodies. On Hot Dudes and Hummus, men are often framed glancing at the camera as if to offer both themselves and their hummus for playful consumption, as if both their masculine physique and their hummus connote virility and desirability. As Dafna Hirsch describes, Israeli culture constructs hummus as a national dish associated especially with men, who are its primary aficionados, obsessives, and purveyors.[10] A 2019 newspaper article puts it this way: "there is perhaps nothing more closely associated with masculinity in Israel than hummus."[11] The Israeli *hummusiya* is a male-dominated space, and when women patronize the *hummusiya*, Hirsch writes, it is typically in the company of men. Hummus has been a plain, cheap, and satisfying food for laboring men, such as Arab workers, who eat it with their hands by wiping or dipping pita bread in a communal dish. The *hummusiya* is thus "a space of informal male socializing."[12]

Hummus is eaten in the home as well as in public, and most hummus in the Middle East, as well as in Europe and North America, is consumed from mass-produced plastic tubs, present in many if not most Hot Dudes and Hummus pics, rather than dishes in a restaurant. Dafna Hirsch and Ofra Tene discuss how the history of the marketing of industrially made hummus in Israel has masculinized and ethnicized the food.[13] One means of achieving this was by picturing male chefs with Mizrahi features and in ethnic dress in hummus advertisements. This contributed to constructing an Israeli national food, an image of Israeli identity based on a conception of the dish as Mizrahi though not Arab, appropriating the culture of a colonized Other. Hirsch develops a concept of "hummus masculinity" in Israeli society that combines an "intertwined politics of settlement and masculinity," such that hummus stands for an Israeli brand of manliness that incorporates the traditional local foodways.[14] The choice of hummus in Hot Dudes and Hummus is thus not just about showing Israeli men and Israeli food, but about claiming hummus as an icon of Israeli masculinity as part of a broader discourse of Israeli identity being defined by this particular gender construction.

We see this claim in the imagery in Hot Dudes and Hummus, especially in the images recognizable as photos of Israel. The young, healthy, physically fit Israeli men posing with hummus in the Instagram posts are images of the nation. The subjects pose against landmarks such as the colorful, modernist Dizengoff Fountain in downtown Tel Aviv or on a giant "I 🖤 Tel Aviv" beach chair. They pose shirtless with their hummus tubs against scenes of the bustling Pride Parade. A September 21, 2017, post shows a man in a tank top seated at a restaurant patio table with an urban streetscape in the background, Hebrew signage visible over his shoulder, and captioned "A happy, beautiful, hot and hummus-filled new year to all of our friends celebrating!! 🍎🖤" The date and the apple emoji indicate that this is a Rosh Hashanah (Jewish New Year) message; apples are eaten in observance of the holiday. This kind of image-caption combination links hummus and youthful, fit masculinity with Israeli and Jewish identity and with the modern, vibrant life of Tel Aviv. A November 25, 2017, post picturing three young men eating hummus in a restaurant is captioned, "Which hottie do you want to share hummus with? Tag your dream hummus partner 😜." Whether fully dressed or shirtless, indoors or outdoors, the men in these images and captions claim hummus as masculine and Israeli. The captions playfully invite the participation of Instagram users to "share" the men and the food offered to them, by extension inviting their participation in the branding of Israel as modern, sexy, and desirable to the global Instagram audience.

These representations of hummus as quintessentially Israeli fly in the face of much consternation within the Middle East and among Palestinians and their advocates around the world. To many on this side of the Israel-Palestine conflict, Israel's claim to hummus is part of a campaign of settler-colonialist erasure. A 2017 essay by the Palestinian American academic Steven Salaita in the New Arab objects to the very notion of Israeli cuisine and to the construction of hummus in particular as Israeli. He sees this as part of a broader effort under Zionism, "a decades-old programme to disappear Palestinians," whether by theft of their land or of their culture, of a piece with Israeli "colonisation or ethnic cleansing" of Palestine alongside "destruction of Palestinian culture."[15] For many advocates of Palestinian independence, hummus is just one element of a broader struggle in which Israel's claim to regional products and customs advances a global legitimation strategy.

FIGURE 1-1. A sample post from @hotdudesandhummus.

Salaita is hardly alone in his views. As Ari Ariel notes in his essay "The Hummus Wars," a Lebanese effort to prevent Israeli companies from marketing hummus abroad zeroes in on this question of legitimacy and ownership. Although they are advocates for Lebanese hummus as a national icon, the Lebanese accept that hummus can be Palestinian as well. However, they reject any Israeli claim. This is an objection not just to Israel's questionable ownership of Levantine culture but to Ashkenazi Jewish culture being compatible with a national project in the Levant, and to the possibility that European settlers could be rightful claimants to the region's foodways. Ariel quotes a Lebanese advocate: "with all due respect, I didn't know German Jews or Polish Jews knew anything about hummus."[16]

Much of this conflict is not just over hummus being a national dish but over the export of Israeli products. This brings us back to Hot Dudes and Hummus, whose identification of hummus with Israel helps promote this Israeli export with a presence in the everyday life of North Americans and Europeans. The unsuccessful campaign against Israeli hummus brought by the Association of Lebanese Industrialists, an NGO, had the ambition of gaining for Lebanon control over packaging and marketing hummus in Europe, denying other countries (in particular Israel) the ability to identify a product by that name.[17] This conflict layers economics, culture, and geopolitics into one campaign over hummus as both a commercial product and a token of Arab identity. Israel does benefit from the sale of hummus abroad, as the Israeli Strauss Group is one of the major players in the global hummus marketplace as the joint owner of the Sabra brand (with Pepsi Co.). As of 2015, Sabra accounted for 60 percent of retail sales revenue for hummus in the United States.[18] Another well-recognized presence in the international hummus market, Tribe, is an Israeli brand under the ownership of Osem, a Nestlé subsidiary that is one of Israel's largest food corporations. So, by pushing hummus as quintessentially Israeli, Hot Dudes and Hummus promotes both Brand Israel on a global scale and one of Israel's successful and growing commercial exports, especially to the United States, where the feed has made the deepest impression.

Hummus in the United States

Hot Dudes and Hummus originated in Israel and its content is Israeli, but its platform and audience are another story. Instagram is owned by a U.S. company, Facebook Inc., which acquired it in 2012. The user base of Instagram is global and skews young, and the followers and commenters of Hot Dudes and Hummus are concentrated in certain locations. Large numbers live in London and New York City, and U.S. users (female Americans ages eighteen to thirty-four in particular) make up the largest number of followers (41 percent). More than 90 percent of the account's followers are outside of Israel.[19]

Like any popular account whose followers were gained by going viral and being spread widely among social media users, the Hot Dudes and Hummus Instagram account succeeded initially by exploiting two common vectors of online publicity: mainstream media attention and influential celebrities. Its creators worked to spread publicity about Hot Dudes and Hummus to journalists and celebrities, gaining considerable attention. The largest boost in publicity came from a solicited recommendation by Mayim Bialik, a Jewish American and vocally Zionist television star who at the time (2016) was appearing on the popular CBS comedy The Big Bang Theory.[20] Bialik's Instagram followers at the time numbered approximately 1.6 million. Some of the Web-based publicity that pushed the virality of Hot Dudes and Hummus followed Bialik's post and mentioned the account, but there were also many other posts and articles in a variety of English-language sources from women-oriented sites like Bustle and Cosmopolitan to LGBTQ+ sites like Gay Times to more celebrity-focused sites like TMZ. Some mentioned Israel, but not all. While perhaps referencing the intention of Hot Dudes and Hummus to show Israel's fun side, the tone of most of these pieces is dominated by horny visual pleasure typical of reception for food porn. Cosmo gives its take of the Instagram account as follows: "Yes. All the yes. Also, dad. Daddy. Daddies. Husbands? Daddy. Mmm." Making no mention at all of Israel, Gay Times offers: "The best combo is hummus, hot guys and LGBT pride."

The reception of Hot Dudes and Hummus outside of Israel, and in particular among its largest audience in the United States, is shaped by shifting meanings within a globalized food culture. Hummus has a different kind of value and a different range of connotations in the United States, where it might have little recognition as a national dish. Furthermore, different communities and consumers in the United States attach varying meanings to hummus. It may be more or less the same puree of chickpeas with tahini and lemon, but it is not always the same hummus.

In the 2015 U.S. Israeli documentary *Hummus! The Movie*, there is a brief segment of rapidly cut interviews shot outside of Israel (or so it appears), where people on the street guess the origins of hummus and fail to accurately locate them in any specific place in the Levant. This is played for comedy. One underlying purpose of the film is to identify hummus with Israel, remedying this evidently widespread ignorance. But it is a revealing moment as it confirms that the global brand of hummus is only weakly identified as Israeli, Lebanese, Palestinian, or Levantine. "Middle Eastern" might be a more general label that can be widely applied, but just as often hummus is understood (as a product of the industry's branding strategy) as Mediterranean, a fuzzier category that could conceivably cover northern Africa, southern Europe, and western Asia. "Mediterranean" also includes white European identities in contrast to the Arab Others of the Middle East, semiotically blurring racial and ethnic categories in an appeal to the mainstream of upscale American consumers. As a marketing strategy, "Mediterranean" has successfully merged a variety of foods, many of them Middle Eastern like hummus, into one category that is "approachable" to U.S. consumers.[21]

A similar account has been told of the "social life of the tortilla," a simple ancient food made from ingredients native to a particular region (maize in Mesoamerica), elevated into a food epitomizing a national (Mexican) culture in the modern era, and spread abroad in an era of industrialization and increasing global trade in mass-produced foods.[22] Both the corn tortilla made by hand on a Mayan *comal*, and hummus made one pot of chickpeas at a time, have been appropriated as elements of a national identity, commodified, exported, and transformed as they are produced on a massive commercial scale. For the tortilla, one shift was from corn *masa* to wheat flour, which is easier to use in mass production and preferable to many U.S. palates. Wheat can also be adapted for preparations such as sandwich wraps that have little relation to Mexican cuisine, and are rarely if ever understood as "Mexican food." Far from its point of origin, hummus has likewise been transformed by the addition of many flavorings and variations. The markets where I shop in a U.S. city carry not only reasonably Mediterranean varieties like olive, pine nut, and "supremely spicy," but also edamame, white bean, beet, avocado, chocolate, Thai coconut, and Buffalo bleu hummus. U.S. hummus is marketed not so much as Middle Eastern or Israeli (or Lebanese or Palestinian), but rather as a healthy, meat-free, dairy-free, and gluten-free alternative to other snacks and dips.[23] Lind and Barham show that industrialized globalization "has often meant distancing the tortilla from its former meanings."[24] This is certainly true of hummus in the West.

The hummus market in the United States in particular has been marked by rapid growth over a period of several decades but especially in the 2010s, as hummus consumption has expanded and its presence in multiple versions in American markets has become a norm. Hummus was a $5 million business in the 1990s in the United States, and by 2018, Americans were spending nearly $800 million on hummus in stores.[25] From 2013 to 2017, as Hot Dudes and Hummus was launched, U.S. farm acres used to grow chickpeas doubled thanks to the hummus craze.[26]

Conversely, in the post-1960s era of activism and alternative politics, hummus was part of a vegetarian diet adopted within some communities as a countercultural statement and a politicized lifestyle choice. Many feminists, including many ecofeminists and lesbians, embraced vegetarianism as a gesture of resistance to patriarchal violence. Hummus, like tofu and brown rice, was a food positioned in opposition to mainstream U.S. foodways.[27] If one didn't prepare it from the recipe in the famous vegetarian *Moosewood Cookbook*, it might be purchased from a health food store or from a restaurant.[28] The hummus served at women's studies department potlucks is the inheritance of this tradition.

But dramatic growth in the U.S. hummus market over the past several decades has not followed from these countercultural, alternative-lifestyle origins. Hummus has become mainstream and has gained traction by being sold as a food that millions of especially female consumers can feel good about choosing as a healthy alternative to other snacks for themselves and their families. Hummus brands such as Sabra have targeted affluent women aged thirty-five to fifty who care for older children and seek nutritious and wholesome snacks and substitutes for dairy and meat.[29] Hummus might be served with fresh vegetables like carrots and cucumbers as an alternative to less healthy-seeming bread or chips. Lifestyle and wellness discussions found online contain thousands of write-ups on hummus and its beneficial qualities under search-engine-optimized headlines like "Is Hummus Healthy?" In one such article, the author extols the virtues of the humble chickpea as an affordable, meat-free, gluten-free, "eco-friendly" food packed with protein and antioxidants. She points to links between chickpea consumption and lower BMI, improved gastrointestinal health, and protections against heart disease, diabetes, and some cancers.[30]

When hummus is linked with the Middle East in popular discourse in the United States, it is often either in coverage of restaurants and cookbooks, or during episodes of political activism. The former tends to be pitched in the up-beat promotional discourse of recommendations and reviews that hype a new restaurant opening or a new book being published. Politics rarely enters into such discussions, but hummus is also sometimes a totem of Israeli culture and industry that can be utilized in campaigns to call attention to the struggle for Palestinian freedom and equality, such as the Boycott, Divestment, Sanctions (BDS) movement, which aims to engage international pressure to force Israel to end its occupation of Palestine. College campus activists in groups such as Students for Justice in Palestine have seized on Sabra as a prominent Israeli brand present in U.S. retail and campus food service environments, demanding that the Israeli product be removed so that students can access hummus without supporting the occupation.[31] Activists on several campuses have called atten-tion to the fact that Sabra's parent, Strauss Group, has been a source of material support for the Israel Defense Forces' Golani Brigade, directly linking the brand and product with Israel's occupation of the West Bank and Gaza.[32] This kind of campaign is precisely the kind of negative branding of Israel that Hot Dudes and Hummus was designed to ameliorate and counteract. Both the campus activism and the hot dudes address the same demographic: young Americans.

Aside from these episodes, localized as they tend to be on elite college cam-puses, the public life and identity of hummus in the United States (and in other markets distant from Israel) is a product of differing contexts and histories of food and consumerism, and contrasting constructions of identity. In redefining hummus as Mediterranean, the product is drained of the political significance of its place of origin, and of its identification with Arab or Israeli identities. In redefining hummus as a healthy snack, the product shifts from working-class and masculinized to upscale and feminized in its prevailing class and gender constructions. In positioning hummus as a mainstream supermarket product, the regional or exotic connotations of hummus are replaced with the familiar-ity of a regular staple of party spreads and refrigerator shelf snack options. Hot Dudes and Hummus is presented as "Israel's yummiest," but the national brand-ing of this appeal, with its emphasis on pleasure rather than persuasion, is easily lost amidst the different connotations hummus has gained in its journey from East to West. Is the U.S. consumer of a Sabra tub purchased at the supermarket really eating the same hummus as the men in Israeli *hummusiyot*? Is it the same as the food eaten by hot dudes from Tel Aviv on Instagram, and as consumed via the sexualized gaze of global social media users?

The Ambiguous Politics
of @hotdudesandhummus

Now that we have canvassed the hummus scenes of both Middle Eastern and U.S. cultures, the Instagram account @hotdudesandhummus comes into focus as an Israeli branding effort that speaks to Israelis in a code that might not be recognizable to its intended audiences abroad in the fullness of its connotations and symbolic value. The masculinized, nation-defining status of hummus in Israel clashes with the feminized identity of hummus in the United States, where it is a "virtuous" snack. Outside of a handful of activist incidents, hummus in the West is rarely linked in popular discourse with its contested status as an Israeli appropriation of Palestinian culture or as an Israeli export underwriting the occupation. This polysemic, multivalent, and flexible appeal is belied by the deceptively simple pictures and words that one finds on this Instagram account of yummy torsos and faces alongside a plate or container of the still humble, beige hummus.

We can see this simplicity in the comments posted on the photos of shirtless men, with their brief bursts of surging emotion: "so much yes in this pic," "oh my," "omg," "I am dead this insta is amazing." Emoji frequently convey the follower's reaction in the lingua franca of social media: hearts, smiling faces with heart eyes, kisses, fire. Most comments are in English, unsurprisingly, with the occasional Spanish and other languages, even some Hebrew. While from time to time there are some references in the photo captions to topics other than dudes and hummus, as we have seen in mentions of the New Year holiday and the sabbath, the themes are very consistently apolitical.

But food in general and hummus in particular are never apolitical, and their cultural politics are the product of the lived experiences and histories of those who produce and consume food, and of the images and stories surrounding it. Hot Dudes and Hummus has an agenda of obscuring the conflict that—among other things—makes hummus a site of struggle and negotiation, and the choice of hummus for this propaganda campaign is telling. But what message might get through its surface appeal of porny pics of bodies and food will depend on the cultural resources of the social media user as much as the strategic communication of the Hot Dudes and Hummus Instagrammers.

Notes

1. Arjun Appadurai, "Gastro-Politics in Hindu South Asia," *American Ethnologist* 8, no. 3 (1981): 494–511, 494.

2. "Social Media Fact Sheet," Pew Research Center, June 12, 2019, www.pewinternet .org/fact-sheet/social-media/.

3. Tal Samuel-Azran, Betti Ilovici, Israel Zari, and Orly Geduild, "Practicing Citi-

zen Diplomacy 2.0: 'The Hot Dudes and Hummus—Israel's Yummiest' Campaign for Israel's Branding," *Place Branding and Public Diplomacy* 15, no. 1 (2019): 38–49.

4. Jon Dart, "'Brand Israel': Hasbara and Israeli Sport," *Sport in Society* 19, no. 10 (2016): 1402–18; Jasbir Puar, "Citation and Censorship: The Politics of Talking about the Sexual Politics of Israel," *Feminist Legal Studies* 19 (2011): 133–42; Sarah Schulman, *Israel/Palestine and the Queer International* (Durham, NC: Duke University Press, 2012).

5. Samuel-Azran et al., "Practicing Citizen Diplomacy."

6. Michael Z. Newman, "*Everyday Italian*: Cultivating Taste," in *How to Watch Television*, ed. Ethan Thompson and Jason Mittell (New York: New York University Press, 2013), 333–34. See also Tisha Dejmanni, "'Food Porn' as Postfeminist Play: Digital Femininity and the Female Body on Food Blogs," *Television and New Media* 17, no. 5 (2015): 429–48.

7. Gil Z. Hochberg, "Introduction: Israelis, Palestinians, Queers: Points of Departure," *GLQ* 16, no. 4 (2010): 493–516, https://doi.org/10.1215/10642684-2010-001; Puar, "Citation and Censorship."

8. Dafna Hirsch, "'Hummus Is Best When It Is Fresh and Made by Arabs': The Gourmetization of Hummus in Israel and the Return of the Repressed Arab," *American Ethnologist* 38, no. 4 (2011): 617–30.

9. Josée Johnston and Shyon Baumann, *Foodies: Democracy and Distinction in the Gourmet Foodscape* (New York: Routledge, 2010).

10. Dafna Hirsch, "Hummus Masculinity in Israel," *Food, Culture and Society* 19, no. 2 (2016): 337–59.

11. Uri Talshir, "From Mundane to Macho: In Israel, Hummus Makes the Man," *Haaretz*, January 1, 2019, www.haaretz.com/food/.premium-from-mundane-to-macho-in-israel-hummus-makes-the-man-1.6802589.

12. Hirsch, "Hummus Masculinity," 349.

13. Dafna Hirsch and Ofra Tene, "Hummus: The Making of an Israeli Culinary Cult," *Journal of Consumer Culture* 13, no. 1 (2013): 25–45; see also Hirsch, "Hummus Is Best."

14. Hirsch, "Hummus Masculinity," 338.

15. Steven Salaita, "'Israeli' Hummus Is Theft, Not Appropriation," *New Arab*, September 4, 2017, www.alaraby.co.uk/english/comment/2017/9/4/israeli-hummus-is-theft-not-appropriation.

16. Ari Ariel, "The Hummus Wars," *Gastronomica* 12, no. 1 (2012): 34–42.

17. Ibid., 37.

18. Statista Research Department, "Hummus Dollar Market Share in the United States in 2006 and 2015, by Brand," Statista, March 23, 2016, www.statista.com/statistics/441085/us-hummus-dollar-market-share-by-brand/.

19. Samuel-Azran et al., "Practicing Citizen Diplomacy."

20. Ibid., 43. It is not known whether Bialik received anything in exchange for reposting from @hotdudesandhummus on her own Instagram in 2016. In 2019, Bialik was a spokesperson for Sabra hummus.

21. Barney Wolf, "Middle Eastern Cuisine Makes Its Move," *QSR Magazine*, De-

cember 2016, www.qsrmagazine.com/menu-innovations/middle-eastern-cuisine
-makes-its-move.

22. David Lind and Elizabeth Barham, "The Social Life of the Tortilla: Food,
Cultural Politics, and Contested Commodification," *Agriculture and Human Values*
21 (2004): 47—60, 48.

23. "Hummus Market Estimated to Reach Market Size of USD 1.104 Billion by
2022 at a CAGR of 9.38%," Market Research Future, August 28, 2017, www.globenews
wire.com/news-release/2017/08/28/1101090/0/en/Hummus-Market-Estimated-to
-Reach-Market-Size-of-USD-1-104-Billion-by-2022-at-a-CAGR-of-9-38.html.

24. Lind and Barham, "Social Life," 56.

25. Whitney Pipkin, "Your Hummus Habit Could Be Good for the Earth,"
The Salt: What's On Your Plate, NPR, July 10 2019, www.npr.org/sections/thesalt/
2019/07/10/739054484/your-hummus-habit-could-be-good-for-the-earth.

26. Megan Durisin and Lydia Mulvaney, "More Hummus, Please: U.S. Chickpea
Acres Seen Climbing to Record," Bloomberg, April 4, 2017, www.bloomberg.com.

27. On countercultural foods, see Warren J. Belasco, *Appetite for Change: How
the Counterculture Took on the Food Industry* (Ithaca, NY: Cornell University Press,
2006); Reina Gattuso, "How Lesbian Potlucks Nourished the LGBTQ Movement,"
Gastro Obscura, May 2, 2019, www.atlasobscura.com/articles/why-do-lesbians
-have-potlucks-on-pride.

28. Mollie Katzen, *The Moosewood Cookbook* (Berkeley: Ten Speed Press, 1977).

29. Michal Clements, "Sabra's Half-Billion-Dollar Hummus Empire Grew One Dip
at a Time," *Market Strategist* (blog), August 10, 2016, http://www.chicagonow.com/
marketing-strategist/2016/08/sabras-half-billion-dollar-hummus-empire-grew
-one-dip-at-a-time/.

30. Cynthia Sass, "Is Hummus Healthy? Here's What a Nutritionist Wants You to
Know," *Health*, May 1, 2019, https://www.health.com/nutrition/is-hummus-healthy.

31. Tamar Lewin, "New Subject of Debate on Mideast: Hummus," *New York Times*,
December 3, 2010, www.nytimes.com; Katie Mulhere, "The Two Hummus Solution,"
Inside Higher Ed, December 10, 2014, www.insidehighered.com/news/2014/12/10/
wesleyan-bring-back-controversial-hummus-brand; Aru Shiney-Ajay and Killian
McGinnis, "More than Hummus: Renewing the Call to Boycott Sabra," *Phoenix*,
March 29, 2018, https://swarthmorephoenix.com/2018/03/29/more-than-hummus
-renewing-the-call-to-boycott-sabra/.

32. Lewin, "New Subject"; Shiney-Ajay and McGinnis, "More than Hummus."

CHAPTER 2

Starving Beauties?

Instabae, Diet Food, and Japanese Girl Culture

TSUGUMI (MIMI) OKABE

Tokyo is home to many dreamy culinary delights, such as cheesy sandwiches oozing with the colors of the rainbow and whimsical parfaits dressed with a cloud of cotton candy. These items reflect a food culture characterized by decadence and excess, one that is increasingly "all for the 'gram." Tokyo has the highest number of posts in the category of "food and drinks" on Instagram of any city, at 42.6 percent, followed by Bangkok (17.7 percent), Berlin (12.8 percent), São Paulo (11.9 percent), and Moscow (8.4 percent).[1] In addition to these Instagram food trends, Japan is known for its traditional cuisines, as well as for its wide variety of Western-influenced dishes, sweets, sake, and tea—all attracting hungry tourists from around the globe. At the same time, Japanese women appear to be obsessed with dieting, as they experience a high prevalence of disordered eating, body image disturbances, and thin ideals.[2] Japan boasts of a culinary culture embracing everything from Michelin-starred restaurants to fast-food chains and food stalls—yet, despite this abundance of food choices, the country is faced with the crisis of an increasing number of underweight women.

One company contributing to, and profiting from, Japan's diet culture is Rivaland Co., established in September 2000. Rivaland sells six products: its original plant-based drinks, Ojsôama Kôso and Ojôsama Kôso Flora, which are sold in bottles or cans; its tapioca-based drinks, Ojôsama Kôso Jewel, Ojôsama Kôso Tropical, and Botanical Tapioca Cleanse, which are sold in six, twelve, or twenty-four individual packets that contain the tapioca pearls in a sugary solution; and Placenta + Collagen beauty supplements, which are sold in packets of sixty capsules.[3] These products are available for purchase through the company website (ojyosama.jp), or on amazon.jp and rakuten.co.jp. Ojôsama Kôso Jewel is the main product featured on the company's primary Instagram account, which boasts ten million packets sold to date. Sold in colorful plastic packets, this product can be combined with water, soy milk, or juice, or used as a topping on yogurt or fruits, and is intended to replace meals as part of one's diet regimen (see fig. 2-1).

This chapter takes up Rivaland's product, Ojôsama Kôso Jewel (hereafter Jewel), as a case study to explore the interplay between *instabae* (Instagram images), food, and body image in relation to scholarship on body image studies in Japan. This examination is timely and important, given growing concerns about the issue of underweight women in Japan and its potential health implications. This chapter briefly presents postfeminist criticism to contextualize the contradictory productions of the feminine self through dieting in Japan. It then explores how the Rivaland Instagram account promotes the connection between hyper-femininity, dieting, and thinness through interrelated themes and visual metaphors of princesses (*ojôsama*), cuteness (*kawaisa*), and sweetness. Throughout this chapter, I ask the following: What does Rivaland's Instagram account reveal about Japanese cultural aesthetics and standards of beauty, including idealized body types? What is the relationship between diet food and the construction of a feminine identity? To answer these questions, I focus on how commercial diet companies such as Rivaland not only sell products, but market a particular brand of femininity that sells ideas of perseverance, encouraging women to attain their body ideals in personally meaningful and even empowering—yet problematic—ways.

Starving to Be "Pretty?"
The Drive for Thinness in Japan

First and foremost, the drive for thinness is not unique to Japan. Some scholars argue that, "similar to European or North American societies, Japanese society seems to value thinness of women's body shape as a sociocultural ideal."[4] This might come as a surprise to some, as cultural anthropologist Laura Spielvogel, who studied fitness culture in Japan, notes that "to the Western eye, many Japanese women who struggle to lose weight appear quite thin or even skinny" and that they strive toward a seemingly arbitrary, but still culturally powerful weight goal between 40 kg and 43.4 kg [88 and 95.5 lb.].[5] These numbers fall within the range of the so-called *shinderera taikei* (Cinderella weight), which represents the ideal weight status desired among some Japanese women. For example, the common formula used to calculate Cinderella weight is (height in m)$^2 \times 20 \times 0.9$. According to this formula, the Cinderella weight for the average height of someone who is 5'1" (157.9 cm) would be around 98.7 pounds (44.8 kg), under 100 pounds, that is, an "underweight" body mass index (BMI) of 18.[6] Such weight goals, which may be "achieved" via disordered eating, are unreasonable and damaging for the average person. However, for some women, to look like a princess or model is desirable precisely because it is aspirational and difficult to achieve. Thus, critics such as Spielvogel emphasize the need to contextualize definitions and standards of ideal body types in culturally specific ways.

The word *daietto*, or diet, in Japanese is an English loan word that makes specific use of its verb form. In this way, similar to the U.S. usage of the term, *daietto* refers to restricting food intake for physical body maintenance, such as consuming low-calorie food to lose weight and/or prevent obesity. In Japan, this inherently fatphobic concept is sold through certain exercise regimens for weight loss, gym memberships, beauty products, and diet food products. In Rivaland's case, the brand specifically utilizes their princess mascot to appeal to a hyper-feminine demographic and justifies *daietto* as a form of self-control and discipline. Naomi Wolf argues that "a culture fixated on female thinness is not an obsession about female beauty, but an obsession about female obedience."[7]

The construction of a feminine identity through food refusal and dieting in Japan is a site of heated debate, including on Instagram. On the one hand, clinical studies have drawn attention to the serious health implications of food refusal and dieting: "Inadequate dietary restrictions can result in undernutrition, which can lead to anemia, menstrual abnormalities, and osteoporosis."[8] Thin idealization has also been linked to depression and is a contributing factor in the development of eating disorders.[9] On the other hand, critics such as Spielvogel posit that "the pursuit of thinness is not simply a quest for beauty, but an active struggle over notions of selfhood, identity, and power. The contradiction between self-denial and self-indulgence reflects a larger struggle over women's roles in contemporary Japan."[10] In other words, Japanese femininity that is defined by a desire for thinness and achieved through food refusal or dieting should be understood on a continuum of obedience and defiance, indulgence and self-control, and empowerment and disenfranchisement.[11] Such contradictions are also found in non-Japanese contexts that show how self-branding in girls' media production in online spaces navigate between the poles of self-disclosure, self-expression, and disempowerment.[12]

Combining such contradictions, Rivaland's Instagram page is a site of *shôjo* (girlish) media content made for young women by other young women that is defined by dainty, princess imagery. In this regard, Instagram can be seen as a powerful platform where like-minded women gather to form an online community to share their dieting secrets and achievements and to empower each other. However, postfeminist criticism would suggest otherwise; that is, online spaces that feed into a "hyper culture of commercial sexuality" risk operating at a level that displaces the goals of feminism, giving but an illusion of female autonomy and agency.[13] Angela McRobbie is among those criticizing the ways in which women have achieved economic independence at the cost of creating a culture of competition over community building that is aligned with neoliberal political discourses of individual responsibility.[14] I argue that Rivaland's Instagram page encourages a culturally specific form of competition and gender surveillance, holding women to a standard of femininity that foregrounds a girliness that diverges significantly from hyper-femininity in other cultural contexts. While Instagram allows women to carve out a space of their own, this online space encourages self-regulation and restriction as it legitimizes starvation to take control of one's own body image through the performance of *shôjo*, or girlhood.

Thin Ideology: How You Consume It and How It Consumes You

In addition to products sold by Rivaland, there is a booming market for diet products in Japan, from fat-burning creams, to gadgets that claim to remove cellulite, to diet food trends like the Konjac Diet, Kombucha Cleanse, diet cookies, and diet ramen. These endless choices are emblematic of the so-called diet craze that mostly targets women in Japan.[15] In her extensive study of diet culture in Japan, Laura Miller found that "many 'diets' involve not ingestion of a product but rather modification of behavior."[16] The success of Instagrammable diet products such as Jewel thus relies on followers and brand ambassadors to help promote the product. Rivaland achieves this by tapping into an online participatory diet culture that targets young women to capitalize on their insecurities about body image.

Rivaland's products, including Jewel, boast of their so-called health benefits. According to the product's homepage, Jewel contains extracts of 107 plant-based ingredients, such as radish, carrot, *myôga* (Japanese ginger), lily root, watermelon, and strawberries. However, the top three ingredients also include glucose-fructose syrup, rare sugar syrup, and domestic konjac flour.[17] Glucose-fructose syrup, which is called high-fructose corn syrup in the United States, is a sweetener mainly used in processed foods and soft drinks and is not typically associated with weight loss.

According to Rivaland's homepage, 80 percent of their consumers have purchased Jewel's six-packet mini-fasting set, which in June 2019 Rakuten.jp ranked as one of the top ten selling diet drinks. Part of its success lies in its use of "functional food ingredients," which refer to ingredients used to justify "products intended to offer benefits beyond their nutritional value," such as capsicum, which has been touted as a "fat burner" because it "induces perspiration." Functional food in Japan "is a $2 billion market, with over two thousand new products launched since 1988."[18] Konjac tapioca pearls (glucomannan) is the main functional ingredient of Jewel; some users have claimed it gives the feeling of *manpukukan* (being full), which Rivaland uses to market Jewel, claiming to be the first in the industry to offer a "tapioca drink diet."[19] Jewel also appeals to consumers with package deals and targeted discounts for first-time buyers, positioning their product as a distinctly affordable means of dieting.

More significantly, Jewel is marketed to women who uphold particular hyper-feminine aesthetics, but with a distinct girliness. By "hyper-femininity," I refer to the "exaggerated adherence to a stereotypical feminine gender role" that takes culturally specific forms.[20] Hyper-femininity, within the context of Rivaland, is connected to the political potential of *kawaii* (cute) gender performance, relying heavily on girly and infantilizing poses and aesthetics defined by the visual tropes of princesses and cuteness seen in Jewel marketing. These include the doe-eyed look and the use of frills, sparkles, and pastel color schemes. This version of hyper-femininity has roots in a Japanese girl culture that celebrates *kawaisa*, or cuteness, even as it risks upholding patriarchal, conventional beauty ideals. Within this cultural context, Jewel offers a way for women to lose weight while retaining their femininity through the consumption of cute food, satisfying "contradictory cultural expectations that women should enjoy sweets but manage to maintain a skinny figure."[21] This view is supported by the characterization, by some users, of Jewel as a snack substitute, while others contextualize Jewel in terms of its cuteness and sweetness.

Packaging plays another significant role in Jewel's commercial success (fig. 2-1). A woman, drawn using anime or manga-style visual tropes, appears on all of Rivaland's products. Her slender, pale body and long flowing hair represent the epitome of Japanese cultural standards of what is considered "beautiful," and sets the tone of the product's feminine appeal. Moreover, although she is un-named, she is depicted as the *ojôsama* (princess) of Rivaland *ôkoku* (kingdom), as shown in a forty-three-second animated commercial uploaded to Rivaland's homepage and YouTube channel. In brief, this short clip, presumably about be-ing at war with yourself, begins with the princess on horseback, dressed in a full suit of armor, as the likeness of Joan of Arc. She tells Sebastian, her right-hand man/butler, "There is no end to the holy war of beauty" and then leads her all-female entourage straight into "battle." The end of the commercial reinforces the importance of persistence in one's dieting. In this scene, the princess is shown stripping off her armor to bathe in a crystal-clear lake, presumably after having won the "war." Her last line, "watashi wo honki ni saseru" (it brings out the seriousness in me), drives home the value of *ganbaru*, or never giving up, which is consistent with the "Japanese cultural model of character building."[22] *Ganbaru* is a culturally specific and semantically complex term that can be rendered into English as "unflagging effort," "doing one's best," or "toughing it out."[23] Rivaland's princess conveys these ideas by suggesting that Jewel offers a solution to those who struggle to stick to their dieting routine.

FIGURE 2-1. Image depicted on the box set of Ojôsama Kôso Jewel (left), which claims that one can lose 6.6 pounds in a matter of forty-eight hours. Individual packets of Jewel (right). © Rivaland Co.

Although, as of this writing, this clip had not been uploaded or saved to Rivaland's Instagram account, it provides important clues about the brand of femininity in which the company is invested. According to Rosalind Gill, "advertisements work by constructing myths in such a way to endow products with meanings which appear to be natural and eternal."[24] It is no coincidence that Rivaland employs the princess motif to promote their diet product. She is a powerful symbol of the *bishôjo* (beautiful girl) or *shôjo* (girl) in Japanese culture. Miller also draws attention to the ubiquity of the Cinderella trope in Japanese popular culture, which relates in fascinating ways to the aspirational Cinderella weight. She found that the story of Cinderella resonates with the Japanese cultural audience because it thematically reinforces the idea that hard work pays off. So, in Japan, "instead of passivity, Cinderella is used to denote individual agency to overcome obstacles or to achieve one's dreams."[25] According to Miller, beauty salons and pageants recuperate this myth through the language of "self-development," "self-mastery," and "self-improvement" to promote drastic weight loss transformations.[26]

While not quite Cinderella, Rivaland employs similar tactics through the image of its own *ojôsama* (princess) who encourages women to take control of their own bodies. This advice is problematic. The Cinderella rags-to-riches tale sells ideas of perseverance that reinforce validation of self-worth through competition—against yourself and others—a notion disguised by the rhetoric of personal achievement. The motivation behind the narrative "to be the better version of yourself" is predicated on individualism and feeds into the neo-liberal vocabulary of "empowerment" that critics such as McRobbie are critical of, and which risks producing the neoliberal female subject who will strive to look "beautiful" at whatever cost.[27]

Branding the Ideal Female Body:
From Moon Princess to Evgenia,
the Princess on Ice

In March 2020, Rivaland's Instagram account had 195 posts and 4,387 followers. It mostly features reposted content from users and from Rivaland's ambassadors, who are most likely compensated. According to information available from public profiles, the demographic of the people being regrammed are all women who appear to be below the age of thirty. These women identify themselves as models; *tarento* (media personalities); mothers; beauty, fashion, or food bloggers; YouTubers; and producers of beauty and/or fashion brands. Only three identify themselves as influencers. Other professions included dancer, dentist, racer, reporter, piano teacher, and trend writer. Rivaland's content is thus created *for* women *by* women.[28]

While Rivaland builds their brand through this form of prosumerism, they are also selective about what appears on their official account, since not all tagged posts are regrammed, which might suggest that the makers of Jewel intentionally discard tagged posts and images that do not express their girly ideal.[29] Original posts by Rivaland include a grid layout that features Jewel and two other posts that advertise the drink. These official posts may have set the aesthetic standard for Rivaland's Instagram account, but the brand's cute visual aesthetic is mostly constructed through regrammed posts that utilize soft, pastel filters and brightly lit settings that convey ideas of opulence and daintiness associated with princess imagery. Typical content of the regrammed posts include selfies posing with Jewel and Kôso, as well as stylized images of these drinks. In fact, without prior knowledge of Rivaland's products, it may be unclear what these women are endorsing because there are more selfies than images that feature Rivaland's products alone.

It is noteworthy that one of Rivaland's brand ambassadors is Russia's two-time Olympic champion figure skater, Evgenia Medvedeva, who initially appeared in six images on Rivaland's Instagram account.[30] Medvedeva gained popularity in Japan after her performance on ice at the 2017 International Skating Union World Team Trophy event in Tokyo, in which she took on the character of and skated to the theme song from the popular *shōjo* manga series of the same name. Medvedeva's tribute to Japan's most iconic heroine on an international stage made her an overnight sensation, capturing the attention of its creator, Naoko Takeuchi, from whom Medvedeva received an autographed portrait of Sailor Moon.

The reference to Sailor Moon is also relevant within the context of Rivaland's branding. Sailor Moon is a cultural icon in Japan, but she is also incredibly popular around the world, as the manga (1991–97) has sold over thirty-five million copies since its debut and generated billions in merchandise sales.[31] The backstory of Takeuchi's heroine, Sailor Moon, who is herself a reincarnated princess, adds to Rivaland's princess motif in interesting ways. According to Anne Allison, a central trope in *Sailor Moon* is transformation, as an ordinary and clumsy girl named Tsukino Usagi turns into a beautiful but powerful sailor warrior, using her "moon cosmic power makeup," which enables her to save the world from evil.[32] Sailor Moon reinforces Rivaland's discourse of transformation, which is central to the princess motif, as does Medvedeva, whom Rivaland describes as "a princess on ice."[33] Rather than "saving the world from evil," however, Medvedeva is living proof that, through discipline and hard work, your dreams will come to fruition.

At an aesthetic level, Rivaland's princess shares certain characteristics with Sailor Moon that are considered particularly desirable in Japan. They are both *bishôjo*, or beautiful girls, who uphold the visual tropes of idealized beauty. They have "a beautiful leg line," which continues to be described in popular magazines and beauty salons as "not only thin (with no unsightly bulges from either fat or muscle), well-pedicured, hairless, and silky smooth, but also perfectly aligned from ankle to hip."[34] They have a small waist, long, silky flowing hair, and often a "white" or fair complexion, as pale skin is considered the ideal image of middle-class women in contemporary Japan.[35] While the ideal of pale, white skin validates "Euroamerican beauty ideology" to some extent, it is not a direct cultural import of racialized beauty standards.[36] This complicates popular assumptions that Japanese women aspire to look like white women. Modern-day beauty practices, such as the application of bright foundation and skin-lightening creams (also known as *bihaku* beauty products), are linked to an ancient "dermal consciousness" visible in centuries-old Japanese beauty standards that "emphasized pale, translucent skin."[37] Even so, the appeal to attain a body sculpted in the image of Medvedeva (i.e., "white," thin, and tall like Sailor Moon) are translated into Rivaland's post that, for example, depicts Medvedeva in a glamor shot wearing an ice-skating costume. She also appears pretty and poised (see fig. 2-2) as she holds a glass filled with Jewel, though she is never shown consuming the drink despite her claims that "it tastes great."[38]

FIGURE 2–2. The first two images depict Evgenia Medvedeva advertising Jewel dressed in a skating costume. These posts are no longer available on Rivaland's account but have been saved on a fan page. In the last image, Medvedeva promotes Jewel on her own Instagram account, which also appeared on Rivaland's main account but now appears in the Tagged posts section.

Consuming Cuteness:
Jewel and the Question of Agency

Rivaland utilizes Instagram as an advertising platform not only to sell diet products but also to define their brand using visual metaphors of cuteness through the princess motif. Cuteness, or *kawaisa*, is evoked by images of women who appear to hide coyly behind the drink packets, a bottle, or a glass cup, while others appear wide-eyed and dress modestly. These women suck or bite on straws, smile, or pucker their lips to convey an innocent look. They are rarely presented in the foreground of the images, and in some images they coyly turn their gaze away from the camera. Only a handful of women are shown in off-the-shoulder shirts, tank tops, or low V-neck tops, as the majority of women wear camisoles and dresses in a range of pastel colors. These visual cues predominantly reinforce an image of cuteness and sweetness over sexiness, indicating how the hyper-feminine, within the context of Rivaland's Instagram account, is characterized by a kind of girlish conservatism rather than overtly provocative sexuality.

The visual tropes depicted in these images reproduce gender stereotypes that infantilize women. In his analysis of a corpus of magazine advertisements from the 1970s, Erving Goffman found that women are often portrayed like children, which is reflective of, and in turn shaped by, perceptions of the subordinate role of women in society. Goffman's central claim is that ads work to instill or re-instill normative gender ideals that ritualize existing stereotypes of both the subordination and the vulnerability of women. He identified six patterns to classify such representation. From Goffman's patterns and based on my observations, some of the most frequently observed poses are the feminine touch, which involves self-touching and/or "using . . . fingers and hands to trace the outlines of an object or to cradle it or to caress its surface"; licensed withdrawal, which refers to poses such as "head eye aversion"; and the ritualization of subordination, which includes gestures such as "canting of head or body" or bashful knee bends.[39] The body language of the women depicted on Rivaland's Instagram account signify ideas of frailty and submissiveness that render women in the likeness of children so that they appear cute, innocent, and even doll-like (fig. 2-3.) These few examples show that Goffman's study can be applied outside of the U.S. context to examine some shared features of gender stereotypes across cultures, but it is equally important to understand these visual codes of subordination in a culturally specific way.[40]

These visual tropes can be understood as examples of *shôjo* performance. In lay terms, "shōjo literally means girl or maiden, but it frequently points to a culturally crafted concept laden with values and history."[41] One way that *shôjo* has been conceptualized as it pertains to girl culture is in relation to feminist discourses of liminality. Conceptually, *shôjo* identity sits on the threshold between girlhood and womanhood, where one is able to free herself from the middle-class life path, responsibilities, and constraints that come with being an adult woman in Japanese society (e.g., marriage, child rearing) by performing girlhood through the consumption of cute aesthetics, dress, and food. Rivaland's *shôjo* utilize *kawaisa* (cuteness), which Simon May calls "a weapon of mass seduction,"[42] through which one can attain control of a certain situation or person. Recent research focuses on the subversive power of cuteness or

FIGURE 2-3. Selected regrammed posts by Rivaland that depict women advertising Jewel in different poses. Clockwise from top left: @erinko0315, @i.am.mell, @ichaaako, and @mau08us.

kawaisa, connecting it to a form of resistance that developed out of Japanese girl culture.[43] For example, while words such as "childlike," "vulnerable," and "weak" have negative connotations, they have also been appropriated in ironic ways by women who uphold *kawaii* cultural aesthetics to "rescue the meaning of cuteness from the male gaze and redefine it as a tool of self-expression for themselves."[44] In this light, as a form of self-expression, *kawaisa* becomes a powerful means to reclaim ideas of immaturity and childishness on social media through personal gratification (i.e., in the form of gaining followers or likes), through monetary gain, or both.

On Rivaland's Instagram account, the performance of *shōjo* through the concept of *kawaii* is visible in the artificiality of cuteness constructed in the images. For example, ideas of sweetness are fused to cute food in images that utilize soft filters and pink and white color palettes. Such girly visual aesthetics are depicted in a regrammed post from @miiannnnn, which displays Jewel in a short glass cup embellished with a gold butterfly stir stick, surrounded by a swirl of sparkles most likely added by an app. In her posts, @sweets_nano captures a romanticized image of the dieting experience that conveys a "Parisian" sensibility for fashion and consumption. Moreover, @yukico_twingram's images present ideas of elegance and opulence, employing string lights to set a calm and dreamy mood, while posts from @chasomama use pearls and other accessories to add a touch of luxury. Notably, cute food is meant to be displayed and photographed rather than eaten. Even in the videos regrammed to Rivaland's account, which show users preparing their drinks, few are shown actually ingesting the tapioca. Combined, these staged images represent the idea that, through the consumption of Rivaland's products, women are not only able to transform into their ideal selves, but they can do so through a fun and girly style (fig. 2-4).[45]

Most importantly, because some of these images share visual aesthetics, it is most likely that users are drawing inspiration from each other's posts, but applying their own interpretations of cuteness to curate Jewel's marketing image in personally meaningful ways. This is particularly evident in comments posted in image captions that reveal the reasons women consume Jewel. User captions on images posted by Rivaland ranged from those who expressed a desire to lose weight in order to fit into a bathing suit and to combat *fuyubutori* (winter weight) (@i.am.mell) to mothers who expressed the convenience of Jewel in their busy lives (@ema.217). Some saw Jewel as a means for women to educate other women about the "health benefits" of dieting or detoxing the body and to share ways to prepare and consume Jewel.

It is through these affinities and tensions that questions of agency are made personally relevant and, therefore, a powerful means of channeling self-determination. Such representations support Susan Bordo's argument that "women

FIGURE 2–4. Selected images regrammed by Rivaland that depict Jewel as "cute food." Clockwise from top left: @miiannnnn, @sweets_nano, @chasomama, and @yukico_twingram.

are not 'cultural dopes'; usually they are all too conscious of the system of values and rewards that they are responding to and perpetrating."[46] Getting the perfect photo takes time and multiple shots. Users then edit their photos, adding filters and using beauty apps to enhance the overall appearance of the image, so they can put their best (or cutest) faces forward. Because women featured on Rivaland's account are creators of their own content, they deliberately position themselves (and the products) to be looked at by inviting or inverting the gaze by staring back. Although their agency over image composition is unquestionable, the extent to which these women demonstrate a clear understanding of the contradictory demands of hyper-feminine consumption remains ambiguous.

Rivaland's Instagram allows for an online community that enables mostly young women to share personally meaningful content with other women who are looking to be inspired to commit to their diet. However, this feminist vision is limited for several reasons. The emphasis placed on youth identity and *shôjo* is a bittersweet reminder of the perceived threat of aging. Social norms demand the curation of the self on social media to align with the cute femininity relevant to a youthful Japanese audience. Curating the self in the likeness of Rivaland's princess also runs the risk of perpetuating harmful stereotypes that privilege thinness and whiteness, signaling a return to conservative beauty ideals in Japan. However, it is not Rivaland's aim to offer alternative modes of beauty. Instead, it capitalizes on youth culture, girly features, and ideas of sweetness and cuteness that are meaningful to a cult of young women who stand at the forefront of the brand's marketing image.

Drawing from Rivaland's Instagram account, this chapter demonstrates how the platform reflects and responds to contradictory productions of the feminine self in Japan. Further research might compare Rivaland to other popular diet food products advertised on Instagram, or conduct interviews with brand ambassadors to obtain an even richer cultural perspective on the role of Instagram, food, and identity politics in contemporary Japan. Rivaland's Instagram frames the relationship between food and gender, utilizing its own *shôjo* princess as a powerful symbol of perseverance emblematic of dieting's hyper-femininity and its war on food consumption. Sadly, not everyone is able to win this fight.

Notes

I thank all the peer reviewers and the editors, Emily Contois and Zenia Kish, for providing thought-provoking and encouraging comments on an earlier draft of this chapter. Also, thanks to Ola Mohammed for encouraging me to submit my work for this book.
1. Lev Manovich, *Instagram and Contemporary Image* (2017), 65, http://manovich .net/index.php/projects/instagram-and-contemporary-image. According to Ma-

novich, "results of computational analysis of subjects of 100,000 Instagram photos shared in Bangkok, Berlin, Moscow, São Paulo, and Tokyo. For dataset details, see http://selfiecity.net/#dataset" (65).

2. Laura Miller, *Beauty Up: Exploring Contemporary Japanese Body Aesthetics* (Berkeley: University of California Press, 2006), 164.

3. Ojôsama Kôso was Rivaland's first product, introduced in June of 2011. Since then, the company has sold over 3.5 million orders. According to the Placenta + Collagen beauty supplements homepage, it contains Italian pig placenta extract; it is marketed as a safe and a high-quality product from Europe that is touted as rich in minerals and amino acids that support one's beauty and health.

4. Yoko Yamazaki and Mika Omori, "The Relationship between Mothers' Thin-Ideal and Children's Drive for Thinness: A Survey of Japanese Early Adolescents and their Mothers," *Journal of Health Psychology* 21, no. 1 (2016): 102, https://doi.org/ 10.1177/1359105314522676.

5. Laura Spielvogel, *Working Out in Japan: Shaping the Female Body in Tokyo Fitness Clubs* (Durham, NC: Duke University Press, 2003), 175–78. See also Tomoki Mase, Kumiko Ohara, Chiemi Miyawaki, Katsuyasu Kouda, and Harunobu Naka-mura, "Influences of Peers' and Family Members' Body Shapes on Perception of Body Image and Desire for Thinness in Japanese Female Students," *International Journal of Women's Health* 7 (2015): 628.

6. Goboutree, "Shinderera taijû no BMI to keisan-shiki! Mitame mo geinôjin gazô de chekku" (How to measure Cinderella weight BMI! Let's take a look at celebrity images), *HAPIEE oshare joshi-muke WEB magajin* (Hapiee: A Web magazine for fashionable women), accessed July 28, 2019, https://hapiee.com/cinderella-weight. Websites about Cinderella weight and dieting such as this one are quite common.

7. Naomi Wolf, *The Beauty Myth: How Images of Beauty Are Used against Women* (New York: Harper Collins, 2002), 187.

8. Mase et al., "Influences of Peers," 625.

9. Mio Yoshie, Daiki Kato, Miyuki Sadamatsu, and Kyoko Watanabe, "The Eating Attitudes, Body Image, and Depression of Japanese Female University Students," *Social Behavior and Personality* 45, no. 6 (2017): 943–50, https://doi.org/10.2224/ sbp.5961.

10. Spielvogel, *Working Out in Japan*, 186.

11. For an insightful exploration of how female consumption mediates between the poles of "desire" and "disgust," see Grace En-Yi Ting. "The Desire and Disgust of Sweets: Consuming Femininities through *Shōjo* Manga," *U.S.-Japan Women's Journal* 54, no. 1 (2018): 52–74. For an exploration of the thematic relationship between normative femininity and self-directed violence, such as in the form of eating disorders in contemporary Japanese narratives and visual culture, see Marianne Gitte Hansen, *Femininity, Self-Harm and Eating Disorders in Japan: Navigating Contradiction in Narrative and Visual Culture* (New York: Routledge, 2016).

12. Sarah Banet-Weiser, "Branding the Post-Feminist Self: Girls' Video Production and YouTube," in *Mediated Girlhoods: New Explorations of Girls' Media Culture*, ed. Mary Celeste Kearney, 277–94 (New York: Peter Lang).

13. Angela McRobbie, *The Aftermath of Feminism: Gender, Culture and Social Change*. (Los Angeles: Sage, 2009), 5.

14. See also Rosalind Gill, "Postfeminist Media Culture: Elements of a Sensibility," *European Journal of Cultural Studies* 10, no. 2 (2007): 147–66, https://doi.org/10.1177/1367549407075898; Angela McRobbie, *Feminism and Youth Culture*, 2nd ed. (New York: Routledge, 2000); Amy Shields Dobson, *Postfeminist Digital Cultures: Femininity, Social Media, and Self-Representation* (New York: Palgrave Macmillan, 2015), 1–22.

15. Miller, *Beauty Up*, 172.

16. Ibid., 165.

17. A brand of sweetener from Kanagawa, Japan.

18. Miller, *Beauty Up*, 164, 162.

19. @rivaland_ojyosamakouso, "#Ojôsama kôso no ribarando desu. Ninki bakuhatsu 1000 manshoku toppa! #Ojôsama kôso Jewel #Ojôsama kôso Toropikaru o hajime daietto gyôkai-hatsu no shin kankaku tapioka dorinku daietto zenshu ga ima dake shokai gentei 399-en de tamese chau 🎵😊" (We're Rivaland of #Ojôsama kôso. We've sold over ten million of our super popular drink! #Ojôsama kôso Jewel. What started with #Ojôsama kôso Tropical, we're now offering a first run limited tapioca diet drink collection set—the first of its kind in the diet industry. You can try it out for only 399 yen), Instagram profile, December 22, 2019, www.ojyosama.jp/angel999/best_selection399/ (www.instagram.com/rivaland_ojyosamakouso/?hl=en).

20. Sarah K. Murnen and Donn Byrune, "Hyperfemininity: Measurement and Initial Validation of the Construct," *Journal of Sex Research* 28, no. 3 (1991): 479.

21. Spielvogel, *Working Out in Japan*, 182. Moreover, Spielvogel posits, "women, like children, are expected and encouraged to relish sweets, and those who do are constructed as cute and childishly attractive" (181).

22. Ivry Tsipy, "Embodied Responsibilities: Pregnancy in the Eyes of Japanese OB-Gyns," *Sociology of Health and Illness* 29, no. 2 (2007): 258, doi:10.1111/j.1467-9566.2007.00475.x.

23. For feminist interpretations of *ganbaru*, see Justin Charlebois, *Japanese Femininities* (London: Routledge, 2014).

24. Rosalind Gill, *Gender and Media* (Cambridge, UK: Polity, 2007), 49.

25. Laura Miller, "Japan's Cinderella Motif: Beauty Industry and Mass Culture Interpretations of a Popular Icon Cinderella," *Asian Studies Review* 32, no. 3 (2008): 394.

26. Ibid., 395–98.

27. McRobbie, *Aftermath of Feminism*, 1.

28. At the time of data collection, there were a total of 156 posts. As of June 9, 2019, Rivaland had 4,910 followers and a total of 702 tagged posts, of which only a selected few are regrammed by Rivaland to their original Instagram page.

29. For more information on corporation branding, see Alvin Toffler, *The Third Wave* (New York: Bantam Books, 1980); Adam Arvidsson and Elanor Colleoni, "Value in Informational Capitalism and on the Internet," *Information Society* 28,

no. 3 (2012): 135–50, https://doi.org/10.1080/01972243.2012.669449; Nicole Buzzetto-Hollywood, "Social Media and Prosumerism," *Value in Informational Capitalism and on the Internet*, no. 10 (2013): 67–79, https://doi.org/10.28945/1796; Comor Edward, "Contextualizing and Critiquing the Fantastic Prosumer: Power, Alienation and Hegemony." *Critical Sociology* 37, no. 3 (2011): 309–27, https://doi.org/10.1177/0896920510378767

30. Although Medvedeva was appointed as one of the ambassadors of the brand as of July 28, 2018 (according to a post on her own Instagram account), her posts no longer appear on Rivaland's main Instagram page, but rather on the Tagged page. As a result, the captions used to regram her posts are no longer available online, but I saved them on a PDF at the time of data collection. Other posts that appeared on the Rivaland's Instagram account have also been moved to the Tagged section. Perhaps Medvedeva's contract with Rivaland has expired, or whoever is running Rivaland's Instagram account selects and regrams relevant images at random.

31. Kris Kosaka, "Naoko Takeuchi: 'Sailor Moon's' Strong-willed Guardian of Girls Manga," *Japan Times*, October 19, 2019, accessed May 27, 2020, www.japantimes.co.jp/culture/2019/10/19/books/naoko-takeuchi-sailor-moons-strong-willed-guardian-girls-manga/#.XnI79KhKjb2.

32. Anne Allison, *Millennial Monsters: Japanese Toys and the Global Imagination* (Berkeley: University of California Press, 2006), 22, 134.

33. @rivaland_ojyosamakouso, "Joshi figyuasukêto-kai de kazukazu no igyô o tassei shite kita medobêjewa-san wa masani kôri no ue no ojôsama!" (Having accomplished a countless number of feats in the women's figure skating league, Medvedeva is what you'd call a princess on ice!). The post has since been deleted on Rivaland's account.

34. Spielvogel, *Working Out in Japan*, 164–65.

35. For an in-depth exploration of the so-called white face within a Japanese cultural context, see Mikiko Ashikari, "Urban Middle-Class Japanese Women and Their White Faces: Gender, Ideology, and Representation," *Ethos* 31, no. 1 (2003): 3–37, https://doi.org/10.1525/eth.2003.31.1.3; see also Miller, *Beauty Up*, 1–39.

36. Miller, *Beauty Up*, 4.

37. Ibid., 35. See also Ashikari, "Urban Middle-Class Japanese Women," 3–37.

38. @jmedvedevaj, "Kicking off the new season with this Japanese famous drink! It tastes great," Instagram photo, July 28, 2018, www.instagram.com/p/BlxoqiCB5__/.

39. Erving Goffman, *Gender Advertisements* (New York: Harper and Row, 1979).

40. See also Mee-Eun Kang, "The Portrayal of Women's Images in Magazine Advertisements: Goffman's Gender Analysis Revisited," *Sex Roles* 37, no. 11 (1997): 979–96, https://doi.org/10.1007/BF02936350; Nicola Döring, Anne Reif, and Sandra Poeschl, "How Gender-Stereotypical Are Selfies? A Content Analysis and Comparison with Magazine Adverts," *Computers in Human Behavior* 55, no. PB (2016): 955–62, https://doi.org/10.1016/j.chb.2015.10.001. According to these critics, gender stereotypes are still prevalent in ads and on social media.

41. Masafumi Monden, "A Dream Dress for Girls: Milk, Fashion and Shōjo Iden-

tity," in *Shōjo across Media: Exploring "Girl" Practices in Contemporary Japan*, ed. Jaqueline Berndt, Kazumi Nagaike and Fusami Ogi (Basingstoke, UK: Palgrave Macmillan, 2019), 219.

42. Simon May, "Cute as Weapon of Mass Seduction," *The Power of Cute* (Princeton, NJ: Princeton University Press, 2019), 1–18.

43. For an in-depth discussion on girl cultures that emerged in the 1990s, see Masafumi Monden, *Japanese Fashion Cultures: Dress and Gender in Contemporary Japan* (New York: Bloomsbury Academic, 2014).

44. Makiko Iseri, "Flexible Femininities? Queering Kawaii in Japanese Girls' Culture," in *Twenty-first Century Feminism: Forming and Performing Femininity*, ed. Claire Nally and Angela Smith (New York: Palgrave Macmillan, 2015), 148.

45. @miiannnnn, "Ojôsama kôso jewel. Tai-appu kyanpên ni sanka shite irunode go shôkai sa sete kudasai" (Let me introduce you to the tie-up campaign), Instagram photo, November 4 2017, www.instagram.com/p/BbE01m6hrq_/; @sweets_nano, "Wadai no Ojôsama kôso@ rivaland _ ojyosamakouso kara atarashî shôhin ga detakara tameshite mimashita" (I've received the popular Ojôsama kôso), Instagram photo, Nov 12, 2017, www.instagram.com/p/BbZePROB5VA/; @chasomama, "Tapioka-iri kōso dorinku mitame ga kawai sugiru" (The tapioca drink looks too cute), Instagram photo, March 23, 2017, www.instagram.com/p/BR-qBZuh6Dt/; @yukico_twingram, "Ima no watashi ni pittari tottemo î mono itadakimashita" (I received something perfect for me), Instagram photo, March 11, 2017, www.instagram.com/p/BRflaSbBHKe/.

46. Susan Bordo, "Feminism, Foucault, and the Politics of the Body," in *Feminist Theory and the Body*, ed. Janet Price and Margaret Shildrick (New York: Routledge, 1999), 250. Also cited in Miller, *Beauty Up*, 7.

CHAPTER 3

#Foodporn

An Anatomy of the Meal Gaze

GABY DAVID AND
LAURENCE ALLARD

This chapter is a ten-course fusion-food meal, *cooked*/built on the outcomes of the colloquium "#Foodporn: The Mobiles of Desire," which we co-organized in December 2018 at the Université Sorbonne Nouvelle Paris 3.[1] The first part of this *meal*/analysis explores the affective and social stakes embedded in the online representation of food porn, particularly on Instagram in France. We then move on to a more open reflection on the notion of food porn and its associated hashtags.

At the crossroads of visual culture, media studies, and cultural studies, we explore and reflect on two main questions: How might people gazing at meals, here defined as the "meal gaze," become the normative way food is looked at, grasped, photographed, and shared in online social networks?[2] Has this way of seeing masked other power relationships?

Hors d'Oeuvres: Introduction

Grow, harvest, cook, and eat. Film, photograph, share, and influence. Post and like. Eat with your eyes. Big corpus, huge data, and then: digital detox. The aphorism says that you are what you eat. But, digitally speaking, in attention ecosystems structured around snack-sized online content, you are what you post and consume—not with your mouth, but with your eyes. Nowadays it is often thought "camera eats first," an expression that illustrates perfectly "how people 'feed' their cameras first by taking photos of their food before feeding themselves."[3] Then, after the camera has had its fill, what happens next, as Terri Senft suggests, is the effort to "monitor, predict and direct the affective flows of user-generated content."[4] For, as we observe who we are, looking at ourselves through how we represent food becomes a pertinent mirror.

In relation to this, Lev Manovich and Alise Tifentale have unsurprisingly written that food is, together with selfies and parties, counted among the most popular shared subjects of social media posts.[5] Indeed, digital ethnography and online research on food reveals that the digital presence of food—in addition to the consumption of *images* of food—is a routine component of many users' online tasks and habitus.

Mouthwatering Aperitifs: Whetting the Appetite

During the writing of this chapter, several striking food-related artsy and media news stories made the rounds. To begin with, a photo exhibition called *Food for the Eyes: The Story of Food in Photography* in Berlin brought together many well-known artists, including Nobuyoshi Araki and Nan Goldin.[6] Subsequently, a banana duct-taped to a wall went on sale at Art Basel Miami Beach, priced at around $120,000. This work, *Comedian* (2019) by artist Maurizio Cattelan, was later eaten by a performance artist and shared endlessly online. Many potential artistic and cultural references could have motivated Cattelan's art piece.[7] For instance, it could refer to Linda Niochlin's *Buy My Bananas* photograph (1972), which is itself a feminist diptych photo reply to a late nineteenth-century popular French magazine photo titled *Buy My Apples*. Together, these works show that the sexualization of women and its relation to food is a very old and established trope.

Yet, Cattelan's edible art banana piece, *Comedian,* provokes reflection and raises the question of the role and price of art, of fresh fruit, of agriculture, but also of Instagram and the social networking sites that amplified the art news story. Across these aforementioned different sites of value production, both the piece itself and the performance of its consumption are rendered art through their intertwined relationships with social media, food representation, food pornification, and visual culture. Apart from being circumstantial, all these artistic coincidences validate once more how food is a timeless topic, depicted artistically, mediatically, digitally, and thus always also visually consumed.

Setting the Table: Rationale

For the purpose of this chapter, and to study its current and latent influences, rather than using "foodporn" as a hashtag tool in itself, we researched and found related associations to some less visible layers of the food industry and food world in France. Our main goal is to offer analytical tools to reflect on the object of food as it relates to this broader sense of the tag #foodporn.

We argue that the online French food visual panorama is a living example of how dominance, and thus authority, can swing from being framed by a "male gaze" to its anagram and pun "meal gaze."[8] For this we define "meal gaze" as a theoretical term that encapsulates the commodity fetishization of images of meals in a digital form. This figure of speech facilitates both a reification of the economy of food production and the representation of meals as sets of habits and practices people enact when cooking, plating, serving, photographing, and sharing images of meals. In this way, we extend the feminist analysis of the male gaze, and the subordination and objectification of women in pornography, to thinking about the pornography of labor in the digital gig economy. Further, we expand this analysis to a place where it intersects with our mediated, Instagrammable, and foodie lives—where images of food become metonyms and motives of desire.

The Entrée:
The Provenance of the Term "Food Porn"

The definition of "food porn" is contested and evades any singular or conclusive meaning.[9] This multiplicity contributes to the interest it evokes throughout the sphere of public discourses and debates. Food porn belongs to the process of making something look desirable, sexy, and eatable: it describes how food can reach out of the screen or page, and grab viewers' attention. Journalist and writer Alexander Cockburn wrote in 1977 that "true *gastro-porn* heightens the excitement and also the sense of the unattainable by preferring colored photographs of various completed recipes."[10] Soon thereafter, Michael F. Jacobson used the term "food porn" in a 1979 newsletter of the Center for Science in the Public Interest. As we discuss below, the term "food porn" was also used by the feminist critic Rosalind Coward in her 1984 book, *Female Desire*, to designate it as a cult of food reminiscent of sexual desire. The staging and advertising of food was seen to incite its consumption and link it to the forbidden: pleasure and passion. The lines between pornography and food imagery quickly became blurred.

More recently, "foodporn" has emerged as a familiar hashtag on social media sites, especially Instagram. However, online the meaning of the term mutates and more often denotes images that are not excessively sexual or pornographic, rich in calories, or even cheesy (melting cheese is an erstwhile classic food porn image). Online, the tag "porn" is a catchy audience strategy. Instagrammers, influencers, and bloggers know it and use it immoderately. Besides, the capaciousness of the category affirms rule 34 of the Internet, which states that "if it exists, there is porn of it, no exceptions."[11] Food, then, does not escape the rule.

The "foodporn" tag does not only index Instagram use in France. Additionally, the mise-en-scène of digital food photography production and consumption also reflects the construction of meaning in French society at large.

A polysemic hashtag like "foodporn" can just as easily caption a photo of a smoothie, a pizza, a chocolate cake, or hummus. Adding the tag "porn" to food-related images acquires potential mouthwatering followers while linking the food to gender pornification and labor pornification. On social media, this hashtag is used differently according to the country and user, although its meaning is shaped more by individuals' tagging strategies than some overarching national symbolism. The aforementioned colloquium we organized showcased very diverse examples of this polysemy. Presentations ranged from visual sociologist Carolina Cambre's keynote, "The Politics of Pleasure: A Tentative Grammar of #foodporn," to "#Foodporn or #foodgore: Visual Notes on Alimentary Desire and Non-Desire" by media scholar Gustavo Gomez Mejia.[12] We also witnessed a presentation by Kévin Poperl on CoopCycle, which is the European federation of bike delivery cooperatives, and one on the LGBTI+ and political reappropriations of hummus by filmmaker Rawane Nassif. This wide-ranging assortment of conference papers not only illustrates that different disciplines (e.g., sociology, anthropology, and cinema) share an interest in the topic, but also signals the diverse approaches being adopted to study food porn in its multiple sociocultural and economic locations (Allard and David forthcoming, 2021).

First Course: On Figures, Hashtagging, Food Porn, and France

Yelena Mejova, Sofiane Abbar, and Hamed Haddadi's "Fetishizing Food in a Digital Age: #foodporn around the World" article classified the top five most distinct food words co-occurring with "food porn" in France to be chocolate, burger, patisserie, gourmandize, and pastry.[13] Similarly, as digital media scholars, we believe that there is value in examining the different patterns manifested in both small and large datasets, invoking questions at divergent scales. Methodologically, we monitored, compared, and included a breakdown of big datasets by compiling data from the social media listening platform Radarly.[14] This software scrapes content from more than a hundred million publications on a daily basis, monitoring over three hundred million sources in sixty languages. It provides data that make sense of the social Web, including social posts and conversations on Facebook, Twitter, Instagram, Weibo, online media, blogs, and forums. We observed the tag #foodporn across all these apps monitored by Radarly from late February 2019 to early April 2019, and focused on its incidences in France.

The software scrape provided a quantitative sample of the use of #foodporn, where the scavenged data are revealed in terms of number of mentions within social media. The analysis revealed that 68.5 percent of #foodporn mentions were in a positive context, 26.8 percent were neutral, 3.7 percent suggested mixed connotations, and just under 1 percent were negative mentions. This is interesting because "smiles" and "likes" are understood to illustrate positive bonds or receptiveness to the commodification not only of the images, but of all user-generated content. Within the content there is also significant use of emojis for communicating the physical embodiment of eating and related affective attachments. These shares and emotional expressions matter to brands and companies that monitor online perception of their products. The relationship between food and sentiment is thus at the heart of the commodity relation signified by foodporn.

In France there are plenty of popular hashtags associated with food imagery, as seen in the tag cloud screenshot (fig. 3-1). Besides #foodporn, users employ many other keywords and concepts that do not exclusively denote food but relate to everyday life and online sharing, for instance, #paris and #photooftheday.[15] Likewise, even if 80 percent of food posts in France are in French, the majority of the hashtags are in English. This represents a desire to be part of a larger, global conversation and indexation, regardless of a potential language barrier. Users seem to reproduce their online habits of using keywords such as fooding, burger, brunch, healthy, and vegan in other platforms, where Instagram usage in France also portrays a globalization of tagging in English.[16] In fact, this tagging in English addresses another population of French eating customers: mainly a younger, Instagram-savvy public that is not as influenced by the Michelin Star ranking system of restaurants. Therefore, it could be said that Instagram redefines French cuisine by inscribing it not only onto the international scale of the platform, but it also reproduces the cuisine as networked food through the self-referential and cross-posting digital practices of younger generations. In this way, we could say that the coupling of the foodporn hashtag with mobile images of food contributes to a global normatization of these types of imagery in the digital ecosystem.

The figures confirm how the digital world reflects the importance of food in France. When talking online about food in French Instagram accounts, the most used language by far is French (80.7 percent of posts), followed by English (9.7 percent), and all other languages comprise a total of 7.8 percent.[17] Moreover, based on 1.01 million posts in France, 12.1 billion impressions, and a reach of 1.66 billion, most of the #foodporn tagged images shared via Instagram show a positive sentiment toward the content of the image, which most of the time is the food itself.[18]

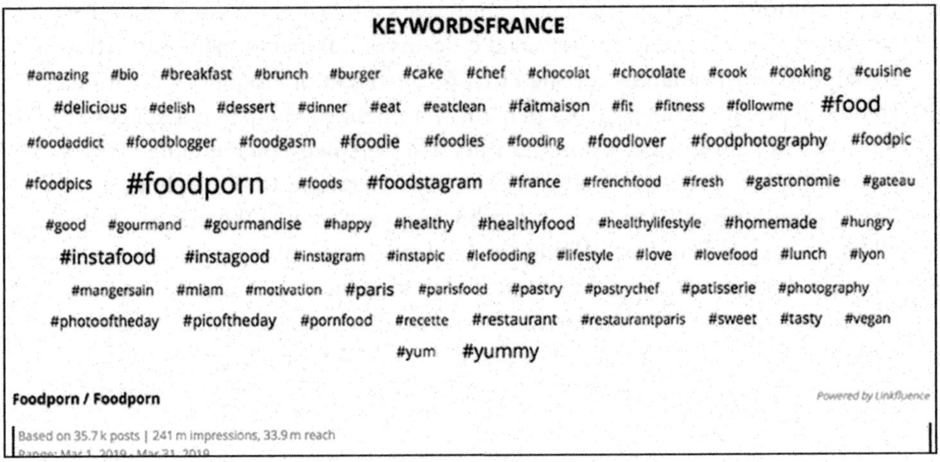

KEYWORDSFRANCE

#amazing #bio #breakfast #brunch #burger #cake #chef #chocolat #chocolate #cook #cooking #cuisine
#delicious #delish #dessert #dinner #eat #eatclean #faitmaison #fit #fitness #followme #food
#foodaddict #foodblogger #foodgasm #foodie #foodies #fooding #foodlover #foodphotography #foodpic
#foodpics #foodporn #foods #foodstagram #france #frenchfood #fresh #gastronomie #gateau
#good #gourmand #gourmandise #happy #healthy #healthyfood #healthylifestyle #homemade #hungry
#instafood #instagood #instagram #instapic #lefooding #lifestyle #love #lovefood #lunch #lyon
#mangersain #miam #motivation #paris #parisfood #pastry #pastrychef #patisserie #photography
#photooftheday #picoftheday #pornfood #recette #restaurant #restaurantparis #sweet #tasty #vegan
#yum #yummy

Foodporn / Foodporn   *Powered by Linkfluence*

Based on 35.7 k posts | 241 m impressions, 33.9 m reach
Range: Mar 1, 2019 - Mar 31, 2019

FIGURE 3-1. Screenshot #foodporn tag cloud, 2019.

With regard to the performativity of how food is represented on Instagram, French food and restaurants are not only predominantly characterized as masculine domains, but they also serve as gendered national identity markers portraying the uniqueness of French culture as we describe next.

Second Course: From Male Gaze to *Faiminisme*

Feminist theory has profoundly changed the way scholars view visual works. In 1975, Laura Mulvey proposed the notion of the "male gaze" to characterize the voyeuristic objectification of women in cinema. Inspired by Freudian theory, Mulvey defines scopophilia as a sexual impulse where the individual takes pleasure in possessing the other through the gaze. This approach coheres with analysis of social roles considered specific to each gender. Western social norms and advertisements long assigned an active role to men, reserving a more submissive role for women. This distinction is still reproduced today in several ways: in clothing that typically presents the female body as more sexualized than the male body; in body discipline norms such as makeup or waxing, which are typically female injunctions; or even in behavioral patterns, such as street harassment, which is predominantly enacted by men toward women.[19] According to John Berger, all these conventions tend to transform the female body into an object, and to reduce women to an image, and thus subject to men's gaze.[20]

More recently, the proliferating norms of gender and sexual expression expand the cultural repertoires described by Mulvey, Berger, and others. Yet, the enduring persistence of Berger's words leads us to examine contemporary gendered mobile practices and how they illuminate and reinforce the integration of the male gaze and pornography into food pornography, further explored by feminist Rosalind Coward in her discussion of food porn and gastro-porn. Coward, for instance, draws parallels between desire, pleasure, and the symbolism of a willingness to serve others.[21]

In the decades following Mulvey's pivotal essay, many researchers have contributed to deconstructing the heteronormative male gaze and the reductive binaries it entails. However, the French mainstream media remains far from changing these old patterns. The patriarchal male gaze is still pervasive in the French food milieu. Sexism is rooted in French culinary culture, where examples of unequal gendered dynamics are still common. A conspicuous example involves the head of the Grand Véfour restaurant in Paris, well-known chef Raymond Oliver, who in the television program *Art et magie de la cuisine* "taught" the program's presenter, Catherine Langeais, how to become the perfect housewife over a fourteen-year run. More recently, on both *Top Chef France* and the French version of *Kitchen Nightmares*, most participants, juries, and all-time winners are all men.

The gendered polarization of French gastronomic visual culture is also conspicuous within the Instagram context. Unsurprisingly, the most followed French Instagram accounts belong to the same established male chefs. Even in the popular cake and patisserie design specialization, where the pastry chefs are mainly women, the most popular patisserie Instagram accounts mainly belong to men. This mirroring of the masculinized televisual representation of chefs within social media obscures the predominantly female workforce in the culinary domain.

Nevertheless, it should be highlighted that in recent years there has been a feminist gastronomic movement in France where cis-women chefs, bloggers, food writers, and food influencers have tried to penetrate the online mediatic food environment dominated by white men, and to emancipate and empower themselves in this sphere. They have somehow opened the industry to small changes by regaining some of this, currently male-only, visibility in the food field. Unfortunately, this gradual shift does not achieve widespread gender parity or gender inclusiveness. But it seems, at least, that providing some visibility to women chefs allows for the possible circumvention of dominant male power roles in the food industry.

However, there are counterexamples and counter powers.[22] In the past, some women have hosted certain French food television programs, like the very famous program *La cuisine des Mousquetaires,* which ran for sixteen years on public television.[23] Some additional examples include the famous female chefs Anne-Sophie Pic, Hélène Darroze, and Rougui Dia. There are also radio programs, like *Plan Culinaire,* hosted by journalist and writer Nora Bouazzani, who also wrote a book called *Faiminisme, quand le sexisme passe à table* (2017)—a pun on the French word *faim* (hunger) and *femme* (woman) because of the pronunciation proximity.[24] The resonance and significance of the pun can be interpreted as a reference to the objectification women suffer in advertisements when represented as if they (we) were fast-food eatable objects, or just placed in the ad to enhance a product. As committed feminists, the authors contest the intimate link between womanhood, food, and sex, where food has long been a means to subjugate women.[25]

Despite these exceptional cases, sexism continues to mark the representation of women in mainstream media production. Indeed, just having women present in the media doesn't inherently combat the patriarchal dynamic. Culturally, however, these illustrations signify that there are at least some counterexamples that challenge, disrupt, and try to offer alternative points of view to the years of male cultural dominance in the French food sphere. These counterexamples are shaping the dominant gendered order of French food culture in various ways. These include visibilization, as well as making space for women to voice their points of view, offering girls new role models, and helping to deconstruct patriarchal French society. If being looked at creates a heightened sense of self-awareness that is contextualized within the gender relations in which the looking occurs, this growing female presence helps to prove the fact that looking plays an important role in the construction of female subjectivity.

On the other hand, the reversal of values is also a way to disrupt the gendered order of French food culture. Unfortunately, this increased visibility is still not enough to counter dominant representations of women primarily as fetish objects of desire. Therefore, following this line of thought, a *faiminisme* activist frame helps us to identify the gendered codes of food production and its cultural representations. Hence, one can speak of meal gaze in an analogical extension of Mulvey's work.

Although she is not French, U.S. artist Stephanie Sarley is well-known in the French food artistic world, as she tries to reverse power roles and gendered schemas consistent with Rosalind Coward's argument. The artist photographs or films herself in metaphorically feminine emancipation poses and relates to fruits and vegetables as if they were depictions of reproductive body parts. For example, the red jelly leaking out of a doughnut in one provocative image suggests menstruation and signals bodily reproductive cycles that do not necessarily direct or signify sexual pleasure (fig. 3-2). Some of her videos personify and empower vaginas through humor and absurdity, which might be understood as having at least two main functions: to enhance and legitimize women to create their own self-representations, and to give more visibility to less sexual representations of feminine genitalia. Throughout her Fruit Art Videos series (since 2015), her artistic style and relationship with food becomes a focal point

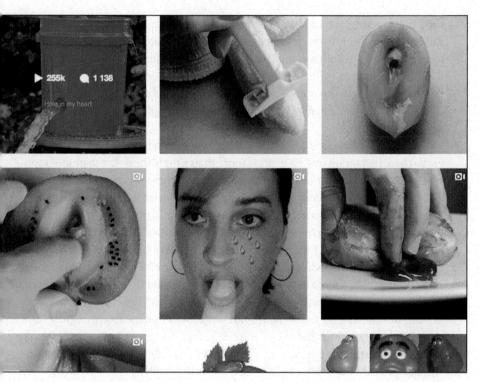

FIGURE 3-2. Screenshot of Stephanie Sarley's Instagram, 2019, www.instagram.com/stephanie_sarley/.

and communication tool for her feminist visual practice. Over the centuries, these images echo what art historian Olivier Leplatre calls "iconophagy," which he defines as the duo of both *food* and the *visuals of food*, which become what we consume, need, and share.[26]

Side Dish: Meal Gaze as Instagrammability

In a visionary article, Ito and Okabe observe that as a result of the multiplying uses of mobile images, the notion of "images worth sharing" has radically changed.[27] Users have begun to attribute much more importance to visually sharing the ordinary objects of everyday life—such as food and pets—and not just photos of birthdays, weddings, vacations, or other extraordinary events that were formerly the central subjects of amateur photography.

Nowadays, the word Instagrammability (or, according to Urban Dictionary, simply "grammability") refers exactly to those moments and places that one might deem worthy of sharing on Instagram. Coupling Instagram and food photographs stages food in a performative sense, as well as increasing its media(ting) power through increased quantitative popularity. In other words, Instagram itself is influencing the way food is consumed. On the one hand, it prompts changes to the aesthetics of the culinary repertoire. On the other hand, these new ways of consuming food lead to different uses of Instagram that shape the visual representation of food on the platform and in broader media arenas as well.

On Instagram, images of food have become metonyms of desire in the meal gaze. These Instagram images express more than simply the desire to photograph images of food but refer also to all the affordances these images enable: the will and need to post, like, comment, and consume them on a daily basis.

How does the meal gaze concept connect with food porn, and more specifically with the #foodporn tag? There is common ground between how women are expected to appear for cis-men and most Instagram food images: they are supposed to look "good." One could ask, how? Similar to Instagram's many makeup tutorials, there are plenty of tutorials that provide tips on how to shoot food better, pornify them, or take advantage of natural light. All this rhetoric around how to take the best food photos underlines that meals are not just supposed to look good for the eye of the restaurant consumer but meant to look good for the camera, which then generates a totally different way of seeing food. Instagram users therefore gaze at those meals differently.

In his famous book, W. J. T. Mitchell asks *What Do Pictures Want?*, finally concluding that images want to "speak to us, sometimes literally, sometimes figuratively."[28] Following his line of thought, we could argue that food wants not only to be eaten but also photographed. To provide an example experienced in our own lives, one night, after we had finished the main course in a Parisian restaurant, we asked the waiter which dessert he recommended. He answered: "Well, one is served warm and is very tasty, but the other one is more Instagrammable." We burst into laughter. We thought that this type of reply was something exceptional, but then, only one month later in Catalonia, Spain, it happened again. A waiter advised us, "The Catalan crème is super, but the mousse is very visual." It seems to be that visuality, or the way that some food appears visually, has increased in importance and can become a game changer parameter to sell the product, a decision-maker. Hence, although not a groundbreaking observation, it could be said that now more than ever, when deciding which dish to order in a restaurant, many customers choose a meal for more than its flavor.

According to the French sociologist Pierre Bourdieu, cultural, musical, and other tastes reflect social class and upbringing.[29] The economics of food porn can relate to a Bourdieusian digital version of what he named the "hierarchy of taste," where people's sensitivities in food and flavor operate as status markers.[30] For instance, in their book *Foodies: Democracy and Distinction*, Johnston and

Baumann explain that affluent versus lower-income users use #foodporn to mark different types of food. For example, a highbrow urban bohemian French bourgeoisie population would tag smoothies and organic food as #foodporn, and a lower-class population will be more likely to tag burgers and kebabs.[31]

The digital version of the social milieu does not strictly reproduce the same hierarchies that Bourdieu's work considered through the notions of social field and economic or cultural capital. Having power in the digital environment means being more connected. This is why it is interesting to couple Bourdieu's theory of distinction with Javier Borondo et al.'s hypothesis of the digital "topocracy." Through an analysis of social graphs of influencers, they demonstrated that far from representing a meritocracy, the socio-technical construction of influence delimits a "topocracy," which is based on the concentration of networked nodes and hubs, whose star-shaped scheme recalls the star system principle.[32] Social dominance in the online world, therefore, presupposes a capital of relational connectivity, and this capital makes it possible to ensure a new form of cultural legitimacy: influenceability. On a site like Instagram where visual talent can be freely expressed and recognized as such, it is necessary to highlight the networked backstage of the influence machinery, which includes influencers, micro influencers, and even nano influencers.[33]

Food Replicas: Insta as Plastic Replica

A final and provocative analogy for food porn could be to compare it to the display of food replicas (*shokuhin sanpuru*), which initially appeared in Japanese restaurant windows in many cities around the world, and are now found in many other types of restaurants. Associated with catchy, kitschy consumer items, these food replicas have contributed to the visuality of (Japanese) food culture in their own way; in other words, they are almost transparently naturalized. They are part of the visual landscape of food and consumer culture belonging to urban decor, but because they are so common, their role is somehow underappreciated in Western haute cuisine restaurants.[34] It could be said that Instagram plays a similar role, but how? Many Instagram photos draw viewers' eyes toward digital food reproductions that show specific dishes available inside restaurants. This mechanism feeds visuality through oversaturated, sometimes beautifully arranged, stylish plating. Both means are visual approximations, meant to lure you in, and show you what you could have.

In contrast to what might remain enigmatic, the plastic food replica dishes do look something like the plates you eat. The visual peculiarities of these replicas makes them even more interesting, and thus analogous to our analysis of Instagram. It is relevant to distinguish between restaurants using these replicas as bait for potential customers and everyday people and influencers posting food pics on Instagram. The latter are not necessarily directly advertising the restaurant. Their Instagram food posts are as much about commodifying their own accounts and personal brands by constructing social media selves that consume particular kinds of foods, communicate an identity, and sell a lifestyle more than an individual dish or restaurant. Moreover, the food replicas are not subjected to the meal gaze, but online food photos result from the digital affordances of sharing, likes, comments, emojis, and so forth.

The digital and particularly visual dimensions of the food industry have impacted the arts of table setting and plating: transforming them into crucial steps for goals beyond pleasing a diner, including advertising, image circulation, engagement, health, branding—and the list could go on. Today, the means to display and order food are proliferating digitally even if food labor is almost, if not totally, invisible. One prominent example is the rise of "ghost restaurants," or online-only restaurants, where people order and receive real food delivered from a restaurant that has no physical space. In a topographic mode, social media like Instagram helps to promote the dematerialization of restaurants—and their workers—into "ghosts," while food influencers promote grammable dishes like plastic replicas for followers to collect like pop figurines and other geek toys.

Paying the Bill: The Invisibilization of Digital Food Labor

Does this "looking at food" reshape restaurant management, marketing, and so on, or does it mask power relationships? The question implies a triangulation between images, mobile app culture, and food delivery workers. What is usually called the "platform economy" should more accurately be called a "mobile economy on demand."[35] The latter refers to digital marketplaces promising immediate access to goods and services frequently delivered by contract, or gig workers. This virtual food system has many impacts on both economic and social fields. First, these Uberized economies, like the American UberEats or the British Deliveroo, have to rely on complex delivery systems. In France, these companies hire workers in precarious situations, including many bicycle couriers, and classify them as self-employed rather than as employees. This freelance status entails no type of insurance or indemnity, effecting huge cost savings for employers.

One can take, for example, advertisements for the food delivery app, Uber-Eats. A simple look at its webpage portrays the invisibilization of the production structures that operate behind it, illustrating nothing other than a nourishing reification of the food commodity. One sees the typical zenithal meal photo but nothing representing the way food is produced or cooked. This is not far from the food influencers' aesthetic and the way of looking at food we describe above. The advertisements sell the image as an effortless Instagram experience, allowing the user to simply order and eat.

As increasing numbers of couriers experienced traffic accidents and other misfortunes, however, workers have begun to protest these working conditions. A legal case filed by the European federation of bike delivery cooperatives, CoopCycle, defending the labor rights of food delivery bikers, eventually won suit in the Cour de cassation (the highest court in France).[36] As a result of these fourteen months of court appearances and negotiations, a new business model for couriers has been accepted. They have created a collectively owned and controlled enterprise, which has become a European federation fostering solidarity between co-ops and reducing their costs, thanks to service pooling and creating a common force to advocate for couriers' rights. This model promises economic and social advantages for the dispatch riders because they promote a circular economy, cultural goods, urban agriculture, and strong value-added and socially responsible deliveries. The Cooperatives Movement platform—developed by Trebor Scholz, a prominent theorist of digital labor—wants to remake our digitally networked society through a solidarity-based economy rooted in free software.[37] Our analysis of the meal gaze undertaken through the #foodporn tag and its scopic ways of understanding food practices becomes an illustration of Scholz's political criticisms. Free software initiatives such as that of the CoopCycle movement are notable examples of how collective actions can become more than simply collective scopic ways of seeing.

This invisibilization of digital food labor took a dramatic turn with the arrival of the COVID-19 pandemic. The deserted streets of big cities are apocalyptic landscapes for couriers, who have, in this case, become hyper-visible, and who are subject to the appalling risk of infection in delivering dishes that will end up on Instagram accounts—alongside homemade bread, the new trend in foodporn at the time of writing.

Dessert *ou digestif*, to Conclude

In this chapter, we show how #foodporn alternately mediates aesthetics, economy, gastronomy, app culture, and of course, users' depictions of their everyday lives. It can be used as a cultural digital ethnographic tool to highlight how food images and habits change eating protocols, norms, and the entire food industry. Nowadays there are many aspects of visuality that have become newly important with the arrival of digital photography. They have become as important as taste in selling food: the likes, tweets, retweets, viralization of images, rankings, comments, and hashtags.

Through this summarizing French food porn voyage, we were able to demonstrate that the French Instagram food panorama is still stamped with a strong male bias. However, some user criticisms and resistance to the mainstream approach to these mobile practices lead to the hope that future influencers with a range of followers might change this situation. Additionally, the proliferation of food apps also helps us imagine that food origin transparency and traceability, food quality, and subsequent changes in eating can all be within easy reach. Now it is time for our mouths and eyes to follow a less normative and repetitive drive, and begin to grow, harvest, collect, buy, and cook more ethical and fair-trade food.

Notes

We thank Emily J. H. Contois, Zenia Kish, and copyeditor Adrian Jordan for helping to sharpen this chapter.

1. "#Foodporn: The Mobiles of Desire," International Symposium Mobile Creation, Université Sorbonne Nouvelle Paris 3, December 2018, co-organized by Laurence Allard and Gaby David, www.mobilecreation.fr/2018/09/20/foodporn -les-mobiles-du-desir-colloque-international-13-et-14-decembre-2018-maison-de-la -recherche-paris-3/.

2. The "meal gaze" was first introduced in Gaby David, "Eating a Popular Corpus, Mapping #Foodporn in France," on "An Undisciplined Discipline: The Challenge of Pop Cultural Studies" panel, Disciplines-Indisciplines, 51st Congrès annuel de l'Association Française d'Etudes Américaines, Nantes, France, 2019.

3. "Camera Eats First," Wikipedia, https://en.wikipedia.org/wiki/Camera_eats_ first.

4. Terri Senft, "The Skin of the Selfie," in *Ego Update: The future of Digital Identity*, ed. Alain Bieber (Düsseldorf: NRW Forum, 2015).

5. Lev Manovich and Alise Tifentale, "Competitive Photography and the Presentation of the Self," in *Exploring the Selfie: Historical, Theoretical, and Analytical Approaches to Digital Self-Photography*, ed. Julia Eckel, Jens Ruchatz, and Sabine Wirth, 167–87 (Cham, Switz.: Palgrave Macmillan, 2018).

6. *Food for the Eyes: Die Geschichte des Essens in der Fotografie* (exhibition), C/O Berlin Foundation, Berlin, June 8 to September 7, 2019, https://co-berlin.org/de/ programm/ausstellungen/food-eyes.

7. "*Comedian* (Artwork)," Wikipedia, https://en.wikipedia.org/wiki/Comedian_ (artwork)

8. Laura Mulvey, "Visual Pleasure and Narrative Cinema," *Screen* 16, no. 3 (Autumn 1975): 6–18.

9. Signe Rousseau, "Food 'Porn' in Media," in *Encyclopedia of Food and Agricultural Ethics*, ed. Paul B. Thompson and David M. Kaplan, 1—8 (Dordrecht: Springer Netherlands, 2013).

10. Alexander Cockburn, "Gastro-Porn," *New York Review of Books*, December 8, 1977, www.nybooks.com/articles/1977/12/08/gastro-porn/.

11. "Rule 34," Wikipedia, https://en.wikipedia.org/wiki/Rule_34_(Internet_ meme).

12. Carolina Cambre proposes ten visual characteristics of foodporning: 1. Ooze (egg, gravy, etc.). 2. Pop (color/saturation/vibrant/exposure/contrast/shallow depth of field), "green is gold." 3. Stack (big/make it look large). 4. Cut and open (cross-section cake, etc.). 5. Multiply (repetition). 6. Invite (fork/close up/hand). 7. Props (backgrounds, tables, "story"). 8. Light: natural, no harsh shadow. 9. Shot: above "flat lay," rule of thirds/close. 10. Plating: staging/framing (fresh). Carolina Cambre, "The Politics of Pleasure: A Tentative Grammar of #foodporn," presented at "#Foodporn."

13. Yelena Mejova, Sofiane Abbar, and Hamed Haddadi, "Fetishizing Food in Digital Age: #foodporn around the World," Proceedings of the Tenth International AAAI Conference on Web and Social Media ICWSM, 2016, www.academia.edu/23513432/Fetishizing_Food_in_Digital_Age_foodporn_Around_the_World.

14. Radarly, https://radarly.linkfluence.com/.

15. A concept offers another way to access relevant posts; for example, at the time of writing, instead of using #Macron, the conceptual #Frenchpresident could achieve a similar or complementary result.

16. For a definition of "fooding," see "Fooding," Wikipedia, https://en.wikipedia.org/wiki/Fooding.

17. Based on 35,700 posts, 241 million impressions, and 33.9 million reach. See the next note for explanations of "impression" and "reach."

18. According to interviews done with some employees of the listening and monitoring enterprise Linkfluence, which provides the Radarly service (October 2019), the "engagement" measure is the number of reactions generated, those being shares, reposts, retweets or likes. The "estimated impression" or just "impression" is the number of times content is displayed on a screen. The "estimated reach" or simply "reach" is the number of different persons reached by particular content, this number being an aggregation of three of the platforms they track (Facebook, Twitter, Instagram). This "estimated reach" represents and is the potential audience. But because users can be the same person participating in multiple platforms, they can be "reached" more than once and consequently counted several times. This can also occur when users have more than one profile on the same platform. The calculation of these positive, negative, and neutral feelings is done through a dictionary of words the software has, and is also assessed thanks to the emojis added within the captions and engagements.

19. F. Vera-Gray, *Men's Intrusion, Women's Embodiment: A Critical Analysis of Street Harassment* (Abingdon, UK: Routledge, 2016).

20. John Berger, *Ways of Seeing* (London: Penguin, 1973).

21. Rosalind Coward, *Female Desire* (London: Paladin, 1984).

22. See, for example, Vérane Frédiani, dir., *À la recherche des Femmes Chefs* 2016, www.filmsdocumentaires.com/films/5797-a-la-recherche-des-femmes-chefs.

23. *Maïté assomme des anguilles*, Archive Institute National Audiovisual (INA), June 1992, is a cult video from a cooking show series. This clip is devoted to a recipe based on eels that Maïté Ordonez, the cook, brutally and directly knocks out in the course of the show, contravening all codes of femininity and domestic cooking. YouTube, posted December 13, 2013, https://www.youtube.com/watch?v=8-lCVMAZBhM&t=151s.

24. *Plan Culinaire* is a radio show, where the similarity in phonemes between the French word *cul*, which literally means "things related to sex," and *culinaire*, referring to topics related to gastronomy, is another pun. *Plan Culinaire*, www.radio .fr/p/planculinaire.

25. Nora Bouazzouni, *Faiminisme: Quand le sexisme passe à table* (Paris: Éditions Nouriturfu, 2017).

26. Olivier Leplatre, *"Un goût à la voir nonpareil." Manger les images, essais d'iconophagie* (Paris: Éditions Kimé, 2018).

27. Mimi Ito and Daisuke Okabe, "Camera Phones Changing the Definition of Picture-Worthy," *Japan Media Review*, 2003, www.dourish.com/classes/ics234cw04/ ito3.pdf.

28. W. J. T. Mitchell, *What Do Pictures Want? The Lives and Loves of Images* (Chicago: University of Chicago Press, 2005).

29. Pierre Bourdieu, "Interview sur les jugements de goût—Sociologie," YouTube, posted October 30, 2017, www.youtube.com/watch?v=09ZI1hkarQk&t=189s.

30. Pierre Bourdieu, *La distinction: Critique sociale du jugement* (Paris: Éd. de Minuit, 1979).

31. Josée Johnston and Shyon Baumann, *Foodies: Democracy and Distinction in the Gourmet Foodscape*, 1st ed. (New York: Routledge, 2010).

32. J. Borondo, F. Borondo, C. Rodriguez-Sickert, and C. A. Hidalgo, "To Each According to Its Degree: The Meritocracy and Topocracy of Embedded Markets," *Nature*, January 2014.

33. Crystal Abydin, *Internet Celebrity: Understanding Fame Online* (Bingley, UK: Emerald Publishing, 2018).

34. Nathan Hopson, "Fake Food: Authentic Japanese Product—On the Rise of Visuality in Middlebrow Japanese Culinary Culture," *Japan Forum* 31, no. 2 (2019): 254–71.

35. Jean-Claude Rochet and Jean Tirole, "Platform Competition in Two-Sided Markets," *Journal of the European Economic Association* 1, no. 4 (2003): 990–1029.

36. Cour de Cassation, November 28,2018, www.courdecassation.fr/jurisprudence _2/chambre_sociale_576/1737_28_40778.htm.

37. Trebor Scholz, *Digital Labor: The Internet as Playground and Factory* (New York: Routledge, 2012); Trebor Scholz, *Platform Cooperativism: Challenging the Corporate Sharing Economy* (New York: Rosa Luxemburg Stiftung, 2015), www .rosalux-nyc.org/wp-content/files_mf/scholz_platformcoop_5.9.2016.pdf.

CHAPTER 4

The South in Your Mouth?

Gourmet Biscuit Restaurants, Authenticity, and the Construction of a New Southern Identity

DEBORAH A. HARRIS AND RACHEL PHILLIPS

In his influential 1987 work, *Southern Food: At Home, on the Road, In History*, writer John Egerton recounts how food has provided an important view into the American South, its people, and its values. The enduring power of food, Egerton notes, allows us a simultaneous "look backward to an Old South since discredited or forward to a New South that always seems to be calling just over the horizon."[1] But how are these Old and New Southern identities performed through food and how do new forms of communication, such as Instagram, help shape these performances? We examine one iconic southern food, the biscuit, and its relationship to this transition from Old to New South. Specifically, we combine ethnographic observations of six biscuit-focused restaurants with content analysis of their Instagram accounts, websites, and news stories to discuss how these restaurants demonstrate a form of authenticity that allows them to draw from traditions representing a southern past while embracing the promise of a New South future. We find that the six southern biscuit restaurants construct notions of regional authenticity that walk a fine line between an imagined "Old South" based on tradition and hospitality and an equally mythical "New South" that features multiculturalism, appreciation of the local, and celebration.

Food, Authenticity, and Instagram

Since its launch in 2010, Instagram and food have been strongly linked.[2] Instagram's visual focus has made the platform especially popular among foodies, and users report they share photographs for recognition, as well as for a sense of reciprocity.[3] In a study of French social media users, researchers found that participants who posted food photographs did so for a variety of experiential reasons, including an altruistic desire to provide publicity to chefs and to illustrate their "passion collecting" memorable meals.[4] These same users also reported symbolic benefits to their social status and presentation of self. These findings align with research on the "extended self" and how it is demonstrated in digital realms. The concept of the extended self originally described how one's possessions become a part of their self-concept, but, in a digital space, the lack of material environment changes this process. In social media spaces like Instagram, users can still showcase their extended selves by sharing photographs to generate likes and affirmations, as well as use tags to help them (and their followers) remember special events and experiences.[5] As food is often tied to these experiences, it makes sense that it would feature prominently in so many Instagram posts.

Instagram has also been embraced by food professionals, including chefs, food companies, and marketers.[6] A chief concern for these groups is how to showcase the authentic experiences many foodies desire using a platform perceived to be filled with filtered and edited images. The companies must find ways to reconcile the concept of authenticity with the Instagram platform. Many social scientists describe authenticity as a social construction "performed" by cultural producers who engage in authenticity "work" that ranges from highlighting membership in certain groups to displaying objects (e.g., fish nets in a seafood restaurant) in order to aid their businesses and reputations.[7] Recent research expands this view and argues the concept should be seen as "emergent, situational, and contested."[8]

How does the process of performing food authenticity fit with Instagram? Research on the platform has found that the company provides routes to authenticity, especially through using "no-filter" hashtags to highlight seemingly more real, authentic products and settings.[9] Instagram food marketing also relies on consumer-generated images in order to bring a sense of authenticity.[10] With smartphones' upgraded cameras and popularity, nonprofessionals can now produce quality food photography while still appearing authentic as they represent "real" meals and experiences of audiences. Among food producers, sharing more information about their history, motivations, and values can market their businesses in a way that feels authentic to their followers and creates relationships (real and perceived) between producers and consumers.[11]

Food, the New South, and Race

Just as "authenticity" is a contested term, so too are the "Old" and "New" Souths. In contrast to the Old South and its associations with poverty, slavery, and racism, the New South is described as a region teeming with economic opportunity, celebrating diversity and multiculturalism, and participating fully in the global society while remaining mindful of its past.[12] In reality, continuing racism, poverty, and unequal development suggest the New South is as much a myth as the Old South, and it continues to represent more of an aspiration than a material and cultural reality.[13]

Southern food has a primary position in the mythmaking of the New South. It represents tradition, comfort, and southern heritage, but also showcases modernization when chefs fuse southern ingredients with other cuisines or transform traditional dishes to more upscale versions. Despite its popularity, the New Southern movement in cuisine also has critics. First, who decides what is authentic food? Often it is those from more advantaged class positions who claim (or are appointed to) this position.[14] This can mean those from less advantaged groups are excluded from discussions about their own foodways. In contrast, Monica Perales points out that authenticity presented as nostalgia and tradition can fuse onto a people, making them seem unchanging and uni-dimensional.[15] Others claim the nostalgia surrounding southern food continues to obscure the reality of the region's history. In her analysis of contemporary southern cookbooks, Lily Kelting found that authors highlighted multicultur-alism but neglected to discuss larger neocolonial power struggles resulting in this creolization of southern food. She argues these works present a South that is much more commensal, interracial, and egalitarian than reality, especially as New Southern food has been accused of aiding in the appropriation of African American culture and creativity.[16] While African Americans have represented a large segment of domestic and restaurant cooks, there is a pattern of white cooks appropriating and profiting from their efforts.[17] Additionally, while there are many references to Sunday extended-family suppers and learning to cook at grandmothers' sides, when New Southern food is deemed award worthy, it is often white male chefs who receive honors.[18]

Biscuits and Identity: A Methodological Approach

Our research began in 2016 in response to media stories about the rise of gourmet biscuit restaurants in several southern cities. Biscuits have long been considered a staple food in the South, and recipes for them have been found in American cookbooks as early as the late 1700s to early 1800s.[19] Over the years, biscuits have taken on different forms due to the development of new leaveners like baking powder.[20] Gender, class, and race have always been tightly tied to the history of southern biscuits because serving freshly made biscuits represented having kitchen help (either from enslaved people or, later, Black domestic work-ers), as well as the ability to purchase flour and other specialized equipment.

We wondered what it meant that this humble food of the South had taken on gourmet status and what this said about the larger region, its food, and its identity. To study the rise of gourmet southern biscuit shops, we selected six restaurants located in southern states: Biscuit Head in Asheville, North Carolina; Holler & Dash in Homewood, Alabama; Biscuit Love in Nashville, Tennessee; the Biscuit Shop in Starkville, Mississippi; the Biscuit Bar in Plano, Texas; and Callie's Hot Little Biscuit in Charleston, South Carolina. We identified these restaurants through a Google search for southern biscuit shops.

Our work employs rhetorical fieldwork that goes beyond analyzing written artifacts.[21] We were also guided by Krishnendu Ray's discussion of restaurant design to focus not only on the physical infrastructure of the restaurants but also on elements like restaurant concept, name, menu, and other ways of connecting what Ray describes as tying "economics to aesthetics."[22] We gathered data by traveling to the various biscuit restaurants to engage in participant observation and create field notes about each scene; collecting media accounts of the restaurants and their owners to see how they created and promoted their restaurants; and visiting Instagram feeds and official websites for each of the restaurants to understand how these businesses represented themselves to customers.

For the Instagram analysis, we collected all Instagram posts from each of these restaurants between January 1, 2019, and March 31, 2019. Among restaurants with multiple locations, we chose to analyze the original or main corporate feeds. We screen-captured each photograph and its comments for analysis. Each author coded the images and comments from the restaurants' Instagram profiles to examine the presentation of the restaurant, its food, and its branding. In addition to photographs, we analyzed the associated captions (including hashtags) and user comments. Analyzing customer messages and comments allowed us to identify not only the values that are important to the restaurants involved in this study, but also the values perceived to be important to their current and potential customers. Throughout our work, we were guided in our analysis by traditional southern archetypes regarding food and culture and theories of "authentic" performance. As we analyzed these posts, we searched for recurring themes relating to how a southern identity was presented in each post.

Showcasing Authenticity and the "Traditional" South

Throughout our analysis, we found that all of the biscuit restaurants highlighted their connections to the South and its traditions through their use of southern idiom, menu items and ingredients, decor, recipes, and production processes. On Instagram, tags like #southern, #southernbaking, #southernstaple, #letseatyall, and #downonthebayou were frequently used along with photographs of biscuits. At Biscuit Head, signs and merchandise instructed customers to "Put Some South in Your Mouth," and Biscuit Love's sign reminds us they were "Born in the South."

The restaurants included southern staples such as pimento cheese, fried green tomatoes, and barbecue on their menus, websites, and Instagram feeds. Restaurants also highlighted well-known southern branded foods. For example, on the walls of Biscuit Love in Nashville were a collection of folksy paintings of Sunbeam bread and Crisco vegetable shortening, which many home cooks use in their biscuit making. At Callie's Hot Little Biscuit, the restaurant displayed bags of White Lily flour, often quoted as being the only "true" flour available to make "real" southern biscuits, assuring customers they would be served authentic southern biscuits, although with the historical connotations of white racial "purity" as well.[23]

Another popular way to demonstrate connection to the South was through decor. At Biscuit Head, the food was served in tin pie plates similar to what one might find in their southern grandmother's attic. Biscuit Head, Holler & Dash, and the Biscuit Bar all served drinks out of canning jars. Several restaurants aimed to replicate the aesthetic of an older, "shabby-chic" home and used reclaimed wood for a rustic feel, while others featured painted wainscoting on the walls and pressed tin ceilings reminiscent of fine older southern homes. The Biscuit Bar featured several of these design elements, including enlarged gingham prints, a modern farmhouse-styled open kitchen with bright yellow cabinetry, and a large farmhouse sink. At Biscuit Love, visitors could purchase new items modeled after traditional flour sack towels and butter churners.

When the restaurant owners described their food and approach to running their restaurants, they often used language relating to "tradition." The owners frequently highlighted their family background and described learning traditional southern recipes (often from mothers and grandmothers) as the beginning of their love of cooking. Not only were the recipes part of the family tradition, but so were the methods for producing biscuits. In contrast to mass-produced biscuits that could be bought frozen or in a can, these biscuits were "100% homemade" (Biscuit Love), "handmade" (the Biscuit Shop), and "[from] scratch" (the Biscuit Bar). The Biscuit Bar is even designed so that customers queue up along windows so they can view the biscuits being made.

On Instagram and their websites, the restaurants would use tags such as #Handmade as well as posting photos of employees making their biscuits by hand, often with close-ups focusing on the white, female hands gently kneading biscuit dough.[24] These images helped demonstrate the authenticity of their product. Each biscuit was handmade, rustic, and distinct from the typical standardized fast-food biscuit. Yet, these images and the description of family recipes also served to whitewash the racial history of biscuits. As numerous writers have pointed out, the history of southern food is filled with the unsung efforts of African American women, who often received little recognition for their efforts even when their food became commercialized.[25] By painting biscuits as the result of a white family history (all of the owners pictured on their websites or Instagram feeds were white), it erases the labor of African American women and shifts the focus to the white hands that produce the biscuits. Although the Instagram feeds rarely featured any people of color at work in the restaurants (an exception were two photos from Biscuit Love featuring an African American male employee), during visits to the restaurants, one of the authors witnessed several African American and Hispanic employees—some directly in charge of making the biscuits.

While these stories emphasized the restaurant's authenticity through the use of family-tested recipes, they also helped promote the idea that the businesses that grew out of these recipes were less about profits and more about "sharing" family (or just general "southern") tradition, both in real-life interaction and social media discourse. Biscuit Love owners describe the restaurant as serving "delicious dishes that honor the deep-rooted tradition of the South" and publicize how they use their restaurant to foster "community, sharing, and connection."[26] On their Instagram feed they posted a picture of four framed prints on the wall of their restaurant that spelled out "LOVE," which they describe as the "secret ingredient" to their food.[27] Such language obscures the commodification of these cultural items and reframes the businesses as helping to save a dying way of life.[28] These restaurant owners described their motivations as driven by a need to share and preserve culture (whether it be specific to their family or the larger southern region) or to please customers to retain their authenticity and evoke feelings of nostalgia.[29]

Making Modern Biscuits

While the physical space of the restaurants aligned with notions of the Old South, their online presence (Instagram and websites) and menus could be quite different. Across the six restaurants, Instagram served as a vehicle not only to showcase their food through both in-house and user-generated photography, but also to craft a modern aesthetic. As we mentioned earlier, many of the restaurants relied on a homey, shabby chic decor with gingham prints, reclaimed wood, and canning-jar glasses. In contrast, their Instagram feeds were marked by crisp, bright images of the food. Many of these photographs centered the food with minimal connections to the more traditional design elements of the restaurants. Instead, their feeds and websites featured numerous food-porn images featuring close-ups of menu items with dripping sauces, large strips of crispy bacon, and colorful backdrops. A typical Instagram post for one of the biscuit restaurants included either a close-up of a dish photographed from the side or above, or a shot of a person (almost always a white female) holding the biscuit in front of a colorful backdrop.[30] These photographs were frequently attributed to customers and helped showcase their fun travels and food adventures, as well as advertise the restaurant.[31]

Featuring customers' photographs on Instagram feeds served multiple purposes. First, it endeavored to provide a more authentic view of their food as the photograph showed a customer's actual order.[32] Second, it created a relationship with the customer who would be tagged in the post and who would often reply with a "Thanks!" or other gratitude for having their photograph published. It also provided a view of the restaurants' clientele for potential customers to get a sense of the scene. Most often, white customers dominated the setting. Across all the images on Instagram, there were rarely any People of Color shown eating the food and all of the hands-focused images were of white women. While this lack of racial-ethnic diversity may relate to who takes and shares this style of photograph, it also helps indicate who "belongs" in certain spaces.[33] Across our three-month analysis, the only post to highlight any racial-ethnic minorities came from the Biscuit Bar. It featured a group of three African American women laughing and smiling together at the restaurant, but it was a rare image among the hundreds of other photographs.[34]

Other ways to interact with current or potential customers on Instagram included using their Instagram feed to advertise soon-to-be opening locations to create excitement among followers.[35] The businesses also used Instagram to interact directly with customers by answering questions and reaching out for more information if someone indicated they had a poor dining experience. Through Instagram, the businesses could encourage followers to visit, make jokes, and respond to compliments about food. These actions allowed the restaurants to perform southern hospitality in a new medium by encouraging visits and engaging in conversation.

The restaurants also adopted social media terms and used them in their Instagram feeds. The Biscuit Shop prepared only a certain number of biscuits each morning and would encourage customers to check their #shelfie status (a play on the #selfie style of photograph) to see if they had sold out of a product before visiting.[36] Other restaurants would frequently use tags like #Eatingforthe Insta to acknowledge some customers seek out photogenic foods they believe will make popular Instagram images.[37] Another popular nod to social media culture included posting well-known memes, such as those featuring *Parks and Recreation* character and known breakfast enthusiast Ron Swanson to encourage customers to come and visit.[38]

Perhaps the best example of combining tradition with modern social media came from Biscuit Head, a restaurant known for their special "cat head" biscuits, named as such because these drop biscuits were said to be about the size of a cat's head. On their Instagram page, the restaurant shared pictures of the "Cat of the Week" and photographs of their newest location, which featured a large mural with a cat's head next to the word "DANG."[39] These images took a traditional southern food (the cathead biscuit) and updated it for the cat-loving Internet. This juxtaposition of tradition with social media modernizes both the food and the larger region by integrating them with a shared Internet culture.

Besides social media, there were other ways the restaurants attempted to align with the modern New South. Sometimes this was done by explicitly describing their restaurant or its food using terms like "modern southern" or "new southern." In other examples, the biscuit restaurants celebrated the past while looking for inspiration in a global society. The Biscuit Head menu offered a chai butter spread and a biscuit sandwich that included brisket topped with barbecue hollandaise and local chèvre. Similarly, at Holler & Dash, international twists on southern classics could also be found in items like the popular strawberry-lemongrass soda.

The restaurants also performed their New South identity by partnering with the local tourism sector. As part of the New South mythos includes economic growth, tourism has become a major industry for many southern cities and the rise of foodie tourism has meant that local restaurants have become major tourist destinations. In Charleston, Callie's Hot Little Biscuit features pictures of their biscuit sandwiches in front of popular Charleston landmarks and uses tags such as #charlestonbound and #explorecharleston, while in Nashville, Biscuit Love encourages followers to enjoy #nashvillebrunch and #visitmusiccity.[40] These promotions seem to be working as followers often responded in ways that suggested these restaurants were as much a part of their trip-planning itineraries as more traditional tourism spots. One comment on a Callie's Hot Little Biscuit post read "this is the reason I want to go back to Charleston," while a Biscuit Love poster commented "we're coming next month and we're so pumped."[41] The tourism-related hashtags make good business sense because potential customers can find out about these restaurants when searching restaurants in these cities. These posts' use of imagery relating to their cities also helps establish a connectedness to place, sending the message to tourists and locals alike that these restaurants are authentic.

Restaurants also highlighted links to places through their ingredient sourcing. Biscuit Head, Holler & Dash, and Biscuit Love had links on their websites to their local farming "partners." On these websites, ingredients ranging from tea and coffee to bacon and cheese were described in lengthy paragraphs. These descriptions highlighted the ingredients' high quality, as well as the importance of supporting small local farmers whose production methods (and their relative closeness) are considered more sustainable than larger, corporate agriculture. Some restaurants also promoted local foods on their Instagram feeds. Callie's Hot Little Biscuit promised customers they use Carolina grits at their restaurant, and the Biscuit Shop highlighted local honey and coffee for sale in several posts.[42] Such language highlights key themes in southern food—connection to agriculture, local land, and very short supply chains—which aligns them with many ideals of the alternative food movement. These choices provide proof of their authenticity by using ingredients that are native or long-produced in the region, but they also appeal to those who value sustainable, local food.

The partnerships with local farmers, farmers' markets, and community-supported agriculture (CSAs) also helped suggest these restaurants' food was fresh and healthy. Southern food has a long history of being viewed as unhealthy and as consisting largely of heavy starches, fatty meats, and fried foods, which has been linked to the region's high rates of obesity and diet-related diseases. To demonstrate that southern food could also mean healthy food, several restaurants had sections of their menu devoted to lighter fare. At Biscuit Head, these options included oatmeal and yogurt for breakfast and salads and grilled chicken for lunch and dinner. One Instagram post by Biscuit Love encouraged customers to "Start the week strong with the protein packed Blacklock Hash."[43] Another post from Biscuit Love's Instagram feed featured their Lindstrom salad composed of shaved Brussel sprouts topped with hazelnuts, parmesan, lemon vinaigrette, and two poached eggs.[44] While a breakfast salad may not be the most traditional southern dish, the use of #Southern to describe it suggests sometimes these restaurants wish to try and expand what is considered southern food to include healthier options.

At other times the restaurants embraced the decadent nature of some of their items and adopted anti-diet language to entice customers to come in and indulge. Because we began our Instagram analysis in January, there were several posts that used jokes like "New Year's Resolutions are all about compromise, right?"[45] Among our sample, the Biscuit Bar's Instagram account was perhaps the most anti-diet and would take an almost daring tone in their posts, such as when they wrote about their Rough Night biscuit: "This biscuit is only for people who like meat. And gluten. And fun."[46] In these posts, the restaurants acknowledge that their food could rarely be considered healthy, but they attempt to reframe their offering from "unhealthy carb-laden southern food" to food that is celebratory and for special occasions, such as brunch with friends and family. The focus on biscuit brunches as celebratory spaces to come together harkens back to traditional southern hospitality experienced in a new way. During the time of a primarily agriculture-based economy, periods of boom and bust were frequent for farmers. When Southerners did have plentiful food, it was shared with family and community members in celebration.[47] Today, people are less likely to come together at church or other institutions, but a brunch with friends and family can still represent a bounty to be shared with one's closest relations.[48]

Biscuits and Instagram

We began this work asking what the rise of upscale southern biscuit restaurants could tell us about the U.S. South today and how these businesses reflected the Old and New Souths.

Virtual spaces, such as Instagram and restaurant websites, aligned the restaurants with modern Internet culture, including southern food-based hashtags and memes, trendy food photography techniques, and direct engagement with customers. They highlighted the increasing role that tourism plays in the economies of many southern cities and positioned their restaurants as a means to try an authentic southern food (the biscuit) but to do so in a hip, trendy environment. These accounts present a New South that is not behind the times, but pulls from familiar southern values (hospitality, family, conviviality) in a more modern, social media–ready setting.

As Perales notes, one problematic aspect of discussing food and authenticity is that it can paint certain cultures as one dimensional and unchanging.[49] Yet, our research finds that these restaurants frequently drew from a version of the South that is filled with foods that can be creative expressions of local culture. They gave credit to the parts of southern food that have become mainstream—the connection to the land and local farmers, and the use of seasonal and fresh ingredients—while minimizing or challenging ideas that all southern food is unhealthy. Simultaneously, they also touted the commensality that has long been associated with southern food and partnered with local tourism offices to promote their food as a vital part of any southern destination. However, this model of the New South is not without its problems. Despite the focus on hospitality and sharing southern culture, the Instagram feeds and websites of these businesses still focus on white knowledge and labor with little acknowledgment of the racialized nature of southern food. While these businesses may focus on the diversity of southern cuisine and highlight the multiculturalism in their menus, these images of their restaurants and its clientele remain mostly white.

Our research indicates that presenting Old South and New South as a dichotomy is not always an accurate representation, especially when the subject at hand is a food with long historical roots. Just as southern history and culture is enriched through its food, additional research into how food helps create what we know as "the South" offers many avenues for exploration. We suggest that food scholars continue the challenging work of addressing the many ways that food can be used to both shore up and challenge certain identities, as well as whose lives and work are centered during these exchanges. Southern food remains complex and these complexities remind us that the New South ideal still remains over the horizon.

Notes

1. John Egerton, *Southern Food: At Home, on the Road, in History* (New York: Alfred A. Knopf, 1987), 3.

2. Sony Kusumasondjaja and Fandy Tjiptono, "Endorsement and Visual Complexity in Food Advertising on Instagram," *Internet Research* 29, no. 4 (2019): 660.

3. Elisa Serafinelli, "Analysis of Photo Sharing and Visual Social Relationships: Instagram as a Case Study," *Photographies* 10, no. 1 (2017): 98.

4. Glyn Atwal, Douglas Bryson, and Valériane Tavilla, "Posting Photos of Luxury Cuisine Online: An Exploratory Study," *British Food Journal* 121, no. 2 (2019): 458.

5. Russell W. Belk, "Extended Self in a Digital World," *Journal of Consumer Research* 40, no. 3 (2013): 488–89.

6. Leigh Chavez Bush, "The New Mediascape and Contemporary American Food Culture," *Gastronomica* 19, no. 2 (2019): 22–23.

7. Dean MacCannell, "Staged Authenticity: Arrangements of Social Space in Tourist Settings," *American Journal of Sociology* 79, no. 3 (1973): 596–97.

8. Cate Irwin, "Constructing Hybridized Authenticities in the Gourmet Food Truck Scene," *Symbolic Interaction.* 40, no. 1 (2017): 64.

9. Meredith Salisbury and Jefferson D. Pooley, "The #nofilter Self: The Contest for Authenticity among Social Networking Sites, 2002–2016," *Social Sciences* 6, no. 10 (2017).

10. Sean Coary and Morgan Poor. "How Consumer-Generated Images Shape Important Consumption Outcomes in the Food Domain," *Journal of Consumer Marketing* 33, no. 1 (2016), 1.

11. Bush, "New Mediascape," 25.

12. Catarina Passidomo, "'Our Culinary Heritage': Obscuring Inequality by Celebrating Diversity in Peru and the U.S. South," *Humanity and Society* 41, no. 4 (2017), 428.

13. Scot. A. French, "What Is Social Memory?," *Southern Cultures* 2, no. 1 (1995): 14.

14. Meredith Abarca, "Authentic or Not, It's Original," *Food and Foodways* 12 (2004): 2.

15. Monica Perales, "The Food Historian's Dilemma: Reconsidering the Role of Authenticity in Food Scholarship," *Journal of American History* 103, no. 3 (2016): 691.

16. Lily Kelting, "The Entanglement of Nostalgia and Utopia in Contemporary Southern Food Cookbooks," *Food, Culture, and Society* 19, no. 2 (2016): 364–67.

17. Toni Tipton-Martin, *The Jemima Code: Two Centuries of African American Cookbooks* (Austin: University of Texas Press, 2015), 4.

18. Passidomo, "Our Culinary Heritage," 439–40.

19. Egerton, *Southern Food*, 18.

20. Linda Civitello, *Baking Powder Wars: The Cutthroat Food Fight that Revolutionized Cooking* (Urbana: University of Illinois Press, 2017), 182–83.

21. Ashli Stokes Quesinberry and Wendy Atkins-Sayre, *Consuming Identity: The Role of Food in Redefining the South* (Oxford: University of Mississippi Press, 2016), 10–11.

22. Krishnendu Ray, *The Ethnic Restaurateur* (London: Bloomsbury, 2016), 60.

23. Civitello, *Baking Powder Wars*.

24. Callie's Hot Little Biscuit (@callieshotlittlebiscuit), "Our team is busy turning some of our favorite Atlantans into biscuiteers this week," Instagram photo, March 27, 2019, www.instagram.com/p/BvhCOUFH7eK/.

25. Tipton-Martin, *Jemima Code*, 4.

26. "The Biscuit Whisperer Karl Worley," Heritage Radio Network, heritageradionetwork.org/podcast/on-the-rise-3-the-biscuit-whisperer-karl-w"orley/, accessed June 3, 2019.

27. Biscuit Love˙ (@biscuitlovebrunch) "Our not-so-secret ingredient," Instagram photo, January 5, 2019, www.instagram.com/p/BsQhQkGBxcM/.

28. Amanda Koontz, "Constructing Authenticity: A Review of Trends and Influences in the Process in Authentication and Consumption," *Sociology Compass* 4, no. 11 (2010): 981–85.

29. Amanda Koontz and Nathaniel G. Chapman, "About Us: Authenticating Identity Claims in the Craft Beer Industry," *Journal of Popular Culture* 52, no. 2 (2019): 352.

30. Holler & Dash (@holleranddash), "The Chicken. Set. Go. is good fo' sho," Instagram photo, February 10, 2019, www.instagram.com/p/BttLlUmjXAI/; Callie's Hot Little Biscuit (@callieshotlittlebiscuit), "Rise TALL like a biscuit, y'all!," Instagram photo, March 12, 2019, www.instagram.com/p/Bu6KqAGHK8R/.

31. Atwal, Bryson, and Tavilla, "Posting Photos," 459.

32. Salisbury and Pooley, "#nofilter Self."

33. Todd Kliman, "Coding and Decoding Dinner," *Oxford American Statesman* 88 (2015), www.oxfordamerican.org/magazine/item/548-coding-and-decoding-dinner, accessed December 1, 2020.

34. The Biscuit Bar (@thebiscuit.bar), "Grab your crew and make plans," Instagram photo, February, 8, 2019, www.instagram.com/p/BtoJqo2HSAw/.

35. Biscuit Head (@biscuitheadavl), "It's been a long time coming," Instagram photo, February, 14, 2019, www.instagram.com/p/Bt2-7UQFsSr/.

36. Krista Olley (@thebiscuitshop), "I spy with my little eye," Instagram photo, March, 2, 2019, www.instagram.com/p/BugbxBjFWr9/.

37. Holler & Dash (@holleranddash), "New Year's resolutions are all about compromise, right?," Instagram photo, January, 21, 2019, www.instagram.com/p/Bs6C6jyDjQm/.

38. Biscuit Head (@biscuitheadavl), "Wise words spoken by a wise man," Instagram photo, December, 30, 2019, www.instagram.com/p/BtQ_R1VFk8x/.

39. Biscuit Head (@biscuitheadavl), "Well I guess we're open. Come on down and try a biscuit," Instagram photo, February, 14, 2019, www.instagram.com/p/Bt3ImPFF4b-/.

40. Callie's Hot Little Biscuit (@callieshotlittlebiscuit), "One of the things we love most about our hometown," Instagram photo, February, 22, 2019, www.instagram.com/p/BuL6MOgHhsb/; Biscuit Love (@biscuitlovebrunch), "Weekend forecast: sunny with a high chance of delicious," Instagram photo, January, 25, 2019, www.instagram.com/p/BtD-kH_A284/.

41. Callie's Hot Little Biscuit (@callieshotlittlebiscuit), "Today is National Southern Food Day!" Instagram photo, January, 22, 2019, www.instagram.com/p/Bs8DqYTj-jo/; Biscuit Love (@biscuitlovebrunch), "It's been four whole years," Instagram photo, January, 21, 2019, www.instagram.com/p/Bs5w2X_g0r3/.

42. Callie's Hot Little Biscuit (@callieshotlittlebiscuit), "How high can you stack it?!," Instagram photo, February, 2, 2019, www.instagram.com/p/BtYdVZtnrQ_/; Krista Olley (@thebiscuitshop), "Who loves honey!!!" Instagram photo, January, 20, 2019, www.instagram.com/p/Bs3GLuxFIPA/.

43. Biscuit Love (@biscuitlovebrunch), "Start the week strong with the protein packed Blacklock Hash," Instagram photo, March, 11, 2019, www.instagram.com/p/Bu3qsRkgNna/.

44. Biscuit Love (@biscuitlovebrunch), "Perfectly poached eggs," Instagram photo, March, 5, 2019, www.instagram.com/p/BuoZyvsB8IK/.

45. Holler & Dash (@holleranddash), "New Year's resolutions are all about compromise, right?," Instagram photo, January, 21, 2019, www.instagram.com/p/Bs6C6jyDjQm/.

46. The Biscuit Bar (@thebiscuit.bar), "THE ROUGH NIGHT: This biscuit is only for people who like meat," Instagram photo, January, 31, 2019, www.instagram.com/p/BtTrBEXH_pZ/.

47. Egerton, *Southern Food*, 84.

48. Sophie Egan, *Devoured: How What We Eat Defines Who We Are* (New York: William Morris, 2016), 135–61.

49. Perales, "Food Historian's Dilemma," 691.

CHAPTER 5

Uncle Green Must Be Coming to Dinner

The Joyful Hospitality of Black Women on Instagram during the COVID-19 Pandemic

ROBIN CALDWELL

Sourdough bread be damned. During the early months of the COVID-19 pandemic, I had no interest in watching another video presentation of how-to or why-to make sourdough bread—or any bread—because I don't bake it or eat it that much to care. I did care about the women making it to feed their families and stretch tight budgets, though. Women who were living paycheck to paycheck; women who were ineligible for stimulus money and unemployment benefits; women who, like me, were new to a pandemic and worried about what that really meant for us financially. But even then, life was more than sourdough to me as I sorted through my feelings following the deaths of Breonna Taylor, Ahmaud Arbery, and George Floyd, in addition to a pandemic that restricted my freedom to breathe anywhere I wished. I found myself craving the familiarity of home. I took up Black people-ing. Read more Black history, watched more Black TV, film, and theater productions on video, talked more to my Black friends and family, and followed more Black people—my people—all over social media. These things were home.

Following established food hashtags comprised the night stop on my midnight train to Instagram, which blessed my weary yet sleepless soul. I'd check in with #blackfoodbloggers, which has more than 120,000 posts, where all of the pretty, staged photos land. Finicky about food photos and good food, I found my joy spot in these images, until it started to feel creepy. I caught myself liking the same people's posts in multiples and daily, so I stopped and sought out on Instagram some of the women I follow on Facebook. They were "regular" like me, less concerned about aesthetics than they were interested in showing off their fare. Freed from following the "top" accounts and "most popular" hashtags, I simply let myself explore to find inspiration from these women, who probably brought their peach cobbler to church functions or hosted family cookouts in their backyards or baked their granny's sixteen-pound pound cake. Those were my home girls.

Within those images, further afield from Instagram's algorithm and its most "liked" posts, I found home. My home and the homes of friends and family. I found kitchen tables and stoves and pots much like the ones my mama and the mothers before her owned. I heard kitchen terms spoken in only the way a Black woman would speak them—translate them. I read the recipes that mostly listed the ingredients and mentioned taste, but gave no discernible measurements and little instruction.[1] "Dust some salt" and "scoop some sugar" were directives that could be understood only by the cook and the mothers who taught her. But more often than not, home showed up in the proud and boastful visual presentation of the day's meal, no matter how sorely lacking the lighting in the photograph or the presence of paper plates. This wasn't about Instagrammability. The food didn't even have to be appetizing to be home, like the countless trays of mac 'n' cheese and gravies—foods I don't like, never have, but love looking at. What made it home was the hospitality, an invitation to receive what was being shared, even if through a screen. A knowing that if I walked into that woman's kitchen, I'd be offered a warm welcome in the form of a plate of food. I simply would be welcomed.

Pandemic conditions restricted gatherings to cook and eat as family, as before. At the same time, the weight of generations of racial inequities and injustice bore down on Black shoulders. The heaviness led Black working women directly to their kitchens. As a result, expressions of love for family and friends played out on social media, particularly on Instagram. Black women used the platform to preserve a heritage of hospitality and joy during a time of social uprisings and widespread illness, when gathering was all the more important yet all the more restricted. Black women upheld and revitalized this heritage through virtual family rituals, such as repasts, reunions, and Sunday dinners. They even extended a sense of family to strangers, like me.

Locating my home girls began on Facebook in two food groups founded by Black women I know: Vegan Soul Food and Black Girl Cooking, which is an extension of the "black girl cooking" food blog. Brooke Brimm and her husband are independent advertising consultants and creative directors who began Vegan Soul Food as a hobby. Kellea Tibbs is a university administrator by day and curator of Black Girl Cooking for like-minded and food-minded

Black women by night. I joined their groups because we are friends, but during pandemic restrictions, the notifications from both groups increased from once a week to several times a day, leading me to pay closer attention.

Brooke's Vegan Soul Food group on Facebook was her "fun" endeavor, where she shared her personal recipes with a handful of women and men to demonstrate veganism's versatility. Different from, for example, the Sistah Vegan Project, the group focused on food rather than ecopolitics, aiming to "keep it happy and encouraging."[2] During the pandemic, Brooke enabled the settings to allow members to post, and the small group grew exponentially to upward of 170,000 members. Kellea Tibbs's story is similar. She started the Black Girl Cooking group on Facebook to meet with other Black women and support her work as a blogger. During stay-at-home pandemic restrictions, the group grew to host 25,000 members.

For me, the constant Facebook notifications were too much, though I was often curious enough to scroll through posts. As is the case with large groups, there were personality conflicts about products and procedures. There were people who threw "shade" and dared to criticize everything from plating preferences to proper eating etiquette. In response, I altered my social media consumption, choosing instead to follow these groups' activity on Instagram, where it is comparatively quiet and the temptation to comment is minimal. I didn't want to chat. I only wanted to see and feel as I had done as a child, moving silently about the kitchen, listening to grown folks talk as I waited to eat.

But on Instagram, I didn't eat. I communed and connected. Brooke's Vegan Soul Food Instagram following grew to over eight thousand as the account's focus shifted to Instagrammable food photos she reposted from other vegan accounts. But I found her own cooking demonstration posts to be a warm replacement for our over-the-phone belly laughs. A video for Tomato, Avocado, and Corn Salad communicates practicality, personality, and intimacy more than the aesthetics of a professional food TV show. The camera is positioned low and zooms quite close, showing just the vegetable ingredients on a wooden cutting board and Brooke's hands as she chops. She speaks to the viewer in a comforting tone as she works. I chuckle as she shares, "This is my breakfast, y'all." I laugh out loud when she says, "Now I'm going to play avocado roulette. Let's see if I win?!" only to cut into an avocado speckled with multiple brown spots. No matter the recipe, no matter the video style, I could see Brooke and hear her voice, and that was home.

Over the course of the pandemic, she and others posted more than a thousand times using the tag #blackgirlcooking. Kellea, who I've known since she was a child, would use the hashtag with her posts on her personal Instagram account, @ivywriter. Even as the hashtag took off, I could tell that her relative "quiet"

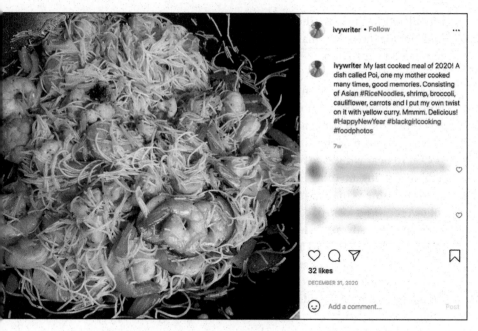

FIGURE 5–1. Kellea Tibbs's #blackgirlcooking Instagram post from December 2020.

on Instagram enabled her to post for her own good pleasure. The inspirational quotes, posts about football and Cleveland, and family photos were for her. Even so, when I wasn't following the hashtag to view the antics of her group's members, I was keeping an eye on Kellea. She'd lost her mother as restrictions began. Keeping an eye on her was akin to the "you good?" call when someone is grieving. On New Year's Eve 2020, Kellea posted a close-up shot of a black skillet, filled with a colorful feast. The caption read: "My last cooked meal of 2020! A dish called Poi, one my mother cooked many times, good memories. Consisting of Asian #RiceNoodles, shrimp, broccoli, cauliflower, carrots and I put my own twist on it with yellow curry. Mmmm. Delicious! #HappyNewYear #blackgirlcooking #foodphotos" (fig. 5-1). As I looked and read, her Instagram food images documented less her cooking than a woman navigating the joys and sorrows of her life. Her hashtag provided entertainment, but her personal Instagram feed provided comfort for her, and for me.

Author Toni Morrison's 1973 essay, "Cooking Out," is a testament to the way Black families sustain hospitality during uncertain times and family upheaval.[3] In the essay, Morrison's Uncle Green represents the past visiting the present and being received as a treasured guest. The rest of the late author's family, as depicted in her essay, represent foundational truths they value together, as articulated in the ways they show hospitality to kin from back "home." You look out for them. You make space for them. You welcome them. These truths resonated in 2020, too.

During the pandemic, on Instagram, I was Uncle Green—the treasured guest—who "was up from Alabama for 20 days with a $500 bill which never broke because nobody—nobody—had change and so he had to borrow whatever he needed until the time he could get to a store big enough to handle it."

Neither Green—"the man who carried his life-savings in one bill deep in his pocket to bear witness to a million sacrifices and tiny thefts"—nor I had to do a thing or bring anything to be treated well, to feel a sense of joy and belonging.

In the same vein, Brooke's and Kellea's Instagram posts, and those of their followers, were a form of communion, where Black women gathered who didn't want to teach anyone how to be decent, a place where Black women needn't explain and translate hurt and disappointment to people who wanted too much at a time when self-care and preservation were more important. As we wore masks for safety in public during COVID-19, there were no masks in these digital homecomings, hiding fake smiles and courtesy in our voices to make others, dealing with their own discomfort in seeing Black people murdered, comfortable with our bodies and being.

One could reckon that Morrison's Uncle Green shared the triumphs and tragedies of "back home" in Alabama in a way his kinfolk understood. One could reckon that he would never speak of those events in the same manner to people who were not his own. It's not a code, it's simply our way to keep a little something for ourselves and not share the family jewels, as my grandmother would say. On Instagram or Facebook, requests such as "Pray y'all, my mama is in the hospital," and simple statements like "I can't attend the funeral" or "I knew they were going to let him off the hook," were enough. Kinfolk understood when those things were uttered through a picture of gumbo with a side of sweet water cornbread or fried chicken livers smothered in onion over a bed of rice.

We only needed our eyes to feast on the familiar, instead of squinting our eyes to look pleasant enough, though we were probably feeling less than.

And most likely we were feeling less than.

But in those food photographs we found no need to explain how some of us Up North thought the sisters Down South were probably better off, or how the ones Down South thought us Up North were doing well. On Instagram, we were all in the same place. No better. No worse. After all, we had arrived in the same manner, using an emotional *Negro Motorist Green-Book*, traveling to meet up. We traveled back roads to find one another, stopping at destinations deemed friendly to us along the way.

Well before Instagram, food and cooking played a significant role in Black women's efforts to create safe spaces, particularly within the home. In her 1990 essay "Homeplace: A Site of Resistance," scholar and critical thinker bell hooks speaks of Black women's labor and its value.

> Historically, African-American people believed that the construction of a home-place, however fragile and tenuous (the slave hut, the wooden shack), had a radical dimension, one's homeplace was the one site where one could freely construct the issue of humanization, where one could resist. Black women resisted by making homes where all black people could strive to be subjects, not objects, where we could be affirmed in our minds and hearts despite poverty, hardship, and deprivation, where we could restore to ourselves the dignity denied us on the outside in the public world.[4]

As numerous scholars would later affirm too, the kitchen proved a vital space for Black women's radical home-place-making.[5] Through cooking, recipes, botanical knowledge, and specialized techniques, Black women claimed home space. They passed it on through generations, even when others attempted to thwart such efforts, or claim them as their own.

Take, for example, B. Smith (Barbara Smith). She died in February 2020, just as the seriousness of COVID-19 began to set in with most of us. She was our guardian of the homeplace, a Black lifestyle guru. She represented what most of us were taught about home and hearth, though she was at times compared to Martha Stewart. In an interview, she responded to this comparison: "Martha Stewart has presented herself doing the things domestics and African Americans have done for years. We were always expected to redo the chairs and use everything in the garden. This is the legacy that I was left. Martha just got there first."[6] In the same article, she also noted that bigots tried to run her car off the road in Sag Harbor, where she owned a home and business. Smith, the woman showing America how to make home better, had to deal with the other America, too.

Some had hoped that Instagram would provide an open, democratic, and perhaps even radical space for community building. As has been repeatedly proven the case for Black women, this coming together, this home making on the platform has interwoven joy and pain, progress and regress.

So was the case during the pandemic. As we did, or did not, discuss our inability to see hospitalized loved ones, attend funerals and the repasts to follow, the cancellation of family reunions and picnics, and the decisions made by jurists regarding the deaths of Taylor, Arbery, and Floyd, or how our people were dying from COVID-19 disproportionately—we safely communed with photos of food. As Morrison writes,

> The day moved then into its splendid parts: a ham, fried-potatoes, scrambled-egg, breakfast in the morning air; fried fish and pan-cooked biscuits on the hind side of noon. . . .

We were all there. All of us, bound by something we could not name. Cooking, honey, cooking under the stars.

And looking, honey, looking over at Instagram.

Notes

1. For scholarship on historical cookbooks and recipes, as well as the embodied knowledge of cooking, see, Anne L. Bower, ed., *Recipes for Reading: Community Cookbooks, Stories, Histories* (Amherst: University of Massachusetts Press, 1997); Janet Theophano, *Eat My Words: Reading Women's Lives through the Cookbooks They Wrote*, 2d ed. (New York: Palgrave Macmillan, 2002); David Sutton, *Secrets from the Greek Kitchen: Cooking, Skill, and Everyday Life on an Aegean Island* (Oakland: University of California Press, 2014); Toni Tipton-Martin, *The Jemima Code: Two Centuries of African American Cookbooks* (Austin: University of Texas Press, 2015).

2. A. Breeze Harper, ed., *Sistah Vegan: Black Female Vegans Speak on Food, Identity, Health, and Society* (Brooklyn, NY: Lantern Publishing, 2010).

3. Toni Morrison, "Cooking Out," *New York Times Book Review*, Summer Reading Issue, 1973. Later quotations from "Cooking Out" are also from this source.

4. bell hooks, "Homeplace: A Site of Resistance," in *Yearning: Race, Gender, and Cultural Politics* (Boston: South End Press, 1990), 41–50, quote on 42.

5. Psyche Williams-Forson, *Building Houses Out of Chicken Legs: Black Women, Food, and Power* (Chapel Hill: University of North Carolina Press, 2006); Rebecca Sharpless, *Cooking in Other Women's Kitchens: Domestic Workers in the South, 1865–1960* (Chapel Hill: University of North Carolina Press, 2010); Jessica B. Harris, *High on the Hog: A Culinary Journey from Africa to America* (New York: Bloomsbury, 2012); Jennifer Jensen Wallach, ed., *Dethroning the Deceitful Pork Chop: Rethinking African American Foodways from Slavery to Obama* (Fayetteville: University of Arkansas Press, 2015).

6. Michael Musto, "B. Smith," *New York Magazine*, September 22, 1997, 38.

CHAPTER 6

Creative Consumption

Art about Eating on Instagram

DAWN WOOLLEY AND ZARA WORTH

This chapter explicates how Instagram has figured as a site, subject, and medium in our respective and collaborative art practices. Instagram, and specifically food on Instagram, is still a relatively unexplored subject within art practice. Since Instagram's early days we were both aware there was a presumption that artists *should* be on that platform, and that, since it was a space for sharing predominantly visual material, artists would naturally be expert users. For both of us, this generalization initially produced a degree of resistance to joining Instagram. Many artists who joined when it first launched blurred the professional and the personal by providing followers with a behind-the-scenes view of their labor and the studio while promoting their artworks. However, what was more interesting to us was how quickly Instagram developed a clear set of behavioral expectations based on interactions between users, and the spectrum of microcultures that took root on the platform.

These newly developed online microcultures escaped geographic restrictions. Moreover, behavioral expectations on Instagram seemed to us to be evidence of a wider shift in values and behaviors toward a more explicitly individualistic, neoliberal culture in which the divide between the personal and the private collapses under the weight of the necessity to self-brand.[1] The imperative to self-brand and the emergence of new microcultures congregating online quickly produced discernible trends identifiable by content type and aesthetic. This is particularly evident when it comes to food, which is both a subjective choice, generally prepared and consumed in the home, and a loaded statement about identity and values. Food has a long history as a signifier of the moral and social standing of the consumer, and it has provided both our artistic practices with a vehicle through which to explore Instagram in the context of wider consumer culture.[2] There is also the obvious appeal of the dual meanings offered by words such as "consume" and "feed" when used in conjunction with social media and food. These words humorously serve to remind us that on social media we play both roles as consumers and producers in an Ouroboros-like cycle of content creation and consumption. What follows is a series of short reflections on artworks we have produced individually and in collaboration, which respond to Instagram food subcultures, with concluding thoughts on using the affordances and restraints social media places on the content and form of our artworks.

[Im]moral Food, a Digital Visual Essay

The *[Im]moral Food* digital visual essay we created together highlights polarized food cultures on Instagram (fig. 6-1). The project was produced for the multimedia academic journal *In Media Res* for a special issue on Food Media.[3] We devised the piece by appropriating images from Instagram that had been uploaded using the tags #cleaneating or #eatdirty. Through this process of collecting and organizing these images, we identified consistencies in aesthetics and ideology. The work was a response to what we felt was a problematic oversimplification of foods being assigned as either clean/good or dirty/bad. *[Im]moral Food* calls attention to these trends, which would usually be confined to their own Instagram echo chambers, by putting them directly in dialogue with each other through visual juxtaposition.

We selected images for the project according to the following rules: searched hashtags had to return at least five thousand posts; they had to be primarily associated with food on Instagram; they must connote either morality or immorality; and the account from which the image was posted must belong to an individual user and not a business. After this selection process, we organized these images in groups of six beneath a screen capture of the search results header containing the searched hashtag. Starting with #eatgood and six images using that hashtag, the digital essay follows an alternating pattern, switching between the good and the bad. As a digital visual essay, *[Im]moral Food* pairs tags from either end of the moral spectrum: #eatgood and #badfood; #eatclean and #dirtyeating; #cleanse and #firemakeseverythingbetter; #feedyoursoul and #sinfulfood; #noguilt and #cheatday; #foodismedicine and #foodcoma; #eatlikeyourlifedependsonit and #eatlikeyoureondeathrow; #makesmewhole and #sizematters; #eatlikeyougiveafuck and #justputitinyourmouth; #eatingyou alive and #foodaddict; #eatyourveggies and #foodporn; #eatmoreplants and #foodbeast.

The process of identifying the hashtags often revealed sexual, aggressive, and dictatorial language, often assuming a pontificating voice that instructed the audience to eat as directed. Moving between variations of alleged "good" and "bad"

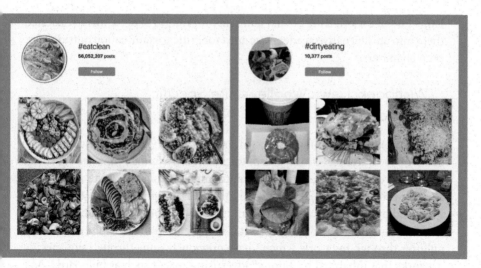

FIGURE 6–1. A slide from the authors' digital visual essay, *[Im]moral Food* (2019).

food emphasizes the visual and linguistic differences between the two Instagram subcultures being cultivated and represented. Throughout *[Im]moral Food* the language of the hashtags on both sides of the moralizing binary escalates; the simple #eatgood crescendos to a dictatorial #eatmoreplants, while #badfood descends to the lurid #foodbeast.

As we anticipated, *[Im]moral Food* also captured the contrasting aesthetic norms of these opposing food subcultures. Each trend offers its audience an allegory. Images tagged as #cleaneating presented foods simply and neatly in a manner reminiscent of commercial food photography, despite not being produced by professionals. In comparison, #eatdirty images adopted close-up shots of messy-looking food, glistening and dripping before the camera in the style of food porn, another trend in commercial food photography, but one that seems to emphasize a candid and unpolished aesthetic. Fruits and vegetables appear frequently in images of "good" food, often in their whole, raw state, communicating ideas of purity and wholesomeness. Images of "bad" food, in contrast, depict large slabs of meat or processed foods that evoke the contradictory archetypes of the hunter-gatherer and the couch potato. The vibrant and varied color palette of "good" food (nearly always featuring a good splash of green) is the antithesis of the homogenous palette of browns, yellows, oranges, and reds that mingle and melt together in photos of "bad" food.

The methodology of *[Im]moral Food* was one of extracting in order to expose. The process of appropriation of language and images from the platform demarcated visual and linguistic commonalities between two online food trends at either end of a moralizing binary. Our reappropriation of these images inserted them into an alternative academic context for critical examination outside their echo chambers.

Wishbook, Dawn Woolley's Site-Specific Work of Art

I (Dawn) resisted joining Instagram, as I was already experiencing a growing sense of pressure, real or imagined, to consistently update my existing social media. I eventually joined the platform to initiate *Wishbook,* a site-specific Instagram project (fig. 6-2). My decision to present this project on Instagram was informed by my earlier writing examining how the personal and commercial coalesce on social networking sites. It is my intention to challenge advertising cultures through my work, which I have previously done through site-specific artworks that inhabited traditional advertising spaces such as billboards. As I researched the use of selfies in and as advertisements, I wanted to intervene in the commercial culture of Instagram.[4] Operating within the spaces that my work critiques is key to achieving a balance between art and activism.

In *Wishbook,* I present individual commodities, such as a Lighter Life diet chocolate bar and a Bombay Bad-Boy Pot Noodle, with a variety of hashtags to highlight gendered ideologies implicit in commercial branding practices on Instagram. For example, #selfie is included in promotional posts advertising a plethora of commodities, from skeins of wool to diet food, in order to place products in users' social media newsfeeds. This creates a seemingly inescapable consumer relation in which the commodity is already assimilated to the viewer's identity before they purchase it, collapsing the hierarchy between commodity and consumer. When included in posts about food, tags such as #cleaneating compound this already-blurred consumer relation by implying that the social media user will assimilate the virtuous characteristics signified by the food.

Hashtags provide a key affordance of social media: connectivity.[5] They can amplify the reach of posts and provide metadata through which online content can be more easily categorized and accessed. This amplification enables hashtags to increase their reach and cultural influence, as demonstrated by #blacklivesmatter and #MeToo. Through the use of shared hashtags, individual posts that seem personal and mundane become part of a bigger conversation. For example, the #cleaneating or #eatdirty tag places a photograph of an individual's food into a wider discourse about values and eating practices. Shared hashtags can form temporary publics, which enables groups of disparate individuals to engage in conversations about diverse subjects, from activism to food. However, as Rambukkana writes in *Hashtag Publics,* commercial companies co-opt the potency of these social and political networks to gain attention and positive publicity.

FIGURE 6-2. *Wishbook*, by Dawn Woolley (started 2015).

"The frictions born from trying to wrest the hashtag away from the hollow articulations of PR and advertising campaigns and maintain this potential for activist content are ongoing," he writes. "But one upshot of this prominence is, perhaps ironically, that at least in this one way, neoliberalism and activism might be speaking the same language, though obviously with different intents."[6] My research found that marketing companies strategically obscure the commercial nature of their posts by employing the language of hashtag publics.[7] The exploitation of shared language through hashtags by companies and activists alike provide *Wishbook* with the same affordances to infiltrate wide and often ideologically opposing audiences.

The title, *Wishbook*, derives from nineteenth-century commodity catalogs such as *The Great Wish Book* and *American Dream Book*, each selling a homogenized version of American culture. The title also alludes to Walter Benjamin's idea that by changing the social value of commodities, consumers are able to inhabit the objects and make them act abnormally. The social and personal values assigned to commodities by advertisements are not inherent to the commodities; furthermore, these values are often problematic and reductive. Benjamin posits that consumers have the power to assign commodities with values more beneficial for the consumer.[8] Accordingly, the ideological values of foods as either "good" or "bad," alluded to by the rhetorics of tags such as #eatclean and #dirtyeating, are not fixed as they might appear. In fact, these values can be disrupted and displaced.

Wishbook questions the ideological meaning attributed to commodities by exaggerating and contradicting the values they express. *Wishbook* posts include tags that repeat advertising rhetoric: #innocent (Innocent Drink Company), #synfree (Slimming World), and #ManFood (Hunt's Manwich), alongside hashtags that I created to critique and explicate the gender ideologies of the products. For example, the inclusion of the tag #boundedpleasure draws attention to the assertion common in advertising that diet chocolates are permissible pleasures *and* naughty indulgences for female consumers, which in turn reinforces #genderstereotypes, and transforms the individual into an #idealconsumer and #neoliberalsubject.

Rather than photograph the commodities in a studio and reproduce the methods of advertising photography, I captured the objects in *Wishbook* using a flat-bed scanner. The scans present the commodity in isolation against a white background, mimicking an advertising aesthetic. However, unlike advertising images, scans have a shallow depth of field: only the surface of the object touching the scanner glass is in focus, and the rest is blurred and warped. If they look like advertisements, they are poor-quality ones. The *Wishbook* commodities are further degraded because they are represented by their empty packaging or half-eaten food, and the white background shows staining and crumbs from previously scanned products. The posts simultaneously depict a desired commodity and discarded rubbish. The images look like they are of the contents of a bin, and the hashtags read like bad poetry. Hashtags enable posts to exist in a limitless number of other user's newsfeeds, allowing them to escape the catalog-like Instagram profile on which they were originally posted. The *Wishbook* posts appear among adverts on Instagram and behave abnormally, challenging the slick advertising aesthetic usually found on Instagram, while the hashtags draw attention to the negative connotations of the commodities.

A Drawing Made by Cutting Up My Body Weight in Celery, Zara Worth's Performance to Video for Instagram

While *Wishbook* explores the ideologies attached to food commodities presented and circulated on social media, *A Drawing Made by Cutting Up My Body Weight in Celery* (hereafter *Celery Drawing*), considers the symbolic significance of a particular foodstuff: celery and its relationship with online "clean-eating" practices. As the title states, I (Zara) cut a quantity of celery equivalent to my body weight into slices on top of the same piece of paper over the course of a year, creating a "drawing" through a mark-making process. For each sliced stem of celery, I uploaded a video recording of the act to Instagram, accompanied by hashtags appropriated from other Instagram posts. To identify hashtags for *Celery Drawing*, I searched for either #drawing, #likes, or #celery, and took

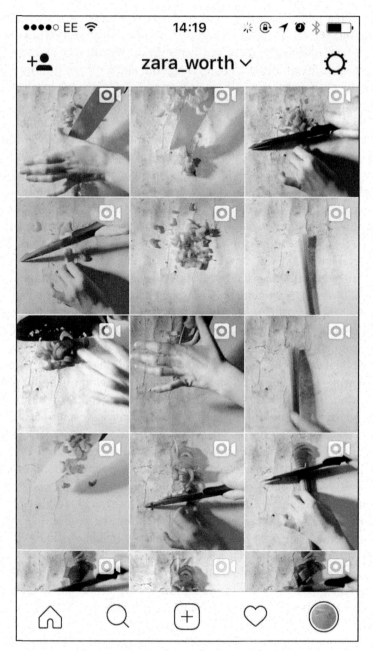

FIGURE 6-3. *A Drawing Made by Cutting Up My Body Weight in Celery*, by Zara Worth (2016–17).

note of other hashtags used in posts recovered through these searches. These three hashtags triangulated key aspects of *Celery Drawing*: creation of a drawing with on- and off-line elements; an interest in the significance of interactions and approval-driven behaviors on Instagram; and an interest in the rise in popularity of so-called clean eating on Instagram, of which celery appeared to be emblematic.

My choice of celery was not arbitrary. Celery already had a compromised relationship with notions of truth, as it is popularly and erroneously believed to be a vegetable that demands sufficient digestive exertion to use up more calories than it provides.[9] Despite the evidence, this falsehood persists—celery remains a symbol of weight-loss-driven dieting and has become a recurrent motif of clean eating on Instagram. The self-styled wellness guru Anthony William (known on Instagram as @medicalmedium) has ignited a resurgence of bizarre celery mythology, claiming he receives information about its "healing properties" from a "high-level spirit." As a white, middle-aged man, William is a comparative outlier as a clean-eating influencer, but is strikingly popular, as evidenced by the swathes of his followers (over two million, including endorsements from Gwyneth Paltrow and Kim Kardashian), who adopt his ideas despite their dubious origins.[10]

Clean-eating influencers and users following (and copying) these food practices are often young women, generally around the age of twenty-five—my age at the time I started developing *Celery Drawing*.[11] Despite the majority of Instagram users sharing clean-eating content having "no formal training in health sciences or nutrition," so-called clean eating impacts the dietary choices of thousands of users and has been linked to triggering obsessive habits, the spread of misinformation, and forms of eating disorders such as orthorexia nervosa.[12] Troubled by the uncritical acceptance of misinformation shared under the auspices of clean eating, Margaret McCartney, a general practitioner, points to the spiritual and vitriolic disposition of the clean-eating trend.[13]

Instagram's designation of users as followers—a synonym of disciple—coincidentally draws parallels between microcultures like clean eating and religious movements or cults. The spread of ideas by influencers like William is rhizomatic: their ideas and values are shared laterally, with the original source often obscured; as opposed to a linear or more hierarchical dissemination of ideas. Many of William's followers adopt his food practice and ideology, then replicate its aesthetics and language in their own posts, spreading clean eating content through the creation of "hashtag publics" that capitalize on the connectivity afforded by hashtags as a means of dissemination and amplification. Like disciples or missionaries, Instagram users themselves who have converted to clean-eating practices become the new proselytizers. These microcultures spread in a chain reaction, as their ideologies and aesthetics are introduced to the personal networks of each user that adopts and replicates its practices.

Through the appropriation of clean-eating language, *Celery Drawing* was able to enter the heartland of the "hashtag publics" it critiqued in order to interrupt the spread of misinformation. The steady flow of over nine hundred videos constituting *Celery Drawing* replicated how microculture influencers drive home ideologies through repetition and the connectivity of hashtags. Although the posts in *Celery Drawing* share similarities with clean-eating posts due to shared hashtags and the presence of celery, they do not make promises of its curative qualities. Instead we see celery as an accomplice to gradual and relentless damage to paper—and metaphorically the body of the consumer. The depiction of slowly progressing destruction warns of the dangers of unfounded ideas about food when they are unregulated and unchallenged.

FEED, Zara Worth's Performance to Video for Instagram

To create *FEED* (2017), I (Zara) printed every photo of food and drink posted on my personal Instagram account on rice paper, which I then ate piece by piece in front of a live audience, while simultaneously filming myself on my smartphone. Despite food's prominence on Instagram, it is unlikely we will get to consume the majority of food we see unless the image is our own. As a consuming presentation, the ingestion of images of food in *FEED* enacts the well-known saying "you are what you eat," encapsulating how symbolic values attached to the food we consume can be read as markers of our character. The rice paper prints of past posts provide a lexicon of social and cultural markers that render legible the identity I wish to portray. For example, homemade chocolate truffles connote creativity, skill, and domesticity, as well as my preference for sweet foods; while a full wine rack and carefully placed bottle of Crémant indicates my middle-class tastes, as well as functioning as an in-joke through its implicit reference to a podcast I like.

Although Erving Goffman's *The Presentation of Self in Everyday Life* was first published fifty years ago, it is uncannily pertinent for considering how we curate images on Instagram. Goffman describes how an individual's everyday performances are articulated as a "front" consisting of any "expressive equipment . . . employed by the individual during his performance," and a "backstage" in which "illusions and impressions are openly constructed."[14] Individuals activate this "front" in an attempt to control other people's opinions of them. The operations between the front and the backstage are analogous with the presentation (the front) and the preparation (the backstage) of an Instagram post.

Although Goffman refers to uses of food as expressive equipment in only a handful of examples, he does not unpack food's symbolic power in any depth. In *FEED* I wanted to expose the contrivance of the backstage preparation of the

FIGURE 6-4. *FEED*, by Zara Worth, 2017.

front, while contending that food's unique quality as a sign can be both external-ized as part of one's front and internalized as a consumable item. *FEED* reduces the displayed original food items to props with which to prepare and present a front on Instagram, and then to rice paper prints, totally removed from any nutritional or flavorsome value. In doing so, *FEED* humorously pulls back the theater drapes between the front and the backstage, using performance art to reveal my own performance of everyday life on Instagram.

Reflections on the Medium

[Im]moral Food, *Wishbook*, *Celery Drawing*, and *FEED* each permeate, dis-rupt, and expose how ideologically driven food subcultures are both produced and circulated on Instagram. We have variously worked with and within In-stagram as a subject, material, and medium, using food trends to reveal the platform's behavioral expectations and the affordances that it offers us as users and artists. We created these artworks to critically engage with the visual con-tent produced and consumed by users on Instagram. As explicated in *FEED*, individual dietary choices on Instagram are detached from gustatory purposes, serving instead as illustrations of one's identity, which typifies how the personal is political.

As we saw with the hashtags in *[Im]moral Food*, *Wishbook*, and *Celery Draw-ing*, these individual words and pithy phrases circulate the posts among hashtag publics in order to connect the individual posting with specific ideologies and values. For us as artists, purposefully written and appropriated hashtags allow our work to enter into other users' newsfeeds, becoming Trojan horses infiltrat-ing unassuming realms. The connectivity afforded by social media, unlike its predecessor mass media, enables two-way communication between content makers and consumers who on social media are one and the same.[15] As a side effect, the artist and the artwork encounter the subcultures being critiqued at the site of its production, which exposes the artist and their work to direct, un-filtered interactions with an audience that has not necessarily come to see art.

In these four works, the medium of dissemination intersects with the material of making. As a subject and tool, Instagram is ripe for appropriation strategies, as it is so easy to take a screen capture, edit, and subvert. The platform offers a predefined set of parameters within which to play, and its aesthetic conventions provide a widely comprehended visual language, which an artist can adopt or rally against as required.

Notes

1. Michel Feher, "The Age of Appreciation: Lectures on the Neoliberal Condition," *Operative Thought Lecture Series* (London: Department of Visual Cultures, Centre

for Research Architecture and Forensic Architecture, Goldsmiths, 2013–15); Alice E. Marwick, "Status Update: Celebrity, Publicity, and Self-Banding in Web 2.0" (PhD diss., New York University, 2010).

2. Eddy de Jongh, "Realism and Seaming Realism in Seventeenth Century Dutch Painting," in *Looking at Seventeenth Century Dutch Art: Realism Reconsidered*, ed. by Wayne E. Franits, 21–56 (Cambridge: Cambridge University Press, 1997).

3. Dawn Woolley and Zara Worth, "[Im]moral Food," *In Media Res*, February 14, 2019, http://mediacommons.org/imr/content/immoral-food.

4. Dawn Woolley, "Critical Clickbait: Artist Interventions in Commercial Visual Culture," *In Media: The French Journal of Media Studies* 7, no. 1 (2018).

5. See J. van Dijck and T. Poell, "Understanding Social Media Logic," *Media and Communication* 1, no. 1 (2013): 2–14, in which they identify connectivity as one of four grounding principles defining social media logic which they position as entangled and distinct from mass media logic.

6. Nathan Rambukkana, "From #RaceFail to #Ferguson: The Digital Intimacies of Race-Activist Hashtag Politics," in *Hashtag Publics: The Power and Politics of Discursive Networks*, ed. Nathan Rambukkana, 29–46 (New York: Peter Lang, 2015), 42.

7. Dawn Woolley, *Consuming the Body: Capitalism, Social Media and Commodification* (London: IB Tauris, 2022).

8. Walter Benjamin quoted in Susan Buck-Morss, *The Dialectics of Seeing: Walter Benjamin and the Arcades Project* (Cambridge, MA: MIT Press, 1991).

9. Kate Dailey, "Who, What, Why: Can Foods Have Negative Calories," BBC News, March 15, 2013, www.bbc.co.uk.

10. Anthony William (@medicalmedium), Instagram account, 2019, www.instagram.com/medicalmedium/.

11. Michelle Allen, Kacie M. Dickinson, and Ivanka Prichard, "The Dirt on Clean Eating: A Cross Sectional Analysis of Dietary Intake, Restrained Eating and Opinions about Clean Eating among Women," *Nutrients* 10, no. 9: 1266, p. 5.

12. Pixie G. Turner and Carmen E. Lefevre, "Instagram Use Is Linked to Increasing Symptoms of Orthorexia Nervosa," *Eating and Weight Disorders—Studies on Anorexia, Bulimia and Obesity* 22, no. 2 (2017): 278; Allen, Dickinson, and Prichard, "Dirt on Clean Eating," 11; Turner and Lefevre, "Instagram Use," 278; Margaret McCartney, "Margaret McCartney: Clean Eating and the Cult of Healthism," *BMJ: British Medical Journal* 354 (2016).

13. McCartney, "Margaret McCartney."

14. Erving Goffman, *The Presentation of Self in Everyday Life* (Edinburgh: University of Edinburgh Press, 1956), 13, 69.

15. van Dijck and Poell, "Understanding Social Media Logic."

PART II

Influence

CHAPTER 7

Picturing Digital Tastes

#unicornlatte, Social Photography, and Instagram Food Marketing

EMILY TRUMAN

The current popularity of "unicorn foods" in North American popular culture begs the question, what flavor is a unicorn? The answer is surprisingly complex, as it is wrapped up in shifting notions of visual taste around food in digital culture. Here, the concept of "taste" refers to both sensory experience (esp. flavor) and culturally informed judgments on quality or style ("good taste" versus "poor taste"). The unicorn food trend embodies key tensions between "tasting" and "looking," played out against new visual practices of mobile photography, food marketing tactics, and consumption habits in relation to the social media landscape. These tensions have conceptual and practical implications for how we think about the appearance and purpose of food in everyday life. An informative example of this is the case of the unicorn latte. This chapter explores a trademark infringement case related to the drink's commercialization as a starting point to engage with its cultural origins and popular representation, framed by the history of the unicorn as popular icon. This exploration of the unicorn latte's digital visibility offers insight into the visual trends that contribute to the creation of new categories of foods in and around social media and digital culture.

#Unicornlatte

In April 2017, Starbucks released a limited-edition Unicorn Frappuccino: a pink and blue blended cream drink made with mango syrup, sour drizzle, vanilla whipped cream, and sweet and sour pink and blue powder topping. This Frappuccino (a registered trademark describing Starbucks' blended drinks) did not contain any coffee products—it consisted of ice, milk, and sugared syrup and powder.[1] The consumption experience was described as a magical spectacle: the pink and blue syrups, topped with "blue fairy powders," were stirred to reveal a purple beverage.[2] The press release also playfully interpreted the drink's origins: "The elusive unicorn from medieval legend has been making a comeback. Once only found in enchanted forests, unicorns have been popping up in social media with shimmering unicorn-themed food and drinks. Now Starbucks is taking the trend to a new level with its first 'Unicorn Frappuccino® blended beverage.' ... This limited time offering is as fleeting as a rainbow ... while supplies last."[3] The limited availability of the drink, for five days only from April 19 to 23, 2017, in the United States, Canada, and Mexico, contributed to a spike in sales and social media posts: the drink sold out in many locations, and it produced 180,000 hits on Instagram in a one-week period.[4] It also reportedly generated 1.3 billion impressions on Twitter and countless photos and videos posted to Snapchat and Facebook.[5] According to Starbucks executive chair Howard Schultz, this beverage was very successful at drawing traffic to stores and increasing awareness and brand affinity.[6] It also generated mainstream news and entertainment media coverage from the *New York Times* and the *Washington Post* to *Jimmy Kimmel Live* and *The Late Show with Stephen Colbert*.[7]

As the press release itself indicated, the viral success of the Unicorn Frappuccino was due in part to Starbucks capitalizing on the existing trend of "unicorn-themed food and drinks" in social media. The popularization of unicorn foods is linked to the 2016 appearance of "unicorn toast" on Instagram: bread covered in pastel-hued cream cheese made with natural food dye from beetroot and blueberries.[8] The roots of this trend were in "natural" ingredients (e.g., fruit and vegetable juices and powders) used to color other foodstuffs, such as smoothie bowls, noodles, rice, cookies, cakes, icing, and hot drinks.[9] One such drink, the plant-based Unicorn Latte created by the End Brooklyn, a café in New York City, gained notoriety in late 2016 and early 2017 through features in the *New York Times*, *Time Out* magazine, and the Huffington Post.[10] It is a predominantly blue beverage made from "superfood" ingredients, including blue-green algae powder (also known as spirulina), maca root, dates, cashews, ginger, and lemon, and topped with colored powder and sprinkles.[11] The drink's popularity led the owners of the End Brooklyn to file an application to trademark the name Unicorn Latte in January 2017.[12] It remains one of the café brand's core products.[13]

Thus, in early May 2017, less than two weeks after the end of the successful run of the Unicorn Frappuccino, the owners of the End Brooklyn, Montauk Juice, filed a $10 million lawsuit against Starbucks for trademark infringement.[14] Widely reported in the press, the complaint alleged that similarities between the names and appearances of the two drinks damaged the plaintiff's trademark.[15] The cause of the harm was the scope of the Starbucks social media–based marketing campaign that, along with press coverage, had made their Frappuccino into "the dominant 'unicorn' beverage overnight" that "eclipse[d] the Unicorn

Latte in the market." Furthermore, this marketing overtook the existing publicity around the Unicorn Latte, which had been carefully cultivated by the owners of the End Brooklyn on social media, as evidenced by the colonization of the hashtag "#unicornlatte" with images of the Starbucks Frappuccino replacing those of the original beverage. The complaint alleged that Starbucks, in associating their Frappuccino with the existing unicorn food trend, intended to create a drink that, just like the Unicorn Latte, was "made for Instagram."[16] The case was settled in September 2017, with the two parties reaching an undisclosed financial agreement.[17]

Picturing Unicorn Drinks

Notably, the #unicornlatte trademark infringement case is about a beverage's name, its appearance, and its visibility—where, how, why, and by whom it was seen on social media. Indeed, news coverage recognized the importance of the Unicorn Frappuccino's imagery, specifically around its photographability and "instagrammable features."[18] It was described as a "digital-age drink" designed to appeal "in the age of likes, snaps, and tweets," and as "Instagram bait"—a meme "geared more toward online sharing than actual consumption."[19] Its status as a viral sensation underlined the primary importance of the visual, resulting in the secondary significance of other characteristics, such as flavor or nutrition. Some stories did highlight its poor flavor, described as "nasty," "the taste of every flavor of popsicle melted together," and "sour birthday cake and shame."[20] Others reported the drink's high sugar content.[21] More frequently, the press discussed the visual appearance of this "social media–friendly product."[22]

It is significant that the trademark complaint itself featured numerous images, including side-by-side full-color reproductions of the marketing images used for the latte and the Frappuccino for comparison (see fig. 7-1); these images accentuate the similarities in core visual characteristics. On the left, the Instagram image of the End Brooklyn's latte presents a predominately pastel blue drink, topped with pink sprinkles served hot in a glass mug, while the press release image of Starbucks' Frappuccino on the right shows a predominantly pastel pink drink, topped with whipped cream, served cold in a tall plastic take-away cup with a straw. The unicorn motif is evoked rather minimally in both cases, primarily through the pastel hue of both drinks, although the product names also identify the theme.

Significantly, the similarities in the names of the drinks mattered as much as the resemblance in their visual representations. This is because the Frappuccino was popularly referred to as a latte by many Instagram users who tagged images of the Starbucks product with the existing hashtag "#unicornlatte," thus associating it with a previously existing product.[23] Online publications followed customers. In addition to having a highly similar name, Starbucks' Unicorn Frappuccino shares

visual similarities to the Unicorn Latte in that both were brightly colored and featured the colors

pink and blue prominently, the below diagram reflects an advertisement for the Unicorn Latte on

the left and the Unicorn Frappuccino on the right:

| Unicorn Latte | Unicorn Frappuccino |

2.   The End began selling the Unicorn Latte in December 2016. Despite the

distinctive name, the Unicorn Latte contained no coffee or milk and was instead a freshly-made

blended beverage containing fresh ingredients such as cold-pressed ginger, lemon juice, dates,

cashews, blended with additional healthy, dried ingredients such as maca root, blue-green algae,

and vanilla bean.

3.   In December 2016, the Unicorn Latte began appearing in articles published by

both traditional and online media outlets, including in the New York Times, the Huffington Post,

and TimeOut Magazine. The press, coupled with advertising efforts and broad social media

2

FIGURE 7-1. Images of the Unicorn Latte and Unicorn Frappuccino compared in *Montauk Juice Factory Inc. v. Starbucks* (p. 2).

suit, also using the "unicorn latte" terminology to refer to the Starbucks product.[24] Thus, the semantics of the "Frappuccino" label mattered little in this case, perhaps because the unicorn theme was a preexisting food trend and not a novel marketing concept created by Starbucks, making proprietary labels less significant to consumers.

The visual results of the conflation of the Frappuccino with the Unicorn Latte are presented in the trademark complaint as depicted in figure 7-2—a collection of

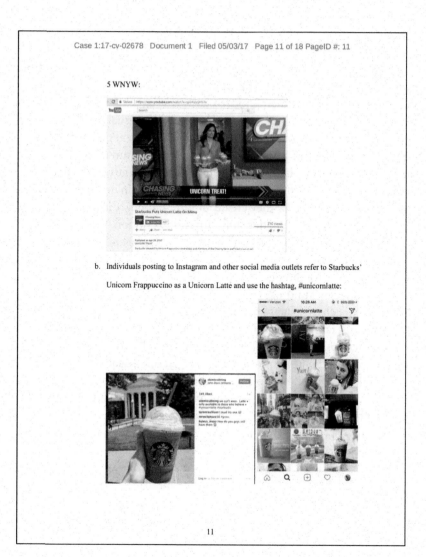

FIGURE 7-2. Examples of images tagged as #unicornlatte on Instagram, in *Montauk Juice Factory Inc. v. Starbucks* (p. 11).

images of the Starbucks drink under the aforementioned hashtag. There is nothing particularly notable about these images, as they feature what are increasingly common promotional content on Instagram: user-generated photos of favored products—in this case, consumers holding, sipping, or displaying the pink drink for the viewer. Yet they represent, through the visual colonization of the hashtag, the epicenter of this trademark dispute: the conflation of two products similar in appearance and name circulating in the same digital promotional spaces.

Conceptualizing Instagram Food

In media coverage about the unicorn Frappuccino, Starbucks claimed that the drink's "look" was an important part of product development.[25] Similarly, the End Brooklyn marketed their Unicorn Latte through styled Instagram photos that highlighted its colorful features. This focus on visual presentation is not surprising, given the desire of food brands and restaurant chains to cater to the behaviors of their target demographics, which for consumers aged eighteen to thirty-four currently includes posting photos online.[26] Indeed, the popularity of social media has changed restaurant and fast-food-chain menus and marketing strategies, influencing how they create and present new dishes.[27]

These changes reflect broader shifts around the notion of social media food imagery as "social currency," by which users document and share their curated food experiences using mobile technology.[28] Such practices contribute to the production of "social photography," what Lev Manovich refers to as "the photo-universe created by hundreds of millions of people" through social media sharing platforms such as Instagram, Flickr, and Facebook.[29] Images of the everyday, such as friends, families, birthdays, and holidays, are the main subject of social photography, captured via mobile photography and shared on Instagram.[30] These images represent the new importance of the "aesthetic society," a concept that describes the "production and presentation of beautiful images, experiences, styles . . . [as] the key propert[ies] of commercial goods and services."[31] The values of the "aesthetic society" influence choices around *how* images of the everyday are captured.[32] This includes images of food, given the widespread popularity of photographing meals and individual food items on Instagram.[33]

The hyper-visibility of foods on Instagram underlines the shifting expectations around their "visuality," or visual characteristics, a lens through which foods become valued for their aesthetic appeal over other attributes. The fetishizing of food imagery is not new, as the concepts of gastro-porn and food porn emerged more than thirty years ago to describe the obsessive devotion to presenting elaborate images of meals in cookbooks.[34] Visual excess defined such images, emphasizing the food's beauty and sensuality for the viewer. With the advent of social media, food porn has proliferated, highlighting the importance of food as artistic creation and thus drawing renewed attention to the visual aspects of its presentation in social photography.[35]

This social, cultural, and digital environment has produced the phenomenon of "Instagram foods," a term describing the prevalence of visual digital expressions of popular food trends and tastes circulating in social media—like the Unicorn Latte. Instagram foods are spectacle with unique visual traits (e.g., color, shape) that contribute to their popularity, such as grilled-rainbow-cheese sandwiches or charcoal-infused ice cream. They are based in broader food trends (e.g., plant-based or "clean food," extreme junk food, or "dirty food") that lend themselves to dramatic visual representation and are popularized through sharing on social media platforms and influencer blogs. This popularity is then exploited by food marketers to create extraordinary food products designed for viral marketing through social media. These are a new phenomenon meant for visual consumption: "made-for-Instagram" foods.

Instagram foods certainly share similarities with other food product fads, including the creation of novel "stunt foods" by fast-food restaurants, such as KFC's Double Down Chicken Sandwich; the scarcity and cachet of popular limited edition products, such as the McDonald's McRib sandwich or Red Velvet Oreo cookies; and the notoriety of "viral foods" that have reached novel levels of fame through circulation on social media, such as the cronut or avocado toast.[36] However, none of these fads was made to be photographed per se, which sets them apart from Instagram foods. Recent changes in food marketing practices signal this shift: some products are now developed specifically to be photogenic and to stand out as visually unique in order to encourage social media sharing.[37] The popular "crazy shakes" from New York restaurant Black Tap Craft Burgers & Beer are a prime example, as these ornately garnished milkshakes (topped with cake and candy) were specifically developed through a partnership between the chef and a social media coordinator.[38] Thus, Instagram foods are, first and foremost, for visual consumption—to be taken in with the eyes, rather than the mouth or stomach. The Unicorn Latte is a prime example of this visual phenomenon. It is a food produced through various practices of looking.

The Unicorn Latte as Instagram Food

The unicorn latte is, principally, a visual trend, both in conception and in practice grounded in social media. It is produced at the intersection of three visual phenomena: the unicorn as cultural icon, social photography practices, and digital food marketing tactics. Each has its own sets of visual practices (e.g., activities or methods) that contribute to the production of cultural representations of food.

The Unicorn as Cultural Icon

The Unicorn Latte and the Unicorn Frappuccino harnessed the iconicity of the unicorn as cultural symbol insofar as they mimicked key attributes of already popular unicorn foods: bright pastel colors featuring pinks, purples, and blues with sparkles or glitter. But how did these visual characteristics in particular come to represent the unicorn? The twenty-first-century Western version of this cultural symbol is built on visual attributes that began to circulate in medieval Europe (fifth to fourteenth centuries), the period in which the dominant image of the unicorn as a white horse with a spiraled white horn was established.[39] Popular representations of the European unicorn began with the animal composite of the Middle Ages (e.g., lion, deer, elephant, goat, or boar parts of various colors), which was replaced by the Renaissance image of the white horned male horse and its associations with purity (religious, sexual, social, medicinal).[40] Key representations of male unicorns from Renaissance Europe include *The Hunt of the Unicorn* tapestries (fifteenth century) and *The Virgin and the Unicorn* fresco by Domenico Zampieri (1605).[41] The unicorn then faded into obscurity in the age of scientific Enlightenment, only to be revived in the Victorian era as a symbol of romantic love (as opposed to religious devotion or courtly love).[42] Children's literature of the time, such as *Grimms' Fairy Tales* and Lewis Carroll's *Alice in Wonderland*, presented visual depictions of a large white animal with a white spiraled horn, thus reinforcing this imagery while also linking it to notions of innocence and modesty.[43]

These representations provided the foundation for the contemporary Western unicorn, now with pastel-colored bodies, rainbow hair, and sparkles as defining features, and more often coded as female or gender fluid.[44] Prime examples include Disney's *Fantasia* (1940), the My Little Pony toys and TV show (ca. 1980s), and stationery and clothing products by the Lisa Frank brand (ca. 1980s–'90s).[45] Built on the Romantic-era unicorn as an emblem of imagination and fantasy, the contemporary unicorn ushered in the new cultural motif of individualism, representing independence, inner strength, uniqueness, and the unconventional—as well as happiness, hope, and a care-free attitude. For millennial audiences, and especially for LGBTQ+ communities, this has also included the adoption of the unicorn as metaphor to represent "otherness" and as a symbol of pride around sexual orientation and gender identity.[46] In this context, the importance of being one's true self is embedded in broader notions of community and allyship.

Nevertheless, the unicorn's current meaning remains rooted in the notion of rarity, a common thread that runs through previous versions. What has changed is the cultural context in which the value of rarity is assessed: in the age of mass production and consumer capitalism, unique objects, ideas, and accomplishments are perceived as rare. Hence, the more recent adoption of the label "unicorn" to describe a start-up company worth more than $1 billion, or to describe a cherished person or thing—the "hypothetical ideal."[47] The notion of uniqueness has, ironically, been co-opted and commodified for mass consumption. The unicorn has been "tamed by consumer culture."[48] It no longer has the quality of the elusive, but it does continue to resonate as a cultural symbol of the unique and the special.

This is the millennial unicorn, not a symbol of divine devotion, courtly or romantic love, but of community and friendship. It is evoked through bright colors and in playful forms and contexts, from consumer products (e.g., pool floats) to marketing campaigns (e.g., Squatty Potty) and media texts (e.g., *My Little Pony: The Movie*).[49] It is this version of the unicorn that is reflected in current food trends. Unicorn foods are food items evoking the iconic characteristics of the unicorn, whether in color (pastel or rainbow hues, or white base), shape (horse face, head, body), or styling (horn, ears, eyes, made with edible substances or nonedible props).

First tied to health food trends, unicorn foods, like the broader trend of rainbow foods, grew out of the popularity of plant-based diets. Healthy unicorn foods use plant-based superfood ingredients, such as beet juice, turmeric, and blue algae, as natural colorants in hot and cold drinks and toast spreads, for example.[50] The use of plant-based dyes to color other edibles then expanded to (typically visually "bland") foods such as noodles, pancakes, bagels, and cheese.[51] Similar to rainbow foods, the popularity of unicorn foods has now surpassed its original health food contexts to include sugar-filled—and artificially colored—foodstuffs made by social media users and food bloggers, such as cakes, donuts, and milkshakes. Indeed, publishers released at least three different unicorn-themed cookbooks featuring desserts and baked goods in 2018.[52] The food industry has also contributed to the spate of sugar-filled unicorn foods, as evidenced by Unicorn Poop® cookies, special-edition Unicorn Froot Loops cereal, Ritter Sport's unicorn chocolate bar, and so on.[53]

Like the mythological creature that inspires them, unicorn foods occupy a unique conceptual space between the natural and the artificial. This category embodies tensions between its health food roots and junk food adaptations. The trademark complaint from the End Brooklyn underlined these tensions in claiming that "consumers who would have been interested in the Unicorn Latte because of the health benefits of the beverage now associate it with the unhealthy ingredients of Starbucks' 'Unicorn Frappuccino' and are deterred from trying it."[54] In fact, such broad categorizations (healthy vs. unhealthy) are oversimplifications, as the ingredients list of the Frappuccino, however sugar-filled, also included some of the same natural plant-based colorants, such as blue-green algae (spirulina), as the superfood Unicorn Latte.[55] Thus, unicorn foods, as a cultural fad, offer a unique example to think through the role of food categorizations in influencing broader cultural conceptions of health and nutrition, such as through the labels of "natural" versus "artificial" and their fluctuating meanings.

Social Photography Practices

The second visual phenomenon contributing to the production of the unicorn latte on Instagram is social photography. As described earlier, this term describes the "photo-universe" created through social media image sharing featuring beautiful pictures of the everyday.[56] Lee Humphreys describes this documentation of everyday ritual as "media accounting," which reinforces the routines of social life for the individual and group.[57] This has come about through shifts in the social uses of photography, which José van Dijck argues occurred in the move away from the purpose of photographs as memory objects toward photographs as experiential texts for sharing everyday life. This shift has reinforced the role of social photography as an "instrument for peer bonding and interaction."[58]

Social photography has also developed its own visual conventions, shaped by the social practices described above, as well as by technology. This "cultural language," as Manovich describes it, consists of "*conventions* and *techniques* that define subjects, narratives, editing, compositions, lighting, sequencing, and other image characteristics." The ability of smartphone camera technology to easily capture images of everyday life, coupled with the new aesthetic expectations for Instagram images, has resulted in new visual "rules" for capturing subjects in photos. In "designed" (or "styled") photos, as defined by Manovich, these rules consist of close-ups, shallow spaces, few details, and feature "the designed environment, as opposed to nature." In photographic practice, this results in the subject or object in the foreground, no background detail, and an emphasis on the visual perspective of the user (often looking down from above). Images may feature objects on a surface (a "flat lay"), body parts (hands, fingers, feet, etc.), or bodies against landscapes/cityscapes. Such images are designed for marketing purposes as influencer content, product placement, lifestyle advertising, and brand marketing.[59]

These visual practices contribute to the production of the unicorn latte as a visual trend by underlining the photographic conventions by which food products are to be captured, documented, and archived in social media. Currently, the multitude of consumer-generated images tagged #unicornlatte and #unicornfrappuccino feature Instagram users holding and posing with the drink, reproducing these visual conventions.

Digital Food Marketing Tactics

Finally, digital food marketing is the third visual phenomenon contributing to the production of the unicorn latte. Social media and digital culture have changed the landscape for brand marketing strategies, requiring new ways of reaching consumers in light of "crowdculture," which operates outside of traditional broadcast technologies.[60] New "cultural branding" strategies must target these crowd cultures and reach them where they interact with and create cultural content in order for a brand to "generate cultural relevance."[61] This is the case for both smaller brands, such as the End Brooklyn, as well as larger companies, such as Starbucks. The End Brooklyn leveraged social media marketing to make consumers aware of their Unicorn Latte, citing "broad social media exposure on Facebook and Instagram" as an important source of the drink's popularity.[62] Indeed, Instagram images were the central photographic content of the drink used in mainstream news coverage (e.g., by Huffington Post and *Teen Vogue*) when it gained notoriety in January 2017.[63]

On a larger scale, Starbucks also paid attention to the importance of "instagrammability" for millennial customers in the promotion of its product. Starbucks is an extremely popular brand on Instagram, with 18.4 million followers. The company has developed viral marketing tactics to reach social media users by engaging them in the process of product marketing: they regularly include re-grammed images of regular people consuming their product in their Instagram feeds.[64] Further, Starbucks has an established history of attention-getting tactics, including seasonal cups, the secret menu, limited-edition drinks, and Frappuccino happy hour. In particular, Frappuccino drinks are historically important to the brand, accounting for 20 percent of sales.[65]

In creating the Unicorn Frappuccino, Starbucks capitalized on its existing marketing strategies to attract attention and increase sales by presenting a limited-time offer that exploited the "growing sense of FOMO (fear of missing out)." In this case, they leveraged social photography practices to encourage customers to promote the brand for free in their social media feeds, as micro-influencers are a useful source of promotion for special "limited edition" products.[66] In keeping with the visual conventions of the designed photos examined above, it is notable that the official press release photos for the Unicorn Frappuccino mimicked those conventions for consumers: the lead image was a picture of the colorful drink held by a human hand, arm extended out of the frame, against a colorful background.[67]

Implications and Conclusion

The unicorn latte is produced at the intersection of three visual phenomena: the millennial unicorn as cultural icon, social photography practices, and digital food marketing tactics. It is significant that these three phenomena are primarily *visual*. The point of the unicorn latte is not its flavor or taste, but its visual presence. As a popular food trend, the hyper-visibility of unicorn foods contributes to the shaping of cultural expectations around food's visuality—how food looks and how it should appear when Instagrammed. Such tensions are further underlined in the case of the Unicorn Latte versus the Unicorn Frappuccino, where questions of authorship and authenticity were raised in relation to the marketplace of ideas around food and food fads. Indeed, in their trademark complaint against Starbucks, the End Brooklyn prohibited the latter from not only infringing on the "Unicorn Latte" mark but also any other "confusingly similar variation" including a rumored forthcoming Starbucks unicorn lemonade.[68] This was an attempt to preemptively block the development of any future products associated with the unicorn label.

The inclusion of such a demand highlights the unpredictability of viral food product marketing: user-generated (free) content promoting the Unicorn Frappuccino was highly beneficial to Starbucks, but it limited the visibility of the End Brooklyn's preexisting product. The flipside of positive user-generated promotional digital content is that brands have little control over its circulation or use. As van Dijck argues, the ability to frame the meaning of a picture can be lost with digital images, which become "prone to unintended repurposing."[69] It is also difficult to gauge the sustainability of such digital marketing tactics; Starbucks has since attempted to duplicate the success of the Unicorn Frappuccino (e.g., with mermaid- and crystal-ball-themed drinks), to no avail.

Digital foods also raise significant questions about "taste." At the level of the everyday, they have the potential to impact our food choices. Recent research on the impact of food imagery on consumption shows that smartphone photos taken before eating promoted "savoring," contributing to increased enjoyment of the food when consumed.[70] Thus, "eating with the eyes" may impact impressions of taste and flavor, pointing more broadly to the increasing (and ironic) influence of food imagery on taste, a topic deserving of more critical attention. Another implication of Instagram foods is the potential influence of limited-edition food products on consumption patterns, although research on this is limited. Additionally, the role of gendered audiences in the production and reception of unicorn foods remains unexplored, especially where issues of taste culture intersect with current representations of the millennial unicorn as feminized or gender fluid.

Overall, "Instagram foods" challenge cultural notions of taste whether in relation to sensory experience or the reasons for the latest cultural craze. The unicorn latte matters both for how (bad) it tastes and for how the circulation of its representations signals the arrival of Instagram foods as a new visual trend in food. Digital food cultures, specifically and significantly, influence food trends, marketing, and product development, but they also challenge expectations of food appearance and tastes in the age of social media. What flavor is a unicorn, then? It looks *and* tastes like rainbows and sparkles.

Notes

1. "Unicorn Frappuccino Blended Crème, Ingredients," Starbucks.com, 2019, www.starbucks.com, accessed July 1, 2019.

2. Ibid.

3. "Starbucks Weaves Its Magic with New Color and Flavor Changing Unicorn Frappuccino," press release, Starbucks.com, April 18, 2018, https://stories.starbucks .com, accessed July 1, 2019.

4. Greg Hoffman, "UBS: The Unicorn Frappuccino Will Drive Starbucks Higher (SBUX)," Markets Insider, April 24, 2017, https://markets.businessinsider.com, accessed July 1, 2019.

5. Jessica Roy, "Unicorn Frappuccinos Are Just the Latest Food Designed with Instagram in Mind," *Los Angeles Times*, April 28, 2017, www.latimes.com, accessed July 1, 2019.

6. Jonathan Maze, "Starbucks Still Rides the Unicorn Wave," *Nation's Restaurant News* 51, no. 8 (May 29, 2017): 24.

7. Liam Stack, "'Unicorn Food' Is Colorful, Sparkly, and Everywhere," *New York Times*, April 29 2017, www.nytimes.com, accessed July 1, 2019; Maura Judkis, "Starbucks' Unicorn Frappuccino Tastes Like Sour Birthday Cake and Shame," *Washington Post*, April 19, 2017, www.washingtonpost.com, accessed July 1, 2019; Kate Taylor, "The Unicorn Frappuccino Completely Revolutionized How Starbucks Invents New Drinks," Business Insider, July 2, 2017, www.businessinsider.com, accessed July 1, 2019.

8. Emily Laurence, "Taste the Rainbow: Why (Healthy) 'Unicorn Food' Is Everywhere," Well+Good, February 27, 2017, www.wellandgood.com/good-food/ unicorn-toast-latte-food-trend-explained/, accessed July 1, 2019.

9. Laurence, "Taste the Rainbow"; Khushbu Shah, "How Unicorn Foods Took over the Internet," Thrillist, April 28, 2017, www.thrillist.com/eat/nation/unicorn -food-instagram-trend-starbucks-frappuccino-superfoods, accessed July 1, 2019.

10. Kat Odell, "A Healing Unicorn Latte, from Brooklyn of Course," *New York Times*, December 19, 2019, www.nytimes.com, accessed July 1, 2019; Alyson Penn, "You Can Now Drink a Unicorn Latte in Brooklyn," *TimeOut*, January 10, 2017, www.timeout.com/newyork, accessed July 1, 2019; Abigail Williams, "These Magical Unicorn Lattes May Be the Prettiest Beverage on Earth," HuffPost, January 19, 2017, www.huffingtonpost.ca, accessed July 1, 2019.

11. Odell, "Healing Unicorn Latte"; the End Brooklyn, "Unicorn Latte," Plant Alchemy Menu, the End Brooklyn, 2019, https://thendbrooklyn.com/, accessed July 1, 2019.

12. Unicorn Latte became a registered trademark of Montauk Juice Factory in 2018.

13. The End Brooklyn, "Unicorn Latte."

14. *Montauk Juice v. Starbucks* [*Montauk Juice Factory Inc., the End Brooklyn v. Starbucks Corporation d/b/a Starbucks Coffee Company*], WL 1747128 (E.D.N.Y. 2017), no. 1:17-cv-02678.

15. Julie Marsh, "Brooklyn Cafe Claims Starbucks Stole Their 'Unicorn' Drink," *New York Post*, May 4, 2017, http://nypost.com, accessed July 1, 2019; Kevin McCoy, "Starbucks Unicorn Frappuccino Sued by NYC Café in Trademark Case," *USA Today*, May 5, 2017, www.usatoday.com, accessed July 1, 2019; "Starbucks Unicorn Frappuccino Slammed by Lawsuit," *CBS News*, May 5, 2017, www.cbsnews.com/news/, accessed July 1, 2019.

16. *Montauk Juice v. Starbucks*, 3, 1, 7, 9.

17. Stipulation of Voluntary Dismissal with Prejudice Pursuant to F.R.C.P. 41(a)(1)(A)(ii), *Montauk Juice Factory Inc., the End Brooklyn v. Starbucks Corporation d/b/a Starbucks Coffee Company*, no. 1:17-cv-02678 (E.D.N.Y. September 5, 2017); Corinne Ramey, "Starbucks and Brooklyn Café Settle Unicorn-Drink Lawsuit," *Wall Street Journal*, September 5, 2017, www.wsj.com, accessed July 1, 2019.

18. Judkis, "Starbucks' Unicorn Frappuccino"; Roy, "Unicorn Frappuccinos."

19. Amy Held, "Unicorn Frappuccino: A Digital Age Drink," NPR, April 19, 2017, www.npr.org, accessed July 1, 2019; Patrick Kulp, "Instagram Bait: Why Starbucks Put a Unicorn Meme on Its Menu," Mashable, April 23, 2017, https://mashable.com, accessed July 1, 2019.

20. Held, "Digital Age Drink"; Danielle Tullo, "Here's What the Unicorn Frappuccino Actually Tastes Like," *Cosmopolitan*, April 18, 2017, www.cosmopolitan.com, accessed July 1, 2019; Judkis, "Starbucks' Unicorn Frappuccino."

21. Elena Cresi, "Unicorn Frappuccino Mania: Starbucks Aims at Instagram," *Guardian*, April 21, 2017, www.theguardian.com, accessed July 1, 2019.

22. Ibid.

23. *Montauk Juice v. Starbucks*, 9.

24. Ibid., 4.

25. Kulp, "Instagram Bait."

26. Roy, "Unicorn Frappuccinos."

27. Kulp, "Instagram Bait."

28. See, for example, *The Waitrose Food and Drink Report 2016*, accessed August 6, 2019, at www.johnlewispartnership.co.uk/content/dam/cws/pdfs/Resources/the-waitrose-food-and-drink-report-2016.pdf.

29. Lev Manovich, "Watching the World," *Aperture* 214, no. 1 (2014), https://aperture.org/blog/watching-world/, accessed August 6, 2019.

30. Lev Manovich, *Instagram and Contemporary Image*, e-book (Creative Commons License, 2017), 30, 31.

31. Ibid., 117.

32. Ibid.

33. Yuheng Hu, Lydia Manikonda, and Subbarao Kambhampati, "What We Instagram: A First Analysis of Instagram Photo Content and User Types," in *Proceedings of the 8th International Conference on Weblogs and Social Media*, ICWSM 2014 (AAAI Press, 2014), 595–98; Ir. Budi Permadi Iskandar and Jessica Arden, "Content Analysis of Food Instagram Account," in *SCBTII Proceeding Book: The 7th Smart Collaboration for Business in Technology and Information Industries* (SCBTII, 2018), 41–45.

34. Alexander Cockburn, "Gastro-porn," *New York Review of Books* 24, no. 20 (December 8, 1977); Rosalinde Coward, *Female Desire: Women's Sexuality Today* (London: Paladin, 1984).

35. Yelena Mejova, Sofiane Abbar, and Hamed Haddadi, "Fetishizing Food in Digital Age: #foodporn Around the World," in *Proceedings of the Tenth International AAAI Conference on Web and Social Media*, ICWSM 2016 (AAAI Press, 2016), 250–58; Patrizia Calefato, Loredana La Fortuna, and Raffaella Scelzi, "Food-ography: Food and New Media," *Semiotica* 211 (2016): 371–88.

36. Kulp, "Instagram Bait"; "Instantly Consumer Poll Reveals America's Love For Limited Edition Fast-Food Products," *Marketing Weekly News* 83 (June 13, 2015); Daniel Levine, "Novelty Foods Are Trending," press release, PR.com, December 14, 2013, www.pr.com/press-release/532831, accessed July 1, 2019; Seth Abramovitch, "Sinful Synergy: How the Cronut Seduced America," Hollywood Reporter, July 10, 2013, www.hollywoodreporter.com/news/sinful-synergy-how-cronut -seduced-583219, accessed July 1, 2019; Jayne Orenstein, "How the Internet Became Ridiculously Obsessed with Avocado Toast," *Washington Post*, May 6, 2016, www .washingtonpost.com, accessed July 1, 2019.

37. Roy, "Unicorn Frappuccinos."

38. Andrea Marks, "Rainbow Bagels and Crazy Milkshakes: What Happens When a Dish Goes Viral," Eater, March 8, 2016, www.eater.com/2016/3/8/11171396/rainbow -bagels-cronut-cruffin-milkshakes, accessed July 1, 2019.

39. Skye Alexander, *Unicorns: The Myths, Legends, and Lore* (Avon, MA: Adams Media, 2015); Kenneth Hunt, "The Lore of the Unicorn," *Colonial Homes* 22, no. 6 (December 1, 1996): 78.

40. Pliny, *Natural History, Book 8, Chapter 31*, trans. John Bostock (London: Taylor and Francis, 1855); "Unicorns, West and East," American Museum of Natural History, 2019, www.amnh.org/exhibitions/mythic-creatures/land/unicorns-west -and-east, accessed August 17, 2019; Boria Sax, *Imaginary Animals: The Monstrous, the Wondrous, and the Human* (London: Reaktion Books, 2013); "Unicorn," in *Chambers Dictionary of the Unexplained*, ed. Una McGovern (London: Chambers Harrap, 2007); Hunt, "Lore of the Unicorn"; Roger Caillois and Scott R. Walker, "The Myth of the Unicorn," *Diogenes* 30, no. 119 (1982): 1–23.

41. Hunt, "Lore of the Unicorn"; Ariane Delacampagne and Christian Delacampange, *Here Be Dragons: A Fantastic Bestiary* (Princeton, NJ: Princeton University Press, 2003), 75–112.

42. Odell Shepard, *The Lore of the Unicorn* (London: George Allen and Unwin, 1930), 155–90; Alexander, *Unicorns*, 129–58; Paul Johnsgard and Karin Johnsgard, *Dragons and Unicorns: A Natural History* (New York: St. Martin's Press, 1982), 104–34.

43. Alexander, *Unicorns*, 159–82.

44. Ibid., 183–204.

45. Ibid.; Arianna Davis, "What's Really Behind Unicorn Fever," Refinery29, May 8, 2017, www.refinery29.com/en-us/2017/05/152423/unicorn-trend-explanation -history, accessed July 1, 2019.

46. Jamie Wareham, "Unicorns Are the Queer Icons of Our Time," GSN, August 17, 2018, www.gaystarnews.com/article/evidence-unicorns-are-queer-icons/#gs.z357rc, accessed July 1, 2019; "What's Happening with the Word 'Unicorn'?," Dictionary.com, 2019, www.dictionary.com/e/unicorn-word-trends/, accessed July 1, 2019.

47. Mark Abadi, "6 Words Americans Are Using Differently than Ever Before," Business Insider, December 12, 2017, www.businessinsider.com, accessed July 1, 2019; "What's Happening with the Word 'Unicorn'?"

48. Alexander, *Unicorns*, 184.

49. Davis, "Unicorn Fever"; Maura Judkis, "This Is Your Food on Acid: Why Edible Rainbows Have Taken Over the Internet," *Washington Post*, April 25, 2016, www.washingtonpost.com accessed July 1, 2019; Alice Fisher, "Why the Unicorn Has Become the Emblem for Our Times," *Guardian*, October 15, 2017, www.theguardian.com, accessed July 1, 2019.

50. Laurence, "Taste the Rainbow."

51. Wency Leung, "Rainbow Food: A Culinary Trend to Dye For," *Globe and Mail.com*, June 2, 2010, www.theglobeandmail.com/life/rainbow-food-a-culinary-trend-to-dye-for/article4348325/, accessed July 1, 2019; Judkis, "This Your Food"; Laurence, "Taste the Rainbow."

52. Clare Swanson, "Hot Topic: Unicorn Food Cookbooks," *Publishers Weekly*, March 23, 2018, www.publishersweekly.com, accessed July 1, 2019.

53. Shah, "Unicorn Foods"; Danielle Jackson, "Kellogg's Is Bringing Unicorn Cereal to the U.S.," *Delish*, December 14, 2017, www.delish.com accessed July 1, 2019; Brinton Parker, "This Sparkly Unicorn Chocolate Is about as Rare as a Real Unicorn, but OMG," PopSugar, November 26, 2016, www.popsugar.com/food/Ritter-Sport-Unicorn-Chocolate-Bar-42750848, accessed July 1, 2019.

54. *Montauk Juice v. Starbucks*, 12.

55. "Unicorn Frappuccino Blended Crème"; Odell, "Healing Unicorn Latte."

56. Manovich, "Watching the World."

57. Lee Humphreys, "Sharing the Everyday," in *The Qualified Self: Social Media and the Accounting of Everyday Life* (Cambridge, MA: MIT Press, 2018), 34.

58. José van Dijck, "Digital Photography: Communication, Identity, Memory," *Visual Communication* 7, no. 1 (2008): 57–76, quote on 62.

59. Manovich, *Instagram and Contemporary Image*, 18, 69, 105–6.

60. Douglas Holt, "Branding in the Age of Social Media," *Harvard Business Review* 94, no. 3 (2016): 40–50.

61. Ibid., 42.

62. *Montauk Juice v. Starbucks*, 2–3.

63. Abigail Williams, "These Magical Unicorn Lattes"; Greg Seals, "This Unicorn Latte Is as Beautiful as It Is Magical," *Teen Vogue*, January 11, 2017, www.teenvogue.com accessed December 14, 2019.

64. Amy Jo Vassallo, Bridget Kelly, Lelin Zhang, Zhiyong Wang, Sarah Young, and Becky Freeman, "Junk Food Marketing on Instagram: Content Analysis," *JMIR Public Health Surveillance* 4, no. 2 (2018): e54.

65. "Frappuccino Turns 20: The Story behind Starbucks Beloved Beverage," Starbucks Stories and News, March 25, 2015, https://stories.starbucks.com/stories/2015/frappuccino-turns-20/, accessed July 1, 2019; Robert Tremblay, "The Unicorn of Trademark Infringement Cases," Bhole IP Law, June 2, 2017, www.bholeiplaw.com/unicorn-trademark-infringement-cases/, accessed July 1, 2019.

66. Natalie Koltun, "Mobile Campaign of the Year: Starbucks Unicorn Frappuccino'" Mobile Marketer, December 4, 2017, www.mobilemarketer.com/news/mobile-campaign-of-the-year-starbucks-unicorn-frappuccino/510799/, accessed July 1, 2019.

67. "Starbucks Weaves Its Magic."

68. *Montauk Juice v. Starbucks*, 17–18.

69. Van Dijck, "Digital Photography," 71.

70. Sean Coary and Morgan Poor, "How Consumer-Generated Images Shape Important Consumption Outcomes in the Food Domain," *Journal of Consumer Marketing* 33, no. 1 (2016): 1–8.

CHAPTER 8

Camera Eats First

The Role of Influencers in Hong Kong's Foodie Instagram Culture

YUE-CHIU BONNI LEUNG AND YI-CHIEH JESSICA LIN

On a sunny day in summer 2013 in Hong Kong, Kelly Chan, a twenty-eight-year-old recent law-school graduate, walked into the central business district and ordered a bowl of fresh-made dumplings and fried noodles with green onion in Shanghai Lane diner. Before she picked up her chopsticks, she decided to snap a digital picture of it and immediately post it on Instagram. The idea of documenting her food in a visual diary suddenly occurred to her as she was thinking about how to share Hong Kong's diverse foodscape on the image-based social media platform she had just joined. From 7 a.m. to 10 p.m. daily, Kelly now enthusiastically uses the camera on her mobile phone to document the details of her breakfast, lunch, dinner, and snacks. In a mere five years, Kelly's food diary on Instagram has attracted 923,000 fans, most of whom are tech-savvy young people in their twenties and thirties. Now, Kelly has built a second career by posting sponsored food photographs in Hong Kong. Her Instagram account was mentioned along with others in an article on twenty Hong Kong foodies to follow on Instagram in the influential online magazine, Lifestyle Asia.[1]

Since the former British colony was ceded to the People's Republic of China in 1997, Hong Kong remains a special administrative region of China. A hybrid food culture has taken root in Hong Kong since the colonial period. According to government statistics, there are currently over 14,500 licensed restaurants in the city, serving a wide variety of food and cuisines from all over the world, 61 of which made the list of Michelin-starred restaurants in 2017.[2] Chefs in this gourmet city are also known to love their food porn, themselves being fans of food photography and celebrating the culture of "camera eats first."[3]

Media reports on Instagram-worthy cafés and restaurants in Hong Kong are also on the rise, amplifying the city's reputation as a gourmet paradise in Asia. Offering comparative insights into the intersections of food and identity, this chapter examines how restaurant-focused influencers capitalize on the affordances of Instagram as a social media platform. Across the region, Hong Kong has the second-highest penetration figures for Instagram after Malaysia, with 70 percent of Internet users on the platform.[4] The relationship between the people of Hong Kong and localism has also been mediated by food, to some degree.

Selina Chan, for instance, argues that *pancai*, a Cantonese traditional festive cuisine found in the walled village culture of the New Territories of Hong Kong, is a symbol of changing identity politics; it embodies socioeconomic transformations due to urbanization, emigration, globalization, and decolonization.[5] *Pancai* ingredients include pork, beef, chicken, shark fin, prawn, dried mushroom, fish balls, eel, bean curd, and Chinese white radish. Served in large basins for communal consumption, *pancai* evokes a sense of imagined nostalgia that is mediated through the commodification and promotion of food by commercial interests and media reports, eventually becoming part of the heritage and identity of all Hong Kong people. Hong Kong tea cafés are another example of local food symbolizing a Hong Kong identity. Local tea cafés display a culture of hybridity and an "entanglement between the multiplicity of Chinese ethnicities and colonial modernity with flexibility, efficiency, choice, and diversity as its features."[6]

While local food culture reflects Hong Kong's history, Instagram users fill their profiles with images of a wide range of foods from different cultures by posting their day-to-day food experience for public consumption. For instance, as of August 6, 2021, there are more than 4.6 million images on Instagram tagged #hkfoodie. In this chapter, we situate the act of sharing food images on Instagram as a sphere where "consumers' private, public, and professional practices interact with technological interfaces and hungry networks to channel, discipline, and unleash desire."[7] We address the following research questions: When influencers subscribe to Instagram expectations to post frequent photos, how does food intersect with diverse performances of identity? And how do individual influencers view their mediations of food, identity, authenticity, or food photography when they harness new media technology and create online foodie communities?

This chapter positions "foodie influencers" on Instagram, like Kelly Chan, as one instance of a larger phenomenon in which trends in offline foodscapes are increasingly mediated by online trends, such as online reviews and user-generated content. We focus on the stories of several of these self-made influencers on Instagram. We analyze their social media strategies and visual aesthetics, while also trying to understand their views on the representation of food on Instagram. We begin by briefly reviewing current scholarship on the digital economy of Instagram and influencers. We shed light on the making of online influencers (as micro-celebrities in their fields) as well as contribute to the understanding of how the megaphone effect works. The megaphone effect refers to the potential the Web poses for ordinary consumers to attract a mass audience through their iterative displays of taste or aesthetic discrimination. Online reviewers who get hold of the microphone are not necessarily trained experts in the industry.[8] In this context, Instagram influencers commenting on food and restaurants do not have to work at or own a restaurant, or be a gourmet. Even without industry expertise, the megaphone effect allows influencers to reach out to an extensive audience with their reviews and comments, possibly influencing public opinion, adoption of innovations, new product market share, or brand awareness.[9] Considering these pathways of influence, we then analyze the accounts of our five informants, as we outline our findings and assess how various aspects of food and identity are mediated or redefined through the use of Instagram. We conclude by considering the intersection of digital culture with traditional food practices, which we discuss in relation to food porn and photography skills.

Food Instagram and Influencers: A Literature Review

The development of Instagram as a social media platform dedicated to visual content relied on the evolution of camera phone technology and the increasing speed of data transmission, which has enabled photography and videos to dominate our daily communication. This imagery is capable of arousing realistic mental associations with convincing power, which can signify in excess of the object itself.[10] This representational power is particularly notable in the rise of everyday amateur food photography.[11]

As Erin Metz McDonnell argues, aesthetic food photography is meant to be seductive and cultivate obsession, a departure from utilitarian food images that function in a denotative, less layered way. For instance, as we look at a food photograph, we may find the food object itself to "materially evoke somewhat pornographic imagery" by perceiving it as a representation of sensuality.[12] Good plating strategies can enhance food photography's pornographic sense and construct a suggestive scene, making use of dressings or vegetables to add extra colors or textures that provocatively enhance the materiality of the food. McDonnell argues that food photography creates fantasy and intimacy for the presumed male viewer, characterizing exotic food as a kind of "femme fatale."

Furthermore, Robert Ibáñez, Anthony Patterson, and Rachel Ashman studied online food image sharing as networks of desire, which they conceptualize as energetic, connective, systemic, and innovative.[13] Tisha Dejmanee's study of digital food porn shows that, in the United States, female food bloggers substitute food for the body and redirect the disciplinary postfeminist gaze from their bodies toward their creative and entrepreneurial capacity.[14] Here digital food porn indicates an aesthetic of excess that is also playful and pleasurable, while postfeminism refers to the ideological shift that emphasizes expressing gendered identity through consumption practices and a neoliberal focus upon individualism, choice, and empowerment.[15] Dejmanee points out that food bloggers in the West often perform femininity in a way that fetishizes the white, upper-middle-class, nuclear family lifestyle while affirming their fulfillment in traditional domesticated roles. But there is a lack of study on food images on Instagram outside the European and U.S. contexts, which this chapter addresses.

Food porn or otherwise, the circulation of highly aesthetized food imagery extends a wider, "'lifestyled' food-media ecology" that includes the rise of celebrity chefs and globally popular reality-style cookery TV formats. Tania Lewis sees "foodie-oriented social media" as the ultimate personalized extension of and engagement with lifestyle media and culture.[16] It is central to the global spread of middle-class forms of lifestyle culture and involves participants in identity-related labor and self-branding.[17] Combined with technologies of geo-location, this digital culture provides a powerful link to people's mobile engagements with food consumption and food tourism. As such, Instagram creates an "emplaced visuality," using geo-temporal tagging to narrate a sense of place embedded with social position and sociality.[18] This emplaced sociality connects with findings by Vicki Molina-Estolano that users see Instagram as satisfying their "desire for fun, relaxation and discovery," as they follow people outside of their immediate social networks.[19]

We refer to our informants as "influencers" because this term generally denotes online social media personalities who mobilize product- or category-specific opinion leadership, although some of our informants do expand their postings on Instagram from food to other relevant fields, such as travel and other types of leisure consumption. Consumers often perceive user-generated content as more trustworthy and credible, leading to more influence on their opinions and consumption behaviors.[20] Past studies have presented diverse perspectives on the roles of influencers on new media, seeing them as doing the jobs of citizen journalists, cultural critics, or even rising market opinion leaders.[21]

While we consider food Instagram influencers, specifically, Arturo Arriagada and Francisco Ibáñez documented that authenticity and entrepreneurship are the two guiding principles of self-branding. Those content creators who become influential often market themselves as "authentic consumer influencers of brands and goods who communicate a brand's values through their authentic experiences."[22] Although Instagram influencer marketing is one of the fastest growing trends in advertising, there have been very few studies on the production side of these influencers themselves (such as their agency and identity), especially in relation to food. Crafted food photos on Instagram, in particular, are seen as performances of personal "culinary capital," which refers to food-related knowledge associated with social status.[23] Lewis further argues that the circulation of food imagery is a performance of lifestyle, aesthetics, good taste, and food photography, in which influencers also engage.[24]

In the digital economy, many consumers, including food Instagram influencers, engage in free labor to produce content online; but they still have enjoyable, rewarding experiences of social production. Kathleen Kuehn and Thomas Corrigan introduced the concept of "hope labor" to describe "un- or under-compensated work carried out in the present, often for experiences or exposure, in the hope that future employment opportunities may follow."[25] When ordinary consumers become social media influencers, they are often then identified as trustworthy, attractive opinion leaders to their users and other content creators. Marketers then utilize these traits to expand brand awareness among their target audiences.[26] More than targeting, such tactics can also create a sense of community. A Euromonitor study found that a rise in blogging about food enhanced public interest and participation in foodie culture, and encouraged individuals to take part in "networks of production and exchange" about food and the dining experience, dynamics in which our informants participate.[27]

Lastly, it should be noted that at certain points in this chapter we use the term "foodie" to refer to influencers on Instagram because they fit the definition of having "a strong interest in or a passion for learning about and eating good food," which transcends factors like gender, age, social class, and having professional knowledge about food, while also operating at different levels.[28] On one level, foodies include individuals who tag themselves as foodies and enjoy the self-pleasing experience of dining. The motivation of another category of foodies is more directed by social desires, and they think of food as a way to reach out and connect with others. Our food Instagram influencer informants document the overlap between these categories.

Studying Instagram Influencers: Methodology

Gaining access to social media influencers for research is difficult. Many guard the secrets of their success carefully and typically avoid researchers, especially as they may see little personal incentive to fit into their busy schedule an in-depth conversation with an unfamiliar researcher. Unlike registered businesses,

Table 8-1. Informants in Hong Kong

No.	Name	Age	Education	Instagram Profile Created	No. of Followers (rounded)	No. of Posts	Career Field
1	Angela	29	bachelor's	May 2016	20,200	1,027	banking
2	Emily	33	bachelor's	February 2011	47,500	4,628	media
3	Mandy	34	bachelor's	October 2011	13,200	4,601	media
4	Kelly	28	master's	March 2013	97,000	2,848	law
5	Stella	27	bachelor's	March 2014	21,900	2,033	advertising

Source: Data as of November 9, 2018.

it is difficult to obtain a full list of Instagram foodies in Hong Kong because user-generated content is created nonstop, 24/7. To make the interview process feasible, we began with a list of Instagram bloggers from "20 Hong Kong foodies to follow on Instagram" published by Lifestyle Asia, a local digital media outlet covering various lifestyle topics, as potential informants.[29] We sent an interview invitation e-mail to every shortlisted Instagram channel owner. Five indicated interest in a conversation about how they manage their food postings on Instagram. On the request of the informants to remain anonymous, we use pseudonyms throughout this chapter and received their permission to use the photos. The informants' backgrounds are summarized in table 8-1.

It should be noted that the bloggers in Hong Kong are divided into two groups: Chinese or local bloggers and expatriates. Most of our informants are local bloggers who grew up in Hong Kong, one is from the United States but now lives in Hong Kong, and all have largely based their careers in Hong Kong. We conducted semi-structured in-depth interviews during August and September 2017 in Hong Kong. The interviews were conducted using open-ended questions to allow the informants to freely share their experiences and observations; we asked them to describe and explain their online choices and behaviors, discuss interactions with followers, and reflect on their status as influential users on Instagram. The interviews were conducted in Cantonese or English and were forty-five to sixty minutes in length. The recorded conversations were transcribed into English by a native Cantonese speaker. We analyzed the collected data with a grounded theory approach in order to find patterns in the respondents' displays of taste and attitudes from their practice and observations during their journey on Instagram. Grounded theory includes several steps to develop a rigorous data collection protocol, to order and analyze data via coding, and eventually produces new theoretical constructs for the phenomenon under study.[30] This method is useful for understanding a research participant's social constructions through an iterative process of generating concepts, categories, and propositions to develop an explanatory theory grounded in the data.[31]

We also asked each informant to select five images that had attracted the most attention (i.e., highest number of likes) from their followers and explain what each image means to them using a visual method known as auto-photography. Auto-photography allows participants to take and choose pictures that best represent their identities and creativity, and allows participants time to reflect on what they want to express.[32]

Our study is limited by our small sample size and by our primary focus on influencers and their perspectives. In future studies, researchers could conduct additional interviews, as well as content analysis of the food photography on Instagram in Hong Kong or study consumer opinions and perceptions to understand which traits of influencers are most attractive. Future studies can also enrich our understanding of food influencers by long-term Internet ethnography, since participant observation over an extended period of time could differ from influencers' self-proclaimed perspectives and agendas.

Cultivating Taste and Building Community

Initial Position

Although our informants differed in some respects, they held a number of views in common. All of our informants began their Instagram blogging as a way to share their dining-out hobby and aspirations to claim a "foodie" identity, as well as to provide information about affordable, everyday food instead of high-priced fine dining. At the time of the launch of their Instagram accounts, these five individuals appeared indistinguishable from the millions of ordinary food consumers in Hong Kong. None of them received any formal academic training in food studies or photography. They simply learned by doing, observing how other foodies acted on social media and developed their own aesthetic sensibility regarding food photography. Some, however, were employed in adjacent fields. Mandy and Emily, for instance, work as food writers in journalism; at the same time, their profiles on Instagram serve as personal showcase spaces for their creative works.

All our informants stressed that the food they consumed and displayed through Instagram was consistent with their personal food preferences, reflecting their personalities and style of photography and writing. These Instagram influencers also exhibit carefree attitudes about broadcasting their personal thoughts and being "authentic" about their taste and feelings. For instance, Emily said in the interview: "I state very clearly that I would have the ultimate control over the content I am going to post. The image and text have to align with my tone and style." Mandy believes that "knowing about food is a way to learn about a community."

Although there is no universal formula for how to produce content, our informants were keenly aware that their Instagram persona is a form of self-branding, which imposes certain expectations and limitations on their content and self-styling. Influencers' success depends on their creative ability to post food photography that is informative, has entertainment value, and displays a unique aesthetic style. Aware of Instagram as a channel of self-branding, all the informants prioritize their autonomy over the monetary rewards they receive from commissioned tasks. Many of them mentioned that they have turned down marketing invitations because they think that the tasks do not fit their own taste or they do not like the brand. Angela typically uses a pun in the caption to promote brands more subtly, whereas Emily emphasizes digging into the "behind-the-scenes" story or communicating her diverse views on trendy food stuffs and restaurants in order to build a niche market for her Instagram account. Mandy states that showing neutrality and independence is important to sustain brand values, an attitude shared by other informants.

Using Hashtags and Curating Content

Since all the informants have produced a significant amount of content on Instagram, they use hashtags as a convenient tool to curate and categorize the content. They believe that their most commonly used hashtags are about restaurant location. Influencers are able to create their own branded hashtags, for instance using #kellyinhongkong to organize all food trips in Hong Kong in one place. In contrast with the general geotags available on Instagram, personalized hashtags can bring an audience to relevant posts created by a specific creator, which is convenient for consumers and helpful for the accounts to increase exposure to new users and networks.

The second important role of the hashtag is to use it as a disclaimer or self-disclosure statement, indicating whether the post is part of a sponsored marketing campaign or not. When it comes to collaborating with restaurants or commercial brands, these Instagram influencers are highly cautious about their content and where to place the marketing messages. On the one hand, they maintained aesthetic styles and tones to match the rest of their posts. On the other hand, they usually disclose the collaboration with tags such as #byinvitation or #ad in order to preserve their credibility. The influencers' biggest concerns are similar: they are afraid of becoming "inauthentic" in the eyes of their followers, or sharing too much irrelevant content and losing their own personal brand niche. They understood that their followers are drawn by their informational content, such as their presumably neutral descriptions of and commentaries on food, the quality of service, and prices.

Diverse Performances of Identity

Our informants are aware of their status as influencers on Instagram, but they identify themselves more as "food writers" who share attention-worthy dining experiences and information from a neutral point of view, instead of "Instagram bloggers." They stress the importance of "autonomy" when they produce their works on Instagram, which means being honest about their dining experiences. "Consistency" is another keyword that the influencers constantly bring up in the interviews as a way for them to build trust with their followers. If the influencer makes substantial changes in their content or style all of a sudden (e.g., featuring a lot of branded materials), it threatens to decrease their "authenticity" and weaken the credibility of their posted content.

Within this mediated foodscape, Hong Kong Instagram influencers construct hybrid identities between the local and the global. In the sample of informants' photographs that attracted the highest number of likes, nonlocal food comprised 60 percent of the photos. This includes a wide variety of cuisines, such as Taiwanese desserts and drinks, Japanese pancakes, Vietnamese sandwiches, and Mexican tacos. Beyond tea cafés and *pancai,* the influencers want to display how exotic food is also part of their diet, reinforcing the notion of Hong Kong as a cosmopolitan city. But the influencers tend to pay more visits, and be more generous toward, the local shops and be more critical of large chain restaurants. In a quantitative assessment of the representative photos provided by our informants, we found about 24 percent of the images were not directly focused on food objects. These photos usually entail a scenic street view or a local restaurant's storefront to help their audiences feel immersed in a shared consumption experience. In these contexts, our informants viewed posting about local establishments as a means to reduce the alienating impact of globalization, such as the inflows of overseas restaurant brands, as well as the public's ever-changing appetite for different cuisines. Mandy uses her Instagram account to promote businesses in the local farmer's market, where she has carefully selected the topic and products for cross-promotions to avoid becoming irrelevant to her audience.

As mentioned earlier, influencers must balance a complex relationship between their commercial and personal interests as the informants constantly receive invitations from restaurants to taste new menus. One of the informants mentioned that her Instagram channel started receiving free tasting invitations once they reached around five thousand followers. Different from offering monetary incentives, tasting invitations do not come with strict terms and conditions, allowing Instagrammers flexibility in terms of their posting style and content creation. The Instagrammer can even decide not to feature the restaurant in their channel if the tasting experience is not satisfying. Some informants have expressed a preference for focusing on positive reviews in the text accompanying their posts after attending free-of-charge tasting events, but they also think that the food photos reveal a certain degree of truth to the audience. In the case that they have few good things to say, they tend to avoid posting about the experience at all, mainly as a form of gratitude for the invitation. When a food blogger gets a larger pool of followers, the remuneration is higher—up to $2,000 per post or more.

All of our informants exhibit very careful attitudes about negative word-of-mouth communication. Emily said: "I rarely criticize a service or restaurant because I don't bother to mention it if it is really awful. But I found people are more reactive when I posted something negative . . . people are leaving comments and they appreciate our conversation on Instagram because it has made the page more alive." Emily shared how a shop owner apologized on Instagram about her lackluster experience, and Emily responded nicely by saying that she would pay another visit soon. Mandy also had similar experiences. Angela found that, in extreme circumstances, her Instagram account empowered her when she experienced disappointing customer service from a famous food provider. She made a complaint on Instagram that led the business to come forward and take responsibility. Mandy said that the best way to offer criticism is to be rational and to be specific about the reasons. If one does not want to destroy the brand on social media, one could just mention the name of the dish and leave out the name of the brand or restaurant.

Techniques of Food Photography

While two informants working in the media industry preferred using a monocular camera for better quality, others credited smartphones and apps for the ability to fine-tune pictures and curate their presentation. Influencers usually enhance the sensuality of food photography with well-adjusted zooming, framing, orientation, and depth of field. Photographs that are zoomed out create a sense of distance, showing the appearance of the food object or cuisine in a whole. Zooming in on the details helps the audience identify with the food object, thus conveying intimacy as if the audience had a bite of the food themselves. Framing and composition are central to how a food object or table setting produce cultural meaning, and influencers use them to construct a fantasy dining experience for their audiences. Last but not least, the orientation of food allows the audience to view dishes from an unfamiliar direction, grabbing viewer attention and offering a new perspective on eating.

For example, instead of posting a still-life or flat-lay photograph, Angela captured the movement of noodles being lifted from a bowl (fig. 8-1). In other photos, she cut open a burger and took close-ups of the stuffing in a dumpling

FIGURE 8-1. Angela's photo of noodles being lifted from a bowl has more visual interest than a flat-lay or still-life photo.

FIGURE 8-2. Stella's framing foregrounds food production and gives the audience more context and access behind the scenes.

FIGURE 8-3. Emily's photo of a cocktail bun in the depth of field, with the bakery storefront as the background, possibly reminds the audience of their experience at a local bakery.

to give her audience a revealing point of view of the food objects. In a photo of a cake, Stella uses her framing skill to highlight that cake baking is a stepped process: she includes multiple finished cakes in the frame, as well as the tool in the chef's hand doing final touch-ups (fig. 8-2). The camera focuses on the nearest cake, so the details of the food object are not diluted in a busy photo. Stella finds that these kinds of behind-the-scenes shots that depict the production of food are very popular among her audience. Angela echoes the view that being able to show the story behind food production is a secret to remaining competitive in this field: "I would like to share my insight or information about restaurants and give the consumers advice for the latest restaurant on the trend."

In contrast, Emily's most popular image focuses on a cocktail bun (a signature local delicacy), with old-style bakery signage in the blurred background (fig. 8-3). The photo represents a purposeful choice by the photographer to evoke a sense of nostalgia in the audience, as the exact time the photo was taken is ambiguous. Emily thought that the image attracted a lot of attention and engagement from the audience because the consumption of a cocktail bun connotes the life experiences of everyday people in Hong Kong, particularly harking back to the 1980s. The purposely clear focus on the bun with blurred bakery signage in the background helps viewers immerse themselves in the scene and recall their experiences buying a local delicacy from a bakery in the neighborhood where they grew up.

A majority of food photographs by our informants clearly adopted techniques for producing the "pornographic gaze," especially through framing, orientation, and depth of field.[33] Even though it is difficult to measure the scope of Instagram's influence, food images are changing the dynamics of the food industry in Hong Kong. Being photogenic is increasingly a priority, reflected in many of the city's restaurants redecorating their interiors in order to create more spots for customers to take attractive pictures to feed social media. However, our informants also expressed their concerns about this visual turn. "Recently, I read an article about the reason people these days have forgotten about 'brown food,'" Mandy shared in our interview. "Brown food, such as red braised pork, is not eye-catching in the world of Instagram, but it could be very tasty. There has been more discussion about how Instagram has destroyed our enjoyment of eating in Hong Kong." Kelly and Mandy were among our informants who mentioned that they do not go for photogenic food in order to counter the trend, but they also understand that the trend is very hard to reverse. After all, as stated by Mandy, "good-looking pictures get published more often."

To respond to this visual turn, some of our informants compromise by posting less attractive food images as "Instagram Stories," which are posted for only twenty-four hours, so that they can maintain better-looking food images on their main page. According to this calculus, the appearance of food determines how much attention it deserves. With this awareness in mind, the influencers also try to highlight the less-known, local shop with fewer resources.

From our interviews, we understand that our informants use similar photographic techniques of food porn that are employed by the food bloggers studied by Dejmanee, but our informants use those techniques for different reasons. Our informants learn to position and style food from other food blogs on the Internet, but they do not affirm women's traditional domestic roles on Instagram. Instead, these young, female Instagram influencers in Hong Kong exhibit more carefree attitudes about showing their independent ideas and being "authentic" about their taste and feelings.

"Camera eats first" has become a global phenomenon but has particular resonance in Hong Kong. This chapter contextualizes how ordinary foodies in Hong Kong emerged to become influential figures via public displays of food and eating on Instagram. We found that these informants began as individuals who enjoyed the self-pleasing experience of dining. In our small sample of Instagram foodie influencers, what appears to be free online labor is also a way to cast their creativity freely. Food influencers prioritize the enjoyment of food tastings; at the same time they get nonmonetary rewards, including free food experience or taste testings. In our sample of influencers, four are quite satisfied with their current status as amateur food connoisseurs as long as they can sustain their sense of creative autonomy. For them, posting on Instagram is a hobby instead of a stepping-stone for their careers. This attitude helps them avoid being overly exploited by the capitalist logics of digital economy, and yet they are still neoliberal subjects. These influencers gradually evolved into a second type of foodie who connects and builds community through the act of posting photos on Instagram. Analyzing the techniques influencers use to produce digital food photography helps us to better understand their agency and digital identity play as well as to gain insights into the process of building a taste community by these once-ordinary Instagram users. As regular Instagram users have come to share their taste and food aesthetic, they have built an audience from the content they create and climbed up the ladder to get ahold of the megaphone. Their channels have become communities while their audience grows and matures, working as a platform for the content creator to interact and exchange ideas with the audience as an opinion leader.

Our study's findings are consistent with others about the megaphone effect in the fashion industry where the absence of institutional mediation is obvious. Food Instagram influencers acquired their initial audience by dint of their own actions. But it is also important not to oversell the megaphone effects observed in food blogging on Instagram. Although the posts of food bloggers might influence their followers' behaviors and create more business opportunities for certain local restaurants, this "visual turn" could also undermine those small businesses without enough capital to renovate the interior designs of restaurants.[34]

We also explored influencers' views on collaborating with corporate marketing, as well as their tactics for hashtag labeling. These influencers deemed sustaining their credibility and authenticity more important than monetary interest when it came to managing their relationships with their audience. It is reflected in their maintenance of a consistent presentation aesthetic while using a mixture of photography skills to foreground new perspectives on food objects. Finally, these locally based food influencers reflect in their posts a longing for a Hong Kong identity that is rooted in both traditional foodways and global cosmopolitanism. Food Instagram has thus far proven a novel space for representing both.

Notes

1. Cindie Chan, "20 Hong Kong Foodies to Follow on Instagram," *Lifestyle Asia*, August 29, 2016, www.lifestyleasia.com/478967/20-hong-kong-foodies-to-follow-on-instagram/.

2. "Restaurant Licenses—Restaurant Licenses" (English), Food and Environmental Hygiene Department (Hong Kong), www.fehd.gov.hk/english/licensing/license/

text/LP_Restaurants_EN.XML, accessed April 10, 2020; Cheryl Tiu, "Michelin Announces 2017 Stars for Hong Kong And Macau: Peninsula Gets Its First Star and Alain Ducasse's Spoon Falls Off List," *Forbes*, November 14, 2016, www.forbes.com.

3. Mischa Moselle, "Taking 'Food Porn' Photos in Hong Kong Is so Popular Even the Chefs Are Doing It," *South China Morning Post*, March 7, 2014, www .scmp.com/lifestyle/food-wine/article/1441916/taking-food-porn-photos-hong -kong-so-popular-even-chefs-are.

4. Marissa Trew, "TNS Connected Life 2016 Study: Instagram and Snapchat on the Rise in APAC," Web in Travel, September 28, 2016, www.webintravel .com/tns-connected-life-2016-kantar-snapchat-instagram/.

5. Selina Ching Chan, "Food, Memories, and Identities in Hong Kong," *Identities: Global Studies in Culture and Power* 17, no. 2–3 (May 13, 2010): 204–27.

6. Selina Ching Chan, "Tea Cafés and the Hong Kong Identity: Food Culture and Hybridity," *China Information* 33, no. 3 (2019): 311–28.

7. Robert Kozinets, Anthony Patterson, and Rachel Ashman, "Networks of Desire: How Technology Increases Our Passion to Consume," *Journal of Consumer Research* 43, no. 5 (2017): 659–82.

8. Edward F. Mcquarrie, Jessica Miller, and Barbara J. Phillips, "The Megaphone Effect: Taste and Audience in Fashion Blogging," *Journal of Consumer Research* 40, no. 1 (2013): 136–58.

9. E. Bakshy, J. M. Hofman, W. A. Mason, D. J. Watts, and Duncan Watts, "Everyone's an Influencer: Quantifying Influence on Twitter," *Proceedings of the Fourth ACM International Conference on Web Search and Data Mining*, 65–74 (2011).

10. Jonathan E. Schroeder, "Visual Consumption in an Image Economy," in *Elusive Consumption*, ed. Karin Ekstrom and Helene Brembeck, 229–44 (Oxford: Berg, 2004).

11. Hu Yuheng, Lydia Manikonda, and Subbarao Kambhampati. "What We Instagram: A First Analysis of Instagram Photo Content and User Types," *Proceedings of the International AAAI Conference on Web and Social Media* 8, no. 1 (2014).

12. Erin Metz McDonnell, "Food Porn: The Conspicuous Consumption of Food in the Age of Digital Reproduction," in *Food, Media and Contemporary Culture: The Edible Image*, ed. Peri Bradley (London: Palgrave Macmillan UK, 2016), 249.

13. Robert Ibáñez, Anthony Patterson, and Rachel Ashman, "Networks of Desire: How Technology Increases Our Passion to Consume," *Journal of Consumer Research* 43, no. 5 (2017): 659–82.

14. Tisha Dejmanee, "'Food Porn' as Postfeminist Play: Digital Femininity and the Female Body on Food Blogs," *Television and New Media* 17, no. 5 (2016): 429.

15. Rosalind Gill, "Postfeminist Media Culture: Elements of a Sensibility," *European Journal of Cultural Studies* 10, no. 2 (2007): 147–66.

16. Tania Lewis, "Digital Food: From Paddock to Platform," *Communication Research and Practice* 4, no. 3 (2018): 212–28.

17. Alison Hearn, "Meat, Mask, Burden: Probing the Contours of the Branded 'Self,'" *Journal of Consumer Culture* 8, no. 2 (2008): 197–217.

18. Larissa Hjorth and Natalie Hendry, "A Snapshot of Social Media: Camera Phone Practices," *Social Media and Society* 1, no. 1 (2015): 1–3.

19. Vicki Molina Estolano, "Facebook and Instagram: A Tale of Two Feeds," Facebook IQ, July 11, 2016, www.facebook.com/iq/articles/facebook-and-instagram -a-tale-of-two-feeds.

20. Susan M. Mudambi and David Schuff, "Research Note: What Makes a Helpful Online Review? A Study of Customer Reviews on Amazon.com," *MIS Quarterly* 34, no. 1 (March 2010): 185–200.

21. Phoebe Maares and Folker Hanusch, "Exploring the Boundaries of Journalism: Instagram Micro-Bloggers in the Twilight Zone of Lifestyle Journalism," *Journalism* 21, no. 2 (2018): 262–78; Nadja Enke and Nils S. Borchers, "Social Media Influencers in Strategic Communication: A Conceptual Framework for Strategic Social Media Influencer Communication," *International Journal of Strategic Communication* 13, no. 4 (2019): 261–77.

22. Arturo Arriagada and Francisco Ibáñez, "'You Need at Least One Picture Daily, if Not, You're Dead': Content Creators and Platform Evolution in the Social Media Ecology," *Social Media and Society* 6, no. 3 (2020): 1–12.

23. Peter Naccarato and Kathleen LeBesco, *Culinary Capital* (New York: Berg, 2012).

24. Lewis, "Digital Food."

25. Kathleen Kuehn and Thomas F. Corrigan, "Hope Labor: The Role of Employment Prospects in Online Social Production," *Political Economy of Communication* 1, no. 1 (2013).

26. Chen Lou and Shupei Yuan, "Influencer Marketing: How Message Value and Credibility Affect Consumer Trust of Branded Content on Social Media," *Journal of Interactive Advertising* 19, no. 1 (February 2019): 58–73.

27. Marwa-Gad Mohsen, "Foodies in the UK: A Sense of Self, Connection and Belonging Beyond the Passion?," in *Creating Marketing Magic and Innovative Future Marketing Trends*, ed. Maximilian Stieler, 457–67 (Cham, Switz.: Springer, 2017); Jonathan E. Schroeder, "Visual Consumption in an Image Economy," in *Elusive Consumption*, ed. Karin Ekstrom and Helene Brembeck, 229–44 (Oxford, UK: Berg, 2004); Audrey Yue, "Eating," in *Interpreting Everyday Culture*, ed. Fran Martin (Oxford: Oxford University Press, 2003), 159.

28. Kate Cairns, Josée Johnston, and Shyon Baumann, "Caring about Food: Doing Gender in the Foodie Kitchen," *Gender and Society* 24, no. 5 (September 22, 2010): 597; Mohsen, "Foodies in the UK."

29. C. Chan, "20 Hong Kong Foodies."

30. Naresh R. Pandit, "The Creation of Theory: A Recent Application of the Grounded Theory Method," *Qualitative Report* 2, no. 4 (1996): 1–15.

31. Juliet Corbin and Anselm Strauss, "Grounded Theory Research: Procedures, Canons and Evaluative Criteria," *Qualitative Sociology* 13, no. 1 (1990): 3–21.

32. Carey M. Noland, "Auto-Photography as Research Practice: Identity and Self-Esteem Research," *Journal of Research Practice* 2, no. 1 (March 2, 2006): 3–4.

33. McDonnell, "Food Porn."

34. Bella Mackie, "Is Instagram Changing the Way We Design the World?" *Guardian*, July 12, 2018, www.theguardian.com.

CHAPTER 9

Repackaging Leftovers

Health, Food, and Diet Messages
in Influencer Instagram Posts

TARA J. SCHUWERK AND SARAH E. CRAMER

"Hands down, vegan brunching is my fave thing to do . . . by far! . . . And [I] didn't go completely bonkers," commented an Instagram influencer about his brunch selection at a restaurant. He made this statement after commenting that he had consumed six medium plates of food for the aforementioned brunch. While dispensing food and health advice in his post, this influencer did not acknowledge portion size, his ability to purchase the food or eat at a restaurant, or his privilege in sharing his experience with a wider audience. This bold, sometimes conflicting, health advice dispensed by social media influencers sparked the analysis in this chapter, which interrogates the food messages influencers deploy on Instagram. Since studying food and Instagram is a fairly new area of scholarship, we approached this research with an interpretivist lens and a desire to better understand how Instagram influencers communicate about food and health.[1] We consider influencers to be social media users with a "sizeable social network" who can shape their followers' decisions through the content they create. Marijke De Veirman, Veroline Cauberghe, and Liselot Hudders assert that influencers are often "trusted tastemaker[s] in one or several niches."[2]

Exploring the food- and health-related messages these influencers circulate is particularly salient considering the carefully edited, ubiquitous images of beautiful bodies and enticing food porn photos that "show you a particular vision of a food world" on Instagram.[3] The abundance of food imagery, discussion, preparation, and storage, as well as the unrefereed nutrition advice on the platform indicate a significant field for study. The need to better understand influencers is supported by diverse scholarly interpretations of Instagram, including the suggestions of scholars that Instagram can be an effective tool to encourage healthy eating in some users, while facilitating *obsessively* healthy eating (orthorexia nervosa) in others.[4] Understanding influencer messages is a necessary foundation for scholars seeking to study processes of meaning making between influencers and their followers. As evidenced in the following research, we argue Instagram influencers repackage the same food and health discourses experienced in mass media (e.g., magazines, television programs) and interpersonal contexts regarding expertise, diets, and identity. Influencers market themselves as experts whose advice should be followed, while ignoring their privilege and how their identities, and the identities of their followers, are intertwined with food and foodways. Their discourse, via images, text, and hashtags, is similar to diet culture discourse that traditionally pushes rigid eating patterns in the guise of health. Additionally, almost all of their posts are firmly rooted in an individualized perspective of food and health with minimal, if any, discussed connection to a larger food system. Finally, because these influencers talk directly to their audiences, there is little accountability or verification of their claims, which represents a diversion from some previous, nondigital discourse.

Research Design for Understanding Instagram Influencers

Our primary research purpose was to improve understanding of Instagram influencers' messages about food and health. Using an interpretive perspective helped make sense of human experience and communication phenomena in context and provided "thick description" about a relatively unexplored area.[5] We entered the field with an investigative intent as complete observers.[6] From this field position, we were not known or noticed by the influencers—this is an easy role to assume in an online, public environment. While complete observers face limitations such as detachment from the scene, in this case our role allowed us to observe influencers' public messages undetected.

In examining food and health influencers on Instagram, we chose to protect the identities of the influencers we studied. Although all accounts we analyzed were public and could be found with tags such as #cleaneating or #healthyfood, we reflected on the ethics of including specific social media posts that included the influencers' information. We considered such questions as these: Do Instagram users expect their posts to be "permanently" archived in a different medium, such as this text? Do regular users, even if they would be considered an influencer, expect to receive scrutiny? Could including usernames or images of social media users in our writing compromise their reputations? The answers to these questions varied, but we considered these social media posts to be intimately connected to the influencers. In essence, we treated influencers and their posts as human participants and deserving of confidentiality.

Table 9-1. Criteria for Sample Selection

Criteria	Notes
Public account	Private accounts were excluded
Accounts with followers in the Mid-tier (20,000–100,000 users) and Macro (100,000–1 million) range	Micro (5,000–10,000 users) and Mega accounts (+1 million) were excluded
Instagram verification symbol was optional	Some influencers were verified, others were not
Accounts promoted or highlighted a company brand or their own personal goods and/or services in their posts	E.g., meal plans, food preparation, fitness coaching, clothing
Accounts with influencer presence: posting selfies, anecdotes about self	Accounts moderated by multiple users were excluded
Accounts with original user-generated content	Accounts primarily reposting other users' content were excluded
Accounts primarily focused on food	Influencer documents food through text and/or images
Accounts promoted a particular way of eating	E.g., paleo, vegan, carnivore, fasting, ketogenic
Posts between May 30, 2018, and May 30, 2019	Timeframe snapshot of recent activity
Accounts must have been active prior to May 30, 2019	Excluded accounts that were created on the last day of post eligibility to try to rule out fake accounts
Influencers offered advice, information, or explanation about food and eating	Accounts that focused exclusively on recipes were excluded (usually did not include user/influencer in relation to recipe); posts of pets or unrelated to food were excluded
Influencers had to have more users following their accounts in comparison to the number of accounts the influencers were following themselves	Focusing on this ratio helped identify the possibility of influence and reach of Influencer
Influencer mentioned fitness through text and/or pictures	Fitness is an aspect of health. However, posts that were exclusively focused on fitness (e.g., gym photos) with no mention of food were excluded in order to keep study focused and manage sample size

Through criterion sampling, we selected twenty-two influencer accounts for analysis.[7] Table 9-1 lists the criteria used in sampling, such as timeframe of active accounts, network size, original content, and diet promotion, as well as exclusionary criteria.[8] We selected these criteria within a framework of understanding how Instagram works, the focus of our research question, and practical measures to limit the sample to a manageable size.

Our sample of twenty-two influencers included thirteen women and nine men who, to the best of our knowledge, all cisgender individuals. Based on physical appearance, the majority of the influencers were white passing—with only four influencers presenting as possibly Asian, Middle Eastern, or undetermined—and most were likely in their early thirties or younger. Reading them as white is noteworthy, with news agencies, bloggers, and consumers questioning why influencers tend be "thin, white, able-bodied, [and] 20-something."[9] The influencers appeared to be living in Canada, the United States, the United Kingdom, and other European countries. There were seven mid-tier accounts and fourteen macro accounts in the sample, with individual posts selected for analysis.

We analyzed the data using a constant-comparative method.[10] The data were initially read to identify food and health messages expressed by Instagram influencers in their posts. We open-coded the posts, including images, accompanying text, and relevant hashtags. Given the assumed role of our sample of influencers as food and/or health educators, many of their posts contained long, explanatory captions, often with links to products, other influencers, or their own websites. This iterative process of analysis allowed us to collect influencers' posts to identify emerging themes and then to review and compare data. Eventually, we collected and analyzed more influencer posts and refined themes.[11] We documented our own elaborate reflections throughout the observation and field-note process, and we later incorporated these commentaries into our coding.[12] We then reconstructed the data by assessing the connections and context among categories through axial coding.[13] This process continued until we reached theoretical saturation, culminating in a total of 213 posts analyzed.[14] The themes that emerged revolved around gender, race, class, and individualism, as well as message incongruity, diet culture/food freedom, and expertise.

Gendered Influencer Performance

There is the risk of assigning gendered essentialism to their respective online presences, or assuming anything about motivation or intent, but many clear patterns nonetheless emerged from the collection of artifacts along gendered lines. Compared to the men, the women in our sample presented a more curated aesthetic and posted more photos of themselves. When the women appeared in the photos, they had neatly styled hair and made-up faces, utilized flattering lighting, and wore well-fitting, stylish clothes. Though this curation certainly required effort, this labor was concealed by the influencers so that it did not compromise the apparent effortlessness of the presentation—makeup is visible but natural looking, for example. The processes of developing a curated effortlessness mirror the trope of the archetypal domestic goddess's "calibration" on her food blog.[15] These visual rules applied even in situations in which the influencers were conveying the most casual of circumstances and settings, like posing in athletic clothing or photographing themselves with an unmade bed in the background. In one post, a woman influencer stands in her kitchen in her underwear. Despite the casualness and intimacy of the outfit, she sports perfectly styled hair and makeup, flawless, hairless skin, and holds a colorful, well-arranged salad. Other women influencers cultivated a consistent aesthetic by always posing in front of the same wall or by color-coordinating their clothing and the food they were holding.

When the women shared images of food, these photos were consistent with scholarly understandings of feminized food, such as sweets and salads.[16] Women presented their meals on round dishes or in round bowls and attended to visual appeal for the viewer by varying and saturating the color palettes of the foods. Sweets (modified to fit influencer-determined definitions of "health," such as chickpea peanut butter "cookie dough") were pictured dripping with sauce or dusted with sprinkles. By reading these images through scholar Tisha Dejmanee's lens, we see that even a food photo without a human subject "metaphorically evokes the female body" through oozing and photo composition, while "sweet food items simultaneously render the sexual female body innocuous."[17]

In contrast, when men posted the rare photos of themselves, they shared images that attempted to convey spontaneity, adventurousness, or authenticity. While women invested energy into creating an appearance of effortlessness, men embraced a (perhaps equally curated) sloppiness, consistent with Wesley Buerkle's findings about heteromasculine fortification.[18] In our study, similar to Buerkle's research, these photos were often less posed, taken outside or during an activity such as snowboarding, or showed the men with ungroomed hair or facial hair. Unlike the women, men were shown eating in restaurants and occasionally consuming alcohol. The men influencers mostly posted infographic-style, instructional images of food that they seemed to have created themselves. These images of food items were presented in hard-lined, box grids that read as masculine and contrasted with the softer aesthetic of the women's posts. In other posts, men also added aggressive text overlay to the images for explanation, using capitalization, bolded fonts, or striking colors for emphasis. The men were more likely to present their food in square or rectangular containers, as opposed to the round bowls and plates of the women, and the men's food contained far more animal protein and higher fat content. These aesthetic conventions reflect previous scholarship on how and why different design elements came to be coded as masculine or feminine.[19] While the women conveyed an "effortless" but clearly rigid attitude toward food preparation, ingredients, and portion size (that, again, concealed the likely extensive invisible labor the follower does not see), posts from the men emphasized flexibility in portion sizes and "breaking the rules."

A final trend from the collection of men influencer posts was a discursive pattern of lambasting. In the language from their captions and the text overlaid onto their photos, the men frequently ventured into outright mocking of other diets, foods, and schools of nutrition advice. They derided the messages and platforms used by other health influencers, while perpetuating the narratives they claimed to critique. The men used curse words, words in all capital letters, and condescension rooted in their claimed knowledge of unspecified evidence-based research to articulate their messages. One caption included this rebuke: "There is no context anymore. Not for the individual who seeks rational guidance on a very simple nutritional goal. Instead they are faced with an exhaustion of irrelevant fear mongering and a bottomless pit of disappointing clusterfuckery—resulting in the curtailment of their goals." As noted in previous scholarship on hegemonic masculinity in dieting, in these lines the influencer discounts the role of emotions, good or bad, in relationships with food and juxtaposed these "silly" emotions with "objective" nutrition science.[20]

One striking attribute common to the posts of both women and men is the absence of any indication of the intersectionality of their gender performance, race, class, and/or privilege. Examining what is absent in these self-curated, gendered posts is imperative.

Privileged Discourses: Race and Class

The majority of the influencers in our sample were white passing, yet none of the influencers engaged with race or color in any explicit way; they did not acknowledge their race or color, or communicate about how that may inform their perspective on food and health. Unfortunately, this is consistent with patterns unique to white culture, especially in the United States, of race privilege and the standpoint in which they view themselves and society.[21] Judith Martin and Thomas Nakayama assert that "white means rarely or never having to think about it."[22] This pervasive whiteness, along with the presumed universal appeal of the influencers' advice, reproduces on Instagram the same problematic, racialized food and health discourses that scholars have previously examined outside the digital realm.[23] While there is certainly a community of food and health influencers of color on Instagram, only a few met the criteria for inclusion in this research. Additionally, though many influencers posted about food or drink items that originated within specific cultural foodways (e.g., kombucha, quinoa), influencers avoided engaging with the items' origins and in effect colonized them to fit their purposes.[24] One post referenced "asian food" (lowercased as in the original) as a good choice for "Eating out for fat loss," and another referenced an influencer's trip to an Indian buffet for lunch as evidence of her food freedom.[25] In these instances, the food in question was not discussed for any cultural significance but rather presented as a means to achieve the influencer's personal health goals. This interpretation of the influencers' posts is in conversation with broader questions about contemporary culinary appropriation.[26]

Like the unacknowledged whiteness among the sample of influencers and their posts, a level of implicit class privilege permeated the posts as well. Beyond sharing promotional codes or links to coupons for branded items, the influencers do not address the fact that food costs money. The influencers did not detail the costs of their meals (either money or time spent), discuss budget-conscious alternatives for their lower-income followers, or mention receiving products for free in exchange for promoting them on their platform. Posts showcased high-quality, expensive, and hard-to-find ingredients and cooking equipment, and included claims that eating healthy is "not complicated!" if you just set aside a few hours on the weekend to plan, grocery shop, and cook. Consistent with Julie Parsons's observations about convenience, class, and healthy family foodways, the curated online presence of many influencers appeared to indicate that they were often home during the day and able to cook lunch for themselves, or if they worked outside of the home they had time to pack an appropriate lunch and a place to store it safely at work.[27] Class privilege was inherent in the Instagram presence of the influencers through their discourses of individual choice and food freedom.

Individualistic Messages

Influencers in this sample perpetuated a food narrative that isolated their personal food choices from the broader food system. With few exceptions, such as a post from one male influencer mocking the criticism that eating meat is "murdering animals and killing the planet!!" or vague advice from another influencer to "source quality meat from local farmers," the influencers did not address the production side of their food choices. Many influencers advocated for a vegan diet while others endorsed the animal protein–rich keto diet; neither set of influencers promoted the respective diet for reasons other than individual health. Even with a diet as political as veganism, the influencers avoided altogether engaging with potential environmental or animal welfare motivations for eschewing animal products.[28] One influencer encouraged consumption of palm oil, even though its production is widely known to be ecologically destructive.[29] Recommendations abounded to eat more avocadoes, despite how environmentally taxing they are to produce.[30] These discourses presented food as nothing more than a means to achieve particular individual, health, wellness, or fitness goals.

Additionally, while there were occasional nods to the cultural significance of food, such as in the rituals of going out to eat or celebrating holidays, even these facets of the broader food system were greatly downplayed. One influencer stated repeatedly in a caption "guys, it's just food," and though this mantra was a response to her own struggles with disordered eating, saying that "it's just food" serves to minimize the extensive and complicated roles food plays in people's lives. In one post, she also sported a shirt that read "My plate. My business."

This is particularly ironic given that her Instagram presence was built on the constant sharing of photos and descriptions of her food.

Incongruence in Influencer Messages

A sense of incongruity pervaded the collection of material we studied. In general, there was an opacity to the influencers' advice. They would express a stance on some food or health topic that seemed straightforward and then backpedal in a way that complicated or potentially negated the advice. For example, after discussing in a photo caption why she was adjusting her diet in order to lose weight, one influencer immediately added in parentheses, "(I'm not saying we as a society should look a certain way 'just for the summer' but I have my own personal goals.)" This post complicated and contradicted the nutrition advice she provided and isolated food and health choices from broader societal forces. Furthermore, it provided her plausible deniability regarding the weight loss message, attempting to absolve her of any responsibility for her post and denying her own role in shaping culture as an influencer with more than forty thousand followers.

Influencers also expressed contradictions as they emphasized "whole foods" or "clean foods" and simultaneously promoted highly processed protein powders, meal replacement bars, and other supplements in the name of, for example, "meeting macros."[31] Finally, most influencers, even those whose words or photos communicated an inflexibility in their nutrition advice, avoided explicitly telling their followers *not* to eat a particular food. One woman influencer posted a photo that was made of three side-by-side images of herself, holding a different breakfast option in each. Though the first two were labeled "a healthy option" and "also a healthy option," the third was labeled "not the best option" rather than something more concrete like "an unhealthy option." The second "healthy option" was not food at all but an empty plate representing "intermittent fasting." While these discursive negotiations may be a reflection of the influencers' desire to not lose followers, they also served to confuse and complicate their messages. Beyond these examples of incongruity that permeated the influencers' messages, we also observed two notable types of contradictions in their online presences discussed below.

Diet Culture Freedom versus Food Rules

At first glance, it appeared that most of the influencers were offering their followers a new path toward health and wellness, one that eschewed traditional diet advice characterized by restraint and anxiety in favor of food freedom. The influencers acknowledged the failures of past dieting guidance, which they attributed to myriad, contradicting reasons, and promised something better to those following their suggestions. Many of them explicitly invoked "diet culture" as the enemy of one's physical and mental well-being, and some even gave "diet culture" human pronouns when referencing it in their captions. In a post that, at the time of our archiving, garnered over twenty thousand likes, one influencer appeared to explicitly address the contradictions of diet culture. The photo showed a three-by-three grid of nine food and drink images with corresponding critical captions representing what various diets might have to say about each image. The caption reads:

> In 2019, if there was a seminar covering nutrition advice for optimal health, it would require 842 PowerPoint slides in font 3 and a Martian to deliver the vocal. Because everything we see or hear is a contradiction. As such, we are creating a venomous dieting culture full of ridicule, self-righteousness and confusion. We have no regulations to expose lies from truth. And we have lost our composure.

Despite this seemingly liberating message, this particular influencer himself offered abundant advice about food and nutrition, and like the woman influencer mentioned earlier, appeared oblivious to the role that his Instagram presence played in perpetuating the diet culture he claimed to so vehemently reject. His criticism of the "ridicule, self-righteousness and confusion" of diet culture was especially incongruent given that we found his language and tone to be among the most abrasive and harsh in our sample.

Many influencers framed the alternative to diet culture as food freedom. One influencer who often referenced her personal achievement of food freedom stated that she arrived there by "IGNORING ALL THE ISH I 'THOUGHT' I KNEW ABOUT NUTRITION" (capitalized as in the original). In a different post, she addressed misconceptions her followers may have about what defines food freedom, writing in the caption that food freedom is "not about losing all control . . . it's about building a happy and healthy relationship with food that allows you to live your best life."

Another influencer proclaimed in a photo caption, "don't let anyone say you can't have any kind of food that you want," and then proceeded to describe exactly why the vegan, gluten-free, vegetable-based cookie she was promoting was a healthier cookie option than others. In yet another post, this same influencer posed provocatively in her underwear while holding a doughnut (bite taken out, but no actual eating shown in any of the three photos), and began her caption, "Me, dreaming of the day we can all live in doughnut land without caring whether it's 'healthy' or not!" The rest of the caption was a confounding back and forth that expressed the sentiment that, while there are no "good" or "bad," foods, one should still eat mostly "whole" and "natural" foods . . . but also not deprive oneself of favorite foods.

When considering the idea of food freedom and what influencers are and are not advocating, it is necessary to revisit the idea of race, class, and privilege. As noted before, here again in this context, influencers abstain from expressing any indication that they recognize that class or privilege may complicate one's food freedom. For example, any follower utilizing the Special Supplemental Nutrition Program for Women, Infants, and Children (WIC), may feel their "freedom" to be curtailed.[32]

While the goal of achieving food freedom and the accompanying liberation from guilt and anxiety-riddled eating is admirable, in the food freedom discourse we found tension and contradiction. Any influencers who fundamentally depend on disseminating food and nutrition advice, while documenting and describing their own meals, will inherently conflict with the notion of food freedom.

Credentials versus Lived Experience

A second major contradiction we observed across the sample of influencers was in the tension between nutrition advice stemming from the influencers' formal professional credentials or from the self-assigned expertise of the influencers' lived experience. Of our twenty-two influencers, ten possessed some sort of formal, relevant, educational credentials. These credentials varied in rigor and ranged from "student of naturopathic medicine" to registered dietician, masters-level exercise physiologist, "National Academy of Sports Medicine Certified Fitness Nutrition Specialist," doctorate-level nutritionist, and medical doctor. We found that influencers with formal credentials broadcasted these in their Instagram bios and often listed their degrees (e.g., MS, RD, PhD) in their Instagram handle or as part of their official name on their profiles.[33]

A trend that spanned the group of influencers was many individuals' histories of disordered eating. At least eight influencers from both the credentialed and lived-experiences camps had a history of disordered eating of some sort that they explicitly disclosed on Instagram (including orthorexia, anorexia, binge eating, food addiction, exercise addiction, and overeating). This shared experience and background certainly informed their promotion of a quest for food freedom. While scholarship has substantiated the value of social media in supporting recovery from eating disorders, these influencers' use of their personal struggles with disordered eating as proof of their expertise and authority to provide advice was noteworthy.[34] Several influencers claimed that they had fully "recovered" from their disordered eating, insinuating through these claims that, first, one *can* fully recover from an eating disorder, and second, they are qualified to show their followers how to do the same.

The tensions concerning who on Instagram is allowed to claim expertise surfaced throughout the discourse as well. There was wide variation among the influencers' epistemologies of health and corresponding language. Some influencers, mostly men, cited empirical research studies in their captions to support their nutrition advice and health claims. Others, mostly women, cultivated an overall more intimate Instagram presence and relied heavily on personal anecdotes and stories of their own health journeys, such as when they engaged in food restriction and the progress they have made. In one caption, a man influencer created a sort of straw man who was giving unsolicited diet advice, such as "bacon is 'fattening' because it is mildly processed," and then went on to aggressively criticize that fabricated perspective. He claimed that media and diet culture have replaced "evidence-based science carried out in unbiased, controlled environments" where nutrition is concerned. His claims bely the scientific reality that it is impossible for any research dealing with humans to be "unbiased" or completely "controlled;" this influencer also did not provide reasons for why his particular voice was a trustworthy source of information when others were not.[35] While men influencers often juxtaposed science (masculine) and emotion (feminine) as a method of rejecting the impact of emotion on food choices, women attempted more frequently to at least acknowledge that eating can be deeply emotional. Still, with this acknowledgment, they also claimed that they themselves had been liberated from emotional eating, and that someday the follower could be, too.

The influencers' use of extensive hashtags to connect their posts to the broader health, wellness, and food communities on Instagram was also contradictory. It was common for a single post to carry twenty to thirty unique hashtags. Though the use of hashtags is not intrinsically good or bad, the combination of hashtags often confused or opposed the very advice given in the post, and the hashtags tended to reproduce the same problematic associations with disordered eating so many of the influencers claimed to reject. For example, in an archetypal list of twenty-five tags that accompanied one woman influencer's post about the healthiest way to eat yogurt with granola for breakfast, she included #eatingwell, #eatwellbewell, #bodypositive, #eatingdisorderrecovery, #flexibleeating, #nondietapproach, #wholefoods, #dietculture, #antidiet, #mindfuleating, #nutritiontip, and #nutritioncoaching. There also were instances in which influencers whose expertise was rooted in their own struggles with disordered eating included tags such as #weightloss, #ketoweightlossjourney, or #getfit into their posts, effectively reproducing damaging narratives about nutrition, health, and weight through this digital conversation.

Repackaging Diet Culture in Influencer Discourse

Close examination of influencer discourses on food, eating, and health on Instagram revealed the intersections of gender, race, privilege, individualism, and contradictory claims concerning food freedom and expertise. Like other forms of social media, Instagram gives users a way to directly communicate and interact with others on a larger scale than face-to-face communication without being accountable to any editorial oversight or fact-checking from professional media establishments. However, Instagram and other new media can be seen as extending or complementing existing media, lending support to the emergent themes in this research such as gender performance in food discourse.[36]

Influencer discourse surrounding food and eating on Instagram reinforced performances of gender, race, and class wherein those with privilege present their experience as the most important and what followers should do. In some cases, the discourse was also complicated by the influencers' experience with disordered eating, which they believed lent them more credibility. Influencers continued to promote "a healthy eating discourse that reframes dietary restrictions as positive choices, while maintaining an emphasis on body discipline, expert knowledge, and self-control."[37] Influencers in this sample promised food freedom and positivity, but in actuality the discourse adhered to a very familiar diet culture that pushes food rules disguised in a false positivity. Both men and women influencers produced messages in their text, pictures, and use of hashtags encouraging acceptance of their expertise and what they deemed to be the correct way to engage with food. These messages of restriction and rule-following were repackaged as healthy choices and food freedom being delivered by "experts" for Instagram followers to consume.

While influencers reproduced broad societal themes of gendered and privileged food discourses and diet culture, they also took this problematic discourse and rebranded it for the larger public by inviting participation by and engagement from a growing following. They also had the added burden of being concerned with how food looks and how to keep their followers engaged. Many of the influencers gave a surface-level impression that meal preparation and creating a perfect meal were effortless. Future studies in this area should include followers' comments and the influencers' interaction with these messages.

Digital communication in these Instagram circles continues to echo diet and wellness discourses in other forms of media, as well as nondigital realms of communication. Many messages encouraged followers to adhere to rules the influencers promoted about what, when, and how much to eat. Following health recommendations from influencers, regardless of their massive following on Instagram, could be dangerous for physical, emotional, and psychological well-being. Consider contradictory posts, such as "this is how you eat clean, you wash your hands before eating any food you F*cking well want." From this analysis, there were indeed more influencers replicating destructive dichotomies that support diet-culture discourse than influencers supporting the dismantling of diet culture.

Notes

We thank Carina Coleman for her assistance in data collection and for her insight during preliminary analysis.

1. Yvonna Lincoln, Susan Lynham, and Egon Guba, "Paradigmatic Controversies, Contradictions, and Emerging Confluences, Revisited," in *Handbook of Qualitative Research*, ed. Norman Denzin and Yvonna Lincoln (Thousand Oaks, CA: Sage, 2011), 97–128.

2. Marijke De Veirman, Veroline Cauberghe, and Liselot Hudders, "Marketing through Instagram Influencers: The Impact of Number of Followers and Product Divergence on Brand Attitude," *International Journal of Advertising* 36, no. 5 (2017): 798.

3. Willa Zhen, *Food Studies: A Hands-on Guide* (London: Bloomsbury Academic, 2019), 28.

4. Chia-Fang Chung, Elena Agapie, Jessica Schroeder, Sonali Mishra, James Fogarty, and Sean A. Munson, "When Personal Tracking Becomes Social: Examining the Use of Instagram for Healthy Eating," in *Proceedings of the 2017 CHI Conference on Human Factors in Computing Systems* (2017), https//doi.org/10.1145/3025453.3025747, 1681; Pixie Turner and Carmen Lefevre, "Instagram Use Is Linked to Increased Symptoms of Orthorexia Nervosa," *Eating and Weight Disorders-Studies on Anorexia, Bulimia and Obesity* 22, no. 2 (2017): 280–82.

5. Clifford Geertz, "Thick Description: Toward an Interpretive Theory of Culture," In *The Interpretation of Cultures* (New York: Basic Books, 1973), 3.

6. Raymond Gold, "Roles in Sociological Field Observations," *Social Forces* 36, no. 3 (1958): 218.

7. Thomas Lindlof and Bryan Taylor, *Qualitative Communication Research Methods* (Los Angeles: Sage, 2019), 145–46.

8. Harshita Agrawal, "The Rise of Nano Influencers: How Many Followers Do You Need to Become an Instagram Influencer?," *Hype-Journal*, March 20, 2019, https://hypeauditor.com/blog/the-rise-of-nano-influencers-how-many-followers -do-you-need-to-become-an-instagram-influencer/.

9. Megan Graham, "Instagram Influencers Are Often White, and Now the Brands That Pay Them Are Getting Pushback," CNBC, August 29, 2019, www.cnbc.com.

10. Barney Glaser and Anselm Strauss, *The Discovery of Grounded Theory: Strategies for Qualitative Research* (Chicago: Aldine, 1967), 105.

11. Ibid.

12. Robert Emerson, Rachel Fretz, and Linda Shaw, *Writing Ethnographic Fieldnotes* (Chicago: University of Chicago Press, 1995).

13. Anselm Strauss and Juliet Corbin, *Basics of Qualitative Research* (Beverly Hills: Sage, 1990) 96.

14. Glaser and Strauss, *Discovery of Grounded Theory*, 112; Strauss and Corbin, *Basics of Qualitative Research*, 212; Lindlof and Taylor, *Qualitative Communication Research Methods*, 329.

15. Alexandra Rodney, Sarah Cappeliez, Merin Oleschuk, and Josée Johnston,

"The Online Domestic Goddess: An Analysis of Food Blog Femininities," *Food, Culture and Society* 20, no. 4 (2017): 695.

16. Kate Cairns and Josee Johnston, *Food and Femininity* (New York: Bloomsbury, 2015b).

17. Tisha Dejmanee, "'Food Porn' as Postfeminist Play: Digital Femininity and the Female Body on Food Blogs," *Television and New Media* 17, no. 5 (2016): 436, 442.

18. C. Wesley Buerkle, "Metrosexuality Can Stuff It: Beef Consumption as (Heteromasculine) Fortification," *Text and Performance Quarterly* 29, no. 1 (2009): 88–90.

19. Miriam van Tillburg, Theo Lieven, Andreas Hermann, and Claudia Townsend, "Beyond 'Pink It and Shrink It' Perceived Product Gender, Aesthetics, and Product Evaluation," *Psychology and Marketing* 32, no. 4 (2015): 423–24.

20. Anna Mallyon, Mary Holmes, John Coveney, and Maria Zadoroznyj, "I'm Not Dieting, 'I'm Doing it for Science'": Masculinities and the Experience of Dieting," *Health Sociology Review* 19, no. 3 (2010): 338–40.

21. Ruth Frankenburg, *White Women, Race Matters: The Social Construction of Whiteness* (Minneapolis: University of Minnesota Press).

22. Judith N. Martin and Thomas K. Nakayama, "Identity and Intercultural Communication," in *Experiencing Intercultural Communication: An Introduction* (New York: McGraw-Hill, 2011), 90–133.

23. A. Breeze Harper, "Vegans of Color, Racialized Embodiment, and Problematics of the 'Exotic,'" in *Cultivating Food Justice: Race, Class, and Sustainability*, ed. Alison Hope Alkon and Julian Agyeman, 221–38 (Cambridge, MA: MIT Press, 2011); Mary Igenoza, "Race, Femininity, and Food: Femininity and the Racialization of Health and Dieting," *International Review of Social Research* 7, no. 2 (2017): 109–18.

24. Ken Albala, "Cultural Appropriation, Authenticity, and Gastronomic Colonialism," *Ken Albala's Food Rant* (blog), January 17, 2019, http://kenalbala.blogspot.com/2019/01/cultural-appropriation-authenticity-and.html.

25. "Food freedom" is often presented as the antithesis of "diet culture" and describes a state a person can theoretically achieve by eliminating rules, weight loss goals, or morality from their relationship with eating.

26. Albala, "Cultural Appropriation."

27. Julie Parsons, "When Convenient Is Inconvenient: 'Healthy' Family Foodways and the Persistent Intersectionalities of Gender and Class," *Journal of Gender Studies* 25, no. 4 (2016): 382–85.

28. Dario Martinelli and Aušra Berkmanienė, "The Politics and the Demographics of Veganism: Notes for a Critical Analysis," *International Journal for the Semiotics of Law* 31 (2018): 501–30; Deidre Wicks, "Humans, Food and Other Animals: The Vegetarian Option," in *A Sociology of Food and Nutrition: The Social Appetite*, 3rd ed., ed. John Germov and Lauren Williams, 281–306 (South Melbourne, Australia: Oxford University Press, 2008).

29. Kanokwan Saswattecha, Carolien Kroeze, Warit Jawjit, and Lars Hein, "Assessing the Environmental Impact of Plam Oil Produced in Thailand," *Journal of Cleaner Production* 100, no. 1 (2015): 150–69.

30. Honor May Eldridge, "Why Our Love for Avocados Is Not Sustainable," *Farming, Food and Culture*, January 31, 2020, https://sustainablefoodtrust.org/articles/why-our-love-for-avocados-is-not-sustainable/; Mark Stevenson, "The Worlds' Hunger for Avocados is Having a Devastating Effect on Mexico," Business Insider, November 1, 2016, www.businessinsider.com/ap-mexico-deforestation-for-avocados-much-higher-than-thought-2016-10.

31. "Macros" is diet slang for macronutrients: fat, protein, carbohydrates.

32. U.S. Department of Agriculture Food and Nutrition Service, "Special Supplemental Nutrition Program for Women, Infants, and Children (WIC)," accessed November 25, 2020, www.fns.usda.gov/wic.

33. We drew conclusions about formal educational experience and credentials from what was included in the Instagram profile, or easily accessible by clicking through a link to a personal website listed in the Instagram bio. The remaining twelve influencers may have also possessed relevant educational experience or credentials, but that information could not be found via the process just outlined.

34. Sarah Kendal, Sue Kirk, Rebecca Elvey, Roger Catchpole, and Steven Pryjma-chuk, "How a Moderated Online Discussion Forum Facilitates Support for Young People with Eating Disorders," *Health Expectations* 20, no. 1 (2017): 98–111; Abby McCormack, "Individuals with Eating Disorders and the Use of Online Support Groups as a Form of Social Support," *CIN: Computers, Informatics, Nursing* 28, no. 1 (2010): 12–19.

35. Charlotte Biltekoff, "Critical Nutrition Studies," in *The Oxford Handbook of Food History*, ed. Jeffrey Pilcher (New York: Oxford University Press, 2012), 173.

36. Signe Rousseau, *Food and Social Media: You Are What You Tweet* (Lanham, MD: AltaMira, 2012).

37. Kate Cairns and Josee Johnston, "Choosing Health: Embodied Neoliberalism, Postfeminism, and the 'Do-Diet,'" *Theory and Society* 44, no. 2 (2015a): 154.

CHAPTER 10

Meet Your Meat!

How Australian Livestock Producers Use Instagram to Promote "Happy Meat"

EMILY BUDDLE

Did my meat live a happy life?

The quotation that follows emerged in an interview that I conducted as part of my PhD research exploring Australian meat consumers' understanding of farm animal welfare.[1] This interview inspired the analysis presented in this chapter about how some Australian livestock producers are using Instagram to highlight their methods for producing what I call happy meat. The quotation, together with this chapter's analysis, demonstrate how and why livestock producers now commonly use social media, particularly Instagram, to share information about meat production, especially against the backdrop of popular representations of industrialized livestock production and mounting public concerns for farm animal welfare.

> I don't really want to support the process of factory farming. I think it is horrific. We don't really have the right to be treating another sentient being like that. I choose to eat meat so I try to make as many good choices around that as I possibly can. . . . We started going to the farmers' market and just by chance stumbled across this lovely producer. I had given up red meat at that stage and I said I am not really keen on this, but my mum was buying some [meat], so I started chatting to the actual farmer and he explained and showed me photos. I actually follow him on Instagram, and he posts everyday about how his cows live and they're literally out in beautiful paddocks, they have a gorgeous dam, they've got gum trees, they have a really beautiful life. I tend to only buy beef through that one supplier because I know they have a good life.

This chapter describes and analyzes the types of images that happy-meat producers share on Instagram and how they assist in creating the reassuring narratives that accompany happy-meat products. The use of imagery is a powerful way to enhance transparency with meat consumers as it links the desire to know that their meat is ethical with evidence for such claims by allowing them to see how the animals are raised using their smartphones.[2] The functionality of Instagram also affords producers the ability to instantly edit and share their images alongside text captions that are used to enhance their narratives. However, as documented in this analysis, happy-meat producers do not share information about some of the more conflictual and increasingly controversial issues that they face, particularly practices associated with slaughter. This absence raises questions about the true level of openness and transparency that these Instagram accounts actually provide. My analysis suggests that, due to the popularity of Instagram in Australia, the platform can serve as an ideal venue for producers of happy meat to increase their transparency by sharing bucolic presentations of their production methods in a cost-effective way. However, the decisions farmers make about what to include and exclude on their feeds also stake out the limits of this visibility.

Background

The "what's for dinner?" question has been complicated in recent decades by an increasing interest from consumers in how food transitions from paddock to plate.[3] Whether consumers are devoted to eating meat; exploring ways in which to reduce their meat consumption for ethical, health, or environmental reasons; or abstaining from meat altogether, one recurring concern amongst many groups is how livestock is treated within the meat value chain. Answers to the problem of what to eat have become less about what is available and more about sourcing food that aligns with one's values, with some consumers questioning the origins of their food and how it was produced, or whether a particular type of food should be consumed at all.[4] Questions about ethical and sustainable meat production, and the role of meat in our diets more generally, have fueled one of the most heated ethical discussions of the twenty-first century to date as a result of increasing attention toward animal welfare, sustainability, environmental footprint, plant-based protein products, and personal health.

Meat consumption has become normalized as a daily staple in high-income countries. Australia's meat consumption remains among the highest in the world. In the relatively short period since European settlement, Australians have been among the world's largest per-capita meat consumers, consuming approximately 220 pounds per capita in 2018.[5] However, many Australian consumers are seeking to reduce their meat consumption, with two and a half million Australians reporting that they consume completely or nearly vegetarian diets.[6] Lenka Malek, Wendy Umberger, and Ellen Goddard suggest that concerns for health and animal welfare are the most common reasons motivating meat avoidance in Australia, including among those who have not been lifelong vegetarians.[7] In addition to reducing meat consumption, many consumers seek meat products accompanied by ethical claims such as free-range chicken or grass-fed beef.[8] Consumers believe that these types of meat have been produced under higher welfare standards because animals lived what are perceived to be "happier lives" compared to animals raised in intensive production systems.[9] Concerns about cage egg production or the use of sow stalls in piggeries are some prominent examples that made recent headlines in Australia, particularly due to the perceived negative impacts that these farming systems have on animals' quality of life.[10]

In part due to the lack of transparency, intensifying media attention, and a growing amount of concern for animal well-being in Australia, meat producers have increasingly become targets of animal welfare activism in recent years. Producers have experienced a rise in trespass on farming properties and rallies have been held in almost every capital city to protest the use of animals in agricultural production. The activist organization Aussie Farms has been particularly prominent in the animal rights space and is known for its publication of an online map listing the locations and details of various farmers and supply chain businesses across Australia and for the group's encouragement of activists to visit these farms in protest.[11] Social media has also become a primary platform for animal-rights activists to communicate with one another and promote their cause to a wider audience.[12] As a result of this expanded media attention and activism surrounding animal welfare, agricultural advocacy bodies, such as the National Farmers Federation, encourage Australian livestock producers to "share their stories" as a means to increase transparency within the industry.[13] Some people involved in agriculture are turning to social media to bridge the supposed urban-rural divide in Australian agriculture.[14] This turn to sharing stories coincides with a growing number of consumers seeking extrinsic information from credible sources to be reassured about the lives lived by their meat sources.[15] In response, livestock producers have begun to adopt social media to share their stories, as it enables users to connect with or find favorable content from actors they regard as trustworthy such as farmers. This assists farmers in building their legitimacy and counteracting the critiques of activists.[16] Social media also enables producers to embrace the benefits of connectivity and visibility to increase transparency.[17] As a result, some meat producers are contributing to the broader adoption of social media by various types of food networks to facilitate transparency of the food system and provide their customers with insights into how they produce meat.[18]

One notable group of livestock producers who have adopted social media to share their story are what Frédéric Leroy and Istvan Praet describe as "happy-meat" producers.[19] Happy meat is generally defined as meat products that are sold with a story—that is, meat that comes from smaller-scale producers who sell not only a product but also reassuring narratives about how that product came to be. Happy-meat narratives emphasize the relationship between humans and farm animals, which "entails that the animal partner indeed lives a satisfactory life and that the human partner feels reassured about it."[20] Indeed, as people continue to be more interested in how their food is produced, the popularity of happy meat has increased.[21] Happy meat is described by Leroy and Praet as coming from animals that have lived a "wholesome life," enjoying their natural diets and environments alongside their responsible and loving farmers.[22] By analyzing images shared on Instagram by Australian happy-meat producers, I highlight how these producers attempt to increase transparency by constructing narratives of how their animals live wholesome idyllic lives, yet they refrain from sharing details of the animals' deaths.

Methods

In order to identify the images and captions shared by happy-meat producers, I conducted an initial exploration of Instagram content in order to identify a set of accounts to be used for this analysis. As Lev Manovich describes, an initial observation and description phase also allows the researcher to rely on her experiences with the platform to explore the way in which images are presented, noting observed patterns from which to form a hypothesis.[23] This preliminary analysis resulted in identification of ten Instagram accounts that use the platform to promote their production of "happy meat" (based on Leroy and Praet's definition) in Australia.[24] I used purposeful sampling to ensure that some producers for each of the dominant meats consumed in Australia (chicken, beef, pork, and lamb) were included in the analysis to ensure I captured any nuances resulting from the different types of animals raised for meat. I collected images that were posted between January 1 and June 30, 2019, as this six-month period captured enough data to reach saturation during analysis.[25] I collected the images and captions posted on these accounts by taking a screenshot on a smartphone for each posting. I printed each screenshot, then used thematic analysis via inductive coding to allow the themes to emerge organically from the content.[26] I analyzed the image and caption as one unit; although as the truism claims an image is worth a thousand words, the use of a caption on Instagram is common to help the content creator provide context and direct how one should read or interpret the image, and hence is critical for this type of analysis. The use of captions was also an important part of the analysis, as captions allow producers to add richness to the narratives they construct about happy-meat production by describing what they are trying to portray in the image. The overall approach to the analysis allowed for a typology to be developed, so I could identify similarities and differences in the narratives appearing on different Instagram accounts.

This approach was not designed to be a comprehensive analysis of all Australian happy-meat producers. Rather, it involved selective identification of active Instagram users—defined by account holders having shared content at least once during the month that data were collected—who use Instagram as a means to communicate about the production of happy meat. The analysis does not aim to be representative but instead seeks to determine and explore commonalities among the types of images that Australian happy-meat producers use to construct their narratives on Instagram as a publicly available forum. Many Australian farming businesses are smaller family-owned enterprises; therefore it is reasonable to assume that a member of the family involved in the business is sharing these images on Instagram, as opposed to a paid social media manager doing the posting. Due to the recent activist backlash experienced by Australian livestock producers, I have anonymized any identifying information from the accounts used in this analysis: thus the account handles and any images or quotes from these accounts are not included in the results presented. My focus here is on how producers used Instagram, rather than how consumers perceived such images. This area remains ripe for future research, particularly using a mixed-methods approach to capture the dynamics between Instagram posts and messaging, and between producers and consumers.

Meet your Meat!

The vast majority of Australian consumers do not live near sites of food production, resulting in what is often described as an urban-rural divide.[27] Many of those who work in food production claim that this distance is the reason for mounting concerns about how food is produced and, in this case, about the ways in which animals are raised for meat. Social media sites such as Instagram may assist consumers who want to know more about their food by helping to reduce the literal and figurative distance between producers and consumers. As detailed in the analysis below, happy-meat producers typically follow a similar set of strategies for sharing images of their livestock animals on Instagram, so that consumers are able to meet their meat virtually. The images shared by producers often focus on the environment in which the animals are raised, with the animals as the main focus of many of the images in order to highlight the "happy life" that the animal experienced before the time of its death. The posts also refer to the animals by name, with captions often describing their individual personalities. The images tend to emphasize the animal breed, the relationship between the animals and the farmer, and the quality of the resulting meat product.

For the happy-meat producer posts that I studied, sharing images of the environment in which their animals live was a common way to provide reassurance to their consumers about the quality of life that these animals experience. These Instagram accounts frequently share images of idyllic, rolling green landscapes and picturesque sunrises or sunsets with animals grazing freely. For example, one producer shared a scenic image of a lush green pasture with tall gum trees in the backdrop flanked by the setting sun, describing the paddock as "a little bit of heaven." All of the farmers included in this study also identified as free-range, grass-fed, and/or organic producers either through their use of hashtags or descriptions of these husbandry practices in their bios. In my previous research, Australian meat consumers described their preference for meat products grown using free-range or grass-fed methods of production, which are more closely aligned to what they consider to be "normal" methods of farming thought to be better for the animal due to a more "natural" quality of life.[28] What Australians consider to be "normal" methods of farming are strongly associated with notions of the "rural idyll," or romanticized notions of agriculture. This idealized pastoral narrative typically emphasizes artisanal farming—particularly smaller family-owned operations that use more traditional methods of production—rather than larger agribusinesses and mass-produced products.[29] These narratives are often reinforced through popular media and marketing campaigns, particularly in attempts to alleviate concerns relating to the perceived risks that modern food production poses to consumers and our ways of life.[30] Happy-meat producers tend to be working at a smaller scale and in the context of a family farm, and hence their products are well-suited to counter these concerns. And Instagram has proven to be an outstanding vehicle for happy-meat producers to share images and stories about the quality of life that their animals experience, situated within idyllic images of rurality that appeal to concerned consumers.

On their Instagram accounts, these happy-meat producers often described the unique personalities of each animal, particularly the breeding animals, identifying them individually by name. Using a number of images over the course of a few days, one producer shared the story of their sow "Wanda" building her nest and giving birth, describing their farm's "lovely girls" as "excellent mummas." Giving names to nonhuman animals has been argued by some to be a symptom of anthropomorphism, namely the attribution of human mental states (thoughts, feelings, motivations, and beliefs) to nonhuman objects or creatures.[31] Humans commonly anthropomorphize things that we love, as opposed to those that we hate or to which we are indifferent. The naming of animals in this instance emphasizes the loving relationship that producers have with their animals—a key feature of happy-meat products—and helps to create a personal connection between the Instagram user and the animal.[32] Happy-meat producers also use these approaches to demonstrate care in their treatment of their livestock in a similar way to how we treat our pets, thus communicating to consumers that these animals are cared for more than those in industrialized, "faceless" herds.[33] While some may question why anyone would want to eat an animal after establishing a personal relationship with it, many Australian consumers consider the idea of treating each animal as an individual important for animal welfare.[34] Providing names to their animals and describing their individual personalities further adds to the narratives constructed on Instagram by happy-meat producers, emphasizing that these animals are thought to be more than a number.

A number of happy-meat producers that I studied produced heritage (also referred to as heirloom) breeds of livestock, a detail captured either within the image itself or the supporting caption and hashtags. The use of heritage breeds can be considered a form of food activism: for many producers and consumers, it is a way to reject the fast-growing livestock breeds used in today's industrial-scale agriculture. The emphasis on heritage breeds by happy-meat producers was particularly evident among pork and poultry producers, which are the industries that have seen the greatest levels of intensification and genetic changes due to their short generation interval relative to other livestock species, such as sheep and beef cattle. Leroy and Praet argue that the use of heritage animals "seems to point towards a form of neo-romanticism and a longing for origins and lost innocence" and ties directly into the rural idyll narrative.[35] The producers using heritage breeds in this study also often emphasized the enhanced flavor of the meat from these breeds, describing the meat provided by modern breeds as bland. Raising heritage breeds can be viewed as a way of demonstrating to consumers that these breeds can still be used in the food supply chain, and supports the rejection of widespread intensive farming methods that require a fast-growing breed that has been developed specifically to reduce the costs of meat production.

Happy-meat images on Instagram also often included the farmers personally involved in the care of the animals. Heide Bruckner, Annalisa Colombino, and Ulrich Ermann suggest that ideas of "good" and "bad" animal welfare manifest themselves when farmers and consumers understand their lives as entangled with the animals that they raise and eat.[36] Paula Arcari suggests that displaying a sense of trust between the farmers and their animals through online images is a "key ingredient in emphasising their pastoral role in caring for the wellbeing of food animals."[37] In the images analyzed, farmers were seen holding animals, often in a close embrace, or standing in the paddock with the animals they were tending to. One producer shared an image of her "morning snuggles" with a lamb, while describing her quest to demonstrate that animal farming can be done with high levels of animal welfare by being 100 percent grass fed and professing her love for what she does. Increasing evidence suggests that people are becoming more concerned about the disappearance of smaller-scale, family farmers alongside the increase of technologically intensive agriculture. In my earlier research, it was evident that the ways in which Australian consumers construct their ideas of what a farmer is are based on the behaviors that they expect farmers to exhibit, such as the provision of high standards of animal welfare in meat production. Further, I found that people involved in intensive meat production were not even considered to be "farmers" in the public imagination due to the perceived lower standards of animal welfare in such systems.[38] In nearly all cases, images posted to Instagram by happy-meat producers tended to show them having positive interactions with their animals, reinforcing the idea that they genuinely care for them.

Not only were farmers featured in many of the images shared on Instagram, but so too were their families. The depiction of families in images associated with more "ethical" types of meat production blend the more open and transparent model of farming with the morality associated in Australia with family, nature, and the rural idyll.[39] Farmers' children were often depicted holding farm animals or enjoying the bucolic lifestyle associated with happy-meat production. One pork producer shared a photo of their children cuddling a piglet with the caption "a calm pig is a happy pig." Another producer shared an image of their child getting grain out of the silo to feed their pigs, coupled with the tag #farmingfamily. By using children as part of the happy-meat narrative, farmers attempt to create personal connections with their consumers, emphasizing that farmers are not so different from their customers, as they also care for their families. These images arguably also convey the message to the potential customer that if this meat is good for the farmer's children to eat, then it must be good for the customer to feed their family. The focus on children also reinforces the view that small family farms are central to the rural idyll construct, particularly in relation to the level of care provided to the animals compared with large intensive agribusiness managers.[40]

Despite producers' desires to share an animal's journey from paddock to plate on Instagram, the point at which the animal is slaughtered and the practices associated with slaughter remain noticeably absent. Censoring the process of slaughter in this way is counter to some attempts elsewhere to promote what might be considered radical transparency in the context of industrialized meat production. For example, some slaughterhouses in Denmark and the United States now have glass walls, the meat industry had produced video tours of slaughterhouses to give consumers who want to know more about meat processing greater exposure to the slaughter process.[41] Various food media are also feeding into this type of transparency by producing television shows that showcase what is involved in raising and slaughtering livestock. Matthew Evans's television program *For the Love of Meat* is just one recent Australian example where Evans follows animals from the farms where they are raised to the slaughterhouse where they are killed.[42] Even though there has been some level of public outcry about such public displays of livestock slaughter, many see these visual representations as beneficial as they provide those that want to know more about the process with the information and transparency which they desire.

Thus, while there have been attempts to increase transparency across the entire meat supply chain, the Instagram accounts analyzed in this research only feature images of animals in paddocks and meat on a plate. The processes that resulted in the happy-meat product essentially are black-boxed: most people are aware of the inputs and outputs of the box (in this case, that an animal dies in order for us to consume meat), but some of the key processes used to arrive at the output remain hidden (in this case, the processes relating to slaughter).[43] The presumption seems to be that if these processes are out of sight, they will be out of mind. Arcari argues that the absence of slaughter in the promotion of ethical meat products is because images that display death may "pollute a visibility constructed to be purposefully benign" and are thus designed to keep the happy-meat narrative positive and unchallenging for the consumer.[44] The practice of slaughter is confrontational and often brings about feelings of guilt relating to the consumption of meat. Australian meat consumers are generally happy not knowing the slaughter details.[45] Despite many acknowledging that slaughter is just "one bad day" in the animal's life (at least for happy-meat animals), it is likely that sharing images of slaughter processes would offend or cause unease for many Instagram users and potential customers. Keeping the process of slaughter absent from their Instagram accounts allows happy-meat producers to maintain a narrative about their animals that is comforting for their audience.

In addition to not sharing images of the slaughter process, none of these happy-meat producers discussed slaughter on their Instagram accounts, which raises the question of whether they may be black-boxing these processes in their own consciousness. More often than not, slaughter occurs off-farm, and thus the process is outside of the control (and arguably out of sight) of the producers themselves, which adds a layer of complexity for them when they attempt to be transparent.[46] However, it was striking that these producers *were* willing to post discussions about death on their Instagram, as long as death had not occurred via slaughter. One producer described the loss of a piglet through its mother crushing it as a reality of "a free-range life." Another producer shared their grief at losing one of her favorite breeding sows to old age, writing a long, almost poetic account of her memories of this sow, signing off with "see you old girl" and a kissing-face emoji. While some may claim that it would be more ethical to have slaughtered and eaten the animal before she died of old age, sharing these stories on Instagram creates a sense of compassion and humanity, and further highlights the personal relationships that are developed between animals and farmers.

Although the slaughter process remains absent from the images on Instagram, posts often feature butchers. Alongside the images of the animal in the paddock are pictures of the butcher who was responsible for breaking down the animal's carcass into the retail cuts provided to the end consumer. The posts that I studied show the butcher hard at work next to the hanging carcass or cutting the meat at the butcher's table, almost always smiling. In response to growing concerns about industrial agriculture and "big food," happy-meat producers highlight their use of local, skilled butchers to emphasize the artisanal qualities of their meat and to put a trusted face to their products.[47] In contrast, technological advances in meat processing—with slaughtering and butchering of livestock becoming concentrated in large-scale, specialized facilities—provide retailers with prepackaged retail cuts ready for the supermarket shelf, reducing the necessity for skilled butchers on site. Including butchers within the happy-meat narrative on Instagram allows producers to further address consumers' concerns about the origins and production methods associated with their meat, particularly as images of the butcher provide additional clear connections to the site of production.

This chapter highlights how Australian happy-meat producers use Instagram to share narratives that accredit their products as better alternatives, particularly in relation to growing consumer concerns about meat and its associated production methods. The use of Instagram by happy-meat producers aligns with increasing use of social media platforms as ways to engage in digital food activism, and other visual methods of representing ethically produced meat.[48] However, despite increasing concerns, mass-produced meat products remain the most commonly consumed forms of meat in Australia due to the majority of consumers shopping in large retail chains where such meat products dominate and their price point (relative to more boutique meat products such as those sold by happy-meat producers) is lower. Happy-meat producers use Instagram to highlight the connections between their families and their animals, show the quality of the environment in which their animals live, and reiterate the popular rural idyll commonly associated with Australian farms. This chapter also demonstrates that happy-meat producers who are using Instagram are not completely transparent, keeping the slaughter process absent in order to maintain a happy, nonthreatening narrative. Instagram ultimately gives producers of happy meat the power to introduce their meat to their consumers in idealistic ways, while still maintaining a certain level of censorship.

Instagram remains an ideal platform for happy-meat producers. It is easy to use, does not require large advertising budgets, is readily accessible by potential and actual customers, and perhaps most importantly, is popular among foodies who are a major target market for these producers. This chapter highlights the need to explore the broader multimedia context in which these happy-meat narratives are constructed. This includes central questions about whether Australian consumer understandings of meat production are changing due to the presence of happy-meat narratives on Instagram, which is widely accessible and highly engaged in Australia, as well as how such Instagram representations interact with happy-meat narratives found in advertising and TV food media. There is also an opportunity to explore whether the increasing number of producers deciding to "tell their story" using social media is influencing public understandings of meat production and their levels of trust in the meat value chain.

Notes

1. Emily Buddle, "Australian Meat Consumers' Understandings of Farm Animal Welfare" (PhD diss., University of Adelaide, 2019).

2. Paula Arcari, *Making Sense of "Food" Animals: A Critical Exploration of the Persistence of "Meat"* (Singapore: Palgrave Macmillan, 2020).

3. Michael Mikulak, *The Politics of the Pantry: Stories, Food and Social Change* (Montreal: McGill-Queen's University Press, 2013).

4. Angela Carlucci, Erminio Monteleone, Ada Braghieri, and Fabio Napolitano, "Mapping the Effect of Information about Animal Welfare on Consumer Liking and Willingness to Pay for Yogurt," *Journal of Sensory Studies* 24, no. 5, (2009): 74–82; Filiep Vanhonacker, Els Van Poucke, Frank Tuyttens, and Wim Verbeke, "Citizens' Views on Farm Animal Welfare and Related Information Provision; Exploratory Insights from Flanders, Belgium," *Journal of Agricultural and Environmental Ethics* 23, no. 6 (2010): 551–69.

5. Katrine Baghurst, "Red Meat Consumption in Australia: Intakes, Contributions to Nutrient Intake and Associated Dietary Patterns," *European Journal of Cancer Prevention* 8 (1999): 158–91; Rachel A. Ankeny, "The Moral Economy of Red Meat in Australia," in *Proceedings of the Oxford Symposium on Food and Cookery 2007*, ed. Susan R. Friedland (Blackawton, UK: Prospect Books, 2008): 20–28; Tim Whitnall and Nathan Pitts, "Global Trends in Meat Consumption," *Australian Bureau of Agricultural and Resource Economics and Sciences (ABARES)*, www.agriculture.gov.au/abares/research-topics/agricultural-commodities/mar-2019/meat-consumption, accessed October 15, 2019.

6. "Rise in Vegetarianism Not Halting the March of Obesity," Roy Morgan, www.roymorgan.com/findings/7944-vegetarianism-in-2018-april-2018-201904120608, accessed October 2, 2019.

7. Lenka Malek, Wendy Umberger, and Ellen Goddard, "Is Anti-Consumption Driving Meat Consumption Changes in Australia?," *British Food Journal* 121, no. 1 (2019): 123–38, https://doi.org/10.1108/BFJ-03-2018-0183.

8. Heather J. Bray and Rachel A. Ankeny, "Happy Chickens Lay Tastier Eggs: Motivations for Buying Free-Range Eggs in Australia," *Anthrozoös* 30, no. 2 (2017): 213–26, https://doi.org/10.1080/08927936.2017.1310986.

9. Buddle, "Australian Meat Consumers' Understandings."

10. Emily A. Buddle and Heather J. Bray, "How Farm Animal Welfare Issues Are Framed in the Australian Media," *Agricultural and Environmental Ethics* 32, no. 3 (2019): 357–76.

11. Chanetelle Francis, "Aussie Farms Map Goes Global," *Melbourne Weekly Times*, August 14, 2019, www.weeklytimesnow.com.au/news/national/activists-aussie-farms-map-goes-global-international-farmers-in-fear/news-story/510da42465c440b7137766e9d9d344a1, accessed August 27, 2019.

12. Emily A. Buddle, Heather J. Bray, and Wayne S. Pitchford, "Keeping It 'Inside the Fence': An Examination of Responses to a Farm Animal Welfare Issue on Twitter," *Animal Production Science* 58, no. 3 (2017): 435–44.

13. Ibid.

14. Courtney Fowler, "The Digital Farmer: Using Social Media to Bridge the Urban-Rural Divide in Australian Agriculture," Australian Broadcasting Corporation, May 27, 2018, www.abc.net.au, accessed December 23, 2019.

15. Fabio Napolitano, Antonio Girolami, and Ada Braghieri, "Consumer Liking and Willingness to Pay for High Welfare Animal-Based Products," *Trends in Food Science and Technology* 21 (2010): 537–43; Frédéric Leroy and Istvan Praet, "Animal Killing and Postdomestic Meat Production," *Journal of Agricultural and Environmental Ethics* 30, no. 1 (2017): 67–86.

16. Wilhelm Peekhaus, "Monsanto Discovers New Social Media," *International Journal of Communication* 4 (2010): 955–76; Cori Brewster, "'Agvocates' for Industry: Citizen-Farmers, Social Media, and the Gendered Production of Food," in *The Ecopolitics of Consumption: The Food Trade*, ed. H. Louise Davis, Karyn Pilgrim, and Madhudaya Sinha (Lanham, MD: Lexington Books, 2015).

17. Tania Lewis, "Digital Food: From Paddock to Platform," *Communication Research and Practice* 4, no. 3 (2018): 212–28.

18. Michael Pennell, "More than Food Porn: Twitter, Transparency and Food Systems," *Gastronomica* 16, no. 4 (2016): 33–43.

19. Leroy and Praet, "Animal Killing."

20. Ibid., 78.

21. Michael Pollan, *The Omnivore's Dilemma: A Natural History of Four Meals* (New York: Penguin, 2006); Catherine Friend, *The Compassionate Carnivore: Or, How to Keep Animals Happy, Save Old Macdonald's Farm, Reduce Your Hoofprint, and Still Eat Meat* (Philadelphia: Da Capo, 2008).

22. Leroy and Praet, "Animal Killing."

23. Lev Manovich, *Instagram and Contemporary Image*, 2017, http://manovich.net/index.php/projects/instagram-and-contemporary-image.

24. Leroy and Praet, "Animal Killing."

25. "Saturation" refers to the point where the researcher is seeing similar instances

over and over again, meaning that no additional themes are emerging, thus the results become "saturated."

26. John W. Creswell and J. David Creswell, *Research Design: Qualitative, Quantitative and Mixed Method Approaches*, 5th ed. (Thousand Oaks, CA: Sage, 2018).

27. Alister Scott, Alana Gilbert, and Ayele Gelan, *The Urban-Rural Divide: Myth or Reality?* (Aberdeen: Macaulay Institute, 2007).

28. Buddle, "Australian Meat Consumers' Understandings."

29. David Bell, "Variations on the Rural Idyll," in *The Handbook of Rural Studies*, ed. Paul Cloke, Terry Marsden, and Patrick Mooney (London: Sage, 2006), 151.

30. Michelle Phillipov, "Media, Supermarkets and the Strategic Manufacture of Consumer Trust," in *Media and Food Industries* (London: Palgrave Macmillan, 2017); Deborah Lupton, *Risk*, 2d ed. (New York: Routledge, 2013).

31. James A. Serpel, "People in Disguise: Anthropomorphism and the Human-Pet Relationship," in *Thinking with Animals: New Perspectives on Anthropomorphism*, ed. Lorraine Datson and Gregg Mitman (New York: Columbia University Press, 2005).

32. Leroy and Praet, "Animal Killing."

33. Rhonda Wilkie, *Livestock/Deadstock: Working with Farm Animals from Birth to Slaughter* (Philadelphia: Temple University Press, 2010).

34. Buddle, "Australian Meat Consumers' Understandings."

35. Leroy and Praet, "Animal Killing," 78.

36. Heide K. Bruckner, Annalisa Colombino, and Ulrich Ermann, "Naturecultures and the Affective (Dis)Entanglements of Happy Meat," *Agriculture and Human Values* 36, no. 1, (2019): 35–47.

37. Arcari, *Making Sense of "Food" Animals*, 225.

38. Buddle, "Australian Meat Consumers' Understandings."

39. Arcari, *Making Sense of "Food" Animals*.

40. Wilkie, *Livestock/Deadstock*.

41. Arcari, *Making Sense of "Food" Animals*.

42. Stephen Oliver, dir., *For the Love of Meat*, TV series, written by Stephen Oliver and Matthew Evans, Special Broadcasting Service, 2016.

43. Bruno Latour, *Science in Action* (Cambridge, MA: Harvard University Press, 1997); Trevour J. Pinch, "Opening Black Boxes: Science, Technology, and Society," *Social Studies of Science* 22, no. 3 (1992): 487–510.

44. Arcari, *Making Sense of "Food" Animals*, 257.

45. Richard W. Bulliet, *Hunters, Herders and Hamburgers: The Past and Future of Human-Animal Relationships* (New York: Columbia University Press, 2005); Heather J. Bray, Sofia C. Zambrano, Anna Chur-Hansen, and Rachel A. Ankeny, "Not Appropriate Dinner Table Conversation? Talking to Children about Meat Production," *Appetite* 100, no. 1 (2016): 1–9; Buddle, "Australian Meat Consumers' Understandings."

46. In Australia, in order for meat to be sold to the public, it must be slaughtered and butchered in a facility that has food safety approvals. There are very few,

if any, farms that have an on-site certified slaughterhouse and, up until the recent introduction of approved mobile abattoirs, farmers had no means to slaughter an animal on-farm for sale to the public.

47. Michelle Phillipov, "Resisting 'Agribusiness Apocalypse': The Pleasures and Politics of Ethical Food," in *Media and Food Industries: The New Politics of Food*, 29–51 (London: Palgrave Macmillan, 2017).

48. Tanja Schneider, Karin Eli, Catherine Dolan, and Stanley Ulijaszek, *Digital Food Activism* (New York: Routledge, 2018); Arcari, *Making Sense of "Food" Animals*.

CHAPTER 11

FreakShakes and Mama Noi

Cases of Transforming Food Industry Influence on Instagram

KATHERINE KIRKWOOD

In 2019, Joe Nicchi, the owner of the Los Angeles food truck CVT Soft Serve, gained worldwide press coverage for the implementation of a new policy: "Influencers pay double." He was fed up with potential customers approaching his ice cream truck, only to claim that they have an extensive following on Instagram, ergo: as an influencer, they would like to have the $4 ice cream for free. In return, these self-proclaimed social media celebrities would post about their experience at CVT Soft Serve on Instagram, providing Nicchi's business with "exposure." When an actor (Nicchi didn't identify her) asked for free ice cream in exchange for posting a picture of herself at Nicchi's truck, the businessman told the actor's assistant, "As much as I'd love to do that, I don't think my kid's school accepts celebrity photos as a form of tuition payment."[1]

Since Instagram was established in October 2010, many in the food industry have been working to understand whether the platform benefits their business or is a source of distraction. Nicchi's point of view is not uncommon, with reports documenting celebrity chefs' displeasure at diners' incessant Instagramming of their meals, including gripes from Heston Blumenthal and David Chang. Blumenthal has said he would prefer if diners "didn't take any photos and just enjoyed themselves at the table."[2] Chang meanwhile banned photography at his Momofuku restaurant, saying "It's food. Just eat it."[3] Others, like Gordon Ramsay, are more supportive of diners photographing their meals. The British celebrity chef lambasted a photography ban at three-Michelin-starred restaurant Waterside Inn. "How bloody pompous!" he said. "It's a compliment to the chef the fact that customers want to take a picture of dishes they've paid for, it's 2017. . . . If I see a great looking picture posted, I'll want to go and eat there immediately, he's [Waterside Inn cofounder Michel Roux] just an old fart who's forgotten to move on!"[4]

The advertising value Instagram offers, as Ramsay alluded to, has even become central to the operation of some establishments. In their study of Instagram, Tama Leaver, Tim Highfield, and Crystal Abidin examine food as one site where "cultures of Instagram bleed from the digital to the physical."[5] They note that eateries have emerged where the decor as well as the food and drink served were geared toward being Instagrammable with props, elaborate and colorful drinks ideal for photographing, as well as staff on hand to advise the best way to photograph certain dishes. As these various examples demonstrate, Instagram is having a polarizing effect on the food industry.

These differing perspectives on Instagram's welcome or unwelcome status at the dinner table reflect tensions between professionals and amateurs and between various actors in the food and food media industries. The above vignettes only consider the views of chefs and restaurateurs, but it is interesting to note that Blumenthal, Chang, and Ramsay also have food media personas as celebrity chefs, which includes Instagram profiles. A confluence of professional and amateur content occurs on Instagram, and the ensuing frictions between these groups have changed what it means to be a food media professional and the types of food media content produced. I argue that Instagram allows for a different type of culinary personality to operate, who is neither a mainstream celebrity chef looking to expand their media empire, nor just an amateur engaging in a pursuit of serious leisure.[6] Rather, this culinary personality type occupies a space between amateur and professional. Instagram's readily accessible affordances, which differ from print or television, are key to the production of such culinary personalities, as the platform creates a space for budding producers to experiment with the long-standing conventions of cooking shows and food photography.

This chapter examines the Instagram dynamics between food industry professionals (including chefs, restaurateurs, and retailers), those working in food media (whether it be in mainstream media or more niche social media channels), and consumers as they respond to this Instagram content. I explore these changing relationships through two key phenomena: food porn (i.e., a specific genre of highly Instagrammable images of food) and prosumption, "a progressive blurring of the line that separates producer from consumer."[7] I explore some of the discomfort members of the food industry are experiencing in response to food Instagram phenomena, while acknowledging Instagram's relative newness. These negotiations of power between professionals, amateurs, and those in-between are still in their early stages. Working in this formative moment, I argue that although Instagram is a site of tension between various existing and emerging actors in the food scene, the platform offers opportunities for new forms of culinary media to become established. This chapter documents the role of food porn on Instagram in shaping food businesses and the opportunities Instagram's affordances offer prosumers for forging food media careers. These are but two ways Instagram is transforming food media and culture.

To explore these timely themes, I present and analyze two case studies. In the first, I examine FreakShakes, the original creation from the Canberra café Pâtissez that went viral on Instagram. To do so, I draw from press coverage and Instagram profiles that document the consequences of placing Instagrammability at the forefront of a food business's operation. This case highlights the role of food porn in culinary posts on Instagram and the tensions it creates with members of the food industry who feel it diminishes the value of their work. It also questions the sustainability of Instagram-driven food businesses from multiple perspectives, including financial implications, health concerns, and food waste. In the second case study, I explore the dynamics of prosumption and personality through the Instagram profile of former *MasterChef Australia* contestant Marion Grasby. Her account illustrates how the platform both adopts and eschews certain aspects of conventional food television. Instagram provides an avenue for Grasby to maintain a profile as a food media personality outside the bounds of legacy media.

Food on Instagram: Food Porn and Prosumption

Given their growing ubiquity, platforms like Instagram are inescapable as "visual media and mobile apps around images and video" become "popular means of documenting everyday life."[8] It was inevitable, then, that Instagram would become intertwined with the food industry where phenomena such as food porn—food depicted as excess, food positioned as an object of desire, or food having "sexy characteristics such as glistening, oozing, or dripping"—can now be captured and shared at every meal.[9] The visual tropes of food porn have become a normalized part of popular food media in the digital age.

Related to the normalized proliferation of food porn images, influencers combine prosumer practices with "a particular kind of micro-celebrity."[10] Their requests for free products from small business owners like Nicchi attract ridicule—as his "influencers pay double" sign demonstrated—but the phenomenon can be read in another way. It can be seen as a consequence of the norms of prosumption practices in the Web 2.0 environment. Influencers' actions can be interpreted as an attempt by consumers to wrest control from brands, which have essentially asked professionals for work without pay in the past, as when LinkedIn asked volunteers to translate the platform into new languages.[11]

In this context, where social media plays a greater role in mediating everyday life, influencers have become a phenomenon because Instagram's affordances are ideal for enhancing user engagement.[12] Here, the social affordances of Instagram are at play. The emergence of Instagram as a visual platform easily accessible to a vast array of users exemplifies how "technology affords social practice."[13] Utilizing their "micro-celebrity," influencers appeal to brands as a promotional avenue because these opinion leaders have done the work of attracting attention and building a sense of authenticity.[14] Having established credibility with their networks, influencers' promotion of brands then capitalizes on users' trust, since users perceive influencer messages as coming genuinely from other consumers rather than as direct advertising from brands.[15] While audiences are becoming more attuned to and skeptical of the brand-influencer dynamic, influencers' ubiquity on Instagram is difficult to ignore and highlights the growth of actors who operate in the space between amateur and professional.

Food blogging is another form of prosumption that proves a useful point of comparison to Instagram. As Lofgren claims, food blogging has made a significant contribution to the popularity of sharing food photos on Instagram and Pinterest.[16] While some scholars view prosumers as exploited—as may be argued with the LinkedIn case above—others assert that some prosumers "seem to enjoy, even love, what they are doing and are willing to devote long hours to it for no pay."[17] This aligns with Isabelle de Solier's assertion that engaging in food blogging as part of a wider foodie lifestyle is a form of "serious leisure," where one devotes a substantial amount of effort to acquiring knowledge and developing skills in a particular interest area. She found that the *production* of cooking a dish in the kitchen or writing a food blog carried "a higher moral value" than just eating food or consuming food media.[18] Following a Bourdieusian approach to cultural capital, Naccarato and LeBesco established the concept of culinary capital, whereby certain culinary behaviors are viewed as exhibiting greater knowledge, prowess, or influence, and therefore function as a marker of a higher social status.[19] As de Solier demonstrates, within our current digital food media environment, consumers seem to value producing food and food media more than simply consuming food. As posting pictures of food on Instagram comprises a way for individuals to assert their identity, culinary capital is a crucial concept for understanding the motivations behind the cultural trend of posting food images.

Although blogging gives amateurs a voice, their emergence in the food scene changed audiences' perceptions of professional food critics' jobs. This reflects tensions that have also arisen in journalism and political communication.[20] In both cases, however, scholars did not observe the rise of amateur content producers leading to the obsolescence of professionals; rather the industry standing of professionals and amateurs was renegotiated to establish complementary roles and fuel innovation.[21] Professional food critics "accommodate" the new norms introduced through digital disruption and the proliferation of online consumer reviews.[22] Morag Kobez cites amateurs' speed to publish as heightening the demand for immediacy in professionals' work, a loss of professionals' anonymity, concerns about the integrity and credibility of amateur food reviews, as well as the increase in listicles and clickbait as key shifts in the professional food writing industry.[23] The dynamics between professionals and amateurs in food writing foreshadows similar tensions that are playing out on Instagram, where existing actors may perceive the platform as threatening long-held norms.

FreakShakes: Food Porn and Instagram Fodder

Since consumer-generated Instagram content has so successfully attracted attention for dining establishments, eateries now attempt to explicitly appeal to Instagrammers. While Instagrammable dishes may look enticing, prioritizing aesthetics can come at the expense of the taste of the dish or the culinary skill required in creating it. For example, Bee Wilson described the rainbow bagel trend (similar to the unicorn trend that Emily Truman examines in chapter 7), as a dyed bread roll "that would look too garish even at a five-year-old's birthday party. Only on Instagram could such a thing seem better than normal bread. It is an idea of joy, rather than actual joy."[24] Instagrammability also drives decor choices, including the placement of lights and selection of wallpaper, tiles, and even plates.[25]

Brisbane sous chef Carlos Gatica noted in our interview that creating Instagram-focused dishes diminished the "theatrical" aspect of plating food for diners because now the act was only geared for the superficial reason of obtaining likes. Leaver, Highfield, and Abidin believe that the sense of theater remains in how chefs present dishes, but the experience of being served is geared toward ensuring diners capture the perfect photo, not necessarily enjoying actually eating the dish. One Singaporean dessert bar even denied a request for whipped cream to be left off a milkshake because it helped the drink look good in photos and "was part of their branding;" this was even after the customer told the server that "we were more keen to eat the item than to photograph it."[26]

Australia contributed to the Instagrammable food phenomenon of elaborately decorated milkshakes dubbed FreakShakes. In Canberra, Pâtissez is credited with starting the craze in 2015.[27] Pâtissez co-owner Anna Petridis stated she wanted to make a photographable product: "I wanted to do some really great shakes, and so ridiculous and over the top that people just had to take a photo of it before they ate it." Petridis far exceeded her objective of creating an Instagrammable treat, as FreakShakes became a social media sensation. "I have people waiting an hour for a table," Petridis said, "and they'll wait 45 minutes for a shake."[28]

Using third-party app Flipagram, a Pâtissez Instagram post from January 28, 2016, shows in a stop-motion-style, time-lapse video how to create their

FreakShake called Pât Gây.[29] Resting a clean canning jar on a saucer (to catch the inevitable drips of FreakShake), one coats the inside of the jar with homemade dulce de leche, along with the outside of the glass from the rim to the top of the jar's handle. That outer coating of dulce de leche is then coated with milk crumb; one then adds the milkshake itself, which Pâtissez claims "is straight up Gaytime in liquid form." A mountain of chocolate mousse that extends high beyond the rim of the jar tops the milkshake, before a Gây Popslide—a popsicle that consists of "a dulce parfait dipped in choc & rolled in loooooots of house made honeycomb"—is nestled on top.[30] By the end of the clip, the finished indulgent milkshake creation rises far above the lip of the jar, with dulce de leche and crumb coating its exterior, and chocolate mousse dripping down the side (fig. 11-1). It fulfills the visual tropes of food porn that depict excess. The gluttonousness of the FreakShake may serve as a fantasy or object of desire, and it materially embodies the oozy, dripping, "sexy" characteristics of food porn.[31]

Although Nathan Taylor and Megan Keating argue that notions of novelty and frivolity should be part of definitions of food porn, as exemplified by items like FreakShakes, questions need to be asked about how sustainable this aspect of food culture is for business, as well as for health and food waste considerations.[32] The viral nature of Pâtissez's FreakShakes garnered lines at the café, prompting Petridis and her mother and co-owner Gina to open a second café by December 2015, before expanding internationally with outlets in Malaysia and Singapore by mid-2016. But novelty only lasts so long. Although the original Pâtissez remained open, by November 2017, the second store was closing and the company that controlled the cafés, Pâtissez Pty Ltd., had gone into liquidation. Arguably referencing the social media frenzy their FreakShakes stirred up barely two months after opening, the café owners spoke about the course their business had taken: "Our situation was pretty unique and we certainly got caught up in the madness!"[33] To date, it does not appear that much has been written about the post-viral lives of Instagram-famous restaurants. But, unlike Pâtissez's misstep, there are some success stories. For instance, Black Tap, a New York City burger spot that similarly went viral for their take on FreakShakes, appears to have managed the hype, expanding to multiple locations in the United States and internationally.[34]

Aside from restaurant owners seeking to maintain sustainable business models, consuming such indulgent items also poses health consequences for customers and food waste concerns. Despite being visually enticing, purchasing and consuming these extravagant treats to populate one's Instagram profile may not be a sustainable practice. Maria Michaelides began serving freakshakes at her London café after seeing Pâtissez's on social media. She believes her version contains about 1,500 calories; not everyone finishes them, but some patrons have a FreakShake with an extra slice of cake.[35] The characteristics of food porn make

FIGURE 11-1. Still of the Pâtissez Pât Gây FreakShake from a Flipagram video.

dishes desirable, especially such items like FreakShakes, and mark a divergence from other simultaneously occurring movements like "clean eating" and general health messaging.[36] In some instances, the vicarious consumption of Instagram-worthy food via images may be enough to sate one's appetite. For instance, a *MasterChef Australia* viewer claimed she surrounds herself with cookbooks, food magazines, and food television, but does not cook the indulgent recipes because she knows eating them would undo the hard physical fitness work she does.[37]

While those who buy FreakShakes only to post photos of them on Instagram will save some calories by not consuming the whole drink, their actions create a different problem of food waste. For example, Leaver, Highfield, and Abidin witnessed diners in Tokyo order repeat servings when they failed to capture footage of a folded marshmallow flower blooming when placed in hot chocolate.[38] Without the compulsion to photograph this moment and share it on Instagram, this food waste could be avoided. These issues around sustainable business models, as well as the health and waste implications of the food in these images, illustrate some of the grim realities food porn Instagram posts gloss over, as food businesses aspire to be Instagrammable.

Forging New Food Careers and Food Media Genres

Just as businesses can use Instagram as a promotional tool, individuals can build and monetize their work or identity using the platform as their primary medium for engaging with their audience and consumers. Unlike legacy media channels, such as television and print, that have high barriers to entry, Instagram, as a Web 2.0 tool, provides an accessible channel through which amateurs, professionals, and those in-between, can publish visual content. Reality television contestants function as a type of liminal prosumer, as they help the program achieve its commercial goals of attracting viewers and advertisers, while also using the program to gain personal exposure rather than direct compensation. Furthermore, it has become increasingly common for everyday people who participate as contestants on these legacy media reality television shows to leverage this exposure to build media careers of their own. Such media careers can take many forms, both on mainstream channels as well as on personal social media profiles. During the early seasons of the popular reality television show *MasterChef Australia*, professionals in the food industry, however, took issue with amateur cooks using the program to shoehorn themselves into a culinary career. Prominent Australian chef Neil Perry was an early *MasterChef Australia* dissenter. He described the contestants as "nobodies with very little experience and [aided by the show] are able to be exposed and have opportunities . . . most go on there to get enough media fame to be able to go on and do more media things."[39] This was somewhat ironic, considering Perry had been on the program as a celebrity chef guest in 2010 and returned again in 2011.[40] The next day he walked back the comments, claiming they had been taken out of context.[41] Although Perry went back on his original comments, this scenario exemplifies some of the tensions Kobez found between professional food critics and amateur food bloggers.

Marion Grasby is a former reality cooking show contestant who has used Instagram's affordances to further establish her presence in the food industry.

Appearing in season two of *MasterChef Australia*, Grasby was a fan favorite and considered a strong contender to win the 2010 title. It came as a shock when Grasby was knocked out a little over midway through the competition, placing ninth.[42] This did not diminish her popularity among audience members, however, and Grasby went on to release a line of meal kits in supermarkets.[43] Of Thai and Anglo-Australian descent, Grasby returned to her mother's homeland, taking up residence in Bangkok in order to be closer to the producers of ingredients for her product lines.[44]

In terms of her media presence since appearing on *MasterChef Australia*, Grasby presented a television program, *Marion's Thailand* (2013), which aired on the Lifestyle Food channel via Australian Pay TV provider Foxtel, and has published two cookbooks, *Marion: Recipes and Stories from a Hungry Cook* (2011) and *Asia Express* (2014).[45] Currently, Grasby is not fronting any television programs, but she takes advantage of social media platforms, including Instagram, Facebook, YouTube, Twitter, and Pinterest, to maintain her media presence. As of August 2021, Grasby had 2.1 million likes on her Facebook page, 1.41 million YouTube subscribers, and 596,000 Instagram followers. Beyond the social affordances of Instagram already discussed, Grasby makes use of Instagram's technological and communicative affordances, as outlined by Taina Bucher and Anne Helmond.[46] For instance, Grasby takes advantage of a range of Instagram's technological affordances, publishing not only photographs of food and her family, but also Instagram TV (IGTV) posts that depict recipes available on her website. IGTV was introduced in June 2018 to enable users to post videos up to one hour long; while accessible via the Instagram app, it also has its own stand-alone app available for download.[47]

Since *MasterChef Australia* and her other television ventures, Grasby has used Instagram to maintain contact with her fanbase and further her culinary activities. The ability to post stills and video and to interact with fans was central in Grasby's promotion of her line of sauces, which launched in May 2019. With flavors like coconut sriracha and coconut sweet chili sauce, the line is available at Coles, one of Australia's two largest supermarket chains. In the lead-up to and following the launch, Grasby posted IGTV recipe videos—many of which feature her mother Noi—demonstrating recipes that use the sauces as marinades, dressings, or dipping sauces. Social media appears to have been the primary vehicle for promoting the products, as a Web search did not capture any press about the launch.

Noi's cooking videos draw visually on the conventions of traditional television cooking shows, using food porn–esque close-ups and slow pans of the cooking process and ingredients. IGTV's 9:16 vertical aspect ratio (smartphone orientation)—as opposed to a horizontal 16:9 (computer and television orientation)—is the key visual difference. Otherwise, IGTV posts depict Noi like many other television cooks, standing in a kitchen presenting to a camera. And like other cooking shows where sponsors' products are used throughout the program, these posts show Noi cooking with Marion's range of sauces. Noi's delivery and personality mark a refreshing deviation from such conventions.

Noi was born and raised in rural Thailand and is a Cordon Bleu–trained chef.[48] Currently, she works as Marion's quality control chef and has become a popular fixture on Grasby's Instagram profile.[49] Grasby, as well as her fans, affectionately refer to her as Mama Noi. A large part of Noi's charm is reminiscent of Julia Child's embrace of imperfections during filming. Unlike contemporary food television broadcasts, Child *had* to absorb and deflect mishaps as her program *The French Chef* (1963–73) was aired live. For example, when Child flubbed flipping a large potato pancake, she owned her mistake, saying "If you're alone in the kitchen, who is going to see?"[50] But in Grasby's Instagram videos featuring Mama Noi, bloopers and off-camera interactions that could be edited out are rather *edited up* with slow motion, animations, and sound effects embellishing these moments. They depict Noi as an endearing Thai auntie.

These production choices are evident in an IGTV video from July 18, 2019, in which Noi presents a recipe for Coconut Sweet Chilli Baked Salmon that uses Marion's sauce. The video starts with Noi on camera and Marion's voice from off-camera. Marion asks, "You got it? You ready?" Noi shakes her head, responding, "No. . . . What about you?" while pointing to Marion and then next to herself, indicating for Marion to come and present the recipe. "No, you. No one wants to see me," Marion replies. Such interactions with off-screen actors are uncommon in television cooking shows. Jamie Oliver was one exception, however. During Oliver's first television show *The Naked Chef*, producer Pat Llewellyn could be heard off-camera asking him about what he was doing in the kitchen.[51] In Noi's case, such interactions do not add further educative elements like in *The Naked Chef*, but rather convey Noi's personality and highlight the bond between Noi and her daughter.

A blooper that could have been edited out, but is instead edited up, occurs when Noi struggles to remember the whole title of the dish, forgetting the word "baked." Noi hesitates, saying, "Today I'm making sweet chilli coconut . . . salmon . . . baked salmon!" The video then shows her laughing and tutting at herself. After basting the salmon with the coconut sweet chili sauce from Marion's product line, Noi jokingly scolds the audience but flubs the name of the sauce: "[If] you don't try sweet coconut chilli, you're crazy." The video was edited so that flames come out of Noi's ears and mouth, followed by one of her catchphrases, "Listen to Noi!" Finally, when Noi completes the dish and holds it up to camera, she finishes with her catchphrase, "Another winner . . ." with Marion and the film crew shouting in unison off-camera, "from Noi!" Noi responds, "You people think you're so funny."

Just as Julia Child charmed audiences with her unflappable nature, showing that she made mistakes like home cooks do, Noi's broad smile and the way in which she does not take herself too seriously has endeared Noi to Marion's followers. Arguably, a conventional cooking program would not have taken such an approach. Grasby, however, has used the agency of her brand of prosumption and the communicative affordances of IGTV to great effect. She recognizes the audience-building potential of Noi's personality, even if it does not match the polished norms of what would be seen on television.

Grasby's success in employing Instagram's affordances and her mother's popularity on the platform illustrates Instagram's legitimate functions in the food industry. Grasby utilized the public profile she developed as a reality television contestant to pursue a career that straddles new media and more mainstream pursuits. While she does not match the legacy media presence of stalwarts of the genre like Jamie Oliver, Heston Blumenthal, or Nigella Lawson, Grasby has established ties with mainstream organizations like the Coles chain. Noi's popularity also highlights ways in which using social media offers opportunities legacy media sometimes cannot. Product placement is a common element of television cooking shows, but Marion utilizes her own Instagram profile to promote her products, coupled with Mama Noi's warm and humorous mode of delivery. This approach feels much less contrived than traditional product placement one might see on a traditional reality or cooking show, or a paid collaboration with an influencer. Grasby's approach to Instagram illustrates how the platform is an invaluable resource that helps her navigate the space beyond an amateur engaging in serious leisure, but on the periphery of mainstream legacy media.

This chapter examines two aspects of how Instagram and food cultures intersect, both of which are related to the concept of prosumption. The cases of Instagrammable FreakShakes and Marion Grasby's charmingly liberated IGTV food show with Mama Noi illustrate that Instagram is more than an auxiliary tool to legacy platforms. Rather, Instagram is a platform where innovative genres of content that are not bound by the norms of mainstream media can emerge. Indeed, Instagram has become enmeshed in various aspects of the food scene, marking a transformative period for the food industry and media professionals, prosumers of varying degrees, and consumers alike. Friction between these actors characterizes this phase, as each experiments with the platform and related emerging trends in food media production. Over time, amateurs and industry stalwarts will negotiate new power structures, as industry innovations will continue to emerge. Considering that Instagram is only about a decade old, the platform's functions alongside the food and legacy food media industries are still in their infancy, but it is already clear that Instagram's affordances both influence and provide novel value for the food industry.

Notes

1. Quoted in Sam Levin, "'We're Anti-Influencer': Ice-Cream Truck Makes Instagram 'Stars' Pay Double," *Guardian*, July 4, 2019, www.theguardian.com.

2. Quoted in Alison Stephenson, "Heston Blumenthal on Taking Photos of Your Food and His Once-in-a-Lifetime Food Experiences," *Daily Telegraph* (Sydney), June 27, 2016, www.dailytelegraph.com.au.

3. Quoted in Grub Street, "Chang Bans Food Photography at Ko; Chefs, Bloggers Prove Resistant," *Grub Street*, June 20, 2008, www.grubstreet.com/2008/06/chang_bans_food_photography_at_ko_chefs_bloggers_prove_resistant.html.

4. Quoted in Sadaf Ahsan, "Gordon Ramsay Says Chefs Who Ban Photos at Their Restaurants Are Pompous 'Old Farts Who've Forgotten to Move On,'" *National Post*, November 6, 2017, https://nationalpost.com/life/food/gordon-ramsay-says-chefs-who-ban-photos-at-their-restaurants-are-pompous-old-farts-whove-forgotten-to-move-on.

5. Tama Leaver, Tim Highfield, and Crystal Abidin, *Instagram: Visual Social Media Cultures* (Cambridge, UK: Polity, 2020), 149.

6. Isabelle de Solier, *Food and the Self: Consumption, Production and Material Culture* (London: Bloomsbury, 2013); Robert A. Stebbins, *Serious Leisure: A Perspective for Our Time* (Abingdon, UK: Routledge, 2007).

7. Alvin Toffler, *The Third Wave* (New York: Bantam, 1980), 267.

8. Tim Highfield, *Social Media and Everyday Politics* (Cambridge, UK: Polity, 2016), 74.

9. Nathan Taylor and Megan Keating, "Contemporary Food Imagery: Food Porn and Other Visual Trends," *Communication Research and Practice* 4, no. 3 (2018): 311–12, https://doi.org/10.1080/22041451.2018.1482190.

10. Catherine Archer, "The Borderless World According to Bloggers: Prosumers, Produsers, Creatives and Post-Consumers Tell Their Side of the Communications Story," in *Proceedings of the World Public Relations Forum*, ed. Marianne D. Sison and Mark Sheehan, 4–7 (Melbourne: Public Relations Institute of Australia, 2012), 4, www.globalalliancepr.org/new-page-61; Susie Khamis, Lawrence Ang, and Raymond Welling, "Self-Branding, 'Micro-Celebrity' and the Rise of Social Media Influencers," *Celebrity Studies* 8, no. 2 (2017): 202, https://doi.org/10.1080/19392397.2016.1218292.

11. George Ritzer and Nathan Jurgenson, "Production, Consumption, Prosumption The Nature of Capitalism in the Age of the Digital 'Prosumer,'" *Journal of Consumer Culture* 10, no. 1 (2010): 13–36, https://doi.org/10.1177/1469540509354673.

12. Elisa Serafinelli, *Digital Life on Instagram: New Social Communication of Photography* (Bingley, UK: Emerald Group, 2018), 106.

13. Hsieh. quoted in Taina Bucher and Anne Helmond, "The Affordances of Social Media Platforms," in *The Sage Handbook of Social Media*, ed. Jean Burgess, Alice Marwick, and Thomas Poell, 233–53 (London: Sage, 2017), 238.

14. Alison Hearn and Stephanie Schoenhoff, "From Celebrity to Influencer: Tracing the Diffusion of Celebrity Value across the Data Stream," in *A Companion to Celebrity*, ed. P. David Marshall and Sean Redmond, 194–212 (Chichester, UK: John Wiley and Sons, 2016).

15. Serafinelli, *Digital Life on Instagram*, 107.

16. Jennifer Lofgren, "Food Blogging and Food-related Media Convergence," *M/C Journal* 16, no. 3 (2013), http://journal.media-culture.org.au/index.php/mcjournal/article/view/638.

17. George Ritzer and Nathan Jurgenson, "Production, Consumption, Prosumption The Nature of Capitalism in the Age of the Digital 'Prosumer,'" *Journal of Consumer Culture* 10, no. 1 (2010): 13–36, https://doi.org/10.1177/1469540509354673, 22.

18. Isabelle de Solier, *Food and the Self: Consumption, Production and Material Culture* (London: Bloomsbury, 2013) 149.

19. Peter Naccarato and Kathleen LeBesco, *Culinary Capital* (London: Berg, 2012).

20. Morag Kobez, "'Restaurant Reviews Aren't What They Used to Be': Digital Disruption and the Transformation of the Role of the Food Critic," *Communication Research and Practice* 4, no. 3 (2018): 261–76, https://doi.org/10.1080/22041451.2018.1476797.

21. Dan Gillmor, *We the Media: Grassroots Journalism by the People, for the People* (Sebastopol: O'Reilly, 2006); Highfield, *Social Media*.

22. Morag Kobez, "'Restaurant Reviews Aren't What They Used to Be': Digital Disruption and the Transformation of the Role of the Food Critic," *Communication Research and Practice* 4, no. 3 (2018): 261–76, https://doi.org/10.1080/22041451.2018.1476797, 269.

23. Ibid., 263.

24. Bee Wilson, *The Way We Eat Now* (London: 4th Estate, 2019), 194.

25. Leaver, Highfield, and Abidin, *Instagram*.

26. Ibid., 167.

27. Lucy Battersby, "Freakshakes Are Hitting Melbourne and Your Waistline," *Good Food*, September 29, 2015, www.goodfood.com.au.

28. Matthew Raggatt, "'Freakshake' Drives Success for Canberra's My Kitchen Rules Duo," *Good Food*, July 11, 2015, www.goodfood.com.au.

29. The name Pât Gây refers to the FreakShake flavor based on the Australian ice cream called the Golden Gaytime, which has been popular for over sixty years. Gaytimes are a popsicle-style ice cream product that consists of vanilla and toffee-flavored ice cream coated in chocolate and biscuit pieces.

30. Pâtissez (@patissez), "The Gâyest of them all! ? currently formulating a whole new range of FreakShakes," Instagram photo, January 28, 2016, www.instagram.com/p/BBE3YhxjysJ/. Milk crumb is made by combining a mixture of milk powder, flour, cornstarch, and kosher salt with just enough melted butter to form a crumb-like texture. This is then baked until dry.

31. Taylor and Keating, "Contemporary Food Imagery," 312.

32. Ibid., 308.

33. Emily Baker, "Pattisez Civic Shop Shut after Freakshake Creators 'Bit Off More than We Could Chew," *Canberra Times*, November 17, 2017, www.canberratimes.com.au.

34. Natalie Sportelli, "Instagram Is Putting Restaurants on the Map, But What Hap-

pens After Their Food Goes Viral?," *Forbes*, March 24, 2016, www.forbes.com; "Locations," Black Tap Craft Burgers and Beer, accessed January 4, 2021, https://blacktap.com/locations/.

35. Hilary Osborne, "Freakshakes: The Rise of a Monstrous Mashup of Drink and Dessert," *Guardian*, August 31, 2016, www.theguardian.com.

36. Ibid.

37. Katherine Kirkwood, "Tasting but Not Tasting: MasterChef Australia and Vicarious Consumption," *M/C Journal* 17, no. 1 (2014), http://journal.media-culture.org.au/index.php/mcjournal/article/viewArticle/761/0.

38. Leaver, Highfield, and Abidin, *Instagram*, 164.

39. Neil Perry quoted in Jonathon Moran, "Neil Perry Slams MasterChef 'Nobodies,'" *Daily Telegraph* (Sydney), July 18, 2010, www.dailytelegraph.com.au.

40. Moran, "Neil Perry"; Karl Quinn, "MasterChef Recap: The Great Airline Food Challenge," *Sydney Morning Herald*, June 13, 2011, www.smh.com.au.

41. Jonathon Moran, "Neil Perry Denies Calling MasterChef Contestants 'Nobodies,'" *Daily Telegraph* (Sydney), July 18, 2010, www.dailytelegraph.com.au.

42. Lucinda Dean, "Marion Is Master of Her Destiny," *Rockhampton Morning Bulletin*, July 19, 2011, www.themorningbulletin.com.au/news/master-of-her-destiny/906024/.

43. Fiona Smith, "Why Being Voted Off MasterChef Was the Best Thing to Ever Happen to Marion Grasby," *Australian Financial Review*, February 13, 2015, www.afr.com.

44. Ibid.

45. Vanessa Williams, "Life's a Feast for MasterChef's Marion," *West Australian* (Perth), April 18, 2013, https://thewest.com.au; Smith, "Why Being Voted off MasterChef."

46. Taina Bucher and Anne Helmond, "The Affordances of Social Media Platforms," in Burgess, Marwick, and Poell, *Sage Handbook of Social Media*, 238.

47. Leaver, Highfield, and Abidin, *Instagram*.

48. "Celebrity Chef Marion Grasby," LifeStyle, 2013, www.lifestylefood.com.au/chefs/mariongrasby/, accessed October 1, 2020.

49. Brooke Hunter, "Marion Grasby Mother's Day Interview," Female.com.au, www.female.com.au/marion-grasby-mothers-day-interview.htm; Angela Saurine, "What My Mum Taught Me about Food," *Daily Telegraph* (Sydney), May 5, 2015, www.dailytelegraph.com.au.

50. Julia Child quoted in Kathleen Collins, *Watching What We Eat: The Evolution of Television Cooking Shows* (New York: Continuum, 2009), 76.

51. Susan Low, "How the TV Chef Was Cooked Up," *Telegraph*, July 20, 2002, www.telegraph.co.uk.

CHAPTER 12

My Life and Labor as an Instagram Influencer Turned Instagram Scholar

KC HYSMITH

I check the calendar and settle on a chocolate layer cake. My next paid Instagram campaign starts in two weeks, and I have three other recipe shoots in the queue. I make a list of ingredients and check the pantry to see if I have open containers of chocolate chips, flour, or sugar. A glance in the fridge to check on the status of unsalted butter, milk, and eggs. If I'm working for a big client, I'll get new versions of everything on the list and expense them. If not, these pre-shopping calculations keep my profit margins high. Most of the time, there is no direct client, so waste not, want not is key in my little kitchen business.

I pocket my list and drive to the grocery store. If I need fresh, photogenic produce, herbs, or other seasonal ingredients, I also stop at the local farmers' market. Bags full, I rush back home before the daylight begins to shift away from the big windows that line one side of my kitchen. Notepad and pen out, I prep the cake batter, jotting down changes to the recipe as I work. I've already figured out the recipe ratios, but I keep my notes handy for any last-minute changes. I add some cinnamon and make a note. While the cake bakes, I make use of that fading light and style some props—spoons, linens, small plates, a silver cake cutter—and snap a few photos. If I didn't already have these props, I would have run to one of my preferred antique shops or home goods stores that let me buy a single dish or two spoons at a time. An entire armoire stores all my photo props and a two-drawer filing cabinet holds linens.

With a few minutes to spare, I wash the chocolate-covered dishes and ready the sink for the next round of recipe testing. I wash most dishes by hand because the dishwasher ruins the hard-earned patina that forms on old metal utensils and serving dishes. Plus, it simply isn't quick enough to keep pace with the timing of my photo shoots. While the cake cools, I make buttercream frosting. I set up my camera and gear. Depending upon the subject, my mood, or the day's light, I might use my smartphone instead, one I've carefully researched and selected primarily for its superior camera and internal storage.

Scene set, cake styled, I snap at least a dozen photos from various angles. Next, I edit. Whether captured on my phone or my camera, I crop the image to size and add editorial features like filters or lighting adjustments. Once the image is on my phone, I pass it through an Instagram planning app that shows me a preview of my current feed along with upcoming images. After making sure it fits into my feed and the other planned images, I upload the image to Instagram along with a thoughtfully crafted caption and any relevant hashtags and handles. My captions are a careful mental calculation of my personal bandwidth, my audience, and the current goings-on in the food world; this creates a range of posts from short-hand recipes sprinkled with food puns to long-form narratives on food and politics.

The work continues after posting. There are e-mails from sponsors about collaborations and campaigns, hashtags to research, comments and likes waiting for replies, online classes on new photo or digital software, finances to monitor, and then it starts all over again tomorrow morning. If there's time, I'll eat a slice of cake.

Despite its name, Instagram is not instantaneous, at least not for most influencers. The publication of a single post can require dozens of steps; days, weeks, or months of planning; and the application of myriad digital and analog skills. Even images that require far less work and happen more organically—like those taken while dining at restaurants, scenes of open-air markets, or more casual dishes that need less setup—go through a similarly exhaustive editorial process. In the end, however, all you see are the perfectly framed pictures of food.

In January 2015, I woke up with over two hundred thousand Instagram followers.[1] I am, according to the numbers, an Instagram influencer. This is the only time I will ever identify as such in print. If you approach me in person and mention my Instagram account, I will try to change the subject. This reaction makes me wonder: why am I embarrassed of my digital work? Why do I struggle to acknowledge the skills that such work requires, such as social media management, culinary technique, photography, and photo editing? Instagram, once a significant portion of my bread and butter, has now become the focus of my scholarly attention.

This chapter examines the personal, political, and professional intersections of being "Instafamous." It also unpacks the careful construction of an Instagram identity and how food-focused influencers navigate the spectacular and the mediated. I use my life—as a woman, as a food professional, and now, as an academic studying the intersections of women's foodways, media, and technology—as a case study. I argue that while influencers cultivate forms of celebrity capital and contrived authenticity through their social platforms, their efforts can also be interpreted as acts of feminist collaboration and subversive resistance to commodity culture—especially for women who have been historically and systemically disenfranchised through traditional capitalist economies. Through a combination of personal reflections, digital ethnographic observations, and cultural critique, this chapter considers how and why the presence and labor of Instagram influencers and the Instafamous have become ubiquitous in the world of food.

The Birth of an Influencer

When I first gained what we now call influencer status, I had recently completed a graduate degree in gastronomy and was working as a freelance food writer, recipe tester, and photographer. Up until that time, my personal Instagram feed was a mix of over-filtered squares featuring my life as a Texan living in New England and the recipes that I tested for national publications and my own social media feeds in my awkward but light-filled rental kitchen. Then one morning, my follower count exploded. One of my first images to break a thousand likes was a shot of an ancho pepper–spiked hot chocolate concoction. Why did this particular image take off? I have a couple of theories. First, a logistical one: a massive blizzard had just swept over the Boston area and the rate of snow-bound Instagram use likely increased in response. Another explanation relies on Instagram's focus on visuality: the aerial angle of the photo and the careful balance between clean, negative space and lived-in messiness were all characteristics of a growing food-photography trend. I look at it now and notice its faults: too blurry, the linens are overexposed, and the dried peppers look like little indiscernible brown lumps. You can even see the lines connecting the four faux-marble floor tiles I glued together to look like a lavish tabletop. Over the next several days my follower count crept upward, reaching over two hundred thousand at one point. I kept waiting for it to disappear, for the glitch to be corrected and my fifteen minutes of fame to be over, but it never happened.

Instagram, the company, does not use the term "influencer." The app refers to users who aim to turn their content into a living as "creators."[2] The term "influencer" is user-generated, platform-agnostic, and applies to users who gain renown and maintain influence through those platforms and generally retain a large number of followers. The term "influencer" is also subjective, as there is no set number of followers that make a user *influential*.

While there are no hard-and-fast rules regarding the analytics that make someone an influencer, some general parameters started to take shape within the influencer marketplace after the introduction of advertising space on the app in the fall of 2013. Digital marketing companies have attempted to categorize influencers by their number of followers: the top tier includes influencers with more than 1 million followers, middle groups include a wide range from 100,000 to 1 million followers, and smaller influencers have anywhere between 1,000 and 100,000 followers.[3] There are a few built-in benchmarks that could denote "influencer status," but they aren't inherently part of being an influencer. For example, users with at least 10,000 followers gain the ability to use hyperlinks in Instagram stories—a particularly helpful digital tool for affiliated link commissions as well as driving traffic to blogs, websites, and online shops.[4] It is important to note that influencers do not necessarily utilize these categories or adopt these subtitles, though they are likely part of the conversation between user and sponsor during transactional negotiations.

Another important difference to note within the categories of influence is the role of the celebrity-influencer—popular figures such as TV chefs, cookbook authors, and food media personalities. While these celebrity-influencers typically possess followers in the millions, they gained their celebrity off-app and came to Instagram with a built-in following. This celebrity feeds their real-world influence and does not necessarily put them on an even footing (or an equally matched paid-content playing field) as an Instagram-native influencer. Consider a food photographer who starts their career on Instagram versus a chef who already had a TV show and several award-winning cookbooks. Social media offers similar tools to both kinds of users, but real-world celebrities bring a higher level of clout (which typically correlates to a higher number of initial followers) than digitally native influencers. This point is significant when it comes to understanding the socioeconomic implications of digital labor. For this study, I rely on Tiziana Terranova's definition of digital labor, or immaterial labor, which sets no parameters for what constitutes knowledge or who, regardless of their perceived influence, can create it.[5]

Before influencers, though, there were popular users with significant followings. Instead of gaining celebrity through crowdsourcing, these popular users were, for lack of a better term, peer reviewed. An early element of Instagram included a "suggested user list" featuring a curated collection of popular users vetted by Instagram officials.[6] When new users downloaded and first signed up for the app, this list would appear and offer suggestions for discovering new feeds. In addition to Instagram's internal selection, popular users with significant followings could also nominate other users for this list. In 2015, I learned that I was nominated by one of my food-photographer peers (I still don't know who), and their influence helped me gain my own.

Before Instagram allowed explicit advertising and promoted posts, popular users with large followings did not necessarily partake in what is now known as influencer marketing and instead participated in collaborations with brands and companies that offered free products and sometimes money in exchange for promotion.[7] My nonmonetary collaborations included posts in exchange for bottles of olive oil, coupons for free yogurt, table linens, and a giant box of enamel dinnerware. As Instagram continued to wrestle with regulation, I and many other popular users turned to the freelance model to create contracts, set rates, and outline publication agreements. While the collaboration method still exists (I recently made a deal to post images in exchange for free kid-friendly cooking kits), newer self-enforced forms of regulation allow popular users, whether they identify as influencers or not, agency over their digital labor. Influencers across the platform—from makeup artists to fitness instructors—perform substantial offline labor to make their digital feeds viable. For food influencers, the majority of their labor is nondigital and takes place in kitchens, markets, and pantries, requiring significant economic planning before a well-lit food photo ever finds its way onto their Instagram feed.

Digital Labor, Emotional Labor

The digitality of Instagram serves as a sort of smoke screen, blurring the individuals and their labor that make its endless stream of content possible. While press abounds on influencers like the Kardashians and their "snake oil" Insta promotions, many homegrown influencers strive for transparency in their digital labor. They clearly mark sponsored posts and offer behind-the-scenes stories that give users insights into the real-life happenings of Instagrammers. As part of our digital practice, influencers commodify transparency in order to communicate a sense of trust and authenticity to our followers. Despite this emphasis on transparency, Instagram remains a precarious and unregulated digital landscape for all levels and category of influencer.

The subjective qualifications of influencerdom also make it difficult to determine the gender (in addition to other) demographics of food influencers. While age is often the first demographic discussed in relation to social media, the concept of the generationally divided user base of apps such as Instagram constantly changes, as new platforms compete for users and older adopters become increasingly comfortable with digital landscapes. The age range of influencers is broad, and that age diversity shapes different types of influence across the platform and within the food world. A 2019 report analyzing three million sponsored Instagram posts found that 54 percent were published by influencers between the ages of twenty-five and thirty-four.[8] However, the age of an influencer cannot compete with the impact of gender.

According to a 2019 report, women make up 77 percent of the total number of influencers across all social media platforms.[9] Another report identifies ten of the most-followed food influencers on Instagram, seven of whom are women.[10] Furthermore, market research indicates women are more likely to be called influencers, while men style themselves as "digital content creators" or other industry-specific terms.[11] Like me, the food influencers in my community eschew these terms, instead selecting titles that accurately describe our labor, like "blogger," "author," or "photographer." This gendered dichotomy, even if perceived, disparages the term "influencer," valuing masculinized creation over feminized influence and obfuscating the fact that influencers do indeed produce content.

Women who manage influential food-focused Instagram feeds labor at the intersection of the digital sector and the food industry, two traditionally male-dominated fields. Unpacking the masculinized narratives that are foundational to both culinary and digital history helps us understand the precarity women face when working in either field. In *Taking the Heat*, food scholars Deborah Harris and Patti Giuffre investigate why women have "lagged so far behind men in professional kitchens" and how the traditionally feminized fields of food and cooking are masculinized in professional settings.[12] Throughout U.S. history, food-related labor has been categorized under traditional gender roles: women cooked domestically, men cooked professionally.

Due to industry-wide structural inequality, women who work in digital spaces also suffer from the devaluation of their digital labor. Looking specifically at digital content creation and management—the bulk of food influencers' work—this disparity centers on a gendered perception of digital labor. Feminist media scholars Brooke Erin Duffy and Becca Schwartz investigated this constructed divide through job recruitment ads and social media employment. Their research found that the ideal digital social media worker possesses a set of features including "sociability and leisure; emotional management; and various types of flexibility." These expectations, they argue, inform and influence the "increasingly feminized nature of social media employment with its characteristic invisibility, lower pay, and marginal status within the technology field." Influencer labor carries an assumption of being "fun" and "hobby-like," in turn marginalizing the predominantly female workforce and their labor.[13] This marginalization reinforces the invisibility of women's digital labor within a larger capitalistic economy that devalues and delegitimizes other work, including food labor, traditionally associated with women.

Building an Identity, Reconstructing Gendered Economies

In practice, this gendered perception results in the expectation that food influencers will produce content—including photos and recipes—for free (or at a lower rate) and perform emotional work (e.g., "liking" and "commenting" especially to users who respond negatively or with extremely personal information) on behalf of their followers.

For example, in response to Texas governor Greg Abbott's decision to opt out of the federal refugee resettlement program, I reposted an old picture (fig. 12-1, top) of a pan of Texas Sheet Cake with bright yellow letters that read "build a longer table, not a higher fence."[14] Multiple users scrutinized my stance on immigration, questioned my use of cakes as a platform for political messaging, and many told me to "stick to baking." This prompted me to post yet another cake with a long caption explaining the importance of women's food labor and the historic role of food in politics.[15] I included a promise piped in buttercream that I would indeed "stick to baking," and all that truly entails. I have kept my promise, especially through the political turmoil of the 2020 U.S. presidential election, with additional cake production (fig. 12-1, bottom), photography, and Instagram management that speak to the ongoing resonance of food politics.[16]

Women who produce content that pushes the limits of these feminized expectations are often met with scrutiny. In the digital market, this scrutiny can cost an influencer their livelihood. Sarah Crawford, a blogger and food influencer known as @bromabakery, posts when other food Instagrammers plagiarize her work. In a post accompanying a photo of cranberry meringue pie, she discusses the issue of accountability and how the theft of intellectual property devalues the work and damages the collective labor of the Instagram food community.[17] Multiple comments beneath Crawford's post question her complaint, arguing that recipes and food photography form a body of work that other users continuously re-create as their own. Other commenters justify Crawford's grievance and suggest practicing proper citation. Plagiarism occurs across all categories of creative content on Instagram, but the fact that users dismiss Crawford's concerns since her work involved *food* demonstrates systemic expectations of gendered labor and the devaluing of food because of its long connection to women. Similar gendered comments followed multiple posts by baker Becca Rea-Holloway, also known as @thesweetfeminist, who manages a feed full of baked goods decorated with feminist messages. This scrutiny encouraged Rea-Holloway to create a cake decorated with alternating blue and pink letters that read "You don't need to know what I do with the cakes."[18] Some users wondered about Rea-Holloway's recipes (whether she used cake mixes to save time and money), others worried about food waste, and many questioned and criticized her use of cakes as a platform for political messaging. This prompted Rea-Holloway to bake yet another cake that spelled out the importance of women's food labor in buttercream frosting: "it's not 'just a cake.'"[19]

All social media relies on willing prosumers, users who deliberately participate in the act of prosumption that involves both the production and consumption of content.[20] Nearly all users—effectively anyone who regularly posts and consumes Instagram content—contribute to the evolving dynamics of prosumption on Instagram. Influencers capitalize on this market. It is possible that certain

FIGURE 12-1. Instagram cake politics.

subgenres of influencer (e.g., users who focus on motherhood, exercise and diet culture, or even food and recipes) purposefully or involuntarily reaffirm gender inequalities through their content. These same subjects, however, also afford many influencers, especially women, an opportunity to make money when their personal or family obligations limit employment options. The impact and the ethical implications of influencers, especially for those who work in areas traditionally associated with outdated gender norms, like food and domesticity, will be a contested issue and area of study in the future.

Building an Identity, Reconstructing Gendered Economies

In building a media identity, Sarah Banet-Weiser explains that "the product in gendered economies of visibility is the feminine body. Its value is constantly deliberated over, evaluated, judged, and scrutinized through media discourses, law, and policy. The dual dynamic of regulating and producing the visible self-work is to not only serve up bodies as commodities but also create the body and the self as a brand."[21] While some scholars argue this economy is simply part of the larger corporate consumer culture, it also highlights the possibility for individual empowerment.[22] Influencers maintain visual lives through the way they curate themselves and their surroundings in order to perform and preserve their influence. Food influencers curate with food and food-related imagery. Shifting the economy of visibility, at least in part, from the body to food forces us to reckon with constructions of gender in different ways. Female food influencers force this shift by using parts of our bodies, specifically our hands, in a calculated performance of femininity that leverages social expectations with feminist agency. While the food and the body remain linked through (mostly) "appropriate" feminine aesthetics—hands gently cupping mugs, touching ornate cakes, cradling delicate produce—this shift allows female food influencers to shape our identity, maintain bodily agency, and navigate labor issues on our own terms.[23]

Female food influencers can be simultaneously empowered and objectified through their relationships with food, all while working to create a more equitable—even wealth generating—gendered economy in which they operate. A picture of a cake posted to Instagram can be both a transaction of digital labor and a feminist act, but it can never be "just a cake."

Notes

1. Since returning to academia and starting my study of Instagram, even though I spend even more time on the platform, my follower count has dropped significantly.
2. @creators, Instagram, www.instagram.com/creators.

3. CMSWire designates these categories as "mega," "macro," and "micro"; Influencers and each possesses its own marketing strategy depending on follower count. Kaya Ismail, "Social Media Influencers: Mega, Macro, Micro or Nano," CMSWire, December 10, 2018, www.cmswire.com/digital-marketing/social-media-influencers -mega-macro-micro-or-nano/; Digital Marketing.org also adds "nano-influencer" to the list, Gary Henderson, "How Many Followers Do You Need to Be an Influencer?" *Digital Marketing* (blog), August 31, 2020, www.digitalmarketing.org/blog/ how-many-followers-do-you-need-to-be-an-influencer.

4. TikTok has a similar benchmark to join their TikTok Creator Fund, a vague fund that pays users an unspecified and dynamic amount based on "a variety of factors" for their content. "TikTok Creator Fund: Your Questions Answered," TikTok, March 25, 2021, https://newsroom.tiktok.com/en-gb/tiktok-creator-fund-your -questions-answered.

5. Tiziana Terranova, "Free Labor: Producing Culture for the Digital Economy," *Social Text*, 63, vol. 18, no. 2 (Summer 2000): 33–58.

6. Trisha Hughes, "How to Get on Instagram's Suggested User List," Eat Your Beets, www.eatyourbeets.com/instagram/suggested-user-list/.

7. Vindu Goel and Sydney Ember, "Instagram to Open Its Photo Feed to Ads," *New York Times*, June 2, 2015, www.nytimes.com; Mona Hellenkemper, "State of the Industry: Influencer Marketing in 2019," *InfluencerDB* (blog), January 14, 2019, https://web.archive.org/web/20191015043214/https://blog.influencerdb.com/state -of-the-industry-influencer-marketing-2019/.

8. A. Guttmann, "Distribution of Influencers Creating Sponsored Posts on Instagram Worldwide in 2019, by Age Group," Statista, January 17, 2020, www.statista .com/statistics/893733/share-influencers-creating-sponsored-posts-by-age/#:~:text =In%202019%20an%20analysis%20of,ages%20of%2018%20and%2024.

9. Lena Young, "How Much Do Influencers Charge?" *Klear* (blog), May 16, 2019, https://blog.klear.com/influencer-pricing-2019/.

10. Though it is important to point out that at least three of these Influencers had gained various levels of celebrity prior to their joining Instagram. This statistic is another example of the subjectivity of influence and who qualifies as an influencer. J. Clement, "Most Popular Food Influencers on Instagram in the U.S. 2019," Statista, October 8, 2019, www.statista.com/statistics/785894/most-followers-instagram -food-usa/.

11. Emma Grey Ellis, "Why Women Are Called 'Influencers' and Men 'Creators,'" *Wired*, May 29, 2019, www.wired.com/story/influencers-creators-gender-divide/.

12. Deborah Harris and Patti Giuffre, *Taking the Heat: Women Chefs and Gender Inequality in the Professional Kitchen* (New Brunswick, NJ: Rutgers University Press, 2015), 2.

13. Brooke Erin Duffy and Becca Schwartz, "Digital 'Women's Work?': Job Recruitment Ads and the Feminization of Social Media Employment," *New Media and Society* 20, no. 8 (2017): 2972—89.

14. Katherine Hysmith, @kchysmith, Instagram, January 13, 2020, www.instagram.com/p/B7RlrKjHB6g/. The caption reads, "#Texas I love you, but you're break-

ing my heart," and at the bottom of the photo a plate holds a Texas-shaped piece of cake.

15. Katherine Hysmith, @kchysmith, Instagram, January 17, 2020, www.insta gram.com/p/B7cTEFYH0Og/.

16. Katherine Hysmith, @kchysmith, Instagram, December 14, 2020, www.insta gram.com/p/CIzGyDQHMwt/.

17. Sarah Crawford, @bromabakery, Instagram, November 9, 2019, www.insta gram.com/bromabakery, accessed January 6, 2020.

18. Becca Rea-Holloway, @thesweetfeminist, Instagram, November 13, 2018, www.instagram.com/thesweetfeminist.

19. Becca Rea-Holloway, @thesweetfeminist, Instagram, June 10, 2019, www.insta gram.com/thesweetfeminist.

20. Ritzer and Jurgenson, "Production, Consumption, Prosumption: The Nature of Capitalism in the Age of the Digital 'Prosumer,'" *Journal of Consumer Culture* 10, no. 1 (2010): 13–36.

21. Sarah Banet-Weiser, "Media, Markets, Gender: Economies of Visibility in a Neoliberal Moment," *Communication Review* 18, no. 1 (2015): 57.

22. Angela McRobbie, *The Aftermath of Feminism: Gender, Culture, and Social Change* (Thousand Oaks, CA: Sage, 2009), 158.

23. Tisha Dejmanee, "'Food Porn' as Postfeminist Play: Digital Femininity and the Female Body on Food Blogs," *Television and New Media* 17, no. 5 (July 2016): 429–48. Appropriate feminine aesthetics can also be interpreted differently; see, for example, the gesture Becca Rea-Holloway makes in her June 10, 2019, Instagram post.

PART III

Negotiation

CHAPTER 13

Transgressive Food Practices on Instagram

The Case of Guldkroen in Copenhagen

JONATAN LEER AND
STINNE GUNDER STRØM KROGAGER

Instagram has become a vibrant digital host to proliferating ethical, environmental, health, and aesthetic movements, spawning diverse online communities. In the context of digital food cultures, Instagram provides a platform for sophisticated aesthetics attributed to middle-class foodie culture[1] and ethical concerns in relation to food consumption.[2] Likewise, restaurants compete to make their food and interiors Instagrammable in order to entice guests to tag and post from their restaurants using tags such as #foodporn or #foodgasm.[3]

Images of food styled to be aesthetically pleasing and enticing is by no means a new genre. The visual arts have depicted food and meals for centuries, such as in classical still-life paintings.[4] However, only recently has it become possible for every social media profile owner to share their everyday meal, Michelin restaurant experience, or coffee on the go. Instagram has become a preferred forum for these posts as the platform's affordances support highly elaborated aesthetic work, and Instagram users mimic the professional food styling genre in their ambition to compose food images that look unconstructed, casual, and yet highly appealing.[5] Thus, the food images permeating Instagram are not random snapshots, such as those typically found on Snapchat, which defaults to deleting posts. On Instagram, the food images tend to be carefully aestheticized, curated, and filtered.

However, some restaurants deploy very different aesthetics and discourses to brand themselves. In this chapter, we discuss how challenging the mainstream Instagram aesthetics can create an incongruous counter-space on social media.

We explore this argument by analyzing an extreme case of this tendency, namely the Instagram profile of chef and restaurateur Umut Sakarya in Copenhagen. Sakarya is the owner of Guldkroen (the Golden Inn), an unusual new restaurant in Copenhagen's vibrant food scene. The establishment sets itself apart by serving heavy, traditional Danish food in a nostalgic kitsch interior at a time when the dominant trend among Copenhagen restaurants tends toward light, vegetable-based foods, served in neatly designed Nordic interiors.[6] On his Instagram profile, Sakarya presents food in a grotesque, humorous, and often provocative manner, accompanied by anti-vegetarian and often sexist discourse celebrating unhealthy and unsustainable food practices.

Sakarya's Instagram practices are particularly provocative due to the antagonistic discourses that coexist on his profile. In one post, he may ridicule right-wing anti-Muslim politicians. In the next, he may be overtly sexist. We argue that using Instagram in a manner that clearly transgresses the aesthetic and discursive food—and social—norms of Instagram works to brand Sakarya and his restaurant as rebellious, distinguishing them from the dominant Copenhagen foodie ideals of sustainability, minimalism, and healthfulness. On the Instagram profiles of restaurants like Radio and Manfreds, which belong to the same mid price range as Guldkroen, one finds pictures of minimalistic, neatly plated dishes, close-ups of in-season produce, and photos of the landscapes where the foods originate—the iconography of the new Nordic cuisine typically associated with Copenhagen.

This chapter contributes to the study of food and Instagram by underscoring how food on Instagram is governed by distinct rules. These rules are largely unspoken but become apparent when transgressed. We furthermore argue that Sakarya's social media performance is particularly provocative because it takes place on Instagram, rather than other platforms such as YouTube, where similar practices have been noted.[7] Finally, we argue that this transgressive use of Instagram works as a branding strategy for Sakarya and his restaurant and can be read as a more general satire of the polished and ethical approach to food dominating Instagram.

Theoretically, we understand transgression as "a deeply reflexive act of denial and affirmation."[8] Transgression is not a direct denial, but a completion of the rule. Hence, transgression depends on the rule or the norm—and vice versa. Building on Michael Goodman and Colin Sage, we expand the concept so that a transgression can also be understood as moving a food ideology from one cultural sphere to another antagonistic sphere, such as slow food's collaboration with supermarkets (which they initially opposed) in order to democratize their ideas.[9] Furthermore, we believe it is important to distinguish between different types of food-related transgressions based on breaking rules or norms related to aesthetics, behavior, and morality. In relation to our case, we have identified two forms of transgression that are central to our analysis of Instagram: transgression of Instagram food aesthetics, and transgression of conventional food discourse on Instagram. As context is central to transgression, we want to contextualize our case in the Copenhagen restaurant scene before we move on to the analysis.

Guldkroen and the Copenhagen Foodscape

Copenhagen has undergone a culinary revolution since the early 2000s. This is not least due to the unexpected success of the New Nordic Cuisine outlined in a manifesto in 2004 authored by Nordic chefs.[10] The goal of the manifesto was to create an innovative Nordic cuisine based exclusively on produce from the region. The manifesto highlighted such values as sustainability, healthfulness, sound production practices, and seasonality.[11] The restaurant Noma, which rigidly follows the dogmas of the movement under head chef René Redzepi, is the flagship of the movement. Noma has received global recognition, earning two Michelin stars in 2007 (and three in 2021) and a position as the best restaurant in the world on Restaurant Magazine's World's 50 Best Restaurants list (W50) in 2010, 2011, 2012, and 2014. The Nordic region, and Copenhagen in particular, was able to capitalize on this global visibility in order to become a hip culinary destination. Restaurants in the capital counted only eight Michelin stars in 2003 when Noma opened. In 2019, Danish restaurants held thirty-four Michelin stars, with the large majority in Copenhagen; two Copenhagen restaurants ranked in the top ten of the W50. This acclaim continues to attract significant traffic to Copenhagen, notably from foodie tourists and young, ambitious chefs from all over the world.

The result was not a mainstreaming of the New Nordic movement but rather a highly dynamic and competitive restaurant scene.[12] Many younger chefs instead engaged in a more globalized style of cooking.[13] Furthermore, the development was not just detectable in the fine dining scene, but also birthed various street food markets with global food options, and supported a strong mid-price restaurant segment and hipster food neighborhoods.[14]

Despite the city's increased international focus and diversification of food cultures, it appears that some of the values from the New Nordic manifesto still dominate. Particularly, the focus on aesthetic minimalism and on ethical food consumption—which promotes sustainability, animal welfare, and healthfulness as essential values—continues to thrive. All of these elements coalesce in the increased focus on vegetable-based food. Vegan and vegetarian restaurants have seen increased popularity in Denmark, particularly in the 2010s with rising public focus on sustainability, especially the negative impact of high meat consumption on climate change. The number of vegan and vegetarian restaurants in Denmark has increased from ten in 2010 to fifty-four in 2019.[15] This trend is particularly strong in the big cities and especially the capital. Here, the area surrounding the Nørrebro neighborhood has seen the highest concentration of vegan and vegetarian eateries with twenty vegan or vegetarian-friendly restaurants within a square mile.[16] Many high-end restaurants have also given vegetables a more prominent role. Another important trend is the focus on organic produce and sustainable production in many restaurants' storytelling. Several restaurants have their own vegetable gardens or collaborate with small organic producers.

Umut Sakarya appeared as something of a shock in the midst of this minimalistic and ethically concerned scene. Sakarya is a trained chef and had his first claim to fame in *Masterchef Danmark* in 2015. He is of Turkish descent and was not brought up on Danish food. Raised in a Muslim family, Sakarya did not eat pork growing up. Nonetheless, Sakarya has a strong love for traditional Danish food. This became clear when Sakarya opened his first restaurant: Grisen (the Pig). The establishment set out to revive and refine traditional Danish *grillbar* (fast) food, characterized by staple "junk" foods such as deep-fried chicken and fish, hot dogs, roast pork sandwiches, and French fries. *Grillbars* were once a feature in every Danish town, serving high-calorie, fatty dishes that would surely be classified as very questionable by modern nutritional standards. In recent decades, the *grillbar* tradition has lost terrain in the fast-food landscape to varieties of international cuisine, such as shawarma and sushi.

Thus, Grisen cultivates a certain nostalgia for this particular food culture, which has fallen out of fashion in the mainstream. We find a similar ambition in Sakarya's next project, Guldkroen (the Golden Inn). This establishment seeks to restore the Danish tradition of *kromad* (lit., inn food), which centers around traditional Danish cuisine—meat, gravy, and potatoes. As in the case of *grillbar* food, this type of meal, too, is some distance from modern standards of healthiness and culinary diversity. Like much twentieth-century Danish food, it is characterized by a lack of vegetables, large amounts of pork meat and fat, and often associated with heavy beer consumption.[17] Meals often consist of one large-portioned dish and a dessert, dispensing with any pretenses to fanciness.

In Guldkroen's case, the revival of this style of eating is taken to the extreme in terms of fat content and portion size. On the menu, we find, for instance, an oversized schnitzel that starts with about 1.3 pounds of meat, then double-breads it and tops it with half a pound of melted butter. In various interviews, Sakarya describes his boredom with the restaurant scene's dominant ideal of elegant minimalism, seasonal vegetables, and healthiness. Instead, he wants to focus on classic foods and abundance. Sakarya does not have any ambition of reinventing *kromad*, preferring to stay true to the tradition. Unlike much of the New Nordic movement, where culinary invention is often miles away from what most Danes associate with Danish food traditions, there are no culinary surprises at Guldkroen.[18]

Another important feature of Guldkroen is its interior design. Sakarya and his partners have taken the refurbished interior of one of many traditional Danish countryside inns to close in recent years and used it to furnish Guldkroen. Such traditional inns are seen as unfashionable by foodie communities and incompatible with modern food ideals as prescribed by health authorities. However, Guldkroen idolizes this unfashionability with an almost museum-like restoration of the traditional inn with green-brown colors, retro wallpaper, and kitsch nature paintings from the *krondyr ved søen* (deer by lake) tradition. This tradition is associated with bad taste and with the unsuccessful attempts of working-class households to be "middle-classing." Guldkroen unapologetically embraces this traditionally unappreciated inn decor.

One of the most idiosyncratic elements of Guldkroen may be that it is located in Nørrebro, one of the trendiest and most politically progressive neighborhoods in Copenhagen. Guldkroen appears radically out of place among the numerous vegan and vegetarian restaurants, but it is exactly this incongruity that Sakarya has used to construct a rebellious image for himself and his restaurant, defying the surrounding trends. Sakarya has also skillfully developed this rebellious image in his online presence to attract attention to his persona and brand. This attention has led to many appearances in traditional media outlets. In October 2018, he became one of the few chefs to ever appear on the front page of *Politiken*, the leading Danish newspaper, and in 2019 the popular public television channel DR3 made a four-episode documentary about him and his emerging restaurant empire based on traditional, meaty food. The program was titled *Tyrkersvin* (Turkish pig), a condescending nickname for Turkish immigrants in Denmark. This appearance in conventional media had a positive impact on his business and boosted his brand.[19] The provocative naming of the program could be read as a politically subversive action reclaiming a pejorative slur similar to the gay movement's reclaiming of the insulting label "queer." Also, the title reflects the crude Danish humor that is frequent in popular culture as well as marketing and advertising in Denmark.[20] The expression is even more strange as observant Muslims do not eat pork.

Methodology

Working with digital and social media calls for comprehensive methodological considerations in regard to the selection of analytical material as digital media provides access to a vast amount of data. Furthermore, working with digital media material requires different ethical considerations. In the following, we elaborate on the identification and collection of our sample.

Our object of analysis is Umut Sakarya's Instagram profile. The number of posts on Sakarya's Instagram profile is immense, and we can by no means conduct a comprehensive analysis of all posts (over eleven thousand). Sakarya has been posting on Instagram since May 2012, and as his popularity (almost forty thousand followers) and number of restaurants have increased, his personal Instagram profile has become more of a professional brand.[21]

We use Sakarya's Instagram profile as a lens to examine the branding of Guldkroen during the first half of 2019. While Guldkroen has been open since mid-2017, due to the high number of posts over this period, we have chosen to focus on this narrower timeframe. This six-month period is significant because it reflects a shift in Sakarya's public persona: it is marked by his rising status following the release of *Tyrkersvin* and by an emboldened reliance on irony and political satire.

To select specific posts for in-depth analysis, we focused on permanent posts rather than the more ephemeral feature Instagram Stories, which are automatically taken down after twenty-four hours, though such stories are also a prominent element of Sakarya's profile. We did not consider stories because they are often less curated than permanent posts, whereas permanent posts leave a lasting mark on the profile. Hence, our interest revolves around the account's enduring content and the themes it reflects.

To identify the themes of the permanent posts, we conducted a thematic mapping of all stored 2019 content on Sakarya's personal profile (not the restaurant's profile, as Sakarya is the brand). The purpose of the mapping is to identify recurring motifs and to ensure variation within the analytical sample. Each of us performed the mapping independently, then we compared the results and, through discussion and consideration of similarities and differences between our analyses, we determined two overall themes characterizing the profile: transgression of Instagram food aesthetics, and transgression of Instagram food discourse (through political satire and both sexualized and sexist content.) Then, we chose representative examples of each recurring theme in an attempt to identify common trends and patterns within the analytical sample.[22]

Transgressing Instagram Food Aesthetics

To analyze the theme of food aesthetic transgression, we have selected four posts for close reading. Two posts are typical examples of vulgar displays of huge amounts of food, most often meat and gravy: March 10, 2019, piles of pork belly; May 25, 2019, a 17.6-pound classic Danish hamburger with gravy. The other two posts are typical cases of how bodies (most often Sakarya's) and food are brought into play in a highly ironic and mocking intertextual way: April 15, 2019, Sakarya sitting in a bathtub filled with gravy (see fig. 13-1); April 30, 2019, Sakarya lying on a table with food served on his mostly naked body).

Celebration of the Grotesque

The March 10 post of heaped meat in the Guldkroen kitchen depicts about a dozen roasting pans filled with thick slices of fresh pork belly. In the foreground, pork belly spans the entire frame. In the background, the line of pork on roasting pans narrows like an infinite road vanishing into the horizon. Apart from the pork belly, only a few large steel kitchen machines are visible at the edges of the photo. Light in the far back of the photo (likely from a window that is not pictured) makes the pork belly almost sparkle at the end of the row of meat.[23]

The image from May 25 is part of a series of seven posts from Sakarya's appearance on *Go' morgen Danmark* (Good morning, Denmark), a morning talk show on TV2. The photo illustrates the Danish-style hamburger that Sakarya cooked in the studio, weighing in at over 17 pounds and soaked in gravy. In the background, the blurred talk show studio is visible, and the huge hamburger fills the foreground. The hamburger is on a large steel tray, and glimpses of melted white and yellow cheese and small green rings of spring onion can be seen between the gravy-soaked bread buns. Apart from this, everything is gravy-brown.[24]

These two photos represent a group of posts of transgressive scenes depicting excessive amounts of food. The depicted foods are always unhealthy—high in saturated fats and calories—as well as unsustainable—with different meats or gravy made from copious amounts of animal fats. The posts are followed by enthusiastic texts and emojis (e.g., 🤤 and 🍴 and ▰ [Denmark]) underscoring Sakarya's passion for traditional Danish food and cooking. These immoderate food scenes are far from the typical Instagram image of Copenhagen restaurants, both in terms of the vulgar content (excessive food quantity and unhealthfulness) and in regard to the lack of thoughtful composition, lighting, and filters.

Alternative Bodily Interaction with Food

The other two posts we examined are typical examples of the intersection of food and the body on Sakarya's profile. An April 15 post reveals him in a bathtub filled with what appears to be brown gravy (fig. 13-1). On the floor of the circa-1950s bathroom is a glass filled with beer accompanied by a beer can, and on the windowsill behind the tub is a potted plant, a small Danish flag, another can of beer, and a bottle of Fernet-Branca next to a glass filled with the same—a popular Italian liqueur that has become lowbrow pub culture. Sakarya is sitting in the bathtub filled with gravy up to his navel. Much of his upper body, with the exception of his arms, is smeared with the viscous brown liquid, as is his head. The gravy is partially wiped from around his eyes and mouth.[25]

In the post from April 30, Sakarya is lying on his back on a table in his restaurant, wearing only skimpy underpants. Sakarya's body is in profile, his head

FIGURE 13-1. Umut Sakarya in an April 15, 2019, post demonstrates a food-body interaction that is uncharacteristic of Instagram. Used with permission.

slightly raised and turned toward the photographer while his forefinger points at the camera. Arranged on his chest are caviar, tartlets, and copious amounts of roasted pork belly. In his lap are a schnitzel, peas, lemon slices, and lettuce, and between his thighs is a glass decanter filled with beer. Behind Sakarya are two men (wait staff from the restaurant wearing identical striped shirts, who recur on Sakarya's Instagram profile). The man seated by Sakarya's chest is bent over him, his eyes wide in a frantic expression, his open mouth ready to bite into one of the tartlets on Sakarya's chest. The other man looks on, smiling. In the background are visible the nostalgic and kitsch interiors of Guldkroen.[26]

Both of these visual performances of embodied immersion in the materiality of food draw on stereotypical and highly sexualized references to film, television, and commercials. The images recall the trope of a typically exposed or naked woman posed in similar settings as an object for the male gaze, albeit often bathing in milk and covered with other kinds of foods.[27] In Sakarya's inversion of this trope, both physical and culinary aesthetic ideals are distorted, and he stages the image to coarsely emphasize its trivialities. In this way, he mocks the original gendered power relation—for instance, with his overweight and hairy body, his moustache, his gesturing finger, and props, such as strong beer and Fernet-Branca, instead of, for example, a flute of refined champagne.

A similar "bro" attitude finds expression in the very popular Canadian YouTube channel Epic Meal Time, which presents grotesque meals similar to Sakarya's. Media sociologist Deborah Lupton argues that these might be seen as a particular kind of food porn, namely gonzo food porn, which "rely for their appeal not on the beauty of the objects depicted, but rather their transgressive nature that disrupts and challenges conventional norms of how these things should look."[28] Similarly, Sakarya's embodied interactions with food focus on their transgressive nature, such as the excessiveness, the ironic playfulness, and presumed working-class preferences for strong alcohol and unhealthy foods. However, Sakarya's total lack of political correctness appears to serve a greater objective—social and political satire, as we discuss in depth in the following section.

Transgression of Instagram Discourse

Political Satire

Compared to a discourse-driven platform such as Twitter, where political debates and hashtag activism are characteristic features, Instagram's political activism finds expression primarily through aestheticized visual representations.[29] Furthermore, aesthetic appeal seems to win favor on Instagram over satire and joking, which are more commonly found sparking political debate on Twitter. Despite this, Sakarya uses his profile to frame his opposition toward Danish right-wing parties in direct and sardonic ways. Prior to the June 5, 2019, Danish election, Sakarya repeatedly used Instagram to mock three Danish right-wing and anti-Islamic parties: Stram Kurs (Hard Line), Dansk Folkeparti (Danish People's Party), and Nye Borgerlige (New Right). These posts consist mostly of ironic imitations of election posters, featuring mock slogans that combine parts of the parties' actual political slogans combined with stereotypical commercial slogans and messages about food, such as "because everyone deserves thicker gravy and crispy crust!" This slogan is accompanied by a picture of Sakarya standing behind a table stabbing a large butcher's knife into the side of half of a fresh pig. In the image, he wears a Photoshopped red cap with the wording "Make flæsk [pork belly] great again."[30]

In all of these posts, Sakarya brings his own Turkish Muslim background into play. In another post from May 7 (fig. 13-2), Sakarya takes the Stram Kurs

FIGURE 13-2. Umut Sakarya's May 7, 2019, post satirizes a Stram Kurs election poster. Used with permission.

(Hard Line, the most controversial and anti-Islamic of the three parties) logo but replaces the party name with "Sprød Kurs" (Crisp Line) and frames himself as

> Umut Sakarya
> The soldier of pork belly
> The light of Danish food culture
> The protector of the hungry
> The hope of Danes
> And Party leader of Crisp Line
> For Denmark
> And against soft crust and
> poorly prepared Danish food.[31]

Sakarya's blunt, even confrontational, deployment of his Middle Eastern ethnicity serves to strengthen his explicit political message. Sakarya belongs to a marginalized ethnic minority in Denmark that is the frequent target of right-wing parties. Complicating matters, however, much of the traditional food culture Sakarya embraces is celebrated by the very same right-wing parties. Sakarya has taken advantage of this affinity before, inviting the long-time leader of the Dansk Folkeparti, Pia Kjærsgaard, to open one of his earlier restaurants celebrating traditional Danish fast food. This generated much media attention, as Pia Kjærsgaard had been persona non grata in Nørrebro, which has a significant immigrant population. While mocking these parties, Sakarya also dissociates himself from his own religious background, which does not condone the consumption of pork or alcohol. Nor does this diet follow the ideals of the left-leaning, cosmopolitan, and "creative class" majority in Nørrebro. Sakarya's intercultural position combined with his political activism is thus filled with contradictions.

Sexualized and Sexist Content

The final theme that we examine in this analysis is the very different modes of displaying sexist and sexualized content.

A recurring figure on Sakarya's profile is his younger girlfriend, Clara. On her twentieth birthday (May 28; Umut was then twenty-nine), Sakarya posted a photo of Clara accompanied by the text: "Happy birthday sweetheart ♥ kind of sad that you are now closer to 30 than 10, but that's life 😂 📸📸📸📸📸 📸📸."[32] Sakarya's joking about his inclination to date (much) younger women deliberately conjures pedophilia, and by drawing on repulsive connotations, he creates a highly politically incorrect provocation.

A post from June 5 consists of two photos next to each other. In the image on the left, an elderly overweight man eagerly kisses and embraces a fit young woman. The woman is clad in a bikini, and the man wears shorts as they stand in the ocean. The photo on the right shows Sakarya and Clara similarly wearing swim shorts and a bikini. The setting is urban, most likely the Copenhagen waterfront. The photo is taken slightly from the side and below, a perspective that emphasizes Sakarya's weight. This is further emphasized by Clara's hand, which is placed on Sakarya's ample belly. Sakarya holds a glass of rosé in one hand, the other hand on Clara's (young, slim, and fit) hip. They are looking into each other's eyes and smiling. In these juxtaposed images, Sakarya ridicules elderly men with a preference for younger women, while paradoxically including himself in this group of men. Both posts frame the stereotypical older and somewhat unappealing man with his younger, beautiful girlfriend, also alluding to cultural narratives of male dominance over female bodies and economic inequality between men and women.[33]

Another type of sexualized post insinuates latent homosexuality and homosociality, frequently combined with ethnicity. In a post from April 26, seven very fit Black men dressed only in underpants surround one skinny white man. This man's head has been replaced with a roughly cut face of one of the wait staff from Sakarya's restaurant (the same man from the April 30 post). In the lower corner of the picture, yellow letters read "Poor little white guy." This image challenges the dominant hegemonic position of white masculinity in Denmark.[34]

A post from April 23 displays Umut Sakarya and another man, Kim (fig. 13-3). The two men eat ice cream while crossing each other's arms. The picture

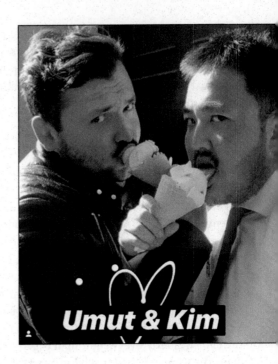

FIGURE 13-3. Umut Sakarya's April 23, 2019, post underscores sexualized food imagery. Used with permission.

shows them biting into and licking their ice creams in a highly sexualized way, while looking flirtatiously into the camera. At the bottom of the picture, a heart appears behind the words "Umut & Kim." The two men's oral movements contribute to the sexualization of the picture.

Other examples of sexist and sexualized posts include a photo of an inflatable Lolita doll accompanied by Sakarya's comment that it has been a crazy weekend with far too much nudity; a video of a female waiter pouring Fernet-Branca into her own mouth while holding the bottle between her breasts, imitating a so called cum shot; a photo of a female stripper serving Fernet-Branca (and almost her breast) directly into the mouth of a male waiter from Guldkroen; a photo of a plate with a sausage, two potatoes, and drops of white gravy, staged as an ejaculating penis; and a close-up photo of a whole, raw chicken taken from an angle that crudely suggests a vagina.[35] These posts all exemplify different ironic ways of portraying men and women, different sexual orientations, and ethnicities in sexualized as well as sexist ways.

Sakarya also combines and plays with a range of positions of power and marginalization. In his criticism of right-wing parties, he explicitly satirizes them from his position as a member of the Turkish, Muslim minority in Denmark. In relation to the sexist or sexualized imagery, he often plays on traditional masculine, racial, and sexual stereotypes, as well as the sexualization of women.

However, he often centers himself in these jokes through distorted sexualization or self-ironic portrayals. Very often, irony and grotesque constellations underline the burlesque tone of his profile. It may be tempting to understand this as a form of hipster sexism where irony is used to mask genuine sexism. Previously, similar strategies have been noted in the sexism of the "lad culture" in British popular culture in the 1990s, where "irony is used as an ideological defense against external attack (only the humorless do not get the joke) and an internal defense against more ambivalent feelings."[36] However, both these forms of hipster sexism and lad sexism were primarily used among white middleclass men. The fact that Umut is also a member of an ethnic minority in the current political climate of Denmark in combination with his criticism of the right wing renders his position all the more ambiguous.

Umut Sakarya's Instagram performance is transgressive on several levels. His performances transgress discursive, aesthetic, and ethical codes of the Copenhagen food scene as well as the dominant cultural codes of most Instagram food profiles. Furthermore, he transgresses social codes for bodily conduct, sexualization, and norms regulating humor. The transgression lies also in the juxtaposition of contradictory discursive repertoires. Sakarya criticizes the extreme right while constantly telling sexist jokes. He praises pork and alcohol while playing on his Muslim background. He frequently exposes his overweight body on a platform often associated with healthy food and fitness.

In relation to the study of food and Instagram, we believe this analysis makes a significant contribution, showing a specific role that the media platform plays for the perception of identity performances. Sakarya's social media performance is particularly remarkable because it takes place on Instagram and not another online platform such as YouTube. Studies of YouTube have noted performances similar to Sakarya's, where crude language, lame humor, sexualization, and oversized, unhealthy food go hand in hand.[37] Tania Lewis finds many features similar to Sakarya's performance in the kitchen in her analysis of YouTube phenomenon Matty Matheson.[38] In contrast, Lewis's analysis of Instagram highlights a different type of men cooking, namely the Insta-dads who use home cooking to brand themselves as modern men and responsible fathers (a kind of "new men").[39] The Insta-dads embrace what we have seen as the dominant aesthetic ideals and sensibility of Instagram, combined with liberal values, but without the laddish, crude humor. What makes Sakarya's Instagram provocative, then, is not the content in itself, which can be found elsewhere, but the fact that this type of content is exposed on Instagram. Were he instead to share this content to YouTube or Facebook, the effect would be less transgressive. Thus, the transgression is found—as noted by Goodman and Sage—also in the transposition from one sphere to another.[40] On Instagram, Sakarya is as out of place as his restaurant is among Nørrebro's many vegan and vegetarian establishments, but this out-of-placeness is central to his recognizability on Instagram and in the highly competitive food scene of Copenhagen.

This can be read as a clever branding strategy, but it may also be construed as a more profound satire of the aesthetic and discursive ideals dominating Instagram and fine dining in Copenhagen. By breaking almost every element of the informal code of conduct followed by most food-related Instagram users, Sakarya highlights the many rules, norms, and restrictions that actually govern the way we are expected to talk about food on Instagram.

Notes

1. Erin Metz McDonnell, *Food Porn: The Conspicuous Consumption of Food in the Age of Digital Reproduction* (London: Palgrave Macmillan, 2016).

2. Jessica Paddock, *Class, Food, Culture: Exploring "Alternative" Food Consumption* (PhD diss., University of Cardiff, 2011), 116.

3. Sony Kusumasondjaja and Fandy Tjiptono, "Endorsement and Visual Complexity in Food Advertising on Instagram," *Internet Research* 29, no. 4 (2019): 659–87.

4. Lise Bek, *Måltidet som stilleben* (Århus: Århus Universitetsforlag, 2018).

5. Tanja Lewis and Michelle Phillipov, "Food/Media: Eating, Cooking, and Provisioning in a Digital World," *Communication Research and Practice* 4, no. 3 (2018): 207–11, doi.org/10.1080/22041451.2018.1482075; Francine Matalon-degni, "Trends in Food Photography: A Prop Stylist's View," *Gastronomica* 10, no. 3 (2010): 70–83.

6. Jonatan Leer, "The Rise and Fall of the New Nordic Cuisine," *Journal of Aesthetics & Culture* 8, no. 1 (2016): 1–20.

7. Deborah Lupton, "Carnivalesque Food Videos: Excess, Gender and Affect on YouTube," in *Digital Food Cultures*, ed. Deborah Lupton and Zeena Feldman, 35–49 (London: Routledge, 2020).

Tania Lewis, *Digital Food* (New York: Bloomsbury, 2020).

8. Chris Jenks, *Transgression: Critical Concepts in Sociology* (London: Routledge, 2006).

9. Michael K. Goodman and Colin Sage, eds., *Food Transgressions: Making Sense of Contemporary Food Politics* (New York: Routledge, 2016); Roberta Sassatelli and Federica Davolio, "Polite Transgression: Pleasure as Economic Device and Ethical Stance in Slow Food," in *Food Transgressions: Making Sense of Contemporary Food Politics*, ed. Michael K. Goodman and Colin Sage, 83–107 (London: Routledge, 2016).

10. Bi Skårup, "The New Nordic Diet and Danish Food Culture," in *The Return of traditional Food*, ed. Patricia Lysahgt, 43–52 (Lund: Lund Studies in Arts and Cultural Sciences, 2013).

11. Håkan Jönsson, "The Road to the New Nordic Kitchen," in Lysahgt, *Return of Traditional Food*, 53–67.

12. Anders Riel Müller and Jonatan Leer, "Mainstreaming New Nordic Cuisine?"

in *Alternative Food Politics: From the Margins to the Mainstream*, ed. Michelle Phillipov and Kathrine Kirkwood, 37–54 (London: Routledge, 2018).

13. Leer, "Rise and Fall."

14. Linda Lapiņa and Jonatan Leer, "Carnivorous Heterotopias: Gender, Nostalgia and Hipsterness in the Copenhagen Meat Scene," *Norma* 11, no. 2 (2016): 89–109; Jonatan Leer, "Copenhagen: Hipster Porridge in the Welfare State," in *Global Brooklyn: How Instagram and Post-Industrial Design are Shaping How We Eat*, ed. Fabio Parasecoli and Mateusz Halawa, 81–95 (New York: Bloomsbury, 2020).

15. Malene Koops Grønbor, "Antallet af vegetarrestauranter femdoblet: 'Vi er med til at skubbe grænserne for den mad, vi spiser,'" DR, March 7, 2019, www.dr.dk/nyheder/indland/antallet-af-vegetarrestauranter-femdoblet-vi-er-med-til-skubbe-graenserne-den-mad-vi.

16. The Danish Vegetarian Association (https://vegetarisk.dk/restauranter/) mapped vegetarian restaurants.

17. Tenna Jensen, "Pork, Beer, and Margarine: Danish Food Consumption 1900–2000: National Characteristics and Common Nordic Traits," *Food and History* 12 no. 2 (2014): 3–37.

18. On Danish food traditions, see Arun Micheelsen, Lotte Holm, and Katherine O'Doherty Jensen, "Consumer Acceptance of the New Nordic Diet: An Exploratory Study," *Appetite* 70 (2013): 14–21.

19. Martin Kongstad, "'Bearnaise er Dyrenes Konge' med digterkokken Chano fra Guldkroen: 'Jeg tjekkede min kærestes beskeder—det er det tarveligste, man kan gøre,'" Heartbeats, interview, February 21, 2020, https://heartbeats.dk/podcast/bearnaise-er-dyrenes-konge-med-digterkokken-chano-fra-guldkroen-jeg-tjekkede-min-kaerestes-beskeder-det-er-det-tarveligste-man-kan-goere/.

20. Jørgen Stigel, "Humor i dansk TV-reklame: Et middel på tværs af livsstil?," *Mediekultur: Journal of Media and Communication Research* 45 (2008): 65–79.

21. Forty thousand followers are a lot for a relatively young chef in Copenhagen. In comparison, one of the long-standing judges in *Masterchef Danmark*, Jakob Mielcke, has twenty-nine thousand followers. However, René Redzepi, one of the big internationally recognized chefs, has over nine hundred thousand followers.

22. Robert K. Yin, *Case Study Research: Design and Methods* (Thousand Oaks, CA: Sage, 1994).

Alan Bryman, *Social Research Methods* (New York: Oxford University Press, 2016).

23. Umut Sakarya (@umutsakarya), Instagram photo, March 10, 2019, www.instagram.com/p/Bu01DnzHUNK/.

24. Umut Sakarya (@umutsakarya), Instagram photo, May 25, 2019, www.instagram.com/p/Bx4nx_7n1MK/.

25. Umut Sakarya (@umutsakarya), Instagram photo, April 15, 2019, www.instagram.com/p/BwRh3EQn_Ag/.

26. Umut Sakarya (@umutsakarya), Instagram photo, April 30, 2019, www.instagram.com/p/Bw4J-gBHjsf/.

27. Laura Mulvey, "Visual Pleasure and Narrative Cinema," *Screen* 16, no. 3 (1975): 6–18.

28. Deborah Lupton, "Understanding Digital Food Cultures," in Lupton and Feldman, *Digital Food Cultures*, 45.

29. Alana Mann, "Hashtag Activism and the Right to Food in Australia," in *Digital Food Activism*, ed. Tanja Schneider, Karin Eli, Catherine Dolan, and Stanley Ulijaszek (New York: Routledge, 2017), 168–84.

30. Umutsakarya (@umutsakarya), "Ud med de bløde svær! Alt i Danmark skal være sprødt! Og det skal være lige nu! 🧋," Instagram photo, May 7, 2019, www .instagram.com/p/BxJxoVBnyFy/.

31. Umut Sakarya (@umutsakarya), Instagram post, May 7, 2019, www.instagram .com/p/BxJxoVBnyFy/.

32. Umut Sakarya (@umutsakarya), Instagram post, May 28, 2019, www.insta gram.com/p/Bx_mpQcHoEr/.

33. Umut Sakarya (@umutsakarya), Instagram photo, June 5, 2019, www.insta gram.com/p/ByU5VPVHPAS/.

34. Umut Sakarya (@umutsakarya), Instagram post, April 26, 2019, www.insta gram.com/p/BwtXBLEn368/.

35. Umutsakarya (@umutsakarya), "Jeg forklare lige om at man skal have tøj på når man kommer til guldkroen 😂😅🙈♂ det gat været en vild weekend på kroen med alt for meget nøgenhed 😅," Instagram photo, May 20, 2019, www.instagram .com/p/BxrqkVUnUhG/; Umutsakarya (@umutsakarya), "Til jobsamtale hos Guldkroen Umut: hvad har du af talenter? Ida: jeg kan skænke fernet og drik det uden at bruge hænder eller shotglas. Umut: Velkommen til guldholdet 🧋😅😅😅 😅😅😅🙈♂😄#wifeymaterial," Instagram video, May 26, 2019, www.instagram .com/p/Bx61_Zjnlhz/; Umutsakarya (@umutsakarya), "Når @chanojorgensenmaxer ud 😅😅😅😅😅😄🙈♂," Instagram photo, May 20, 2019, www.instagram.com/p/Bxrq JXFHy-c/; Umutsakarya (@umutsakarya), "Tag en ven som elsker pølser 💜," Insta gram photo, June 12, 2019, www.instagram.com/p/ByncwKsnlAT/; Umutsakarya (@umutsakarya), "Elsker tyrkisk kyllinger!," Instagram photo, July 19, 2019, www. instagram.com/p/B0Go18vHsB0/.

36. Peter Jackson, Nick Stevenson, and Kate Brooks, *Making Sense of Men's Magazines* (Cambridge, UK: Polity Press, 2001).

37. Deborah Lupton, "Carnivalesque Food Videos: Excess, Gender and Affect on YouTube," in Lupton and Feldman, *Digital Food Cultures*, 35–49; Tania Lewis, *Digital Food* (New York: Bloomsbury, 2020).

38. Lewis, *Digital Food*, 93.

39. Rosalind Gill, "Power and the Production of Subjects: A Genealogy of the New Man and the New Lad," *Sociological Review* 51 (2003): 34–56.

40. Michael K. Goodman and Colin Sage, eds., *Food Transgressions: Making Sense of Contemporary Food Politics* (New York: Routledge, 2016).

CHAPTER 14

Posing with "the People"

The Far Right and Food Populism on Instagram

SARA GARCIA SANTAMARIA

As social media become key communication platforms connecting political leaders and their audiences, populist leaders have been experimenting with the use of everyday cultural tropes that spark emotional connection with their followers. Flipping through their Instagram posts, one such trope stands out for its familiarity: food. In fact, food has started a few battles on social media. In Italy for instance, Matteo Salvini, former deputy prime minister, sparked a "Nutella battle" in late 2019. A self-declared fan of the chocolate nut spread, Salvini announced that he would stop eating it because it contained foreign hazelnuts—not just Italian—only to pose with a Nutella jar on Instagram the next day.[1] Similarly, Brazilian president Jair Bolsonaro has sparked a "poop war," asking climate change defenders to protest less and eat less, so they poop every other day and reduce waste. These examples represent the use of food as a political tool for defending both nationalist and class-based values: national production and restraint. But they also indicate the problematic nature of using food as part of populist friend-and-foe narratives. This chapter explores a set of questions related to political communication in the digital era: How do far-right populist leaders use Instagram food posts as a way of bypassing elite and expert mediations between the leader and "the people"? How do far-right populist leaders respond to (and even instrumentalize) Instagram foodie trends? These questions are relevant for understanding how food becomes a cultural trope taken up within populist performances of class and national identity.

Food, as a cultural product, helps to create and reinforce social divisions that organize our image of the social world and our place in it. In his social critique of taste, Bourdieu considers that it "functions as a sort of social orientation, a 'sense of one's place.'"[2] The particularity of populist discourses is that they are played out in an antagonistic register of friends against foes—that is, in a moral register. "In place of a struggle between 'right and left' we are faced with a struggle between 'right and wrong.'" Populist discourse constructs a coalition between the leader and the people in order to defend themselves from an outside menace, an Other (whether the elites, a "dangerous" marginalized group, a set of policies, and so forth), that threatens peoples' (allegedly natural) predisposition to attain well-being.[3] One of the ways in which leaders achieve closeness to the people is by instrumentalizing comfort food such that it serves friend-versus-foe narratives. More specifically, comfort food becomes a tool for staging a two-way rebellion against perceived enemies: the traditional, snobbish, foodie elite but also left-wingers who sacrifice the joy of simple food in the name of health and environmental claims. Politicizing the desire for authentic, traditional food, populists advance food puritanism as an alternative to Instagram food-porn dominant aesthetics. The term "food puritanism" refers to the representation of familiar and traditional food that is stripped of all excess and embellishment, both in terms of culinary and photographic techniques.[4]

This chapter analyzes the use of food photographs in the official Instagram accounts of Matteo Salvini (member of Italy's Lega party) and Jair Bolsonaro (head of Brazil's Partido Social Liberal) for one year, following the beginning of their respective electoral campaigns. Both far-right populist leaders ran for office in their country's general elections almost simultaneously in 2018 and coordinated a great part of their campaigns through social media.[5] This chapter analyzes Instagram posts—both images and text—from a qualitative perspective, drawing on sensitizing topics of discourse theoretical analysis.[6] Through these lenses, food appears as a familiar cultural trope that fulfills the role of an empty signifier. An empty signifier, for Ernesto Laclau, is an element that is able to encompass meaning beyond its immediate definition.[7] Using food as an empty signifier means that food is able to stretch its immediate meaning and, in this case, to stand for "a people" in terms of national and class-belonging. Therefore, when food is mobilized in posts, so is a particular sort of people that identifies with it, whether it is Italian pizza or Brazilian mangoes.

Populist leaders do not post images of food by chance. Salvini and Bolsonaro show a clear preference for comfort food—food that is local, simple, and traditional. Comfort evokes feel-good memories of home, family, and childhood, making us feel cozy and secure. Therefore, comfort food is used as a means to perform authenticity and unpretentiousness, to defend the "democratic taste" of the common people.[8] In Italy, a country with rich culinary capital and great national pride, the type of food represented, and the degree of elaboration of its cuisine, is different from that of Brazil, where gastronomy is less linked to national identity.[9] Matteo Salvini uses his Instagram account to assert the symbolic power of food-as-nation, presenting himself as a gourmand fighting to defend "Italy first." In fact, it was his leadership that helped to shift Lega from northern regionalism to an "empty nativist nationalism."[10] While Jair Bolsonaro appeals to national values, he does so by foregrounding the role of the working classes. The Brazilian president presents himself as a humble man who lives in a modest house and has a taste for simple food, approaching food-as-class as a way of sharing the socioeconomic struggles of the common people. This is done even though his appeals contrast with his voters' socioeconomic base—statistics show that he has little support from the poor.[11]

Food and Populism: What's at Stake?

This chapter explores how far-right populist leaders use comfort food on Instagram as a way to appeal to "the people" both in terms of class (the common people) and nation (the national people). In doing so, it makes a series of ontological assumptions by defining populism as a specific logic of articulation of "the people" and their identity.[12] Benjamin de Cleen and Yannis Stavrakakis observe that the "thinness" of populism makes it compatible with other political ideologies, such as nationalism.[13] The importance of articulating nation and class-based communities lies precisely in their apparent naturalness, capable of quickly mobilizing people around a reservoir of shared emotions.[14] Populist leaders appeal to the apparent naturalness of national comfort food as a way of evoking a shared, familiar connection that brings them closer to the people, thus mobilizing them emotionally.

Populist leaders present themselves as the authentic representatives of the people in a context in which the traditional elite seems to have distanced itself too much from popular interests. In political communication terms, populist leaders curate an image of authenticity and familiarity that allows them to engage, allegedly, in an unmediated conversation with citizens. Therefore, populist leaders have been quick to use social media for showcasing their everyday life, entering people's private space while opening the doors of their homes to their followers.[15] Previous studies in Italy and Brazil have shown that populist leaders present themselves as "champions of the people" and the common "man on the street," opposed to the elite and ostracized Others.[16] While it is clear that populist leaders want to be considered part of the people, systematic knowledge remains sparse on the way in which they construct this closeness on social media. This is why it is important to understand the use of everyday cultural tropes, such as food, and their emotional power to help bind leader and followers together.

By appealing to tradition and authenticity through unsophisticated comfort dishes, populist leaders construct a popular identity that defies Instagram food porn trends. Amanda Simpson defines food porn as whatever makes you drool, inviting ephemeral consumption and creating a desire that cannot be satisfied.[17]

Similarly, Anne McBride looks at the concept of food porn as posting "sexy" and appealing photos of food online.[18] The association of food to porn is twofold: pictures of food are shown in an unrealistically attractive way, and there is a connotation of indecency in the obsession for good-looking food in such an unequal world. What is clear is that the idea of porn refers to "an aesthetic of excess," of "obsession, waste and playfulness."[19] This excess is portrayed not only in the qualities of the food represented but also in the way they are curated: a "precise, delicate setting," "bright and propped," showing off the perfection and the glossiness of the food that is presented.[20]

The styling of food porn contrasts with the austere performance of populist leaders' food-centric posts, who share seemingly uncurated photos of comfort food that looks familiar yet unappealing. This can be easily seen in the analysis that follows, which examines apparently unedited pictures that are technically flawed both from a photographic and a culinary perspective. The portrayal of often-blurry images with inadequate color balances reinforces the unappetizing side of bland and messy-looking food. Embracing amateurism and imperfection can be seen as a way of reinforcing the leaders' authentic self-representation, indicating a clear strategy rather than a simple lack of skills. The arousal of emotions through recognizability, rather than aesthetics, raises questions about how to interpret far-right leaders' posts set against Instagram's curated landscape of mouthwatering food. In a rebellion against "food porn," "food populism" evokes authenticity and puritanism against the curated millennial aesthetic. In a way, Salvini and Bolsonaro's appeals to tradition, familiarity, and austerity bring "food populism" close to "food puritanism."

Emotions are particularly important for mobilizing people's support for right-wing parties. While research on food and social media focuses mainly on identifying positive emotions, scholarship on populism tends to focus on negative ones. Some works suggest that invoking negative emotions is effective in appealing to the insecurities of the so-called "losers of modernization," who some identify as the main supporters of populist leaders.[21] More particularly, the notion of *ressentiment*, or the way in which negative emotions, such as fear, are repressed and then translated into anger, has proved an important element in far-right support. Looking at populist political strategies of emotionalization and boundary-making, Mikko Salmela and Christian von Scheve argue that *ressentiment* can be mobilized through identity-evoking symbols, and then externalized through anger toward "other" identities.[22]

The data presented below show that, while food becomes an empty signifier that connects emotionally with the people, the accompanying text of food posts evokes *ressentiment*. The combination of food photographs and text sheds light on far-right leaders' political communication strategy: first, mobilizing support through identity-evoking symbols, such as comfort food, then turning those symbols against an "other," whether the intellectual left or activists—from Carola Rackete to Greta Thunberg.

Matteo Salvini, a Happy Italian Gourmand

Since 2013, Matteo Salvini has been the federal secretary of Lega, a far-right regionalist party from northern Italy that achieved national reach during his leadership. Salvini served as Italy's deputy prime minister and minister of the interior from June 2018 to September 2019, trumpeting Euroscepticism, nativism, and anti-immigration policies. The nationalist elements of Lega are ubiquitous in Salvini's Instagram account. There, food appears as an empty signifier that encompasses Italian nationalist values and traditions as opposed to foreign trends and perceived threats.

The contrast between national versus foreign, and traditional versus trendy foods, is palpable not only in the photos that Salvini shares on Instagram but also in the accompanying captions. His captions are actually never food related but use images of food to call attention to broader sociopolitical debates aligned with his political interests. For example, he repeatedly sets comfort food against healthy eating habits. Not only is healthy food almost absent from his posts, but he often makes sarcastic comments about his health while posting images of tasty traditional dishes. Posting a photo of gnocchi with sausage, which he jokingly refers to as "a light lunch," he addresses a question to his followers: "Will you still love me if I gain weight?"[23] Love and food go hand in hand.

As we have seen, Salvini's food posts reject conventional representations of healthy eating and go one step beyond. The leader suggests that an excessive preoccupation with health leads to unhappiness, and unhappiness is precisely what distinguishes the political left. According to this sequence, the leader poses as an unabashedly happy Italian gourmand and often mocks his opponents by stressing his enjoyment of traditional Italian dishes. Meanwhile, his political opponents, among them journalists or professors, are portrayed as depressed, starving wannabes who attack him out of pure (food) envy. Therefore, appeals to health or climate change are dismissed as the moralizing discourses of a hubristic political elite who despise the little joys of everyday life.

The recurrent posts of a smiling Salvini holding a bottle of iced beer or sniffing a steamy pasta serve as a means to construct boundaries of belonging. In one of his posts, the leader evokes unity through a cold bottle of beer from the Veneto region that reads: "Birra di tradizione Italiana" (Italian traditional beer). Salvini uses this identity-evoking symbol as an empty signifier that gets people's attention so he can pursue his real goal: to mobilize citizens' *ressentiment*. This is clear from the text accompanying the photo, in which he waves at "those who want to hurt Italy." In the post, Salvini presents himself as a leader who defends Italian heritage against foolhardy enemies: "I don't give up."[24] At times, the construction of an evil "other" takes a historical magnitude. For instance, in another post a smiling Salvini holds a bottle of Birra Nursia, an Italian beer, and shows off his latest *tonno pugliese* pasta while criticizing the Yugoslavs who massacred the Italian people during World War II.[25] In doing so, Salvini presents himself as a leader ready to protect citizens from all their past and present enemies.

Salvini's enemies are not always clearly identified. The Other who steals people's enjoyment of Italian food is often obliquely evoked, left to people's imagination. This can be seen in the post in figure 14-1, in which a smiling Salvini poses with a jar of Nutella, the sweet par excellence that can spark Italians' joy and recall childhood memories. The jar reads: "Today will be better than yesterday"—to which Salvini replies, "Good morning Friends. For many, but not for everyone." The aesthetics of the image are in keeping with Salvini's selfies, with no filters, a canted angle and a close-up that cuts part of his face out of the frame. All these elements contribute to a narrative of authenticity by which the leader communicates with his followers in an apparently unself-conscious manner: direct, spontaneous, and seemingly uncurated.

In the examples above, Matteo Salvini appeals to classic Italian products while drawing clear boundaries of belonging between his followers—often referred to as *Amici*, "Friends" with a capital *F*—and evil enemies, who thrive by attacking the leader and, by extension, his friends. The enemy is often clearly identified as left-wingers and intellectuals. For instance, a photo of tortellini in sausage sauce appears next to a message in which Salvini paradoxically states that he doesn't want to offend any left-wing journalists or professors (which he calls *professorone*).[26] The word *professorone* applies not just to university professors but to those who pretend to know it all, including what is morally wrong and right. Surprisingly, the post ended up offending some of his followers who, in the name of tradition, reminded Salvini that his tortellini recipe does not exist—tortellini should always be eaten in broth. This is not the first time that ostensibly heretical pasta dishes sparked heated debates over Italian values. In fact, in October 2019, the archbishop of Bologna, Matteo Zuppi, served a chicken-stuffed tortellini (instead of pork) to the poor with the goal of making the meal more inclusive. This prompted Andrea Indini, editor of the conservative paper *Il Giornale*, to write an opinion piece defending tortellini and tradition. This op-ed supported Salvini's puritan defense of Italian tradition against ideas of multiculturalism or interculturalism—that is, nationalism against foreign values.[27]

Salvini's eating habits and food nationalism have become a matter of public debate in Italy. In an Instagram post, Salvini holds up for the camera a newspaper article in which a doctor questions his health habits—a Nutella toast, in this case.[28] In the post, the journalist is portrayed as taking pleasure in the image of a sick Salvini, suffering from clotted arteries. The remedy for the left's misery?

♡ ◯ ▽   🔖

102,593 likes

matteosalviniofficial Buona giornata Amici.
Per molti, ma non per tutti 😌

FIGURE 14-1. The composition of Matteo Salvini's (#matteosalviniofficial) posts deliberately suggests folksiness. February 12, 2019.

Enjoying more daily pleasures. In fact, Salvini suggests that if the "female doctor" ate more Nutella, she would be a happier person and would stop criticizing him. This post exemplifies how Salvini positions his visible enjoyment of unhealthy pleasures as sparking the envy, but also the reprobation, of leftist moralists.

Salvini acknowledges that he uses food pleasures as a means to overcome leftist and elitist attacks. In one illustrative example, he posts a photo of zuppa inglese, a desert from Piemonte, which comes to represent comfort food as a common ground that unites all Italians against daily struggles. He writes: "the more they attack and threaten me, the more they give me energy and the desire to work to defend Italians."[29] After another long day, he shows off his hearty polenta to his friends, which he claims helps him disconnect from the "insults and disappointments" that he received throughout the day (fig. 14-2).[30]

The frequency of Salvini's food posts proves a useful tool for melding his love for food and for his followers. Perhaps the clearest example of this is his post of a heart-shaped fried egg (fig. 14-3). The misshapen heart illustrates his love

43,585 likes

matteosalviniofficial Per dimenticare insulti e delusioni una bella cassoeula con polenta, piatto tipico lombardo con le parti povere del maiale, verza, cipolla, sedano e carote.
Come passate la vostra serata Amici?

FIGURE 14-2.
Matteo Salvini (#matteosalviniofficial) poses hearty, traditional Italian dishes as cures for the Left. January 26, 2019.

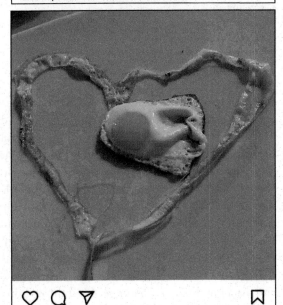

56,071 likes

matteosalviniofficial Ovetto dedicato a voi Amici! 😊

FIGURE 14-3.
Matteo Salvini (#matteosalviniofficial) uses an egg to express his love for Italians. June 3, 2019.

73,074 likes

matteosalviniofficial La tradizione non si tocca! 😊

FIGURE 14-4. An example of a Matteo Salvini (#matteosalviniofficial) post that connects himself to traditional values. January 1, 2019.

for Italians, a love that might look imperfect but is at least authentic. As with many of his food posts, the unvarnished picture visually conveys his relatability through a blemished aesthetics that differs from the bright, proper, and glossy characteristics of Instagram food trends.[31] In this particular post, the dish is dirty, the egg burned on the edges and barely resembles a heart.

Shot in poor lighting, the posts in figures 14-2 and 14-3 imply that there has been no effort to make the food look appealing. Rather, they look spontaneous and authentic while hiding a carefully curated logic of unpolished comfort food and unembellished love. The post in figure 14-4 shows a vaguely unappetizing dish of *cotechino con lenticchie* (lentil stew with sausage) invoking the imperfection of homestyle cuisine. Eating lentils is a New Year's tradition in Italy, and Salvini's campaign deploys *cotechino con lenticchie* to suggest that he will protect Italian Christmas values. "You don't touch tradition!" he writes, followed by a smile emoji.[32]

Italian traditions are opposed to the image of a foreign Other that is explicitly omitted from his food images but often referenced in the accompanying text. Even from a composition perspective, Salvini frequently posts photos of people the right vilifies, such as refugees, left-wingers, and human-rights defenders, among them Carola Rackete (fig. 14-5).[33] These images appear with photos of pepperoni pizza or Italian wine. This is the clearest example of Salvini's politicization of food in a way that serves his political goals. The post in figure 14-5

FIGURE 14-5. By juxtaposing images of left-leaning activists with traditional Italian foods, Matteo Salvini (#matteosalviniofficial) politicizes food. January 17, 2020.

shows the extent to which food is seamlessly integrated into quotidian far-right visual displays of who is—and who is not—perceived as belonging in the national body.

Jair Bolsonaro, a Humble Brazilian Survivor

Jair Messias Bolsonaro is a Brazilian politician and former military officer who was elected as Brazil's president in October 2018. Although he represented the state of Rio de Janeiro as a deputado federal (Chamber of Deputies) between 1991 and 2008, he was practically unknown nationwide, something he used to his advantage by presenting himself as a political outsider. Just like Donald Trump and Matteo Salvini, Bolsonaro despises political correctness and campaigned for the presidency on a platform of conservative values and law-and-order policies. There are in fact stark similarities between Trump's "Make America Great Again" slogan and Bolsonaro's 2018 presidential campaign slogan, "Faça o Brasil grande de novo" (Make Brazil Great Again). This type of nostalgic nationalism is also present in Salvini's 2018 presidential slogan, "Prima gli Italiani" (Italians First!). While Salvini is almost twenty years younger than Bolsonaro, and might be more adept in his digital skills, both leaders represent themselves on Instagram in line with far-right nationalistic, anti-immigration, religiously conservative, and antiliberal imaginaries. Labeled a racist, homophobe, and misogynist by some, Bolsonaro was stabbed during his presidential campaign in September 2018, which required him to continue campaigning first from the hospital and then from home.[34] Due to his strong social media presence, this gave Bolsonaro's followers a window into the private space of his home.

When Bolsonaro posted images of his health recovery, the Other that re-surfaces is the evil enemy who stabbed him once and keeps trying to damage his persona. Comfort food is visible in the background yet is key for capturing people's attention for his divisive discourse. In one of Bolsonaro's first videos from the hospital, he poses barely covered by a hospital gown, showing some of his scars to the camera in front of a tray with unappetizing hospital food. In the accompanying text he acknowledges that most Brazilians could not afford his treatment and promises more funding. But more importantly, he uses his semi-naked, scarred body as a vehicle for thanking the federal police for the investiga-tion of the "terrorist act" that almost cost him his life. In the posts, Bolsonaro creates boundaries of moral belonging between good and reckless Brazilians, such as delinquents, by emphasizing crime and revenge. What is curious is that felons are at the same scale of evil as his other enemies: the political left.

Like other far-right populist leaders, Bolsonaro sees himself as the victim of a leftist conspiracy against him, and against the nation. An analysis of his captions shows the degree of his deep contempt for a political and intellectual elite that is always unhappy, always fretting about negative things like sexism, racism, or climate change. A left that, with their extreme moralism, steals people's enjoy-ment of simple, everyday pleasures. This can be seen in figure 14-6, captioned "Too much racism and homophobia together . . . no more political correctness. Please comment and share."[35] The ultimate goal of the post seems to be to show that Bolsonaro has supporters of color, refuting progressive politicians and intellectuals' accusations of racism.

Bolsonaro's self-styled persona goes hand in hand with his antiestablish-ment discourse. In fact, images of Bolsonaro eating simple food reinforce a discourse based on economic austerity, religious asceticism, and health recovery. The president's professional mise-en-scène defies that of traditional politicians: posts of him working show him as often in suit and tie as working at his desk in shorts and a T-shirt, with some breadcrumbs stacked up against his computer and the aroma of coffee almost palpable. Food is never the point in Bolsonaro's posts but rather an empty signifier that directs people's attention toward his political goals, just like Salvini's. However, both far-right leaders differ starkly in how they present food. While food is visually central in Salvini's posts, with many close-ups of traditional Italian dishes, it is backgrounded in Bolsonaro's

242,110 views

jairmessiasbolsonaro - Muito racismo e homofobia juntos... - Chega do politicamente correto. - Peço comentar e compartilhar.

FIGURE 14-6.
Jair Bolsonaro's (#jairmessiasbolsonaro) posts position leftist criticisms of social problems as destroying simple pleasures. April 14, 2018.

Instagram account. Bolsonaro poses with mundane commodities such as coffee, bananas, a slice of bread with condensed milk, or other simple dishes. The element of comfort comes not from traditional savoir faire but from a simplicity that resonates emotionally with people's little daily pleasures.

While Bolsonaro's fondness for fast food is well-known, the way he curates his Instagram account is quite different. Putting health recovery above indulgence, simple food constructs his humble persona but also his victory—personal and political. Posing in a hospital bed next to a bowl of dull soup and exposing his scars, Bolsonaro embodies the wounds of a nation deeply affected by violence, insecurity, stark inequality, and economic stagnation. In this sharing of both the people's suffering and the people's small pleasures, the leader presents himself as authentically Brazilian (fig. 14-7). During his recovery, Bolsonaro expresses his yearning for "real food," especially bread with condensed milk, which he often eats for breakfast.[36] Through the contrast between food posts and food yearnings, we can feel the extent to which the attack deprived Bolsonaro of simple everyday pleasures. Joys stolen by his aggressor, who directly stabbed him, but also by the political left that the attacker is associated with—and whose permanent attacks threaten the humble gratifications of his everyday life. A political outsider, Bolsonaro is himself just another victim of Brazil's somber reality. However, once home, he is able to surrender to simple comforts, such as a cup of home-brewed coffee or an ice cream on a hot day, which become markers of his recovery.

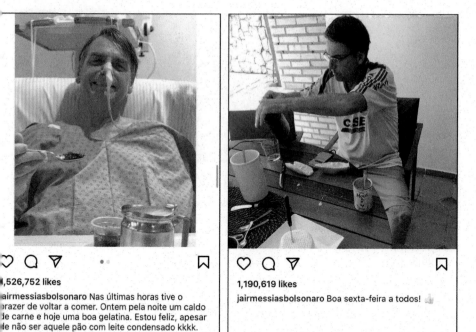

FIGURE 14-7. Jair Bolsonaro (#jairmessiasbolsonaro) used his recovery to solidify perceptions of himself as a political outsider and as one of the people. February 8, 2019, and October 19, 2018.

While Salvini seems to cherish food by engaging with it sensorially—by looking at it, smelling it, and touching it—Bolsonaro displays indifference to the substance of his food. Fruit, rolls, tea, some sweets in the background . . . that is all he reveals. The only full meals he shares are ones with blue-collar workers who represent people's security, whether policemen or firefighters. Therefore, food as an empty signifier acquires various meanings: recovery and austerity, but also a love for law and order. The post in figure 14-8 shows a Bolsonaro who loves hard-working Brazilians who work for the country as well as for his family. In return, he offers many kisses: "kkkkkkkkk."

When Matteo Salvini poses on Instagram wearing an informal shirt from his favorite football team, he is always well-groomed. Bolsonaro's posts, however, are characterized by a sort of unapologetic messiness. This is reflected in his physical appearance, whether posing semi-naked in a hospital gown, shaving shirtless in the bathroom, or having breakfast with still uncombed hair. This messy aesthetic is also visible in his personal spaces, such that the leader is not embarrassed to show his dirty terrace or sink full of crumbs and food leftovers. In fact, Bolsonaro's modest and seemingly uncurated aesthetics recall Gauber

FIGURE 14-8. When Jair Bolsonaro's posts (#jairmessiasbolsonaro) show him eating a full meal, he is typically with blue-collar workers. October 30, 2018.

1,255,429 likes

jairmessiasbolsonaro Lanche presidencial com o @choque_bpchq . Estar perto, tratar bem e ouvir faz parte de quem deseja o bem de seu time! É uma satisfação, Guerreiros!

Rocha's influential essay on the "aesthetics of poverty," which refers to the "poverty porn" aesthetics that permeate most foreign representations of Brazil.[37] Bolsonaro's poorly taken photographs, often blurry and out of focus, either too light or too dark, are part of his performed, unstudied aesthetic; they convey his efforts to represent himself as an authentic man of the people, rather than a polished politician. By rejecting photographic skills and Instagram filters, he seems to renounce all excess, both in the food he eats and in the way he visually represents it, adding to the aura of puritanism that characterizes his social media persona.

It is legitimate to wonder, though, to what extent Bolsonaro's social media persona corresponds with his real-life habits. A parallel anonymous Instagram account, #bolsonaro.comendo, shows the president enjoying fast food, such as a hamburger or pizza—a contrast from the bland diet he chooses to pose with. This fake anonymous Instagram account impersonates the president and is written from an ironic standpoint in which an imagined Bolsonaro makes fun of himself. While it is not openly critical, the account shows what is constantly evoked but missing from Bolsonaro's official posts; it includes irony and humor, and reveals his "real" yearnings, which are not so healthy.

The fake account includes a few memes that combine images of Bolsonaro and climate activist Greta Thunberg. While in one post (14-9, top), they are mutually accusing each other of stealing their enjoyment—Thunberg's dreams and Bolsonaro's doughnuts—another post shows them sharing a Brazilian breakfast at Bolsonaro's place in complete harmony (fig. 14-9, bottom). The casual humor of the scenes contrasts with the stark reality. Bolsonaro has in fact been widely

FIGURE 14-9. The anonymous account that impersonates Jair Bolsonaro (#bolsonaro.comendo) ironically juxtaposes Bolsonaro with climate activist Greta Thunberg. September 28 and 27, 2019.

criticized by climate change advocates for his management of the 2019 Amazon rain forest fires and for accommodating farmers' demands for more cropland, one of the major causes of deforestation.[38] And Greta Thunberg has been the object of Bolsonaro's hatred, just as another activist, Carola Rackete, became one of Salvini's obsessions.

The doctored posts of Bolsonaro with Greta Thunberg evoke a moralizing left that is constantly worried about virtue and political correctness. Bolsonaro's stances against what he calls "cultural Marxism," "gender ideology," or "environmental psychoses" align with his Instagram attacks against a leftist elite whose mood seems to be permanent discontent.[39] Some Brazilian scholars believe that Bolsonaro's creation of a symbolic culture war comes from the lack of a clear political program beyond championing guns and police control—something otherwise common among populists. Therefore, Instagram food posts can be seen as Bolsonaro's strategy for presenting himself as a humble, authentic leader who cares for the people, calling attention to everyday cultural tropes that connect with the people while backgrounding his political inconsistencies.

From Food Porn to Food Populism

This chapter examines the use of food posts in the official Instagram account of two prominent far-right populist leaders: Italy's former deputy prime minister, Matteo Salvini, and Brazilian president Jair Bolsonaro. The analysis has shown that political leaders' food posts are never just about food. Salvini and Bolsonaro both take an exclusionary populist and antielitist stance by posting food images in the name of "the people"—that is, a nation represented as a mythical unified whole that existed in a past era in which cultural habits and conventions did not need to be justified. Far-right politicians' Instagram accounts use food as an empty signifier to invoke both positive emotions of familiarity and negative emotions of *ressentiment* against the political and intellectual elite. The emotional appeal of food serves as a way to connect with citizens who feel compelled by both the enjoyment of tradition, or "food puritanism," and fear of a globalizing world that seems to be leaving them behind—such as the food porn images of exotic, good-looking dishes that are beyond their reach.

The analysis reveals that, while we can find elements of national pride and popular culture in both cases, Salvini uses his Instagram account in a way that foregrounds the symbolic power of food-as-nation, as a return to a preglobalization era that values nativism, heritage, and products "made in Italy." In Bolsonaro's case, shared images of food become a strategy for positioning himself on the side of the humble Brazilian masses, as someone who shares their socioeconomic struggles in a quasi-aesthetics of "hunger."[40] Therefore, the images of Salvini, the Italian glutton, and Bolsonaro, a humble Brazilian president, construct food as a cultural trope that mediates the symbolic connection of far-right leaders with their voters.

Making familiarity-based arguments allows political leaders to create boundaries by demarcating authenticity as a marker of inclusion, while excluding the foodie, intellectual elite who are accused of failing to properly perform nationalism.[41] In fact, the simple and apparently spontaneous aesthetics of the posts contrast starkly with Instagram's highly polished and curated images of food porn. Salvini and Bolsonaro operate within a sort of food puritanism: both are committed to tradition, authenticity, and immediacy beyond aesthetic values. Both Salvini's self-indulgence and Bolsonaro's abstention are characterized by raw, unappealing aesthetics. Far-right populist leaders demonstrate how Instagram can be a site for food porn, but also for food populism—that is, for the use of food as an empty signifier that embodies polarizing populist discourses. Food is not the message itself, but a means to convey the leaders' political stances.

Matteo Salvini and Jair Bolsonaro are not alone in doing this: Nigel Farage in the United Kingdom and Tomio Okamura in the Czech Republic also use food as an empty signifier. And of course, using food as a means of bonding with "the people" is not only a far-right strategy. One only has to follow U.S. representative Alexandria Ocasio-Cortez on Instagram to realize the importance of everyday popular culture, such as food, in connecting politicians with their followers. All in all, this analysis underscores the need to consider the role of cultural tropes, from food to sports to pets, in connecting politicians and their followers, and positioning them against elites. The politicization of everyday familiar symbols sheds light on the use of popular culture as an empty signifier that serves populist, simplistic yet flashy recipes for solving people's problems: to stop eating Nutella if you can, or to poop every other day, if you can. This is just as important as understanding whether cultural tropes can also be mobilized in a way that supports "authentic" democratic politics.

Notes

1. The popular hazelnut spread Nutella belongs to the Italian brand Ferrero, which uses Turkish hazelnuts because Italian production was insufficient for meeting Nutella's demand.

2. Pierre Bourdieu, *Distinction: A Social Critique of the Judgement of Taste* (Cambridge, MA: Harvard University Press, 1984), 466.

3. Chantal Mouffe, *On the Political* (New York: Routledge, 2005), 5, 16.

4. In Anne E. McBride, "Food Porn," *Journal of Food and Culture* 10, no. 1 (February 2010): 38–46, food critic Richard Magee delineates the idea of "food puritanism" in reference to traditional, conservative ways of representing food, such as that of Martha Stewart.

5. The Italian elections were held on March 4, 2018, and the Brazilian ones on October 7, 2018.

6. Nico Carpentier and Benjamin de Cleen, "Bringing Discourse Theory into Media Studies," *Journal of Language and Politics* 6, no. 2 (January 2007): 265–93.

7. Michael Kaplan, "The Rhetoric of Hegemony: Laclau, Radical Democracy, and the Rule of Tropes," *Philosophy and Rhetoric* 43, no. 3 (January 2010): 253–83; Ernesto Laclau, *On Populist Reason* (London: Verso, 2005), 71. Signifiers can only represent totality by stretching their own meaning, losing their specific sense and becoming what Laclau calls an "empty signifier."

8. Emily Contois, "Welcome to Flavortown: Guy Fieri's Populist American Food Culture," *American Studies* 57, no. 3 (January 2018): 150, 152.

9. Sara Garcia Santamaria, "The Italian 'Taste': The Far-Right and the Performance of Exclusionary Populism during the 2019 European Elections," *Trípodos* 49, no. 1 (2021): 129–49.

10. Daniele Albertazzi, Arianna Giovannini, and Antonella Seddone, "'No Regionalism Please, We are Leghisti!' The Transformation of the Italian Lega Nord under the Leadership of Matteo Salvini," *Regional and Federal Studies* 28, no. 1 (September 2018): 1–27.

11. Andres Schipani, "Brazil: Jair Bolsonaro pushes culture war over economic reform," *Financial Times*, August 24, 2019, www.ft.com/content/f470734e-c41a-11e9-a8e9-296ca66511c9, accessed September 10, 2019; Daniel Aldana Cohen, "Stop Eco-Apartheid: The Left's Challenge in Bolsonaro's Brazil," *Dissent* 66, no. 1 (November 2019): 23–31. Bolsonaro's austere eating habits cannot hide his politics of "eco-apartheid" that have sparked a war over the Amazon's natural resources, including food production, threatening the livelihood of the poorest.

12. Laclau, *On Populist Reason*, 153.

13. Benjamin de Cleen and Yannis Stavrakakis, "Distinctions and Articulations: A Discourse Theoretical Framework for the Study of Populism and Nationalism," *Javnost—The Public* 24, no. 4 (July 2017): 301–19; Cas Mudde, "The Populist Zeitgeist," *Government and Opposition* 48, no. 2 (September 2004): 542–63.

14. Margaret Canovan, *Nationhood and Political Theory* (Cheltenham, UK: Edward Elgar, 1998), 68.

15. Sven Engesser, Nicole Ernst, Frank Esser, and Florin Büchel, "Populism and Social Media: How Politicians Spread a Fragmented Ideology," *Communication and Society* 10, no. 8 (2017): 1109–26; Nicole Ernst, Sven Engesser, Florin Büchel, Sina Blassnig, and Frank Esser, "Extreme Parties and Populism: An Analysis of Facebook and Twitter Across Six Countries," *Information, Communication and Society* 20, no. 2 (May 2017), 1–18.

16. Wendy Hunter and Timothy Power, "Bolsonaro and Brazil's Illiberal Backlash," *Journal of Democracy* 30, no. 1 (January 2019): 68–82; Roberta Bracciale and Antonio Martella, "Define the Populist Political Communication Style: The Case of Italian Political Leaders on Twitter," *Information, Communication and Society* 20, no. 9 (May 2017): 1310–29; Engesser, Ernst, Esser, and Büchel, "Populism and Social Media."

17. Yasmin Ibrahim, "Food Porn and the Invitation to Gaze: Ephemeral Consumption and the Digital Spectacle," *International Journal of E-Politics* 6, no. 3 (July

2015): 1–12; Simpson in Cari Romm, "What 'Food Porn' Does to the Brain," *Atlantic*, April 20, 2015, www.theatlantic.com, accessed October 16, 2019.

18. McBride, "Food Porn."

19. Tisha Dejmanee, "'Food Porn' as Postfeminist Play: Digital Femininity and the Female Body on Food Blogs," *Television and New Media* 17, no. 5 (December 2015): 2; Krishnendu Ray, "Domesticating Cuisine: Food and Aesthetics on American Television," *Gastronomica: The Journal of Critical Food Studies* 7, no. 1 (February 2007): 58.

20. Stephanie Shih, "Current Food Photography Styles and Trends: A Cake Case Study," *Desserts for Breakfast* (blog), June 12, 2012, www.dessertsforbreakfast .com/2012/06/current-food-photography-styles-and.html, accessed January 12, 2019.

21. Mikko Salmela and Christian von Scheve, "Emotional Roots of Right-Wing Political Populism," *Humanity and Society* 42, no. 4 (October 2018): 434–54; Minkenberg, "The Renewal of the Radical Right: Between Modernity and Anti-Modernity," *Government and Opposition* 35, no. 2 (April 2003): 170–88.

22. Salmela and von Scheve, "Emotional Roots."

23. Matteo Salvini (@matteosalviniofficial), Instagram post, February 17, 2019, www.instagram.com/p/Bt_Ih5ZBYar/?utm_source=ig_web_copy_link.

24. Matteo Salvini (@matteosalviniofficial), Instagram post, July 7, 2019, www .instagram.com/p/BznaSj8IMMH/?utm_source=ig_web_copy_link.

25. Matteo Salvini (@matteosalviniofficial), Instagram post, February 8, 2019, www.instagram.com/p/BtoiSM6Bajt/?utm_source=ig_web_copy_link.

26. Matteo Salvini (@matteosalviniofficial), Instagram post, December 22, 2018, www.instagram.com/p/BrsAxFPhK0x/?utm_source=ig_web_copy_link.

27. Andrea Indini, "In Difesa dei Tortellini (e della Tradizione)," *Il Giornale* (blog), October 1, 2019, http://blog.ilgiornale.it/indini/2019/10/01/in-difesa-dei-tortellini -e-della-nostra-tradizione, accessed October 21, 2019.

28. Matteo Salvini (@matteosalviniofficial), Instagram post, December 27, 2018, www.instagram.com/p/Br55sewBOW6/?utm_source=ig_web_copy_link.

29. Matteo Salvini (@matteosalviniofficial), Instagram post, May 6, 2019, www .instagram.com/p/BxHGwWrn-le/?utm_source=ig_web_copy_link.

30. Matteo Salvini (@matteosalviniofficial), Instagram post, January 26, 2019, www.instagram.com/p/BtHBbCTh6xO/?utm_source=ig_web_copy_link.

31. Shih, "Current Food Photography."

32. Matteo Salvini (@matteosalviniofficial), Instagram post, January 1, 2019, www .instagram.com/p/BsGt7yNhjyx/?utm_source=ig_web_copy_link.

33. Carola Rackete became the target of Matteo Salvini's anger when the German ship captain, who rescues immigrants at sea for Sea-Watch, docked a rescue ship with fifty-three migrants in Lampedusa, Italy, without governmental authorization on June 29, 2019.

34. Elaine Brum, "How a Homophobic, Misogynistic, Racist 'Thing' Could Be Brazil's Next President," *Guardian*, October 6, 2018, www.theguardian.com, accessed September 17, 2019

35. Jair Bolsonaro (@jair_bolsonaro_presidente), Instagram post, April 14, 2018, www.instagram.com/p/BhjmDOxDplA/?utm_source=ig_web_copy_link.

36. Jair Bolsonaro (@jair_bolsonaro_presidente), Instagram post, February 8, 2019, www.instagram.com/p/B29uiwrHx5u/?utm_source=ig_web_copy_link; Jair Bolsonaro (@jair_bolsonaro_presidente), Instagram post, October 19, 2018, www.instagram.com/p/BpHLNk_nZtV/?utm_source=ig_web_copy_link.

37. Gauber Rocha, "Uma Estética da Fome," *Revista da Civilização Brasileira* 3, no. 1 (July 1965): 165–70.

38. "Amazon Fires Increase by 84% in One Year—Space Agency," BBC, August 21, 2019, www.bbc.com/news/world-latin-america-49415973, accessed October 28, 2019.

39. Schipani, "Brazil."

40. Rocha, "Uma Estética da Fome."

41. Tuukka Ylä-Anttila, "Familiarity as a Tool of Populism: Political Appropriation of Shared Experiences and the Case of *Suvivirsi*," *Acta Sociologica* 60, no. 4 (2017): 342—57.

CHAPTER 15

Farming, Unedited

Failure, Humor, and Fortitude in Instagram's Agricultural Underground

JOCELINE ANDERSEN

In spring 2019, a local farmer was driving through the winding highways of the Pacific Northwest when a load of crates flew off their truck. Losing these recycled crates from a local flower producer, picked up on an hours-long return trip, represented valuable time away from the farm and lost investment in supplies. Small-scale organic farmers are typically dependent on marginal profits, and sustainable, low-impact agricultural methods may be applied to quarter-acre plots with crews of just one. While this loss could have been just another setback in the unpredictable world of organic farming, when the farmer reported the loss back to their business partner, the immediate reaction was not simply one of concern. Instead, finding the silver lining to this crisis, the partner texted back, "this could be darkgram goooold!" Immediately, the farmer uploaded a photograph of the roadside jumble of crates to a private Instagram network, known colloquially to these farmers and their community as darkgram, the darkside, or darkmedia (see fig. 15-1).[1] Fellow darkgrammers, who follow each other's private accounts and make up what I will refer to as the farmer darkgram network, quickly posted comments, ranging from profanity to offers to keep an eye out for crates on that hairy stretch of road.

This exchange on Instagram illustrates the kind of content that a group of local farmers in the Pacific Northwest (PNW) are privately sharing about their community on the darkgram, in stark contrast to what appears on their farms' public Instagram accounts. Crises, failures, and panic-inducing moments abound on the farmer darkgram in visual form, with comments that provide sympathy, similar stories, and, most importantly, advice from local farmers as they share what one private account profile calls "unedited farming."[2] Ultimately, the farmer darkgram is not only a space for complaining about mishaps

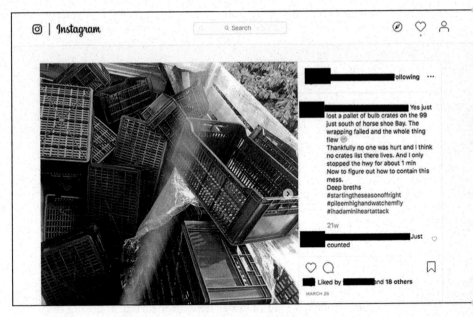

Following ···

Yes just lost a pallet of bulb crates on the 99 just south of horse shoe Bay. The wrapping failed and the whole thing flew 😩 Thankfully no one was hurt and I think no crates list there lives. And I only stopped the hwy for about 1 min Now to figure out how to contain this mess. Deep breths #startingtheseasonoffright #pileemhighandwatchemfly #ihadaminiheartattack

21w

Just counted

♡ ○   🔖

Liked by ▮▮▮ and 18 others

MARCH 26

FIGURE 15-1. A sample post from the Pacific Northwest farmer darkgram.

and "oops moments," but also for knowledge sharing among a group of local and experienced farmers that is free from the pressures created by Instagram's dominant incentives to intensify visual branding and global reach.[3] Demonstrating community-specific practices in social media similar to those Elisabetta Costa has revealed in her study of Facebook users in Turkey, the PNW farmer darkgram demonstrates an adaptation of the affordances of Instagram for local, situated use.[4]

Media scholars note the potential for Instagram to provide transparent access to and education about food systems to consumers who are alienated from food production, creating global networks that are not restricted by proximity.[5] As Michael Pennell points out, photos of food being prepared in a local restaurant allow chefs the opportunity to connect with consumers who might patronize the restaurant, and link them to the producers who harvested the pictured food.[6] This synthesis of production and consumption has created new awareness about the interconnectedness of food systems, which food activists have harnessed, since they see education about food sources to be integral to food justice.[7] Food justice means not only universal access to healthy food, but the rights of farmers and producers to grow organic food in ways that ensure continued viability of larger agricultural systems both financially and ecologically.[8] While some critics assert that sharing on social media has a weak relationship to real-world change in consumer habits and policy, there is no doubt that farmers and food producers have found exposure on Instagram in a way that was impossible before social media.[9] Social media creates a network where consumers expect to not only receive information about the brands, products, and lifestyles they are interested in, but, as Jenkins, Ford, and Green point out, they expect to be able to interact as active participants in shaping those brands as cocreators with an "emotional and moral investment."[10] Connected to myriad other Instagram posts through hashtags, Instagram messages can spread far and wide.

However, Instagram's potential for creating social relationships and supporting the complexity of local food systems is not necessarily realized through global online visibility and mass participation alone. As Pennell suggests, sharing photos of prepared dishes as #foodporn has given chefs and farmers the opportunity to speak about their role as food producers.[11] Yet many of those public conversations are aimed at a consumer audience unfamiliar with, uninterested in, or overwhelmed by the details of food production. Scholars of agriculture have pointed out that small-scale farming is a ritual and rhythmic performance that is highly contingent on seasonal and geographical conditions, but social media extends the scope of that performance.[12] Farmers on Instagram need to perform and adapt their practice not just for different weather and land conditions, but for different audiences, from local customers looking for produce updates to global followers interested in sustainability and environmental impact to experienced farmer peers.

To open a space for specialist dialogues about food production that is grounded in local experience rather than global flows of information, a group of organic farmers in the PNW are using private Instagram accounts to create restricted networks that allow a frank sharing of information about farming. Nancy Baym and Joshua McVeigh-Schultz have examined similar uses of social media as microsocial hubs, where small groups rather than large networks are brought together.[13] Facebook's affordances for boundary management, as noted by Baym, Kelly Wagman, and Christopher Persaud, are also present in Instagram's architecture, creating the potential for communication that is only open to a restricted group.[14] As these farmers balance the extent to which they share on Instagram failure, uncertainty, or exasperation with the demands of the sustainable farm brand, farmers must make choices about what kind of transparency, authenticity, and realness is appropriate to express on their public-facing accounts. On the private farmer darkgram network, they share farming's horror stories and, with the aim of overcoming those failures, its technical demands. Through these local networks limited by personal and reputational familiarity, small-scale organic farmers of the PNW make use of Instagram's affordances for privacy to sustain the darkgram as a unique online community of expertise.

This chapter compares the public and private Instagram accounts of small-scale organic farmers in order to understand the affordances of Instagram as a space for knowledge sharing beyond branding. I examine in detail one organic farmer darkgram account in the Pacific Northwest, which I call Farm A. I assess the content shared by this account in these posts as well as the unique ways in which the farmer darkgram network utilizes Instagram's affordances to maintain privacy and protect their public brand while building a local community of expertise. To make sense of the content shared on this private network in a comparative context, I look at the public Instagram accounts of twenty small-scale organic farmers across North America, including a detailed analysis of posts by Laughing Crow Organics and Plenty Wild Farms in Pemberton, British Columbia, Sassafras Creek Farm in Maryland, and Tree House Farm in Massachusetts. I also interviewed Sassafras Creek's co-owner, David Paulk, and corresponded with a former darkgram member from Farm X. Like farmer darkgrams, public farmer Instagram accounts have coalesced around a community of potential customers and fans who are concerned with food justice but are more focused on attributes of sustainability like beauty, health, and purity rather than on technical farm processes. By comparing the private and public faces that farmers allow themselves to show on Instagram, I examine the unfolding of an alternate use of Instagram for intimate, local, and selective sharing that creates a specialized space for learning and innovation.

Branding, Aesthetics, and Realness on Farmer Instagram

Aesthetics played an important role in the ascendancy of Instagram, which grew from a group of photographers sharing photos in 2010 to become increasingly focused on social networking and community building.[15] As a microblogging site, the Instagram platform offers the possibility for individuals and businesses to market their brands directly and globally. For Sarah Banet-Weiser, branding "attaches social or cultural meaning to a commodity as a means to make that commodity more personally resonant to the consumer." Branding has long been associated primarily with corporations, but for many social media users branding has also become a way of expressing the self.[16] Those social media users who aspire to influencer status and the paid work that could accompany it are especially concerned with curating their own brand, transforming cultural labor into a business practice, and vice versa. Social media creates a relationship for users with the purchased, material product as well as the opportunity to interact with the immaterial brand that surrounds that product.[17]

Farmers use social media and branding to market their products and their experiences as individuals connected to rural locations and food production in a time when much of the world's population is concentrated in cities. For these farmers, lifestyle and product are interchangeable: they post images of sunsets over tidy fields and cozy farm staff lunches alongside images of carrots and beets for sale. Consumers who choose organic products from farmers markets often pay a premium to support local producers who cannot offer the economies of scale of agroindustrial corporations, nor the yield of farms that use conventional pesticides, herbicides, and fertilizers. As part of an activist movement for food justice, many consumers embody an almost "missionary-like zeal" for education about sustainability and its connection to food.[18] Connecting with these consumers on Instagram, outside of retail transactions, has allowed farmers to participate in the educational aspect of food justice as they offer to show consumers what farms look like on a day-to-day basis.

While education may be part of the goal, the use of Instagram as an extension of the farmer's brand to showcase commodities to potential consumers has limited the kind of information shared on public-facing Instagram accounts. Many farmers themselves feel uneasy about the split between education and marketing on Instagram. On the two farmer darkgrams I followed, posts made on public Instagram that are focused on selling farm wares to customers are referred to as "bragagrams."[19] For these farmers, bragging about quality and bounty for the purpose of increasing sales is central to their economic success; however, it is also an object of ridicule that they set apart from the other conversations about food justice, sustainability, and expertise they share on Instagram. The darkgram allows these farmers a space to negotiate and find respite from the tensions between community and consumer demands encountered by many professional users of social media.[20] Darkgram is free of bragagrams, a space where farmers can communicate without the need to express purely positive messages about their food and experiences as growers.

Analyzing 3.5 million posts on Instagram about organic food, Ladislav Pilar et al. reported that these posts most commonly referenced three attributes of organic food: health benefits, superior taste, and aesthetic beauty.[21] Clean food, or purity, was another highly ranked attribute. Organic farmers have benefitted from these associations by exploiting the potential of Instagram as a direct marketing service. Many farms have a public Instagram account where they post photos of beautiful, tasty, and healthy food, advertisements for their subscription services, or notices of the local markets they are attending. For example, organic farmers Laughing Crow Organics (@laughingcroworganics) post images of their produce lovingly laid out in mesmerizing mandalas to advertise their weekly subscription boxes.[22] Based in Pemberton, British Columbia, and farming on a little over five acres of leased land, Laughing Crow is a small-scale organic farm that sells vegetables through two weekly markets, on-farm sales, and direct-to-consumer subscriptions, as well as to local restaurants. As of August 2019, their public Instagram had over 2,700 followers, and mixes images of farmers working in mountain valleys with those of market stands and sales flyers.[23] If

FIGURE 15-2. A sample post of beautiful, organic produce from Laughing Crow Organics.

Instagrammers are looking for beauty from posts about organic food, the picturesque Pemberton Valley in the Coast Mountains fulfills that requirement. Wild landscapes framing productive farms are a common theme in public farmer Instagram. In the foreground of snaps of mountains and forests, orderly rows of organic crops are tended by happy farmhands showing humans and nature in harmony in a way that embodies the tenets of sustainable farming (fig. 15-2). Such images capture organic farming as a holistic practice, where beauty is felt in the juxtaposition of wild and tamed lands.

While beautiful shots of idyllic and immense landscapes are important in the visual marketplace of Instagram, part of the platform's appeal is also the presumed yet constructed transparency it offers. Many studies of social media identify authenticity as a key characteristic online users seek from brands. Alexandra Rodney et al. suggest that food bloggers need to balance aesthetic values, like attractive presentation of dishes, and their claims of expertise as cooks with a sense of authenticity, which might mean blogging a flopped soufflé or two.[24] Examining connections between food producers and local communities, Pennell emphasizes that revealing "the back end" of food production is an important component of the transparency that social media offers small business owners.[25] Farmers likewise experience expectations to keep it real. This operational aesthetic, whereby viewers are curious about not just the finished product but the labor behind it has long been exploited, from events like the World's Fair, which began its exhibits of new technology in the mid-nineteenth century, to craft-based reality TV such as *The Great British Bake Off* (2010–) and *Top Chef* (2006–).[26] Sites like Instagram and Twitter fulfill the same function. Allowing viewers access to behind-the-scenes trials and tribulations is part of the appeal of following experts on social media. On her Instagram, farmer Katy from Tree House Farms sporadically features #farmerfashion, where she shows her chicken-tending outfits, consisting of tie-dyed and tattered shorts, a far cry from the cowboy boots and spotless overalls featured in curated spaces of rural life like the Canadian soap opera *Heartland* (2008–).[27] At other times, Tree House Farms does tap into a more aestheticized image of country life, using vintage linens and hand-painted signs to deck out Katy's farmers' market table.[28] The balance of realness and fantasy is an important part of the public address of Instagram farmers.

The audience for public farmer Instagram accounts represents a diverse demographic. Comments on Instagram posts suggest an audience made up of consumers, novice and expert farmers, friends, hobby gardeners, farm equipment manufacturers, and even curious fans. Consumers post questions about product availability at markets, while hobby gardeners ask general questions about buying seeds and which pesticides are approved for organic use.[29] Farmers on Instagram are expected to serve as knowledge resources for people who know little about farming. Pierre Bourdieu links the purchase of commodities to the affirmation of the cultural capital of individuals, but on Instagram users assert their cultural capital through interactions with an immaterial brand rather than consumption of physical commodities.[30] This farmer network makes food justice visible, but it also places demands on busy farmers. David Paulk, an organic farmer from Maryland with 10,800 followers (August 2019), posts on Instagram as Sassafras Creek Farm on average ten times per week, a high frequency among the public farmer Instagram accounts I looked at. In contrast, Laughing Crow Organics posts up to five times a week during their high season. While farmers like Paulk welcome the opportunity to create community on Instagram, in our interview, Paulk acknowledged that he is more likely to respond to people on Instagram who seem serious or who he knows personally.[31] Despite the fact that Instagram opens up farmers to a global community of users, small-scale organic farmers like Paulk are still looking for local, peer connections, and darkgram is one way of making those connections possible.

As Paulk suggests, serious farmers follow public Instagram accounts. Paulk's public Instagram features photos of his market stand, but it also heavily represents the technical side of farming that one would expect to interest only a professional audience. Videos of farm machinery with hundreds of views are met by questions and suggestions from fellow farmers fluent in suppliers and automated processes.[32] Unlike the food justice brand of the PNW farmers I examined, Paulk's Instagram is focused on farmer-to-farmer, or as he describes, "peer-to-peer" discussions. Talking about public farmer accounts, Paulk says that the national visibility afforded by Instagram is perhaps most beneficial in terms of sharing information about farm equipment. While climate zones mean that information about planting times or pest pressures can't necessarily translate across the continent, engines work the same everywhere. Laughing Crow similarly shares photos of their farm machinery.[33] However, some serious questions might be lost in the mix. Vetting the serious farmer is difficult at a distance, and questions from nonlocal farmers can be lost amid a general audience of thousands. For example, a Laughing Crow post from July 2019 featured two questions about market logistics that were unanswered.[34] For nonfarmers, these technical posts show expertise and efficiency in farming, building an image of competency. Rodney et al. point out that, while providing glimpses of their authentic lives, bloggers writing about food need to be able to support their claims as experts as well.[35] Performing farmer life for many different audiences at once means complying with all kinds of demands to share details about farmer knowledge and lived experience.

Knowledge Sharing and Affordances on Darkgram

The power of the photorealistic image to represent the world as it has been seen is an important hallmark of the photograph. Images that appear to convey directly what words mediate through language endow photographs with a power to represent the real world seemingly without interpretation or intermediary.[36] From nineteenth-century portraits cataloging human bodies for judicial purposes to motion pictures recording medical procedures for distant classrooms, photographic images have long been seen as enabling efficient training in industry, trades, and skilled professions.[37] Educational visual media promised to improve retention of subjects, increase the speed of learning, and use teaching resources efficiently through asynchronous formats, as techniques and teaching are recorded, multiplied, and distributed to be shared far and wide, and at a time chosen by the viewer.[38]

Instagram is distinctive in the social media ecology due to its ease of image sharing, which is one of the platform's most evident affordances. Peter Nagy and Gina Neff have critically expanded the definition of affordance beyond its common usage denoting "qualities, features, or cues within a technology" that enable what many have identified as normative behaviors.[39] They emphasize instead the relational and contingent nature of affordances for users, where users draw on their understanding of other platforms and outside contexts as they engage with their online environment. Further, the platform affordances of Instagram can be perceived as remediating social relationships with visual media created by earlier image-sharing technologies.[40] Although on the one hand Instagram has taken up the banner of advertising, allowing the creation of complex brand identities through carefully constructed and meaningful images, it also embraces the image's capacity for transparency and effective teaching. Like older educational media mentioned above, the so-called farmer darkgram privately linking PNW farmers on Instagram uses these affordances to create opportunities for knowledge sharing that conforms to the farmer's schedule. Rather than describing pests, dropped flowers, or awkward growth patterns, farmers on darkgram can simply show them to each other, making use of Instagram's continuous, asynchronous distribution of images. For these small-scale organic farmers, where much of the expertise of growing is based on feedback from sight, smell, and touch, the immediacy of images as a communication medium is undoubtedly appealing. Once shielded from the public imperatives of self-branding, a space like the farmer darkgram shows the continued value of images for community teaching and learning.

While scholarly discussions of social media have suggested that its affordances reinforce values like connectedness and searchability, Nagy and Neff's imagined affordances place the user at the center of choices about social media engagement.[41] Demonstrating this nonnormative use of affordances in action, Baym has documented how users describe a need to limit their connection, or over-connection, on social media, and use privacy settings to control their sharing.[42] Likewise, the two accounts I follow on farmer darkgram show distinct choices and adaptation of Instagram's affordances away from unbounded connection, driven by the need for sharing situated knowledge about a geographic space and work practices.[43] Costa argues that affordances are highly locally and culturally dependent, which she demonstrates through the example of Turkish users' management of multiple Facebook accounts in order to respect socially prescribed behaviors toward different groups, from relatives to friends to political factions.[44] Rather than reproducing normative experiences of social media, for Costa affordances-in-practice create opportunities for diverse and individualized engagement with social media. Clearly there is space on social media for private sharing.

Privacy on social media takes many forms, from anonymity to secrecy. Private, so-called fake Instagram accounts, or Finstas, have been documented, especially among teens and young adults who curate Finstas for small groups of friends, sharing goofy or risqué images that might not fit the public brand that is expressed on their "real" Instagram account.[45] As described by Brooke Duffy and Ngai Chan, Finstas allow control over audience, content, and connection, while promising freedom from surveillance by their public followers.[46] On Instagram, the affordances of private networks make it possible for private accounts to screen requests to follow their image feed. In this way, a private network can be created that explicitly restricts audience. Looking at private and secret groups on Facebook, Urszula Pruchniewska examines how women use Facebook to create spaces where they can express concerns and questions that push against consumerist and neoliberal visions of success by expressing doubt and uncertainty.[47] Creating a similar space on their private darkgram, this small network of farmers keeps their conversations about struggles with their technical operations out of the public eye.

By taking to private networks rather than simply following each other on public Instagram accounts, farmers on the darkgram demonstrate a need for productive privacy. Food justice and sustainable farming practices may emerge from the same overarching standards of value and unite farmers, customers, and activists, but the discussions farmers want to have with one another do not always align with the interests of other groups. In the darkgram farmer community, members are able to advocate for sustainable practices while also expressing concerns about profitability and the demands on their time and labor. Trying to achieve a consensus within a wider inexpert group about effects of water pH on seedlings would be as difficult as relating to nonfarmers how late-night meals of Kraft macaroni and cheese fit into ideals of low environmental impact.[48] Dark is not always synonymous with failure: instead, farmer darkgram can be seen as a muted space where the chatter of nonexperts can be faded out.

On the darkgram farmer community that I examined, there are a few different kinds of posts. Because all darkgram posts are private, the farmer accounts I looked at developed their online connection as a result of face-to-face relationships. Unlike the members of Instagram communities studied by Elisa Serafinelli, who experience connection online as a first step toward consolidating a social relationship with a real-world meet-up, most of the members of the darkgram already know each other either reputationally or personally.[49] For new accounts, there is a process of introduction where a farmer darkgram member creates a post that vouches for the new user and asks other darkgrammers to follow them. Each darkgram feed differs depending on which accounts one follows. Posting on the farmer darkgram is much more infrequent than on farmers' public Instagram accounts because it is free from the imperative to affirm weekly relationships tied to market schedules and growing the brand. Since 2016, when the farmer darkgram was initiated, a network of roughly thirty to seventy active accounts have contributed as few as 6 or as many as 350 posts. Taking advantage of the affordances for disconnection and asynchronicity on social media, busy Farm A disappeared from darkgram for a whole season, only to reappear with a post or comment and an apology for the absence.[50] Curiously, although not connected to the wider Instagram, many of these posts use hashtags that serve to provide brief, humorous, and often one-off summaries of the sentiments expressed in the post. In this private space, hashtags, usually used to connect images to searchable categories, are adopted simply as vestigial elements of the Instagram environment, rather than as affordances for connection.

While Serafinelli suggests most Instagram users are photographers first and social media members second, the farmer darkgram is not about pleasing aesthetics but instead about highly transparent images that efficiently convey information, sometimes consisting of graphs of greenhouse temperature control readouts or screenshots of text messages.[51] Some of the photos are visually different from the poster's public account, with underexposed images, poor composition, or dreary colors, but often it is the comments made by the initial poster that sets them apart. Text serves a bigger role in darkgram than on public Instagram because the layering of comments and backtalk are foregrounded. On public networks, the potential of a captivating image to circulate beyond the community is more important. Kathleen Rodgers and Willow Scobie suggest that images widely spread on social media serve as symbols that condense layers of meaning and emotional impact to create complex visual messages rather than transparent, instructive communication.[52] Yet Instagram clearly has the potential to allow users to create images that serve both purposes.

Many farmer darkgrammers have taken pains to ensure that followers looking for their public Instagram accounts do not stumble across their darkgram accounts. While affordances for privacy exist through closed accounts on Instagram, there are no secret and unsearchable groups as on Facebook. Even if they are private, Instagram account avatars and bios are visible to anyone searching Instagram. But, because non-verified Instagram names and accounts can be generated with little more than an e-mail address, users are able to create darkgram-specific accounts that use clever naming practices to counteract searchability. Darkgram accounts often have parody names that use rhyming games to create handles that are unlikely to pop up in a search of the farm's name or keywords, yet are recognizable to those who are already familiar with the farms in question. Though irreverent, these farmers are cognizant of the network as a hub for many potential viewers, and adjust their names accordingly. One poster changed a name that suggested drug taking when they invited their niece to the group. These fake names are important for protecting the farmers from public Instagram followers who are not the desired audience for the darkgram. Because authenticity and transparency are part of the public farmer brand, even the existence of a second private account could suggest farmers have something to hide from their customers.

Like private professional Facebook groups, benefits to posters range from technical to less tangible support.[53] Farmers can boast about craft-focused accomplishments that are insignificant to the general public, but that hold value for other like-minded farmers: a good tool rack, for example.[54] Many posts on the darkgram are explicitly seeking specialist and geographically specific knowledge by posting questions about the pests, plants, or equipment featured in the post's image.[55] The privacy of the network allows conversations to be streamlined, creating space for knowledge sharing that can be expressed without concern for the curation of an individual's brand. Recounting some of the fallout of transparency, Pennell describes how a set of tweets with images of a cheese shop brought a Rhode Island cheesemonger to the attention of the local food authority for code infractions.[56] The darkgram's farmers can be open about their questions, needs, and processes because they are engaging with a closed community.

So what is dark, secret, or bad about farming? Any message that doesn't fit into the brand of healthy, beautiful, and tasty is shared on farmer darkgram accounts rather than public farmer Instagram accounts. The mistakes that are documented may be as simple as a messy shed.[57] Other problems are more dire, like coyote-destroyed crops or seeding trays killed by overfertilizing.[58] Some are frustrating, like recurring plant diseases that can't be treated with sprays as simply as conventional producers can. Waste such as rows of crops damaged by flooding or snow, or crops abandoned due to weed pressure or end of season are another dark secret not deemed fit to talk about on public farm Instagram accounts.[59] Because zero waste has become part of the accepted practice of sustainability, farm losses are characterized as part of the dark side. On the darkgram, farmers weigh the benefits of DIY against ready-made solutions to farm problems, speaking freely about equipment and suppliers.[60] Recurring themes of slightly dangerous tractor jaunts and jury-rigged power or plumbing systems are also seen as bad farmer practices.[61]

Unique to the darkgram is the frank discussion of pests. Where there is food, there are pests. Because organic and sustainable agriculture standards preclude many of the most effective and deadly deterrents, these farmers need to be vigilant about crop-destroying pests. Many posts show rodent ingress and address low-impact prevention and elimination strategies with advice and even referrals to online resources.[62] One post balances snark about another member's "savage moves" with advice about pest-specific dog breeds and statistics on pest population forecasts.[63] Pests and decay have a long-standing association with disgust. Even Dutch masters of the Renaissance included images of vermin and rot in their paintings as reminders of death. Vegans, who avoid animal products and condemn violence against animals, even pests, make up a large part of the audience for organic food brands: on Instagram, #vegan was the fourth most common pairing with #organic found by Pilar et al.[64] Thus, pest posts can be fully disclosed only on the darkgram, and they often feature less snark

FIGURE 15-3. On the farmer darkgram, Farm A complained about insects preying on crops with this image of a bug-filled sticky trap.

and more serious advice than other posts. One question about deer that were eating crops received detailed advice about electric fencing voltage and deer fencing height, as well as solutions that involved shooting and killing the deer. Because their shared community thrives on a commitment to sustainability and considering lifecycle impact, harvesting any venison was also suggested. Vegans and vegetarians on the farmer darkgram had outed themselves in another deer pest post, but they didn't simply reject the death of the deer. Aligned around farming first, they expressed a desire to protect their livelihood while seeking other strategies that are in keeping with sustainable practices.[65] In a similar vein, Farm A complained about insects preying on crops in a post with an image of a bug-filled sticky trap, but when another commenter pointed out beneficial insects, the poster opined that it "really makes you think hard about non selective pesticides" (fig. 15-3).[66] Pest posts are an important site of knowledge sharing on the farmer darkgram, where users reaffirm their environmental goals by seeking advice on low-impact solutions while sharing farm experiences that defy the sanitized, sustainable farmer brand promoted on public accounts.

Snark is an invaluable part of the language of this local farmer darkgram. Anjali Vats has documented the use of Instagram for detournement, where parody of posts, memes, and branding is used to create political commentary on economic and political inequality.[67] Similar critique of the imperative for self-branding is present in darkgram. The farmer darkgram posts offer satires of the carefree scenic images presented on public farmer Instagram accounts, some of which may even include their own bragagrams. In other cases, some posts criticize farmers who have totally transferred their attention from the material products of agriculture to the immaterial value created by branding. A series of videos made by Farm A parodied the success of two organic farmers with idiosyncratic small-scale methods who have become social media superstars through platforms like YouTube.[68] As a result of their successful branding, these farmers now make income not only from farming, but from tutorials, webinars, books, and workshops where they share their methods and their equipment recommendations. Making fun of the promises of success and profit by using specific cultivars or planting methods, Farmer A's videos mock the idea of a globally applied, one-size-fits-all solution for any farmer. Farmers are invested in making their businesses profitable; on darkgram, they speak frankly about marketing trends such as juicing packs, precut salad mix, or farm visits.[69] But in this case, other farmers are criticized for embracing too wholly the logic of branding and jumping from the material, local, and specific to the immaterial, global, and general. The farmer darkgram fights back against these tendencies in organic farming, using this private space to reaffirm community, diversity, and the usefulness of failure. They celebrate situated and local farming culture rather than global agricultural stardom.

Not everyone finds the farmer darkgram to be a productive community. Many accounts on the local network have only a handful of posts. In an e-mail, a producer who has deleted their darkgram account said that managing two accounts was too time-consuming.[70] Instead, they have chosen to show measured transparency on their public account, tagging these posts as #fails. While Costa suggests that some Facebook users juggle multiple accounts regularly, for the darkgram's farmers, the labor involved in managing two accounts means they must make decisions about transparency, authenticity, and audience, deciding what is more appropriate for public or private conversations.[71] Some conversations migrate between darkgram and public Instagram accounts. One account's darkgram secret, such as time devoted to stacking bins in elaborate towers, could be innocuous and playful content for another public account.[72] Yet, regardless of brand and audience, there are some conversations that are notably absent even on the most farmer-friendly public-facing Instagram accounts, such as pests or open discussion of the farm brand. In Maryland, Paulk, who is not part of the farmer darkgram network I examined, suggested that he would rather pick up the phone or consult an e-mail Listserv than commit these discussions to Instagram.[73] For some users, Instagram is a platform with affordances for public and open conversation, but e-mail and the telephone provide direct, local, and immediate responses required by farmers. For others negotiating Instagram's landscape, Instagram networks afford private, situated, asynchronous, and focused engagement with knowledge communities through image sharing.

Speaking Locally

On the one hand, it is clear from public Instagram accounts that small-scale organic farmers think conscientiously about the greater impact of their farm practices and respect the need to share this information with consumers. On the other, the burden of making farm and food labor visible and accessible to Instagram viewers continually rears its head on the farmer darkgram. Excited viewers that press farmers with questions about everything from lettuce to kohlrabi are lightly lampooned on the darkgram, as are others who are enthusiastic about the importance of local foods but strangers to the implications of seasonality or climate zones.[74] Farmers with markets in metropolitan regions may find their public Instagram conversations are more often linked to followers familiar with the ideals of food justice rather than the realities of agriculture. Is it the duty of farmers, as producers, to educate consumers about sustainable agriculture? Do small-scale farmers selling to local markets need to speak with followers, or even farmers, the world over? Navigating Instagram as a site of "lived practices of communication" as they negotiate visibility and privacy, as well as local and global flows of information, farmer darkgram demonstrates how users exploit the affordances of social media that address their local and community needs.[75]

The farmer darkgram shows that Instagram is not just a public network encouraging users toward the denser connectivity that makes branding possible for small-scale producers around the world; it can also serve as a private space enabling productive conversations for farmers as they navigate the values of sustainability and the possibilities offered by social media. Through Instagram, a global audience has turned to small-scale farmers for their perspectives on food production, and with this attention comes pressure on farmers to present the public image of an idyllic prosperous farm. At the same time, Instagram's members-only networks allow efficient sharing of technical knowledge and farming-specific skills that only experienced, local farmers would be able to provide. For this group of small-scale organic farmers from the PNW, the farmer darkgram provides a space to post about sustainable agriculture and its challenges, using the capacity of the image for transparency and teaching to seek advice, testify to experience, and reflect on farming, unedited.

Notes

1. Farm A, "Yes just lost a pallet of bulb crates on the 99 just south of Horse Shoe Bay . . .," Instagram, March 26, 2019, www.instagram.com/p/BvfW1OsA5iubs5a Fg3Y0Coer8EH927FZL7EImM0/.

2. Farm B, profile, Instagram, March 29, 2020.

3. Farm A, "Ok It's been a hectic spring and we haven't been sharing the oops moments . . .," Instagram, June 28, 2019, www.instagram.com/p/BzRjE_rH0ZCdZ13A dkJZSfB6V_jUXsAs4wNxTQ0/.

4. Elisabetta Costa, "Affordances-in-Practice: An Ethnographic Critique of Social Media Logic and Context Collapse," *New Media and Society* 20, no. 10 (October 1, 2018): 3641–56, https://doi.org/10.1177/1461444818756290.

5. Elisa Serafinelli, "Analysis of Photo Sharing and Visual Social Relationships: Instagram as a Case Study," *Photographies* 10, no. 1 (January 2, 2017): 91–111, https://doi.org/10.1080/17540763.2016.1258657; Michael Pennell, "More than Food Porn: Twitter, Transparency, and Food Systems," *Gastronomica: The Journal of Critical Food Studies* 16, no. 4 (November 1, 2016): 33–43, https://doi.org/10.1525/gfc.2016.16.4.33; Helena C. Lyson, "Social Structural Location and Vocabularies of Participation: Fostering a Collective Identity in Urban Agriculture Activism," *Rural Sociology*, September 1, 2014, https://doi.org/10.1111/ruso.12041.

6. Pennell, "More than Food Porn," 37.

7. Serafinelli, "Analysis of Photo Sharing."

8. Kathy Lynn et al. "The Impacts of Climate Change on Tribal Traditional Foods," *Climactic Change* 120, no. 1 (2013): 545; Philip McMichael, "Historicizing Food Sovereignty," *Journal of Peasant Studies*, 41, no. 6 (2014): 935.

9. Kathleen Rodgers and Willow Scobie, "Sealfies, Seals and Celebs: Expressions of Inuit Resilience in the Twitter Era," *Interface* 7, no. 1 (June 2015): 79.

10. Henry Jenkins, Sam Ford, and Joshua Green, *Spreadable Media: Creating Value and Meaning in a Networked Culture* (New York: New York University Press, 2013), 17.

11. Pennell, "More than Food Porn," 37.

12. Dominic Glover, "Farming as a Performance: A Conceptual and Methodological Contribution to the Ecology of Practices," *Journal of Political Ecology* 25 (2018): 688.

13. Nancy K. Baym and Joshua McVeigh-Schultz, "Thinking of You: Vernacular Affordance in the Context of the Microsocial Relationship App, Couple," *Social Media and Society*, December 2015, 1—15.

14. Nancy K. Baym, Kelly B. Wagman, and Christopher J. Persaud, "Mindfully Scrolling: Rethinking Facebook after Time Deactivated," *Social Media and Society* 6 (May 1, 2020), https://doi.org/10.1177/2056305120919105.

15. Serafinelli, "Analysis of Photo Sharing."

16. Sarah Banet-Weiser, *Authentic™: The Politics of Ambivalence in a Brand Culture* (New York: New York University Press, 2012), 4, 8.

17. Jenkins, Ford, and Green, *Spreadable Media*, 7.

18. Lyson, "Social Structural Location."

19. Farm A, "Oh. . Yeah. This one was totally meant to go bragagram not dark-gram," Instagram, September 13, 2017, www.instagram.com/p/BZAp4nOlhbICqv EoArUNtGci3dy5ioapqpH9zo0/.

20. Hector Postigo, "The Socio-Technical Architecture of Digital Labor: Converting Play into YouTube Money," *New Media and Society*, 2014, 9.

21. Ladislav Pilař, Lucie Kvasničková Stanislavská, Stanislav Rojík, Roman Kvasnička, Jana Poláková, and George Gresham, "Customer Experience with Organic Food: Global View," *Emirates Journal of Food and Agriculture* 30, no. 11 (November 2018): 921, https://doi.org/10.9755/ejfa.2018.v30.i11.1856.

22. Laughing Crow Organics (@laughingcroworganics), "CSA Box 7. We're really proud of this one . . .," Instagram, August 9, 2018, www.instagram.com/p/BmQjO Evlzko/.

23. Laughing Crow Organics (@laughingcroworganics), "Our CSA is filling up! Sign up . . .," Instagram, April 16, 2019, www.instagram.com/p/BwU1NG7FVbK/.

24. Alexandra Rodney, Sarah Cappeliez, Merin Oleschuk, and Josée Johnston, "The Online Domestic Goddess: An Analysis of Food Blog Femininities," *Food, Culture and Society* 20, no. 4 (2017): 685–707, https://doi.org/10.1080/15528014.201 7.1357954.

25. Pennell, "More than Food Porn," 38.

26. Neil Harris, *Humbug: The Art of P.T. Barnum* (Boston: Little, Brown, 1973).

27. Tree House Farms (@treehousefarms), "#farmerfashion is not realizing your shirt . . .," Instagram, August 26, 2019, www.instagram.com/p/B1laINGAtLA/.

28. Tree House Farms (@treehousefarms), "We made it! The table is groaning . . .," Instagram, July 18, 2019, www.instagram.com/p/B0ERGFHA_JU/.

29. Laughing Crow Organics (@laughingcroworganics), "We will be at @squamishfarmersmarket Saturday and . . .," Instagram, July 6, 2019, www.instagram.com/p/Bzk5ylDgoxa/; Plenty Wild Farms (@plentywildfarms), "Yesterday's market set up at the Wednesday . . .," Instagram, August 1, 2019, www.instagram.com/p/B0pW7U MAR5j/; Plenty Wild Farms (@plentywildfarms), "Our first pick of kale (and lettuce) is heading to . . .," Instagram, May 24, 2019, www.instagram.com/p/Bx3eCZZhUU8/.

30. Pierre Bourdieu, *Distinction: A Social Critique of the Judgement of Taste* (Cambridge, MA: Harvard University Press, 1984), 3.

31. David Paulk, interview with author, August 14, 2019.

32. Sassafras Creek Farm (@sassafrascreekfarm), "Last planting of beets #ticktock," Instagram, August 28, 2019, www.instagram.com/p/B1rqi5IAs-9/.

33. Laughing Crow Organics (@laughingcroworganics), "Cultivating tractor has been down for a couple key weeks here. So glad . . .," Instagram, July 9, 2019, www .instagram.com/p/BzuKDPlAHKp/.

34. Laughing Crow Organics (@laughingcroworganics), "Hey friends we've spent months," Instagram, July 20, 2019, www.instagram.com/p/B0JaWrtgyHo/.

35. Rodney, Cappeliez, Oleschuk, and Johnston, "Online Domestic Goddess."

36. Devin Orgeron, Marsha Gordon, and Dan Streible, *Learning with the Lights Off: Educational Film in the United States* (New York: Oxford University Press, 2012), 21.

37. Haidee Wasson, "The Elastic Museum: Cinema Within and Beyond," in *Useful Cinema*, ed. Haidee Wasson and Charles Acland (Durham, NC: Duke University Press, 2011), 196.

38. Orgeron, Gordon, and Streible, *Learning with the Lights Off*, 21.

39. Peter Nagy and Gina Neff, "Imagined Affordance: Reconstructing a Keyword for Communication Theory," *Social Media and Society*, December 2015, 3.

40. J. David Bolter and Richard Grusin, *Remediation: Understanding New Media* (Cambridge, MA: MIT Press, 2000).

41. Nagy and Neff, "Imagined Affordance," 4.

42. Baym, Wagman, and Persaud, "Mindfully Scrolling," 2.

43. Donna Haraway, "Situated Knowledges: The Science Question in Feminism and the Privilege of Partial Perspective," *Feminist Studies* 14, no. 3 (1988): 575–99, https://doi.org/10.2307/3178066.

44. Costa, "Affordances-in-Practice," 3646.

45. "Does Your Kid Have a 'Finsta' Account? Why It's a Big Deal," *USA Today*, www.usatoday.com, accessed April 29, 2019.

46. Brooke Erin Duffy and Ngai Keung Chan, "'You Never Really Know Who's Looking': Imagined Surveillance across Social Media Platforms," *New Media and Society* 21, no. 1 (2019): 127, https://doi.org/10.1177%2F1461444818791318.

47. Urszula Pruchniewska, "'A Group That's Just Women for Women': Feminist Affordances of Private Facebook Groups for Professionals," *New Media and Society* 21, no. 6 (2019): 1366, https://doi.org/10.1177/1461444818822490.

48. Farm A, "Championing healthy farm lunch today KD with broccolini, sweet onion . . .," Instagram, September 26, 2017, www.instagram.com/p/BZhIMO6lgEt5 FWbl0oB51TNRjxNLlL-IWM_bto0/; Farm A, "Deer oh dear we have a problem or more accurately . . .," Instagram, June 2, 2018, www.instagram.com/p/BjjGmRbA xbJ6ZeXQtdyjaPe-5bG1I0arGQ7kds0/.

49. Serafinelli, "Analysis of Photo Sharing."

50. Farm A, "Ok rats! Fucking rats! We've never had them . . .," Instagram, December 1, 2018, www.instagram.com/p/BpLuWcchA8H8OxO28SkwWqlKo9_ 5jwGT1ZzMqY0/.

51. Serafinelli, "Analysis of Photo Sharing"; Farm A, "I didn't stop to ask . . .," Instagram, May 28, 2018, www.instagram.com/p/BjY1D7jAcf4amizE7gYVZBpGF kSyugphRqFGmY0/.

52. Rodgers and Scobie, "Sealfies, Seals and Celebs."

53. Pruchniewska, "Group That's Just Women for Women."

54. Farm A, "This bragagram post is shining light through cracks . . .," Instagram, April 11, 2018, www.instagram.com/p/B-duVL3DwQaohB4rNNwv_-iVM7mId7fF -Vpakl0/

55. Farm A, "Deer Oh Dear."

56. Pennell, "More than Food Porn," 41.

57. Farm A, "Cows entry—pic one is about to become . . .," Instagram, April 6, 2018, www.instagram.com/p/BhPHprkFhbEoN8yxXEPKDomBi8PPrpKdul9tww0/.

58. Farm A, "We too had salt issues . . . again . . .," Instagram, April 22, 2018, www.instagram.com/p/Bh5oA47gKQKU-fFAR4VaCEXoZwnrHI-qOWBlsI0/.

59. Farm A, "Ooops mowing madness takes over #cleanitup," Instagram, November 5, 2018, www.instagram.com/p/BnXWFJDgX5l8er5ZbGqbF2NfIDjvd4NZ c3TWKM0/.

60. Farm A, "I didn't stop to ask."

61. Farm A, "Well we certainly weren't going to spring for a sprinkler stand . . .," Instagram, June 6, 2017, www.instagram.com/p/BVBMAYAl756-NZM29UxvQ rREGU5PNZj22IVNzE0/; Farm A, "Hey remember this crappy project . . .," Instagram, April 29, 2018, www.instagram.com/p/BiKZHwxAbF06iJE0yjdWRFT58cIXnq _dzmF8G00/.

62. Farm A, "Sound on it's very different when they're alive . . ., April 1, 2020, www.instagram.com/p/B-duVL3DwQaohB4rNNwv_-iVM7mId7fF-VpakI0/.

63. Farm A, "Ok rats!"

64. Pilař, Stanislavská, Rojík, Kvasnička, Poláková, and Gresham, "Customer Experience with Organic Food," 921.

65. Farm A, "Ok so we are having deer probs for the first time . . .," Instagram, June 3, 2018.

66. Farm A, "Geez. These sticky traps make me real nervous . . .," Instagram, July 7, 2018, www.instagram.com/p/Bk8zcPWApNxKNinOpWHw7fOT3SZrCt4h Fm5WZE0/.

67. Anjali Vats, "Cooking Up Hashtag Activism: #PaulasBestDishes and Counternarratives of Southern Food," *Communication and Critical/Cultural Studies* 12, no. 2, http://www.tandfonline.com/doi/abs/10.1080/14791420.2015.1014184, accessed August 23, 2019.

68. Farm A, "Carrot carrot beet beet carrot beet beet," Instagram, May 20, 2018, www.instagram.com/p/BjBaryUgYvXD9uMmzi-Owqss6wvb3svgXTFKsk0/.

69. Farm A, "Ooops mowing madness"; Farm A, "Feeling the heat? Cool down with our slip n slide," Instagram, June 21, 2018, www.instagram.com/p/BkTINW eghnJwpTpGUITfbVCfE5-mzQiyeQUdzo0/.

70. Farm X, "Re: new message via your website," Instagram, June 27, 2019.

71. Farm A, "Oh. . Yeah."

72. Farm A, "Binz in the hood . . . the secret hiding spot of Bin Laden . . .," Instagram, September 29, 2017, www.instagram.com/p/BZpfbJAFO64zTeMN qYxOlVEBFlwgY2-meH9OV80/.

73. Paulk, Instagram and agricultural training research project.

74. Farm A, "Ooops mowing madness."

75. Baym and McVeigh-Schultz, "Thinking of You," 1.

CHAPTER 16

The Surprisingly Long History of Feminist Eateries on Instagram

ALEX KETCHUM

In addition to managing her chocolate shop and commissary, vegan anarchist-ecofeminist chocolatier Lagusta Yearwood actively posts on Instagram. As founder of both Lagusta's Luscious and Lagusta's Commissary in New Paltz, New York, and cofounder of Confectionary in New York City, she often shares five or more Instagram stories and at least one grid post a day on the accounts of each of her businesses. These stories include her views on the politics of feminist veganism, the sources of her ingredients, discussions of labor rights, and advertisements of upcoming events and new products. As Yearwood demonstrates, Instagram provides a communication space for the owners of feminist eateries: the restaurants, cafés, coffeehouses, bakeries, and sweetshops whose founders explicitly referred to themselves as feminist in interviews, written materials, or advertisements. These owners communicate with customers about how their menu and restaurant or shop space reflects their feminist ideals within a multiplicity of feminisms: radical, radical lesbian, socialist, liberal, and anarchist.[1]

This chapter is particularly interested in the communication media of feminist eateries. Feminist food enterprises have long produced literature making connections between food, feminism, and their businesses. The operators of feminist eateries in the 1970s and 1980s actively produced books, articles, flyers, calendars, and other materials covering topics similar to the Instagram posts of feminist eateries in 2019. In this way, Instagram practices should not be seen as entirely new or unique, but analyzed for the important ways they function as an extension of a longer and more complicated lineage of feminist literary and communication culture around food. The technological affordances of Instagram have not changed how the founders of feminist food enterprises continue to communicate and explain their business decisions. Nor has Instagram changed the ways that these founders have sought to be vulnerable and authentic with their customers and audiences. Feminist food eateries from the 1970s to the present have done the work to make the personal (and the interworkings of the business) political. Rather, what is new is that Instagram has expanded digital and affective labor demands, as the operators of current feminist eateries must produce feminist writings about food on multiple platforms simultaneously. The interactivity built into social media platforms means that while having to manage and respond to multiple audiences, operators of these accounts are also exposed to trolls and critics. Instagram, then, has a mixed impact on feminist eateries, since it offers new possibilities for feminist visual communication while being challenging to sustain from a labor perspective.

Feminist Media and Communications

This chapter contributes to the fields of feminist media and communications studies, feminist history, and food studies. I build on the work of historian Margaret Finnegan, who in *Selling Suffrage* showed the links between feminist activism, consumer culture, and publicity in the early twentieth century.[2] My analysis shows how these themes continued into the second half of the twentieth century and early twenty-first century. Women who have run feminist eateries during this time period in the United States always produced more than food to eat, contributing to the creation of feminist media. I focus on the 1970s to the present, as this periodization is useful for comparing a pre-Internet era to the current digital surround of Web 2.0.

From food studies, I look to the work of sociologist Stacy Williams, who has shown how feminist activists have used their writings about food to work toward gender equality.[3] Although Williams focuses on the early twentieth century and thus does not address Instagram, her work demonstrates the importance of taking the genealogies of feminist media communications seriously. In addition, sociologist Deborah Lupton has studied how, "while people uploading images of their restaurant or home-cooked meals to a social media platform may not seem overtly political, it represents the micro-political level of participatory culture on social media as users attempt to generate meaning and to portray their food practices (and, by extension, themselves) in a certain light."[4] Here, Lupton highlights social forces that tend to depoliticize the work women do in the kitchen or in restaurants, even when women themselves see it as political. It is because of this depolitization that owners of feminist food businesses make explicit the political content within their work. Instagram enables activist groups, dissenting voices, and marginalized food cultures to be visible to potentially very large audiences in novel ways. Yet the kinds of content produced by feminist eatery owners on the platform is far from unprecedented.

I also draw on the work of communications studies scholars Cait McKinney and Elizabeth Groeneveld, who demonstrate that despite changing technological formats, a desire for feminist communications remains.[5] In "Online Feminism Is Just Feminism," sociologist Alison Dahl Crossley notes the symbiotic relationship between online and offline feminism, and the constancy of networking in many forms to sustain feminist movements. She argues that while the creation of separate spaces has been crucial to women's lives, "feminist networks need not be face-to-face to be impactful, as exhibited by the exchange of feminist zines (i.e., handmade photocopied pamphlets distributed by mail in the 1990s and penpal networks)."[6] As such, while the physical space of feminist eateries and their analog publications of calendars, cookbooks, and periodicals have been crucial to the feminist movement, so too is the work that feminist eateries, old and new, foster online on Instagram.

Analyzing Instagram in Feminist Historical Context: A Methodological Approach

In order to understand the historical context of the media produced by the founders of U.S. feminist eateries, I examine materials from the 1970s until the present. I resist over-relying on the term "business" in order to emphasize that the founders were not solely, or even primarily, motivated by profit. Rather they used or use food as their feminist activism. First I analyze the kinds of past materials feminist eateries produced, such as periodicals, flyers, cookbooks, and calendars assembled from my research at fourteen archives across the United States.[7] After discussing the major themes that emerge from these materials, I show how parallel themes are displayed on feminist food eateries' Instagram accounts. I have focused primarily on the accounts of U.S. feminist eateries founded in the 1970s and 1980s, and the twenty-first-century businesses of Lagusta Yearwood (@lagustasluscious, @llcomissary, @confectionarynyc), since these accounts speak to the genealogy of feminist media over several generations.[8] Instagram has not replaced the older forms of media publicity, but food professionals have adopted it as part of a larger media toolkit. Yet, while Instagram has expanded the options for feminist food enterprise creators to communicate, it is not without drawbacks.

Feminist Eateries' Communications of the 1970s and 1980s

In the 1970s and 1980s, the founders of U.S. feminist restaurants, cafés, coffeehouses, and food enterprises produced extensive printed materials as part of their political projects.[9] These materials included event calendars, cookbooks, and periodical articles. These publications acted in part as advertisements, but they accomplished more than that. These pre-Internet strategies educated readers about the politics of the business and business owners, while also acting as platforms to share information relevant to their activism. For example, some eateries produced flyers for primarily local customers explaining the culinary and feminist significance of their ingredients and techniques. The aesthetic of such flyers and posters ranged from handwritten to typed, most with an amateur, cut-and-paste, photocopied texture. On occasion, these publications circulated beyond the local context, which was useful for traveling lesbian feminists who might make pilgrimages to feminist restaurants such as Bloodroot in Bridgeport, Connecticut. These texts simultaneously worked to spread theories about food and business practices that could inspire other activists and restauranteurs.

Newsletters, particularly those with event calendars, were key to influencing customers and community members beyond the plate. For example, Las Hermanas of San Diego produced a newsletter beginning in 1975 called *Feminist Communications,* which always included an event calendar filled with activities by and for their community of primarily working-class Latina feminists.[10] The newsletter also included notes, event descriptions, ads for local feminist businesses, and articles on topics ranging from the value of feminist credit unions (January 1979 issue) and sterilization (August 1975 issue) to an editorial on the state of the women's movements in San Diego (December 1978). Likewise, Mama Bears bookstore and coffeehouse of San Francisco produced *Mama Bear News,* which informed readers about upcoming feminist events at both their establishments.[11] In addition, these newsletters created transparency to distinguish them from other kinds of political groups and eateries. Kay Lara Schoenwetter, editor of A Woman's Coffeehouse of Minneapolis's newsletter *Coffee Klatch,* explained that "this newsletter will be put out quarterly (or so) to publicize 'behind the scenes' information about how A Woman's Coffeehouse is run."[12] By making this information public, the coffeehouse collective hoped women would feel a greater connection to the institution and also be empathetic to some of the organizational difficulties that the collective encountered, such as insufficient funding.[13] Positioning announcements about feminist workshops, book launches, and poetry readings among information about coffee and snacks demonstrated to readers that feminist food politics engaged beyond the dish to the politics of labor, meat consumption, environmentalism, access to space and resources, and the topics covered by touring feminist authors, artists, and speakers. These newsletters were integral to the feminist food businesses' understanding of themselves as political, while also serving to advertise the spaces.

Longer publications, such as cookbooks and articles in feminist and lesbian periodicals, provided more space for these owners to elaborate on the meaning of what it meant to be a feminist eatery and to explain how their businesses reflected these principles. In the Bloodroot Collective's first cookbook, *The Political Palate* (1980), the collective wrote: "Feminism is not a part-time attitude for us; it is how we live all day, everyday. Our choices in furniture, pictures, the music we play, the books we sell, and the food we cook all reflect and express our feminism."[14] Bloodroot's Selma Miriam and Noel Furie have also elaborated on these ideas in popular lesbian publications, such as *Heresies*, *Lesbian Ethics*, and *Sinister Wisdom*, as well as in vegetarian magazines.[15] However, even articles published in feminist and countercultural periodicals had to be approved by other editorial committees. The women of Bloodroot decided to start their own press, Sanguinaria, in order to publish their first four cookbooks (the last three cookbooks were published by Anomaly Press). As demonstrated by the author of *The Feminist Bookstore Movement*, Kristen Hogan, feminists created their own presses and distribution networks in order to control their own political narratives—an ethic also taken up by founders of feminist eateries.[16]

The founders of feminist food enterprises produced media by and for themselves—primarily self-published or published in feminist, lesbian, or countercultural periodicals—that advanced feminist food and business practice. This media promoted their enterprises and related businesses, while creating pre-Internet feminist communications networks centered on food production and consumption. Forty years later, founders of feminist food enterprises continue to do similar work, but Instagram is now part of their toolkit.

Is Instagram Really That Different?

Regardless of medium, the emphasis of feminist eatery owners in publications from the 1970s and 1980s was primarily on written text. Reproducing images was costly. Digital technologies, like Instagram, have changed this in the twenty-first century. Scholar KC Hysmith (who also contributed chapter 12) argues that "no other social media platform will allow you to tell a story through images as powerfully as Instagram. This is what the app was designed to do."[17] One of Instagram's most evident contributions is that the distribution of images is now relatively free. The power of the image is foregrounded on the platform, requiring the operators of feminist eatery Instagram accounts to be creative with how to draw the viewer's attention to the text. While visuals help keep audiences engaged, feminist eatery operators focus on words as the most significant part of their messaging. In grid posts, words are integrated into the images themselves, with longer descriptions captioned below. This is not to say that these accounts do not share beautifully crafted Instagram posts and stories—they do. However, all of the accounts surveyed draw audiences in with visuals that are accompanied by captions stretching one or more paragraphs.

In this way, these proprietors unite the power of Instagram (cheap and quickly distributed images) with the long-standing feminist practice of heavily relying on text to express their political perspectives around feminism and food.

Chocolatier Lagusta Yearwood regularly posts beautiful photos of her sweet creations, the raw ingredients she sources from local farmers, and smiling images of the workers and her dog at her businesses. Despite this visual baseline, Yearwood's posts use lengthy captions to explicitly engage the politics of the images. For example, on June 23, 2019, Yearwood shared a series of @lagusta-luscious Instagram stories about U.S. Immigration and Customs Enforcement (ICE) and deportations. The stories re-posted images of puppets from @kore-angry explaining what legal rights people have in case ICE comes to their home. Yearwood added the following captions to the series of posts: "Oh and if you don't like that I post about politics on a business account . . . [next story] this business is political [next story] so if you're uncomfortable you're going to be uncomfortable with everything we do."[18] Yearwood writes about how occasionally her longer political posts lead to a loss of some followers. However, for her, the point of creating her own business was and continues to be explicitly political. Making her politics material, she then added that the red cards mentioned in the stories, for people to slide under the door if ICE knocks, are available for free at Lagusta's Luscious headquarters.

Social media platforms, such as Instagram, enable speedy dissemination, which feminist eateries use to readily and cheaply communicate with followers (to the extent that global digital users have access to the Internet and to Instagram). Such accessibility is useful for a business that can ship its chocolate products to many parts of the world (although Yearwood only ships within the United States), but it is worth questioning how important it is that someone on the other side of the world knows about a restaurant, café, or small food business that keeps its business local. Followers are not the same as customers. This wide potential distribution can foster the discussion of feminist food politics, but it is not as necessary for the financial side of the business if customers mostly come from the nearby region. However, the cost-benefit analysis of disseminating this kind of publication to larger audiences is similar to the kinds of analysis required by workers in feminist eateries of the 1970s and 1980s. Not everyone could visit Connecticut to dine at Bloodroot, but the collective still wanted to widely share its ideas about its restaurant through print. In this way, Instagram, like the writing of articles, is not about profit; rather, it is an extension of the founders' politics. Here, feminist media is about creating a collective community—an idea not wholly at odds with a feminist vegan anarchist such as Yearwood.

Instagram enables Yearwood and other founders to share raw thoughts immediately with followers. In a set of Instagram stories from January 30, 2019, Yearwood reflected on her own business in detail:

I feel ashamed to live in this country and don't know what to do about it when I'm so exhausted at the end of the day trying to run my world that is still exploitative but hopefully not as much. [Story 2] I've been thinking about wealth inequality so much lately because I'm reorganizing the financial structure of the businesses (which is, incidentally exhausting in new and wild ways I've never before experienced, namely my brain pulsating in actual pain from reading fine print and learning new systems) and seeing how a nice middle class business owner with good credit has access to so much that others don't: financial systems and advice and opportunities and capital and bankers and people being nice to her because she looks young and is white and a woman. [Story 3] It's still incredibly hard, every day, to keep these businesses financially healthy, but I'm doing it, we're doing it together and I'm more mindful than ever of the sneaky ways income inequality worms its way into every corner and the advantages I have and how best to use them to remake the system in the name of fairness. [Story 4] Let's beat it into submission, let's use the tools of rich people and make them work for us, let's Robin Hood our way out of this trash. Things are not Ok.[19]

She finished this thread of stories with an exhortation: "Let's talk about it, all the time. How broken the system is. What we're going to do about it."[20] Stories such as these are not rare on Yearwood's Instagram accounts. She often posts about worker rights, for instance. Yearwood goes into great detail about the decisions she makes in operating her business, especially about how to be an anarchist and a boss, how to try to avoid reinforcing all the problematic issues of operating a business under capitalism, and how to ethically source products. The stories utilize a gray background with white text and either pink or red highlights. Although the operators of feminist food enterprises may take advantage of the instantaneous and inexpensive publication of images on the platform, written political discourse remains dominant on these accounts.

Instagram is a social network, yet the kinds of cross-pollination and sharing that happens on Instagram between feminist enterprises is not wholly new. Feminist enterprises have long supported one another by cross-promoting events and sharing information about one another in what I have previously called the "feminist nexus."[21] This practice of sharing, amplifying, and supporting the political work of other feminists continues on Instagram. For example, Yearwood, like founders of feminist eateries of the past, regularly promotes other women-owned businesses and artists (e.g., Yearwood's mention of @koreangry on June 23, 2019). In an April 28, 2019, story, Yearwood posted about how she is "psyched about a cool woman owned beer spot RIGHT NEXT DOOR and the cutest pupper for my cutest pupper to be friends with . . . yay @mcfoxlins."[22] The Instagram format, however, allows for connection to be made with something as simple as a tag and hashtag. The medium has shifted, yet alliance building and connection continues.

lagustasluscious • Follow
New Paltz, New York

lagustasluscious I'm hand lettering every recipe title for #lagustaslusciouscookbook. I've watched all of Please Like Me, Special, and Shrill so far while doing it. For some reason I have to do like three versions of every word. Anyway, top tier TV, all of it, in case you too have a large project to work on. PS: big announcement about this book situation coming this TUESDAY. Xoxo Lagusta #sweetxsaltybook

93w

ethicalveganlife Eeeek! I can't get your chocolates and they're basically my favourite thing ever so I am so unbelievably ridiculously excited for this cookbook!!!

208 likes

MAY 17, 2019

Add a comment...   Post

FIGURE 16-1. Yearwood shared her hand-lettered recipe title cards on Instagram.

It is most productive to understand Instagram as part of an interweaving timeline. The cultural production of feminist eateries of the 1970s and 1980s continues to influence new generations of feminist food workers. Yearwood reflects: "I bought a Bloodroot cookbook in college and fell in love with it. I wrote a fan letter to Noel and Selma and they wrote back, encouraging me to come visit."[23] She later decided to cook at Bloodroot during her culinary school internship and continued working there after. Furthermore, she worked alongside Selma and Noel to produce some of their cookbooks. This kind of interplay between generations and the relationship between old and new media is evident in Yearwood's Instagram posts—particularly the posts that reference her own cookbook or capture her sign making work.

Instagram adds to the past forms of cultural production that the creators of feminist food enterprises utilized in the 1970s and 1980s. In fact, Instagram can actually bolster old media forms such as cookbook writing. Most notably, Instagram is the main platform Lagusta Yearwood uses to advertise her cookbook.[24] In a May 17, 2019, post, Yearwood shows title cards with the caption, "I'm hand lettering every recipe title for #lagustaslusciouscookbook" (fig. 16-1).[25] On January 11, 2019, she posted the story "the original manuscript was supposed to be 35–50k words." Second story: "it ended up being 70k words."[26] Yearwood regularly updates followers on the cookbook progress. As she discusses on podcasts such as *Sagittarian Matters* and *Meatless*, despite her blog and daily posts, it is through the cookbook that she feels she is "being a real writer."[27] Although Yearwood acknowledges the importance of new media, she still finds traditional book publication to be legitimizing.

Instagram Downsides

While old and new media intertwine, these methods differ in their sustainability and lifespans. The material presence of cookbooks, which are often referred to as old media, can linger on bookshelves and be rediscovered, thereby influencing the next generation of feminist food business owners.[28] One must wonder what the impact of Instagram productions will be on the next generation, especially given the ephemeral nature of the technology. Instagram stories disappear after twenty-four hours, and the proprietary nature of this platform threatens future access to grid posts. A larger discussion of the ephemerality of social media and the threat of the digital dark ages is beyond the scope of this chapter, yet this challenge reiterates the importance for feminist food eatery founders to produce a wide range of communications materials.

Although Instagram offers the creators of feminist eateries benefits, such as cheap access to their customer base and instantaneous publication, using the platform has its disadvantages. The ability to connect with readers quickly can also expose one to harassment.[29] For example, Lagusta Yearwood has had a troll make fun of her gender presentation.[30] Creators are vulnerable to wider audiences and the violence that comes with being a woman, gender nonconforming, or racialized person online. They are also not compensated for the physical and emotional labor of producing posts and mitigating harassment.

While feminist eateries in the past produced written materials and wrote articles that were issued over longer time periods, such as monthly newsletters, Instagram and other social media work requires near constant attention. On April 6, 2019, Yearwood wrote about this phenomenon in her own Instagram stories:

> Sometimes the social media aspect of running three businesses can be overwhelming. [Story 2] Each business has a Facebook, Instagram, and Twitter. And DMS [direct messaging] for all of them. We've got an unused Pinterest, a Tumblr, a blog, a website. [Story 3] Probably more I'm forgetting. [Story 4] including personal accounts, to which business inquiries get tossed surprisingly frequently, it's about 12 mailboxes to remember to check daily. [Story 5] I've tried all the apps and services to manage it, but what's worked best is our two GMs [general managers], Kate and Rachel, keeping an eye out in

addition to me. They're great. We've never had a social media manager (U can tell// for that I take pride) or publicist of anything. Just diy diy diy diy diy.[31]

Instagram is not the sole cause of this communication labor. Yearwood chooses to post on numerous social media accounts, produce the podcast *Thank You in Advance*, and write cookbooks, in addition to running multiple businesses. Yet the features of Instagram stories require near constant attention. It is a useful tool, but in order to remain at the top of followers' story feed, the operator of the account must release at least one new story every twenty-four hours. The ever-present demand on the owners to post stories and grid posts in order to stay relevant to the algorithm coordinating user feeds forces the owner of the restaurant to become part of the product itself. While owners of feminist eateries in the past had at times revealed intimate sides of themselves—as when the women of Bloodroot posed naked in the lesbian journal, *Common Lives, Lesbian Lives* in 1986—the slowness of print publishing enabled more deliberate reveals of the personal.[32] Instagram's speed does enable the women who run these enterprises and accounts to control their own narratives. However, the platform demands that account operators often reveal intimate and personal details in order to generate enough new content quickly, which fuses with the demand for authenticity. In this way, the platform extracts additional affective labor and results in a capitalization of intimacy.[33]

Performing this digital labor further burdens feminist eateries' tight operations.[34] On June 16, 2019, the @LagustaLuscious account published photos of Yearwood editing her cookbook with her dog sitting on her lap with the caption "Why yes, I did make Kate [her general manager] take photos of me editing a book that I wrote with my dog on my lap. I'm still kinda blown away that I WROTE A BOOK." In this post she makes readers feel invested in the process of creating her book. Yearwood uses Instagram to advertise her endeavors while also displaying her politics through the intermixing of old and new media. The post reveals the behind-the-scenes process both of book publishing and of maintaining Instagram accounts, including asking a staff member to photograph her. She also speaks to the politics of authenticity by revealing what appears to be an unretouched, true representation of the process. The images show the handwritten text in her cookbook, digitally reproduced. The post illustrates how Instagram is not just a way to promote work, but is work in itself that is not directly compensated. In further Instagram posts and stories that promoted the cookbook, Yearwood's photos and videos exposed intimate details of her life by showing her home, wardrobe, makeup, dog, and herself at all hours of the day and night. The visuality of these accounts highlights both expectations of authenticity in the digital age and the work required to do so, and the particularly taxing affective labor of not only producing content for the twenty-four-hour audience, but also of making oneself (potentially) vulnerable to the public *all the time.*

Instagram and other social media change the kind of labor required of food businesses—and not just the feminist ones. Part of what links feminist eateries' cultural productions from the past and present is their relationship not only to politics but to authenticity. Over 25 million businesses are on Instagram as of the spring of 2019, and many of these businesses rely on Instagram for advertising.[35] While speaking about shopping features on Instagram, the product manager at Instagram, Layla Amjadi, says that one reason Instagram advertisements are so successful is that brands can market themselves in a very specific way that feels genuine.[36] Marketing director Mark Choisi spoke to this idea, remarking that Instagram allows his company to "really engag[e] our audience in an authentic way."[37] Especially for small businesses, Instagram can make a brand's marketing feel deeply personal. However, inculcating this feeling of intimacy for small businesses and their owners is not just about authenticity, but vulnerability. Instagram has not altered the choices feminist food enterprise founders make to explain their business decisions, nor how they are both vulnerable and authentic in their interactions with their customers. Instead, Instagram demands such affective labor from other food businesses as well, who might not have initially done this work.

Instagram is part of a long history of feminist communication practices. Lagusta Yearwood creating an Instagram post about workers' rights while promoting this Wednesday's ramen should be taken seriously as a form of feminist political media, just like a magazine article, newsletter, or cookbook. Feminist food businesses have used various forms of media to communicate about their businesses since the 1970s. Whether a handwritten event poster, newsletter, cookbook, or Instagram story, old and new media both serve to articulate the ways the owners of feminist eateries position their work in relation to their activism. Though endowed with particular affordances, each kind of media could be employed to communicate with existing and potential clients, as well as community members, about available products as handily as they can explain the inner-workings of the business. What is changing feminist practice now is that the nature of new media platforms demands more consistency from business owners. It also demands a greater level of transparency and vulnerability. Instagram transforms the format, places more emphasis on the visual, and requires near-constant engagement. It thus raises questions around undervalued—indeed, sometimes unpaid—feminist digital and affective labor. In such ways, the images and texts on the Instagram accounts of feminist eateries *are* political activism.

Notes

1. It is beyond the scope of this chapter to explain the various feminist movements. For more information on the history of feminist movements in the second half of the twentieth century and the twenty-first century, see Benita Roth, *Separate Roads to Feminism: Black, Chicana, and White Feminist Movements in America's Second Wave* (New York: Cambridge University Press, 2004), and Alice Echols, *Daring to Be Bad: Radical Feminisms in America* (Ann Arbor: University of Michigan Press, 1989).

2. Margaret Mary Finnegan, *Selling Suffrage: Consumer Culture and Votes for Women* (New York: Columbia University Press, 1999).

3. Stacy J. Williams, "A Feminist Guide to Cooking," *Contexts* 13, no. 3 (August 2014): 59–61, https://doi.org/10.1177/1536504214545763.

4. Deborah Lupton, "Cooking, Eating and Uploading: Digital Food Cultures," in *The Handbook of Food and Popular Culture*, ed. Kathleen LeBesco and Peter Naccarato (London: Bloomsbury, forthcoming), 151, https://ssrn.com/abstract=2818886.

5. Cait McKinney, "Newsletter Networks in the Feminist History and Archives Movement," *Feminist Theory* 16, no. 3 (September 2015): 309–28, https://doi.org/10.1177/1464700115604135; Elizabeth Groeneveld, *Making Feminist Media: Third-Wave Magazines on the Cusp of the Digital Age* (Waterloo, ON: Wilfrid Laurier University Press, 2016).

6. Alison Dahl Crossley, "Online Feminism Is Just Feminism: Online and Online Movement Persistence," in *Nevertheless, They Persisted: Feminisms and Continued Resistance in the U.S. Women's Movement*, ed. Jo Reger, 60–78 (New York: Routledge, 2019), 63, https://doi.org/10.4324/9780203728628.

7. The Sallie Bingham Center for Women's History and Culture at Duke University, the Schlesinger Library on the History of Women in America of the Radcliffe Institute at Harvard University, the University of Iowa Archives, the University of Minnesota Archives, the San Francisco GLBT Archives, the San Francisco Public Library Archives, Northeastern University Archives, Smith College Archives, New York University Fales Archives, New York University Archives of the Tamiment Libraries, John J. Wilcox Jr. Gay Archives at the William Way Center in Philadelphia, the San Diego LAMBDA Archives, the Lesbian Herstory Digital Archives, and Yale University Archives.

8. In order to respect her privacy, with one exception, I do not cite Lagusta Yearwood's personal account, although it is also public and reveals how her work affects her personal life.

9. For a full list of over 250 feminist eateries in the United States, see thefeministrestaurant.com.

10. Las Hermanas Coffeehouse, *Feminist Communications*, June 1975, Las Hermanas box, LAMBDA Archives of San Diego.

11. Mama Bear Coffeehouse, *Mama Bear News*, San Francisco LGBT Business Ephemera Collection (#BUS EPH), GLBT Historical Society of San Francisco Archives.

12. Kay Lara Schoenwetter, "A Women's Coffeehouse History," *Coffee Klatch*, 1, 1976, box 1, Jean Nickolaus Tretter Collection in GLBT Studies of the University of Minneapolis Libraries and Archives, A Woman's Coffeehouse Collective Records 1976–1985.

13. Similarly, the Women's Coffeehouse of Cambridge, Massachusetts, in May 1988 began publishing *The Coffeehouse News*, stating, "We've been looking for a way to keep in touch with new participants and veteran coffeehousers [*sic*] for updates and invitations." The writers also emphasized that the coffeehouse was a nonprofit, volunteer-run women's collective organizing free feminist cultural events on Friday evenings at the Women's Center in Cambridge. (Women's Coffeehouse of Cambridge, Massachusetts, "About," *Coffeehouse News*, May 1988.)

14. Bloodroot Collective, *Political Palate: A Feminist Vegetarian Cookbook* (Bridgeport, CT: Sanguinaria, 1980), 1.

15. In Other Words: Portland's Feminist Community Center, *Remembering Our Roots*, July 31, 2009. https://inotherwordsbooks.wordpress.com/2009/07/31/remembering-our-roots/.

16. Kristen Hogan, *The Feminist Bookstore Movement: Lesbian Antiracism and Feminist Accountability* (Durham, NC: Duke University Press, 2016).

17. Katherine Hysmith, "#FreeFireCider: Folk Herbalists, Feminist Hashtags, and the Instagram Modernity," *Penknife* (blog), July 10, 2017, www.penknifekitchen.com/blog/firecider.

18. Lagusta Yearwood (@lagustaluscious), Instagram story, June 23, 2019.

19. Lagusta Yearwood (@lagustaluscious), "I feel ashamed to live in this country," Instagram story [story 2, story 3, story 4], January 30, 2019.

20. Lagusta Yearwood (@lagustaluscious), "Let's talk about it, all the time. How broken the system is," Instagram story, January 30, 2019.

21. Alexandra Ketchum, "'The Place We've Always Wanted to Go But Never Could Find': Finding Woman Space in Feminist Restaurants and Cafés in Ontario 1974—1982," *Feminist Studies* 44, no. 1 (2018): 126–52.

22. Lagusta Yearwood (@lagustaluscious), "Psyched about a cool woman owned beer spot RIGHT NEXT DOOR," Instagram story, April 28, 2019.

23. Yearwood, personal communication with author, e-mail April 16, 2015.

24. These posts are also cloned on her Facebook accounts.

25. Lagusta Yearwood (@lagustaluscious), "I'm hand lettering every recipe title for #lagustaslusciouscookbook," Instagram photo, May 17, 2019, https://www.instagram.com/p/Bxk0u8Ij_em/.

26. Lagusta Yearwood (@lagustaluscious), "The original manuscript was supposed to be 35–50k words, it ended up being 70k words," Instagram Story, January 11, 2019.

27. Nicole J. Georges, interview with Lagusta Yearwood, "Lagusta YEARWOOD Talks Veganism!!!" episode 95, part 1 of 2, *Sagittarian Matters* (podcast), January 12, 2018, https://sagittarianmatters.podbean.com/e/episode-95-lagusta-yearwood-talks-veganism-part-1-of-2/; Nicole J. Georges, interview with Lagusta Yearwood and Beth Pickens, "Lagusta Yearwood & Beth Pickens!!!" episode 97, part 2 of 2,

Sagittarian Matters (podcast), January 26, 2018, https://sagittarianmatters.podbean
.com/e/episode-97-lagusta-yearwood-beth-pickens-part-2-of-2/; Alicia Kennedy,
interview with Lagusta Yearwood, "Lagusta Yearwood," episode 2, *Meatless: A Podcast about Eating* (podcast), June 11, 2018, https://www.stitcher.com/podcast/alicia
-kennedy/meatless-a-podcast-about-eating/e/54855659.

28. There are various debates about the differences between old and new media,
including Lev Manovich, *The Language of New Media* (Cambridge, MA: MIT Press,
2001).

29. Karla Mantilla, "Gendertrolling: Misogyny Adapts to New Media," *Feminist
Studies* 39, no. 2 (2013): 563–70, www.jstor.org/stable/23719068.

30. She described the troll experience in her personal account's stories. Lagusta
Yearwood (@lagusta), Instagram story, June 2019.

31. Lagusta Yearwood (@lagustaluscious), "Sometimes the social media aspect
of running three businesses can be overwhelming," Instagram story, April 6, 2019.

32. Noel Furie, "Mes Amies, les Amantes," *Common Lives, Lesbian Lives: A Lesbian
Journal*, no. 20 (Summer 1986): 15–21.

33. Tobias Raun, "Capitalizing Intimacy: New Subcultural Forms of Micro-Celebrity Strategies and Affective Labour on YouTube," *Convergence* 24, no. 1 (2018):
99–113.

34. Stephanie Anne Brown, "Digital Labor: The Internet as Playground and Factory," ed. Trebor Scholz, *Transformative Works and Cultures* 15 (2014).

35. Layla Amjadi, "What Have You Bought on Instagram?" *Why'd You Push that
Button* (podcast), November 21, 2018, https://podcasts.apple.com/ca/podcast/what
-have-you-bought-on-instagram/id1295289748?i=1000424284144, 38-minute mark.

36. Ashley Carman, "Instagram Is Creating a 'Personalized Mall' for Everyone,"
Verge, last updated November 21, 2018, www.theverge.com/2018/11/21/18105006/
instagram-shopping-e-commerce-whyd-you-push-that-button.

37. Ibid.

CHAPTER 17

How to Think with Your Body

Teaching Critical Eating Literacy through Instagram

SARAH E. TRACY

When I was teaching at the University of California, Los Angeles, in fall 2017, a student approached me, wanting to write her paper on activated charcoal, which she had repeatedly seen on Instagram. She wanted to explore whether it was actually healthy or just photogenic. Her final project analyzed the science behind activated charcoal, a visually charismatic health trend of the late 2010s and an example of food functionalism—an approach based on consuming foods explicitly for their health effect, or functional benefit, in the body. Activated charcoal illustrates the digitally saturated frame of reference my students on both coasts have brought to our classroom discussions of U.S. food culture. Constantly inundated with information about food and nutrition, students nonetheless found themselves asking: What kind of diet is truly healthy? And what kind of diet just *looks* that way?

In the spirit of Daniel Bender et al.'s commentary on "Eating in Class," this chapter provides a brief reflection on the task of "asking students to historicize themselves" by reflecting on their own participation in the performative food culture of Instagram.[1] I thank my students for our enriching conversations and the opportunity to reflect on their work in this chapter. Teaching at UCLA and the New School in New York City, I have encountered what my friend and scholar of food and indigeneity, Hi'ilei Hobart, has called "Food Studies 2.0," which she defines as classrooms full of students for whom food's cultural, ecological, and political importance is self-evident. Between 2016 and 2019, I have developed courses at UCLA and the New School on the history of food science and culture. They reflect two of my main intellectual projects: to clarify how food operates as a technology (applied science) and as a technology of the self (one in a set of pressures to transform oneself in the pursuit of greater happiness, health, or success.)

For these interdisciplinary, upper-level elective classes, my students critically interrogate topics ranging from the neurobiology of food porn and the racial politics of appropriative health trends like matcha, to how to contextualize the unattainable body image standards of Instagram models and Influencers. These queries are grounded in insights and methods from science and technology studies, food studies, sensory studies, and media studies. Self-directed learning modules and final projects invite students to interrogate the role of vision, as a sensory modality, in everything from the scientific method to food marketing. In other words, students meditate on the proverbial claim that seeing is believing.[2] We take inspiration from literary critic Kyla Wazana Tompkins, who forwards a queer practice of "reading orifically" in her influential work on racialization, nationalism, and eating in nineteenth-century America.[3] For Tompkins, this means attending to the eating body's many sites of incorporation and vulnerability, and refusing patriarchy's alienation from the body below the neck. We focus on how food concepts and materials circulate in our moods, in our noses, in our hands, in our desires, and in our guts.

I understand Instagram as a vibrant digital ecosystem whose algorithmic and commercial contrivance is masked by vivid, user-generated content. It is reality, bent.[4] As a class, my students and I explore how the tension between cynicism and earnestness shapes our visual consumption. In our assignments, students reflect critically on how the platform amplifies dietary trends: they trace how marketers and digital entrepreneurs can tactically create an optics of health, in which health is conflated with dominant cultural ideals of beauty and affluence. We watch this manifest in the association of gluten with weight gain, for example, or in the equation of LA's juicing culture with slimness and virtue.[5] Students choose topics like Flamin' Hot Cheetos and craft brewing, not to mention trendy restaurants like Media Noche in San Francisco, Christina Tosi's Milk Bar, or the Dominique Ansel Bakery of cronut fame. I invite students to examine the cultural assumption that underpins the Instagram economy: that our eyes give us accurate purchase on the world. As a result, they may over-determine our beliefs and consumption practices. Can we better serve our health by opening our eyes to how vision drives aspiration, and aspiration drives commercialism? What do we learn when we look inward, and eat, instead, with our entire bodies?[6]

Unboxing a Food Trend

My upper-level elective at UCLA's Institute for Society and Genetics was titled "Food. Power. Money. Science." A special course capped at seventy students, it drew mainly juniors and seniors from the institute's interdisciplinary Human Biology and Society major. The final assignment for the course was called "Unbox a Food Trend," inspired by the digital entrepreneurship unboxing phenomenon. Alternately characterized as a democratizing force or just "aspirational thrill-seeking in recessionary, digitally mediated times," unboxing predates the platform that made it famous: YouTube.[7] In the early 2000s, websites like Unbox.it and unboxing.com offered a venue for young adults to participate in virtual unveilings of the latest electronics—sometimes dubbed "geek porn."[8] Other videos featured telegenic children in the grip of a newly unwrapped toy, or young women hypnotically trialing beauty products.

My students' task was to examine a selection of written and visual representations of one dietary trend using French sociologist Bruno Latour's concept of the "black box." With the concept of the black box, Latour challenges us to follow scientists around—in their labs, in their field sites, in their clinics—to address how scientific knowledge gets made. This approach makes explicit how much work—how much debating, silencing, and (self-)promoting—goes into the acceptance of a scientific theory or practice. Not every nutritional claim or theory, for instance, becomes black boxed or rendered "invisible by its own success." Latour's argument was that "the more science and technology succeed, the more opaque and obscure they become."[9] In other words, dominant ideas seem natural and inevitable, rather than products of history, politics, or chance. I enjoyed the wordplay of unboxing a black box, and I hoped it would prove a useful technique for following the structural influences behind digital content that appears raw, spontaneous, and user-generated.

To unbox a trend, students needed to contrast online representations of a dietary or lifestyle vogue with relevant peer-reviewed literature in the life sciences, social sciences, and humanities disciplines. They were invited to integrate their own embodied experience of the food product or trend into their analysis. How did it sit with their own bodies? What meaning did the food hold within their own traditions, identity, and wellness? If Instagram did not exist, how would the food's value change? I received fascinating papers peeling back label claims on trendy food products and their bioactive properties, including KIND granola bars, craft beer, matcha tea, gluten-free bread, and West LA's ubiquitous raw-juice bars. One of the most intriguing submissions was this chapter's opening example: the essay on the Instagram footprint of then-trending activated charcoal. This student scrutinized the more zealous popular claims about activated charcoal's suitability as a prophylactic detoxifier. She referenced the health product's most frequent applications in her feed—in baked goods and other products that carry charcoal's dramatic pigment well: ice cream (both dairy and nondairy variants), vegetable juices, teas, and lattes (fig. 17-1).[10] She concluded that activated charcoal had established therapeutic use in acute cases of poisoning or drug overdose, but that its prominence in the visual culture of clean eating was more a product of hype and beauty than science. She herself did not perceive any effect of activated charcoal-containing

FIGURE 17-1. Rawnice (@rawnice), "Stunning and inspiring galaxy bowl."

products on her sense of wellness, digestion, or mood. These reflections helped her explore the theoretical inspiration for this assignment, in that she found visual appeal to play a sophisticated role in driving consumption of purported health foods, as well as that of high-fat, high-sugar, or high-calorie offerings customarily considered food porn.

Managing Your Feed:
How to Think Holistically in a Visual Society

In my adaptation of a food studies core course called Food and the Senses at the New School in New York, upper-year food studies, design, and communication majors explored the hypothesis that U.S. food culture is particularly visual.[11] Their final Unessay Project was informed by Constance Classen's critique of the patriarchal elevation of sight and hearing (coded as masculine) over smelling, tasting, and touching (coded as feminine). We grounded this argument with, for example, business historian Ai Hisano's research on artificial color chemistry and the leading reliance of the U.S. food industry on food dyes throughout the twentieth century. Food dyes, we learned, obscured consumers' ability to discern between products of varying quality or provenance, such as butter versus margarine and fresh versus aging meat. In this way, we explored the interplay of visuality and health claims in U.S. food culture. This meditation combines the gendered exploitation of feminist critic Laura Mulvey's famous "male gaze" with the distorting effect of what sociologist of science Hannah Landecker calls the "scientific gaze:" one that reduces whole foods and their ecologies to single bioactive ingredients, such as cholesterol or medium-chain triglycerides.[12] U.S. food culture exhibits a broad spectrum of guilty to virtuous eating experiences, all of which are conveyed with visual signifiers whose purpose is to incite consumption.[13]

The final submissions for this assignment were inspiring. They included food diaries and cooking videos, and a private "anti-Instagram" account chronicling the author's raw inner monologue while eating out with Lyme disease and amid the toxicity of misogynistic online dating culture. Rather than rosy captions and flattering filters, the student used blurry images narrated through ennui, self-doubt, body dysmorphia, and—in many cases—indigestion. Another student mused on their emotional (and financial) investment in the recommendations of @foodiemagician, a magician and influencer named Josh Beckerman whose every meal is eaten out and documented in luscious detail for his 82,600 followers (as of August 2021). The student illustrated Beckerman's aesthetic using three recent images from the magician's Instagram account (fig. 17-2).[14]

Alarmed by findings like those of one restaurant management firm that only 12 percent of study respondents took issue with influencers like Beckerman receiving compensation for promoting products on social media, the student resolved to take in future food recommendations with a proverbial grain of salt.[15] Vivid reflections also came from one student who analyzed the #cleaneating trend through the well-publicized struggle of lifestyle blogger and former vegan Jordan Younger (@thebalancedblonde, with 232,000 followers as of August 2021 fig. 17-3),[16] with orthorexia nervosa (a form of disordered eating characterized by a fixation on pure or righteous eating). She concluded that zealous pursuit of virtue and beauty was as likely to produce dysregulated eating as sustainable wellness.

At UCLA and the New School, it has been my hope that deconstructing food and diet culture on Instagram would demonstrate the catharsis of critical media consumption. I am encouraged that student evaluations strongly indicated that the unboxing and unessay assignments realized two key learning outcomes of

FIGURE 17-2. Josh Beckerman's (@foodiemagician) images of A Taste of Maine, the Holy Donut, and Dim Sum To Go.

FIGURE 17-3. A curation of Jordan Younger's Instagram posts by student Ella MacDonald (#Eatclean).

my classes: a high level of student ownership of course content, and increased competence in nuanced, interdisciplinary research and analysis. I have never received so many office hour visits as I did at UCLA during the weeks when students were preparing their unboxing research essays. Students seemed deeply invested in their projects—perhaps because it was an opportunity to bridge two of the most powerful forms of authority in their lives: science and social media. In the words of one New School food studies major, "I still need that craving of sensory input to be fed via the endless late night scrolls. Don't get me wrong. I think that it is great that we have access to all of this material, but . . . it's important to question the motives behind the posts, and to dig a little bit further than a quick look and double tap. Some may continue to eat with their eyes first, but I am content to leave that task to my mouth."

Notes

I am grateful to Giselle Greenbaum, Ella MacDonald, and three other students (who have remained anonymous) for their permission to share their intellectual products. My deep thanks also go to Emily Contois, Zenia Kish, and two anonymous reviewers for their helpful suggestions on improving this chapter.

1. Daniel Bender, Rachel Ankeny, Warren Belasco, Amy Bentley, Elias Mandala, Jeffrey M. Pilcher, and Peter Scholliers, "Eating in Class: Gastronomy, Taste, Nutrition, and Teaching Food History," *Radical History Review* 110 (2011): 198.

2. Lorraine Daston and Peter Galison, "The Image of Objectivity," *Representations* 40 (1992): 81–128; Constance Classen, *The Color of Angels: Cosmology, Gender, and the Aesthetic Imagination* (New York: Routledge, 1998); David Howes, "How Capitalism Came to Its Senses—and Yours: The Invention of Sensory Marketing," Center for Sensory Studies, June 29, 2017, http://centreforsensorystudies.org/how-capitalism-came-to-its-senses-and-yours-the-invention-of-sensory-marketing/.

3. Kyla Wazana Tompkins, *Racial Indigestion: Eating Bodies in the 19th Century* (New York: New York University Press, 2013), 3.

4. Natasha Dow Schüll, *Addiction by Design: Machine Gambling in Las Vegas* (Princeton, NJ: Princeton University Press, 2012); Hilary Andersson, "Social Media Apps Are 'Deliberately' Addictive to Users," BBC News, Technology, July 4, 2018, www.bbc.com/news/technology-44640959.

5. Marshall McLuhan, "Inside the Five Sense Sensorium," in *Empire of the Senses: The Sensual Culture Reader*, ed. David Howes, 43–54 (Oxford: Berg, 2004); Esther Rothblum and Sondra Solovay, eds., *The Fat Studies Reader* (New York: New York University Press, 2009).

6. This critical stance may remind readers of intuitive eating, an anti-diet lifestyle approach based on eschewing shame-based calorie counting and instead honoring the body's internal cues. Intuitive eating is itself a branded lifestyle concept that would make an interesting focal point for pedagogical discussions on capitalism's ability to incorporate its own critiques. Intuitive Eating, www.intuitiveeating.org/10-principles-of-intuitive-eating/.

7. Merielle Silcoff, "A Mother's Journey through the Unnerving Universe of 'Unboxing' Videos," *New York Times*, August 17, 2014, www.nytimes.com.

8. E. Steel, "At New Video Sites, Opening up the Box Is a Ritual to Savor," *Wall Street Journal*, December 7, 2006, www.wsj.com; David Craig and Stuart Cunningham, "Toy Unboxing: Living in a(n Unregulated) Material World," *Media International Australia*, no. 163 (2017): 77–86.

9. Bruno Latour, *Pandora's Hope: Essays on the Reality of Science Studies* (Cambridge, MA: Harvard University Press, 1999), 304. See also Bruno Latour, *Science in Action: How to Follow Scientists and Engineers through Society* (Cambridge, MA: Harvard University Press, 1987), and Heather Paxson, "Rethinking Food and Its Eaters: Opening the Black Boxes of Safety and Nutrition," in *The Handbook of Food and Anthropology*, ed. Jakob A. Klein and James I. Watson, 268–88 (London: Bloomsbury, 2016).

10. Rawnice (@rawnice), "'Remember to look up at the stars and not down at your feet. Try to make sense of what you see and wonder about what makes the Universe exist.'—Stephen Hawking. Stunning and inspiring galaxy bowl from my girl, Laura @laurastencel 🌌 Pigments from our all-natural powders 💜💜💜 #activatedcharcoal #galaxysmoothie #breakfast #foodstyling #bbg #dairyfree #fitfood #cleaneating #foodlover #healthyfood #blueberries #wholefoods #feedfeed #foodie #thrivemags #foodpics #foodphotography #healthyeating #vegansofig #eeeeeats #foodporn #glutenfree #zdrowo #smoothie #bestofvegan #śniadanie #vegan #ewachodakowska #dessert #smoothiebar." Instagram photo, September 17, 2019, www.instagram.com/p/B2g-IIaHmOA/.

11. Ai Hisano, "The Rise of Synthetic Colors in the American Food Industry, 1870–1940," *Business History Review*, no. 90 (2016): 483–504; Daniel Paul O'Donnell, "The Unessay," University of Lethbridge, September 4, 2012, http://people.uleth.ca/~daniel.odonnell/Teaching/the-unessay; Hayley Brazier and Heidi Kaufman, "Defining the 'Unessay,'" Digital Humanities at the University of Oregon, April 2, 2018, https://dh.uoregon.edu/2018/04/02/defining-the-unessay/; Emily Contois, "Teaching the Unruly Unessay," May 10, 2019, https://emilycontois.com/2019/05/10/unessays/.

12. Hannah Landecker, "A Metabolic History of Manufacturing Waste," *Food, Culture, and Society* 22 (2019): 530–47. See also Charlotte Biltekoff, "Critical Nutrition Studies," in *The Oxford Handbook of Food History*, ed. Jeffrey M. Pilcher, 172–90 (New York: Oxford University Press, 2012).

13. Jeannine Delwiche, "You Eat with Your Eyes First," *Physiology and Behavior* 107 (2012): 502–4; J. R. Georgiadis and M. L. Kringelbach, "The Human Sexual Response Cycle: Brain Imaging Evidence Linking Sex to Other Pleasures," *Progress in Neurobiology* 98 (2012): 49–81; Allison Kugel, "How 'Food Porn' Posted on Social Media Has Become an Industry," *Entrepreneur*, June 1, 2017, www.entrepreneur.com/article/295126; Lev Manovitch, "Designing and Living Instagram Photography: Themes, Feeds, Sequences, Branding, Faces, Bodies," November 2016, http://manovich.net/index.php/projects/designing-and-living-instagram-photography; Anne McBride, "Food Porn," *Gastronomica* 10 (2010): 38–46; Charles Spence, Katsunori

Okajima, Adrian David Cheok, Olivia Petit, and Charles Michel, "Eating with Our Eyes: From Visual Hunger to Digital Satiation," *Brain and Cognition* 11 (2016): 53–63; Charles Spence, "From Instagram to TV Ads: What's the Science Behind Food Porn?," Guardian, March 19, 2019, www.theguardian.com.

14. Josh Beckerman (@foodiemagician), "Dim Sum To Go. @hutongnyc #foodiemagician #nyc," Instagram photo, January 31, 2021, www.instagram.com/p/CKuo DwklQVI/; Josh Beckerman (@foodiemagician), "Incredible Donuts in Portland, Maine. @holydonutmaine—Maine Blueberry/Dark Chocolate Sea Salt. Outstanding. I woke up like this. #foodiemagician #foodiemagicianeatsportlandmaine #stilleating #stillsingle," Instagram photo, August 20, 2019, www.instagram.com/p/ B1Y8L-Sl196/; Josh Beckerman (@foodiemagician), "A Taste Of Maine, In Maine. @biteintomaine—Lobster Roll Perfection! Wow. #foodiemagician #foodiemagicianeatsportlandmaine," Instagram photo, August 20, 2019, www.instagram.com/p/ B1ZFNr5lI0M/.

15. Lizzy Saxe, "How Are Food Influencers Changing the Restaurant World?," Forbes, December 7, 2018, www.forces.com.

16. Ella MacDonald, "#Eatclean," December 2019, https://macde105.wixsite.com/ eatclean.

Food Instagram's
Next Course

EMILY J. H. CONTOIS
AND ZENIA KISH

Instagram's rapid growth and cultural influence have outpaced sustained scholarly inquiry into its significance. The goal of this book is to contribute to the emerging study of Instagram through the prominence of food across the platform's photographic social worlds. We seek to foster new conversations at the intersection of food and digital media, acknowledging that there remains much more to see, critique, and connect. As Sarah Tracy discusses in chapter 17, additional interdisciplinary perspectives from science and technology studies and sensory studies, among others, could also open up new ways to analyze food Instagram. We propose a number of pressing areas for further exploration, although this brief catalog is intended to be suggestive rather than exhaustive.

While this book aims for global reach and includes case studies from twelve countries (United States, Canada, United Kingdom, France, Italy, Denmark, Australia, Hong Kong, Thailand, Japan, Israel, and Brazil), we note the unfortunate absence of submissions addressing Instagram and food in Africa, most of Latin America, mainland China, and India, among other significant regions. Our attempt to map out the interrelated elements of food Instagram's value chain indicates the importance of transnational linkages in the production and distribution of food and digital media. Our work also suggests that media scholarship at this intersection could further explore comparative and connected Instagram geographies, particularly the relationship between local, national, and global identities. This volume lays such groundwork. Yue-Chiu Bonni Leung and Yi-Chieh Jessica Lin (chapter 8) explore Hong Kong food culture within a global foodscape guided by "foodie" aesthetics, while Michael Newman (chapter 1) considers how images of hummus, a food with both local and global resonance, attempt to construct a desirable national brand. Deborah

Harris and Rachel Phillips (chapter 4) analyze how Instagram photos of biscuits seek to represent the New South, an identity and a space that changes with the transcultural flows of people and traditions that immigrate to the U.S. South and collide with its histories.

Such analysis opens larger questions about space, place-making, and identity practices on Instagram. There is much to explore concerning the platform's coproduction of food and place: from qualitative analysis of regional food Instagram content, to ethnographic study of place-based production and consumption of digital food, to quantitative investigation of geographical differences and convergences in culinary representation. Future research could ask: How does the at-times soil-bound concept of terroir circulate on the platform to create cultural capital, economic currency, and marketing opportunities in digital environments? How is food imagery taken up in spatially mediated projects of community formation, nation building, travel, and gentrification? How have the quarantine conditions of the COVID-19 global pandemic altered our relationship with home cooking, virtual food tourism, and cultural traditions involving cooking and eating in shared spaces?

Such analysis also calls on scholars to further embed the study of food Instagram in critical approaches to race and racial capitalism, postcolonial critiques, and unequal global digital infrastructures. What would a decolonial approach to food Instagram look like? Is such a question even legible against the backdrop of Instagram and Facebook's model of monetizing user data, recurrent privacy scandals, and widespread surveillance, bots, and fake accounts?

As various campaigns to #quitFacebook have demonstrated in recent years, social media platforms face widespread skepticism, especially on issues of privacy and surveillance, and yet they continue to rapidly grow their user base despite scandal after scandal.[1] Instagram has shown greater immunity to public criticism than its parent company. In addition to analyzing influencers and other content creators, further study of everyday food Instagram users would illuminate how consumers themselves navigate these controversies and exercise agency when they engage with, and make meaning on, social media.

This book presents numerous methodologies for analyzing food Instagram, from expansive data sets to small intentional samples, from discourse analysis to feminist digital ethnography to historical assessments of change and continuity over time. We see opportunities for exciting mixed methods approaches, particularly for considering the interplay between words and images, individual expression and community building, personal branding and commerce on Instagram. The contributors to this book closely consider Instagram grid images, caption text, and hashtags, but future studies could explore food within Instagram's shopping feature or analyze profile descriptions, perhaps adapting Carrie Helms Tippen's approach to cookbook recipe headnotes to more deeply understand how account owners wish to be seen.[2] Katherine Kirkwood (chapter 11) analyzes one content creator's use of IGTV, and we see rich potential for deeper exploration of this mobile food TV format, and of Reels content, particularly when situated within the historical lineage of food programming on broadcast television, streaming services, and YouTube.

That said, Instagram research can be challenging. Jill Walker Rettberg notes that "Snapchat is a conversation, not an archive"—offering communication possibilities for users, but also seeding a number of issues for social media researchers.[3] Studying digital content necessarily begins from a state of overwhelm given the vast array of available material.[4] In chapter 16, Alex Ketchum draws some of her evidence from Instagram Stories, which poses methodological difficulty because this ephemeral content is only available for twenty-four hours. Researchers must *create* an archive of Instagram Stories via screenshots in order to study it. Just as Ketchum and KC Hysmith (chapter 12) both discuss, generating and monitoring Instagram content necessitates significant, constant, and often invisible and feminized labor.

Even within the somewhat more static Instagram grid, we must address what the food Instagram archive contains and what it does not, what it can tell us and where it is silent. In our conversations with students about how they use the platform, they openly discuss how they regularly delete images, whether ones that feature failed romances they'd rather forget or posts that simply didn't get enough likes. In such ways, the Instagram archive is always unstable. Furthermore, despite Instagram's affordances, which provide all users the means to capture and share everyday moments, much of food Instagram in the 2010s remained tied to the aspirational and exclusionary dynamics of food porn. Culinary historian Laura Shapiro calls for Instagrammers to capture the ordinary, the messes, failures, and leftovers, in part because food Instagram photos "don't speak up. Or rather, they all say the same thing—'Look at this amazing food!'"[5] As chapters 13 and 14 reveal, anti-food-porn trends on Instagram offer new research possibilities, even as these images remain curated and mediated.

Finally, the political economy of food Instagram invites deeper engagement. Siva Vaidyanathan argues that scholarly debates about social media's political economy have produced a still-incomplete framework for understanding how these platforms organize production and create value. Our inherited analytic tools in media studies and cultural studies lag behind the sector's dynamic intersections of digital labor, industry concentration, monetization of attention and data, online influencers and advertising, and other key elements of platform capitalism.[6] It is important for media studies to adapt our thinking to these fast-changing conditions, particularly to remain relevant in public and regulatory discussions about the pleasures and dangers of platforms like Instagram. Similarly, our food system is experiencing an unprecedented rate of change with the introduction of new technologies from lab-grown meat and robotic farmworkers to microbiome reengineering and vertical farms. Indeed, digital technologies are becoming increasingly integrated into all stages of food production, indicating that media and food supply chains are converging in surprising ways. Our understanding of these technological and economic revolutions increases to the extent that scholars in food and media studies build stronger interdisciplinary conversations together.

When we first proposed the idea of a book about food and Instagram, someone questioned whether the focus on this single platform would be too narrow. After completing this book, we can confidently attest that by exploring the significance of Instagram through its food-related content, producers, and audiences, we have opened a rich yet nascent dialogue between scholars who have much to learn from each other. May the questions and insights shared in these pages go on to nourish future inquiry and feed our more-than-digital imagination—and appetites.

Notes

1. Brooke Erin Duffy and Ngai Keung Chan, "'You Never Really Know Who's Looking': Imagined Surveillance across Social Media Platforms," *New Media and Society* 21, no. 1 (2019): 119–38.

2. Carrie Helms Tippen, *Inventing Authenticity: How Cookbook Writers Redefine Southern Identity* (Fayetteville: University of Arkansas Press, 2018).

3. Jill Walker Rettberg, "Snapchat: Phatic Communication and Ephemeral Social Media," in *Appified: Culture in the Age of Apps,* ed. Jeremy Wade Morris and Sarah Murray, 188–96 (Ann Arbor: University of Michigan Press, 2018).

4. Kathleen Franz and Susan Smulyan, "New Media, New Networks, New Content, New Methodologies: Popular Culture's Past Illuminates Its Future," in *Major Problems in American Popular Culture,* 441–42 (Boston: Wadsworth, Cengage Learning, 2012).

5. Laura Shapiro, "Instagram Your Leftovers: History Depends on It," *New York Times,* September 2, 2017, www.nytimes.com/2017/09/02/opinion/sunday/instagram -your-leftovers-history-depends-on-it.html.

6. Siva Vaidyanathan, "The Incomplete Political Economy of Social Media," in *The Sage Handbook of Social Media,* ed. Jean Burgess, Alice Marwick, and Thomas Poell (New York: Sage, 2017), 213–30; Nick Srnicek, *Platform Capitalism* (Malden, MA: Polity, 2017).

Contributors

EMILY J. H. CONTOIS is Assistant Professor of Media Studies at the University of Tulsa. She holds a PhD in American studies from Brown University. In addition to numerous articles, she is the author of *Diners, Dudes, and Diets: How Gender and Power Collide in Food Media and Culture* (2020). She serves on the board of the Association for the Study of Food and Society and is book review editor for *Food, Culture, and Society*. As a public scholar, she has written for *NBC News*, *Jezebel*, and *Nursing Clio* and has appeared on *CBS This Morning*, *BBC Ideas*, and *Ugly Delicious* on Netflix. Learn more about her work at emilycontois.com or connect on social media (@emilycontois).

ZENIA KISH is Assistant Professor of Media Studies at the University of Tulsa. She earned her PhD in American studies at New York University and was a postdoctoral fellow at Stanford University. Her work explores global digital media, sociotechnical imaginaries of food and agriculture, and philanthrocapitalism and has been published in journals including *American Quarterly*, *Cultural Studies*, and *Environment and Planning A*. She is a member of the Agri-Food Technology Research (AFTeR) Project and is the reviews and commentaries editor for the *Journal of Cultural Economy*, as well as serving on the board of the *Journal of Environmental Media*. She is writing a book on philanthropic media cultures.

LAURENCE ALLARD is Assistant Professor at the Université Lille and a Researcher at the Institut de Recherche sur le Cinéma et l'Audiovisuel (IRCAV), Université Sorbonne Nouvelle. She specializes in mobile communication technologies and expressive culture, social media, influencers, and critical approaches to data. She cofounded and codirects the research group Mobile Création. In addition to numerous articles, she coedited *Téléphone mobile et création* (2012; Mobile phone and creation) and *Mobiles, enjeux artistiques et esthétiques* (2018; Mobiles: Artistic and aesthetic issues), both with Laurent Creton and Roger Odin, and authored *Mythologie du portable* (2010; Mythology of the cell phone).

JOCELINE ANDERSEN is Assistant Teaching Professor of Journalism, Communication, and New Media Studies and of English and Modern Languages at Thompson Rivers University in British Columbia. She holds a PhD in communication studies from McGill University. Her research focuses on audience reception, educational film, and Internet viewing. She is the author of *Stars and Silhouettes: The History of the Cameo Role in Hollywood* (2020).

EMILY BUDDLE is Visiting Research Fellow at the University of Adelaide. Her PhD explores Australian consumer understandings of farm animal welfare. Her research interests include how media representations are helping to shape public understanding of agriculture, and how the growth of social media is changing how people access information about food and food production.

ROBIN CALDWELL is an Independent Researcher and Public Historian who has transitioned from a career as a public relations and marketing specialist in the food, hospitality, and beverage space, to writing and fact-checking on the primary topic of Black culinary history. A native Midwesterner with Gullah and Geechee, Appalachian, and Creole roots, she endeavors to degeneralize racial mythologies and to humanize enslaved Africans and their descendants by writing about their everyday experiences. Visit robincaldwell.com and @ robinmcaldwell on social media to learn more about Robin's interests and recent projects.

SARAH CRAMER is an Assistant Professor in Sustainable Food Systems at Stetson University, where she teaches introductory food studies courses and an upper-level course on race, class, and gender in the food system. She holds a PhD in agricultural education and a master of public health degree, both from the University of Missouri. Her research agenda includes garden-based learning, critical food systems pedagogy, gender and agriculture, and food communication.

GABY DAVID is a Lecturer and an Affiliated Member at Transferts Critiques anglophones (TransCrit) at the Université Paris 8. She is also a Research Fellow at the Institut de Recherche sur le Cinéma et l'Audiovisuel (IRCAV), Université Sorbonne Nouvelle, where she is an active member of the research group Mobile Création. She holds a PhD from the École des Hautes Etudes en Sciences Sociales (EHESS) in Paris and a master in fine arts from the Université Paris 8, Saint-Denis. She serves on the board of the International Visual Sociology Association. She has published articles in journals including *Social Media+Society*,

Ubiquity, and *Visual Studies*. She coedited a special issue of *First Monday* titled *Shame, Shaming, and Online Image Sharing* (2021) with Amparo Lasén, and is coediting *#Foodporn: Les mobiles du désir* (2021) with Laurence Allard. Her work explores social media, visual culture, and serious games.

SARA GARCIA SANTAMARIA is a Lecturer at Universitat Jaume I and Universitat Ramon Llull in Spain, where she teaches courses in journalism studies, political communication, and intercultural communication. She holds a PhD from the University of Sheffield. Her research, teaching, and publications address populist performances on social media, with special attention to the creation of caring ecologies, as well as journalism in restricted contexts. Some of her latest articles include "The Italian 'Taste': The Far-Right and the Performance of Exclusionary Populism during the 2019 European Elections" and "Politicians 'Stay Home': Left-Wing Populism and Performances of the Intimate Self on Social Media during the COVID-19 Pandemic."

DEBORAH HARRIS is Professor of Sociology at Texas State University. Her research focuses on inequalities within various sectors of the food system. She is coauthor with Patti Giuffre of *Taking the Heat: Women Chefs and Inequality in the Professional Kitchen* (2015). Her work has been published in a number of journals, including *Gender Issues, Symbolic Interaction*, and *Humanity & Society*. She also serves on the advisory board for gender initiatives for the James Beard Foundation.

KC HYSMITH is a PhD Candidate in American Studies at the University of North Carolina at Chapel Hill. Her academic research looks at the intersections of food history, gender, technology, and social media. She also has a professional background in food writing, food photography, and recipe testing. See more of her academic work at kchysmith.com and her professional work on her Instagram feed (@kchysmith).

ALEX KETCHUM is the Faculty Lecturer of the Institute for Gender, Sexuality, and Feminist Studies of McGill University, where she earned a PhD in History. Her work integrates food, environmental, and gender history. She organizes the Feminist and Accessible Publishing, Communications, and Technologies Speaker and Workshop Series, and cofounded both the Historical Cooking Project and Food, Feminism, and Fermentation. To learn more about her work, visit alexketchum.ca.

KATHERINE KIRKWOOD holds a PhD in Media and Communication from Queensland University of Technology. Among other publications, she is coeditor with Michelle Phillipov of *Alternative Food Politics: From the Margins to the Mainstream* (2019). Her research investigates popular culture's relationship with everyday Australian food culture and how media and cultural texts inform and shape Australians' approach to food, their culinary interests, and their concerns.

JONATAN LEER holds a PhD in food culture and is Head of Food and Tourism Studies at Professionshøjskolen Absalon (University College Absalon), Roskilde, Denmark. He has published widely on food culture, notably on the New Nordic cuisine, food mediations, and the gendering of food practices. He coedited *Research Methods in Digital Food Studies* (2021) with Stinne Gunder Strøm Krogager and *Food and Media: Practices, Distinctions and Heterotopias* (2016) with Karen Klitgaard Povlsen.

YUE-CHIU BONNI LEUNG received a Master's degree from the International Master's Program in International Communication Studies from National Chengchi University in Taipei, Taiwan. She was born in Hong Kong, where she now works in marketing and communications.

YI-CHIEH JESSICA LIN is Associate Professor of the Department of Journalism at National Chengchi University in Taipei, Taiwan. She holds a PhD in anthropology from Harvard University. She has published a number of articles exploring food, sustainability, and culture in *Food, Culture, and Society, Journal of Rural Studies, Taiwan Journal of Anthropology, Communication Research and Practices,* and in edited volumes.

MICHAEL Z. NEWMAN is Professor in the Department of English at the University of Wisconsin–Milwaukee, and in the programs in Film Studies and Media, Cinema, and Digital Studies. His publications include *Video Revolutions: On the History of a Medium* (2014) and *Atari Age: The Emergence of Video Games in America* (2017). He has also written on food and media in "Everyday Italian: Cultivating Taste," in *How to Watch Television* (edited by Ethan Thompson and Jason Mittell, 2020).

TSUGUMI (MIMI) OKABE is a Lecturer at the University of Alberta, where she earned a PhD in Comparative Literature. Her research examines discourses of identity, nation, and youth culture in Japanese detective manga in the 1990s. She also conducts research on women's participation in the Japanese video game industry. For more information, visit her website (mimiokabe.com) and Instagram feed (@mimirellaz).

RACHEL PHILLIPS is pursuing a Master's degree in Sociology at Texas State University. Her research involves issues of crime and deviance, recently focusing on public reactions to instances of mass violence. Her most recent work examines social movement activity on Twitter through an analysis of the March for Our Lives movement online, which focuses on collective behavior, the public sphere of rational-critical debate, and political process theory.

TARA J. SCHUWERK is Associate Professor and Chair of Communication and Media Studies and the Program Director for Sustainable Food Systems at Stetson University. She earned her interdisciplinary PhD in communication from the Hugh Downs School of Human Communication at Arizona State University. Her research explores food within intersections of communication, health, culture, and identity, as well as the scholarship of teaching and learning.

STINNE GUNDER STRØM KROGAGER is Associate Professor in the Department of Communication and Psychology at Aalborg University. She has published on children, food, gender, and methodologies in a number of publications, including *Critical Food Studies, Trends in Food Science and Technology*, and *Nordicom Review*. She is also editor in chief at the Nordic journal *MedieKultur: Journal of Media and Communication Research*. With Jonatan Leer, she coedited *Research Methods in Digital Food Studies* (2021).

SARAH E. TRACY holds a PhD in the History of Science and Technology from the University of Toronto. Her work brings feminist science and technology studies and critical race approaches to the study of food and flavor, and has been published in *Food, Culture, and Society, the Senses and Society*, and *Global Food History*. Her first book, *Delicious: A History of Monosodium Glutamate and Umami, the Fifth Taste Sensation*, is forthcoming.

EMILY TRUMAN is a Postdoctoral Fellow in the Department of Communication, Media and Film at the University of Calgary. Her research examines food literacy theorization and implementation, as well as visual cultures of food, nutrition, and health, with a particular interest in cultural icons and symbols. Her research has appeared in *Appetite, British Food Journal*, and the *Canadian Journal of Communication*.

DAWN WOOLLEY is a Visual Artist and Research Fellow at Leeds Arts University. She completed her PhD by practice in fine art at the Royal College of Art (2017). Her solo exhibitions include "Consumed: Stilled Lives," Blyth Gallery, London (2018), Ffotogallery, Cardiff (2018), Ruskin Gallery, Cambridge (2017), and Dyson Gallery, London (2016); "Visual Pleasure," Hippolyte Photography Gallery, Helsinki, Finland (2013), and Vilniaus Fotografijos Galerija, Lithuania (2012). Learn more at dawnwoolley.com.

ZARA WORTH is an Artist and Doctoral Researcher at Leeds Beckett University. Recent exhibitions include "Fields of Perception," THE CUBE, London (2018); "Zara Worth: FEED," Vane, Newcastle upon Tyne (2018); "Instagram Expo," Atelier, Montreal; "AVBody," Judaica Project at the University of Huddersfield (2018); "Four Words," Platform, Leeds (2017). Worth was an Engagement Artist for the 2019 "Yorkshire Sculpture International" festival of sculpture. Learn more at zaraworth.com.

Index

Page numbers in *italics* refer to figures

amateurs. *See* professional v. amateur

Amhadi, Layla, 270

Andersen, Joceline, 11, 14, 17

animal rights and welfare, 154, 163–66, 169–70, 207, 252–53

anti-food porn, 8–9, 285

anti-selfies, 14, 16, 124, 199

Appadurai, Arjun, 33

Arcari, Paula, 169, 171

Ariel, Ari, 39

Arriagada, Arturo, 135

art, 66, 101, 103–4, 111

art practices, 67, 101–11

Ashman, Rachel, 135

attention economy, 10, 15, 19, 125

Aussie Farms, 165

Australia, 164–65, 166, 170, 172, 175n46, 181, 283. *See also* Grasby, Marion; *MasterChef Australia*

Australian farmers, 13, 163–73

authenticity: agriculture, 243, 254; biscuits/biscuit restaurants, 81–82, 84, 85, 86–90; Bolsonaro, Jair, 232, 234–36, 237; brands, 246, 251, 270; comfort foods, 222; consumers, 82; feminist food enterprises, 260–61, 269–70; food blogs, 246, 248; food images, 82; food Instagram, 8, 13, 14, 82, 269–70; food production, 82; gender, 152; hashtags, 82; hummus, 37; influencers, 133, 135–36, 138–40, 144, 145, 152, 180, 192–93, 195; Instagram, 270; populism, 223–24, 237; Salvini, Matteo, 226, 227–29, 237; scholarship, 82; social class, 83; social media, 16, 246; the South, 81, 84–86, 90; unicorn latte, 126

auto-photography, 138

Banet-Weiser, Sarah, 199, 244

Barham, Elizabeth, 42

Barthes, Roland, 7

Baumann, Shyon, 74–75

Baym, Nancy, 243, 249

beauty, 48–54, 60, 244, 245–46, 252, 275, 278

Beckerman, Josh, 278, *279*

Bender, Daniel, 274

Benjamin, Walter, 5, 105

Berger, John, 70–71

Bialik, Mayim, 40

bicycle couriers, 68, 76–77

biscuit restaurants, 18, 81, 83–90

biscuits, 18, 81–91, 283–84

#blackgirlcooking, 6, 95, 96–97

Black Girl Cooking, 95–96

Black women, 6, 10, 85–86, 87, 94–100

Bloodroot (restaurant), 263, 264, 265, 267, 269

Blumenthal, Heston, 177–78, 187

bodies, 124, 211–13. *See also* anti-selfies; selfies

body image, 47–48, 50, 61n11, 275

Bolsonaro, Jair, 221, 222–23, 224, 230–37

Bordo, Susan, 58–60

Borondo, Javier, 75

Bouazzani, Nora, 71–72

Bourdieu, Pierre, 74–75, 221, 247

Brand Israel, 17–18, 35–36, 40, 44

brands: agriculture, 243–48, 251, 253–54; authenticity, 246, 251, 270; biscuit restaurants, 84; celebrities, 14–15, 16–17; consumers, 244; digital food cultures, 124–25; emojis, 69; farmers, 244–48; food blogs, 10; food Instagram, 242; #foodporn, 69; FTC, 19–20; gender, 104, 105–6; hashtags, 12; Hot Dudes and Hummus, 44; hummus, 283; influencers, 2, 12, 20, 134, 135–36, 139, 141, 179–80, 194–95; Instagram, 5–6, 11, 244, 249, 253, 255, 270; restaurants, 205, 210; Sakarya, Umut, 206, 209–10, 218; social media, 124–25, 243, 244, 246; social photography, 124, 125; transgression, 206; unicorn foods, 116–17; users, 126, 244; visuality, 120; women, 199. *See also* self-branding; *and individual brands*

Brazil, 8, 17, 221–23, 230–37, 283. *See also* Bolsonaro, Jair

Brimm, Brooke, 95–96, 98

Bruckner, Heide, 169

Bucher, Taina, 185

Buddle, Emily, 13, 14, 17

Buerkle, Wesley, 152

Buy My Bananas (Niochlin) (photograph), 66

Caldwell, Robin, 6, 10

Cambre, Carolina, 68, 79n12

Cattelan, Maurizio, 66

Cauberghe, Veroline, 148

celebrities: advertisements, 14–15; brands, 14–15, 16–17; the demotic turn, 16–17; food, 17; food images, 15; food Instagram, 9, 14–15, 19; Hot Dudes and Hummus, 34, 40; influencers, 192–93, 194, 200n10; politicization, 17

celebrity chefs, 71, 135, 177–78, 184, 194. *See also individual chefs*

Celery Drawing (Worth), 106–9, 111

Chan, Kelly, 132, 133

Chan, Ngai, 249–50

Chan, Selena, 133

Chang, David, 177–78

chefs, 1–2, 71, 132–33, 242–43. *See also* celebrity chefs
Child, Julia, 186, 187
Choisi, Mark, 270
Cinderella trope, 48–49, 52
Classen, Constance, 277–78
clean eating: *Celery Drawing* (Worth), 106–9; consumers, 105; diet culture, 108; food Instagram, 11, 108; food trends, 120–21, 276, 278; FreakShakes, 182–83; hashtags, 106–8; *[Im]moral Food* (Wooley and Worth), 102–4; influencers, 108, 155; users, 108; visuality, 276–77
#cleaneating, 102–3, 104, 149, 278
Cockburn, Alexander, 67
Coffee Klatch (Schoenwetter) (newsletter), 263
Colombino, Annalisa, 169
Comedian (Cattelan) (art), 66
comfort foods, 222, 223–25, 227, 231
commodification: biscuits, 86; food, 5–6, 133; food Instagram, 15, 76; #foodporn, 69; influencers, 76; meal gaze, 7; photography, 5; *Wishbook* (Woolley), 105–6
communities, 20, 138–45
consumers: advertisements, 105–6; agriculture/organic farmers, 242–43, 245, 247, 255; animal rights and welfare, 169; authenticity, 82; brands, 244; chefs, 242; clean eating, 105; feminism, 261; food Instagram, 2, 7–8, 17, 101–2, 178, 180–81, 268, 284; food markets, 124–25; food production, 82, 163–68, 242–43; food systems, 18; happy meat, 163–66, 168–73; hashtags, 243; influencers, 135–36, 138, 139, 180; localism, 245; negotiations, 21; scholarship, 138, 167; social media, 101–2, 111; Starbucks/unicorn latte, 125; sustainability, 245, 255; unicorns, 122–23; *Wishbook* (Woolley), 104, 105
consumption: feminist food enterprises, 264; food images, 126; food Instagram, 74, 275; food systems, 18–20; health, 277; identities, 135; influencers, 135; media, 278; unicorn foods, 115–16; visuality, 275, 277–80; waste, 20. *See also* prosumption
"Cooking Out" (Morrison), 97–98
CoopCycle/Cooperatives movement, 68, 77
Copenhagen, 8, 206–9, 211, 215, 217–18
Corrigan, Thomas, 136
Costa, Elisabetta, 242, 249, 254
COVID-19 pandemic, 10, 14, 77, 94–100, 284
Coward, Rosalind, 67, 70–71, 72
Cramer, Sarah E., 12, 17, 18
Crawford, Sarah, 197

credentials, 108, 149, 151, 157–59, 162n33
Crossley, Alison Dahl, 262
Cruz, Ariane, 8
culinary appropriation, 6, 83, 85–86, 103–4, 153, 275
cultural politics. *See* politicization
cultural tastes, 115, 126

Danish food, 206, 208, 211
darkgram, 241–44, 245, 247, 248–55
Darroze, Hélène, 71
data, 15, 16, 19, 26n59, 137
David, Gaby, 7, 9, 14
de Cleen, Benjamin, 223
Dejmanee, Tisha, 135, 144, 152
Denmark, 17, 170, 207–9, 215, 217, 283. *See also* Copenhagen
de Solier, Isabelle, 2, 180
De Veirman, Marijke, 148
Dia, Rougui, 71
dietary trends, 275. *See also* food trends
diet brands, 16. *See also* Jewel (Japan)
diet culture, 47–60, 148–59; advertisements, 106; clean eating, 108; femininities, 48, 49; food freedoms v., 161n25; identities/Japan, 47–60; influencers, 149, 150, 151, 154–59; influences, 148–59; nutrition, 49
digital food cultures: art practices, 102–3, 111; brands, 124–25; food images, 1, 65–66, 180; food Instagram, 3–4, 111, 178, 205; food markets, 124–25; Hong Kong, 132–33; politicization, 221–22; unicorn latte, 115
Digital Food: From Paddock to Platform (Lewis), 2
digital food images. *See* food images
dirty eating, 102–4, 105, 120–21
disordered eating: clean eating, 108; health, 148–49; influencers, 157–58, 159, 278; Japan, 47, 48–49, 61n11
distribution, 18–20
Drawing Made by Cutting Up My Body Weight in Celery, A. See Celery Drawing (Worth)
Duffy, Brooke Erin, 196, 249–50

Eastman, George, 5
#eatdirty, 102–3, 104
eating literacy, 274–80
economics: aesthetics, 84; bicycle couriers/Cooperatives Movement, 76, 77; biscuit restaurants, 88, 90; food Instagram, 3, 6, 284, 285–86; food labor/food systems, 76–77; #foodporn, 77; gender, 196–99, 215; influencers, 145, 199, 285; scholarship, 134;

unicorn latte, 117–18, 121, 124–25; users, 126; visuality, 275

food media, 178–79, 184–87

food politics. *See* politicization

food porn, 7–9; aesthetics, 8, 9, 135, 224; anti-food porn, 8–9, 285; art, 66; biscuit restaurants, 86; Cambre, Carolina, 79n12; elitism, 7–8; feminism, 135; fetishization, 7, 68; food blogs, 8, 67, 144; food consumption, 9; food industries, 179; food Instagram, 4, 7–9, 67, 178–84, 285; food/labor, 8, 9; food production, 9; food replicas, 75–76; food systems, 9; France, 65, 68–70, 77–78; FreakShakes as, 182; gender, 8; Grasby, Noi, 185; hashtags, 65, 67–70; Hong Kong, 132–33; Hot Dudes and Hummus, 7, 40–41, 44; identities/power, 9; *[Im]moral Food* (Wooley and Worth), 103; influencers, 67, 148; Instagram, 5–6; Instagrammability, 8, 9; male gaze, 70–71; meal gaze, 7, 74; neurobiology of, 275; photography, 134, 144; populism, 236–37; scholarship, 9, 68–70; sexualities, 67; social class, 7–8, 74–75; social media, 120; sustainability, 182–84; as term, 7–9, 67–68, 179, 182, 223–24; transgression, 213; visuality, 79n12, 120; waste, 182–84

#foodporn, 65, 66, 67–70, 74–75, 77, 243

"#Foodporn: The Mobiles of Desire" (colloquium), 65, 68

food production, 16–18; advertisements, 76–77; agriculture, 242–43, 255; animal rights and welfare, 170; authenticity, 82; chefs, 243; consumers, 82, 163–68, 242–43; farmers, 244; feminist food enterprises, 264; food images, 167–73, 242; food Instagram, 16, 167, 242–43; food justice, 242; food porn/#foodporn, 9, 243; food systems, 16–18; gender, 72; geographies, 284; globalization, 243; happy meat, 163–73; heritage breeds, 169; influencers, 142–43, 154; localism, 246; photography, 142–43; scholarship, 167, 286; social media, 173, 242–43, 246

food puritanism, 222, 224, 234, 236, 237

food replicas, 75–76

food studies: eating literacy, 275; feminist food enterprises, 261; food cultures, 277–80; food systems, 13; media studies, 3–4, 13, 17; scholarship, 286; social media, 17

food styling, 205

food systems, 13–22; agriculture, 17, 285–86; consumption and distribution, 18–20; economics, 76–77; food images, 18; food

Instagram, 13–22, 242–43; food markets, 18; food porn, 9; food production, 16–18; food studies, 13; happy meat, 165; influencers, 149, 154; media studies, 242; raw inputs, 13–15; waste, 20–21

food tourism, 88, 90, 135, 284

food trends, 115–21; clean eating, 120–21, 276, 278; cultural tastes, 126; food Instagram/ influencers, 120–21; FreakShakes, 181–82; identities, 276; social media, 120–21, 280; "Unbox a Food Trend" (course assignment), 275–77, 280; unicorn foods, 115–19, 123, 125–26

food workers, 9, 13–14, 76–77. *See also* labor

Ford, Sam, 243

France, 65–78; bicycle couriers, 76–77; feminism, 70–73; food images, 69; food industries, 66; food Instagram, 65, 69, 77–78, 283; food porn, 65, 68–70, 77–78; #foodporn, 66, 67–70, 75; gender, 70–73; 77–78; globalization, 69; hashtags, 69; identities, 70; male gaze, 70–73; meal gaze, 67; nationhood, 70; Radarly, 68; restaurants, 14; sexualities, 70–71; social class, 75; social media, 82; uberization, 14, 76

FreakShakes, 14, 20, 179, 181–84, 187, 189nn29–30

Fruit Art Videos (Sarley), 72–73

FTC (Federal Trade Commission), 19–20

Furie, Noel, 264, 267

gastro-porn, 8, 67, 70–71, 120. *See also* food porn

Gatica, Carlos, 181

Gauber, Rocha, 233–34

gender: advertisements, 56, 70, 72, 105–6; aesthetics/authenticity, 152; biscuits/Southern food, 83; brands, 104, 105–6; celebrity chefs, 71; cultural tastes, 126; economics, 196–99, 215; feminist food enterprises, 261; food industries, 71, 196; food Instagram, 3–4, 18, 50, 77–78, 104, 197; food porn/#foodporn, 8, 68; food production, 72; France, 70–73; 77–78; Hot Dudes and Hummus, 34–35; hummus, 37–38, 42, 43–44; identities, 16, 21, 44, 135; influencers, 12, 71, 78, 151–53, 157–59, 195–99; Instagram, 2, 6; labor, 195–96; male gaze, 70–71; media, 72; Rivaland Co., Ltd, 50, 51, 56, 60; Sakarya, Umut, 213; Sarley, Stephanie, 72–73; sexualities, 216; social media, 196; textuality, 12; transgression, 215; unicorns/foods, 122, 126; users, 78; visuality, 277–78; Yearwood, Lagusta,

Nakayama, Thomas, 153
Nassif, Rawane, 68
nationalism, 221–23, 225–26, 229–31, 236–37, 275
nationhood, 21, 33–34, 36–41, 70, 284
Neff, Gina, 9, 248–49
negotiations, 21–22; agriculture, 241–55; consumers, 21; eating literacy, 274–80; farmers, 21; the far right, 221–37; feminist food enterprises, 260–70; food Instagram, 4; politicization, 21; populism, 221–37; transgression, 205–18
Newman, Michael Z., 7, 17–18, 283
New Nordic cuisine, 8
New South, 18, 81–91, 283–84
Nicchi, Joe, 177
Niochlin, Linda, 66
Noma (restaurant), 207
Nordic cuisine, 207–8, 211
nutrition: clean eating, 108; diet culture, 49, 156, 158; food cultures, 274; influencers, 18, 152–53, 156–58; Jewel (Japan), 50; Latour, Bruno, 276; scholarship, 148; unicorn foods, 117, 123

Ocasio-Cortez, Alexandria, 237
Ojôsama Kôso Jewel (Princess Enzyme Solution Jewel). *See* Jewel (Japan)
Okabe, Daisuke, 73
Okabe, Tsugumi (Mimi), 10
Okamura, Tomio, 237
Old South, 82–83, 90
Oliver, Jamie, 186, 187
Oliver, Raymond, 71
O'Neil, Molly, 7
"Online Feminism Is Just Feminism" (Crossley), 262
organic farmers: advertisements, 245; animal rights and welfare, 252–53; consumers, 245, 255; darkgram, 241, 243–44, 249, 254, 255; food Instagram, 243–44, 245–46; food justice, 242; food markets, 245; food systems, 17; localism, 247

pancai (Cantonese cuisine), 133
pandemic. *See* COVID-19 pandemic
Parasecoli, Fabio, 11
Parsons, Julie, 154
Pâtissez, 181–83
Patterson, Athony, 135
Paulk, David, 244, 247–48, 254
Pennell, Michael, 242, 243, 246, 252
Perales, Monica, 83, 90

Perry, Neil, 184
Persaud, Christopher, 243
pests, 252–53, 254
Petridis, Anna, 181, 182
Phillips, Rachel, 18, 283–84
photography: aesthetics, 134, 138–39; chefs, 132–33; commodification, 5; education, 248–49; flat lays, 11, 124, 141–42; food Instagram, 4, 134, 138, 178, 181; food porn, 134, 144; influencers, 124, 133, 138–45; Instagram, 120, 134; sexualities, 134; social photography, 115–26; unicorn latte, 117. *See also individual exhibits and individual photographs*
Pic, Anne-Sophie, 71
Pilar, Ladislav, 245, 252
plagiarism, 197
PNW (Pacific Northwest), 241–42, 243, 248, 249, 255
Political Palate, The (Bloodroot Collective), 264
politicization: aesthetics, 213; celebrities, 17; digital food cultures, 221–22; feminist food enterprises, 12, 261–64, 265–66, 270; food, 197, 221–22, 229–30, 236–37; food Instagram, 21, 197, 213–15, 269, 270, 285; hummus, 33, 35–36, 37–38, 40, 42–44, 68; identities, 111; Instagram, 253; negotiations, 21; Sakarya, Umut, 8, 210, 213–15; social media, 221, 261; visuality, 213
Poperl, Kévin, 68
populism, 221–37; aesthetics, 224; anti-food porn, 8; authenticity, 223–24, 237; comfort foods, 222, 223–25, 227, 231; elitism, 223, 225, 227; empty signifiers, 224–25, 231, 233, 236–37; food, 224; food porn, 236–37; food puritanism, 222, 224, 234, 236, 237; globalization, 236; identities, 223, 224–25; nationalism, 223, 225–26, 229–31, 236–37; *ressentiment* (anger), 224–25, 236; scholarship, 224; social media, 223. *See also* Bolsonaro, Jair; Salvini, Matteo
power, 3, 6, 9, 18, 19
Praet, Istvan, 165–66, 169
Presentation of Self in Everyday Life, The (Goffman), 109
professional v. amateur, 178–79, 180–81, 184, 187
prosumption: definitions of, 7, 178; food blogs, 180; food chain, 18–19; food Instagram, 178–81, 197–99; Grasby, Marion, 187; influencers, 179, 197–99; reality television, 184; Rivaland Co., Ltd, 53; social media, 197
Pruchniewska, Urszula, 250

influencers, 148, 179–80, 244; Instagram, 6, 248–49; labor, 246–47, 268–70; livestock, 165–66; localism, 255, 265; meal gaze, 65; media studies, 17, 112n5, 285; politicization, 221, 261; populism, 223; prosumption, 197; Radarly, 68–70, 79n18; restaurants, 120; scandals, 284; scholarship, 2, 224, 246, 249, 285; social photography, 120, 124; the South, 90; Starbucks, 125; "Unbox a Food Trend" (course assignment), 280; unicorn foods, 115–17; unicorn latte, 121, 125; users, 120, 244, 248–49, 284; visuality, 120–21; Woolley, Dawn, 104. *See also individual social media*

social photography, 115–26

Southern food, 81–91. *See also* biscuits

Southern Food: At Home, on the Road, in History (Egerton), 81

Southern restaurants. *See* biscuit restaurants

Spielvogel, Laura, 48–49

staged authenticity. *See* authenticity

Starbucks, 20, 115–20, 125–26

Stavrakakis, Yannis, 223

supply chains, 13–22, 169, 171, 286

sustainability: agriculture, 243–46, 250, 252–53, 255; consumers, 245, 255; food Instagram, 179, 182–84; food porn, 182–84; happy meat, 164; media, 268; Nordic cuisine, 207–8; restaurants, 182, 207–8; Sakarya, Umut, 206, 211

Systrom, Kevin, 14

Tagg, John, 4–5

Taking the Heat (Harris and Giuffre), 196

Tasty videos (Buzzfeed), 5

Taylor, Nathan, 182

technologies, 9–10, 20–21

temporalities, 9, 10, 25n42, 268, 285

Tene, Ofra, 37

Terranova, Tiziana, 194

textuality, 9, 11–13, 166–67, 192, 213

thinness, 48–53, 60, 275. *See also* diet culture

Thunberg, Greta, 224–25, 234–36

Tibbs, Kellea, 95–97, 98

Tifentale, Alise, 16, 66

Tippen, Carrie Helms, 284–85

Tompkins, Kyla Wazana, 275

tortellini, 226

tortillas, 41–42

Tracy, Sarah E., 7, 283

trademarks, 20, 115–19, 123, 126. *See also* brands

transgression, 205–18; aesthetics, 206–7,

210–13, 218; brands, 206; food discourse, 206–7, 210, 213–18; food images, 212–13; food Instagram, 205–18; food porn, 213; gender, 215; negotiations, 205–18; Sakarya, Umut, 206, 208–18; sexism/sexualities, 206, 210, 215–18; social class, 213

Tree House Farms, 247

Truman, Emily, 20, 181

Trump, Donald, 230

Turner, Graeme, 16–17

Twitter, 2, 6, 19, 79n18, 116, 213, 247

Tyrkersvin (documentary), 210

UberEats, 76–77

Umberger, Wendy, 164–65

"Unbox a Food Trend" (course assignment), 275–77, 280

Unessay project, 277–79

unicorn foods, 115–26

unicorn latte, 14, 20, 115, 117–19, 121–26

#unicornlatte, 115–19, 124

unicorns, 121–23, 125

US (United States), 33–34, 40–44, 151, 153, 170, 277–78, 283

users: affordances, 248–49; biscuit restaurants, 84; brands, 126, 244; clean eating, 108; Facebook, 19, 284; food images, 120; food markets, 126; #foodporn, 77; gender, 78; globalization, 69; Hot Dudes and Hummus, 34, 35, 44; IGTV, 185; influencers, 133–34, 196, 244; Instagram, 6, 11, 19, 40, 82, 158–59, 251, 285; Instagrammability, 73; Radarly, 79n18; Rivaland Co., Ltd, 53, 58–60, 62n28; social media, 120, 244, 248–49, 284

users and food Instagram: aesthetics/identities, 3; affordances, 9–10, 21, 111, 179–80; algorithms, 275; art practices, 111; authenticity, 81–82; clean eating, 108; credentials, 149; demographics, 1–2, 5, 40; France/hashtags, 69; Hong Kong, 133, 136–37; influencers, 3, 133–34, 136–37, 193–95; microcultures, 101, 108; monetization, 284; prosumption, 197; scandals, 284; scholarship, 149–51; selfies, 1; sociality, 135; social media, 9–10, 13, 66; temporalities, 10

Vaidyanathan, Siva, 285

van Dijck, José, 11, 124, 126

Vats, Anjali, 253

vegan and vegetarian restaurants, 96, 207–8, 209, 217–18

veganism, 96, 154, 252, 260, 265

The University of Illinois Press
is a founding member of the
Association of University Presses.

———————————————

University of Illinois Press
1325 South Oak Street
Champaign, IL 61820-6903
www.press.uillinois.edu